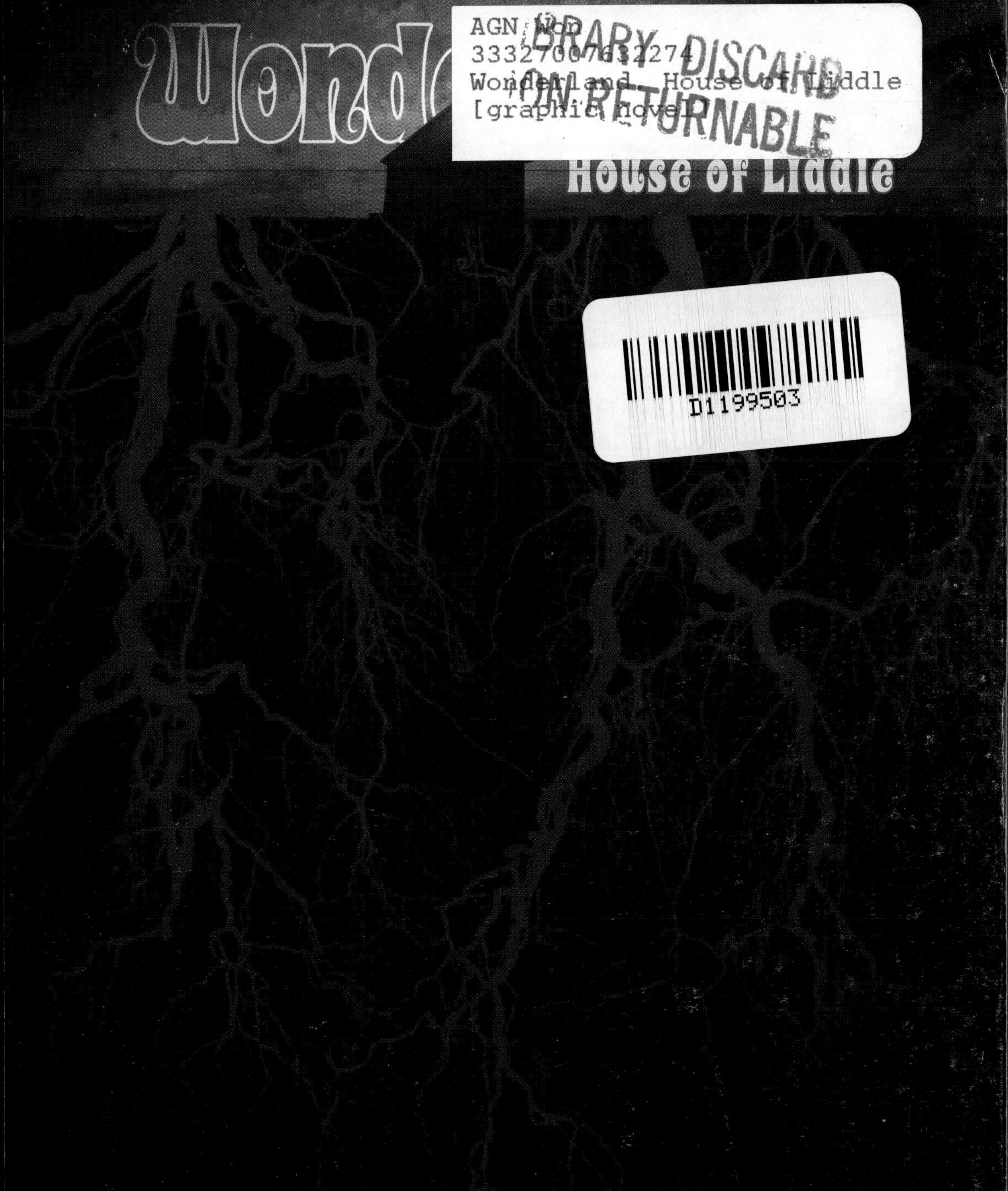

Wonde
House of Liddle

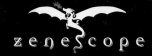

zenescope

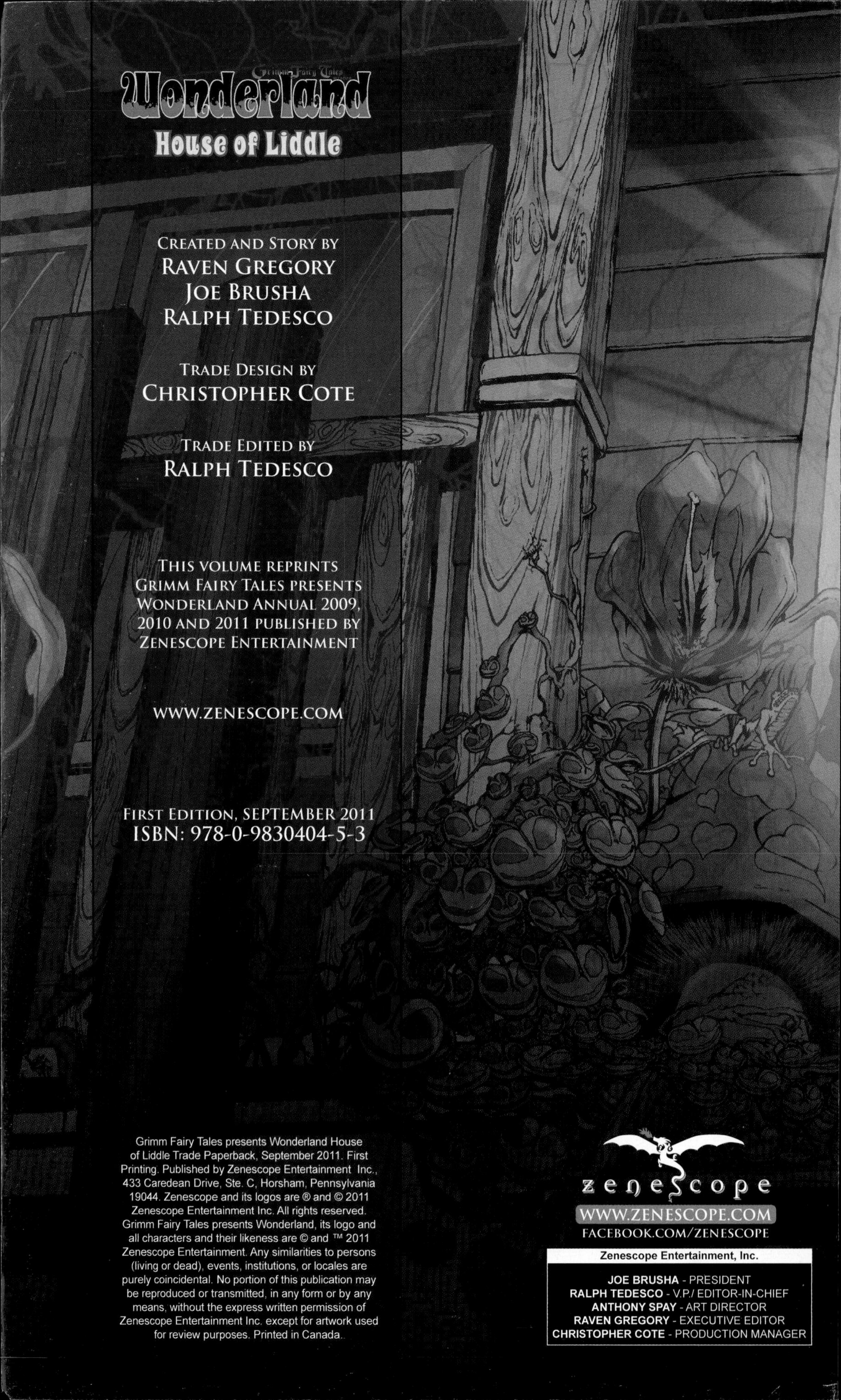

Wonderland
House of Liddle

CREATED AND STORY BY
RAVEN GREGORY
JOE BRUSHA
RALPH TEDESCO

TRADE DESIGN BY
CHRISTOPHER COTE

TRADE EDITED BY
RALPH TEDESCO

THIS VOLUME REPRINTS
GRIMM FAIRY TALES PRESENTS
WONDERLAND ANNUAL 2009,
2010 AND 2011 PUBLISHED BY
ZENESCOPE ENTERTAINMENT

WWW.ZENESCOPE.COM

FIRST EDITION, SEPTEMBER 2011
ISBN: 978-0-9830404-5-3

Grimm Fairy Tales presents Wonderland House of Liddle Trade Paperback, September 2011. First Printing. Published by Zenescope Entertainment Inc., 433 Caredean Drive, Ste. C, Horsham, Pennsylvania 19044. Zenescope and its logos are ® and © 2011 Zenescope Entertainment Inc. All rights reserved. Grimm Fairy Tales presents Wonderland, its logo and all characters and their likeness are © and ™ 2011 Zenescope Entertainment. Any similarities to persons (living or dead), events, institutions, or locales are purely coincidental. No portion of this publication may be reproduced or transmitted, in any form or by any means, without the express written permission of Zenescope Entertainment Inc. except for artwork used for review purposes. Printed in Canada.

zenescope
WWW.ZENESCOPE.COM
FACEBOOK.COM/ZENESCOPE

Zenescope Entertainment, Inc.

JOE BRUSHA - PRESIDENT
RALPH TEDESCO - V.P./ EDITOR-IN-CHIEF
ANTHONY SPAY - ART DIRECTOR
RAVEN GREGORY - EXECUTIVE EDITOR
CHRISTOPHER COTE - PRODUCTION MANAGER

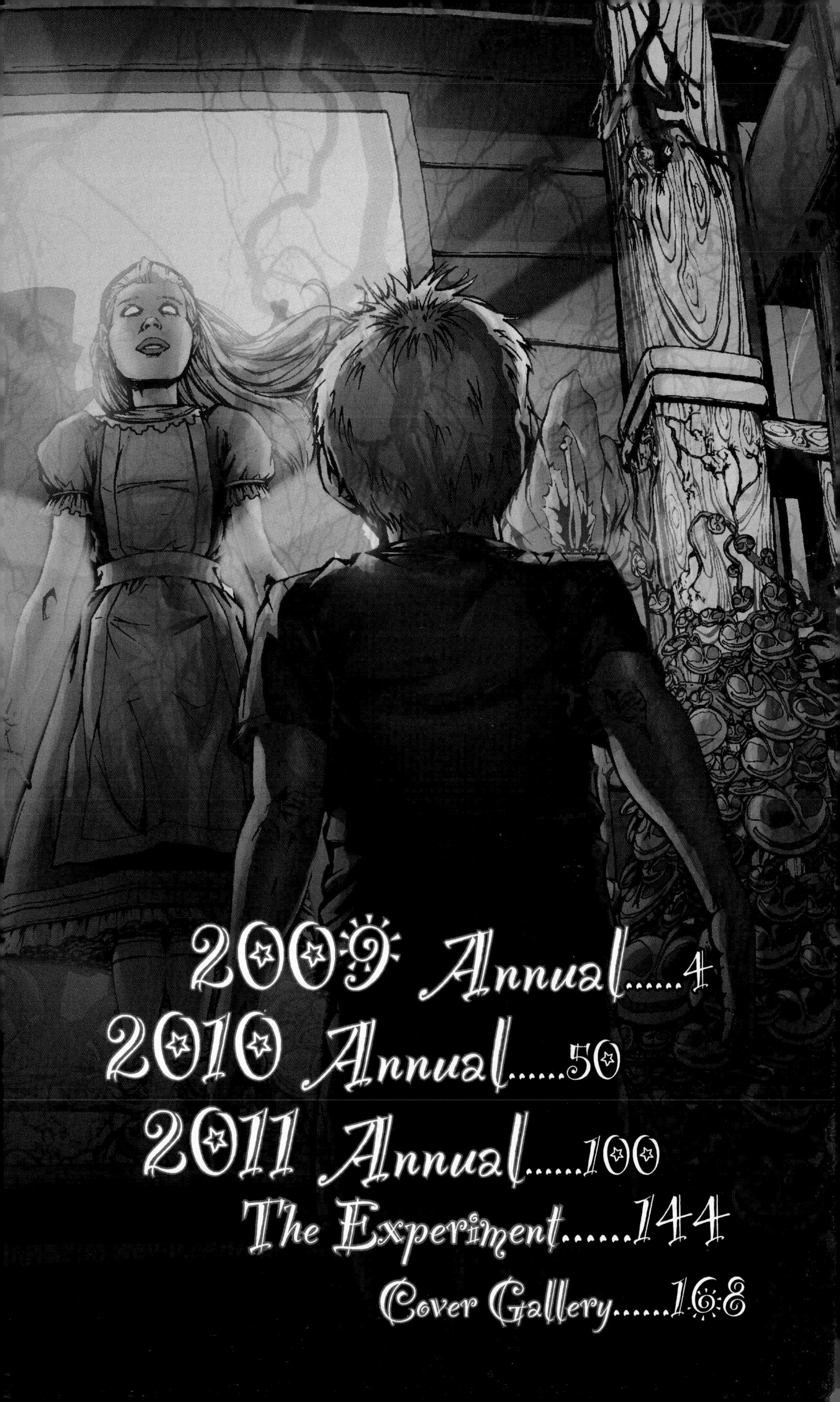

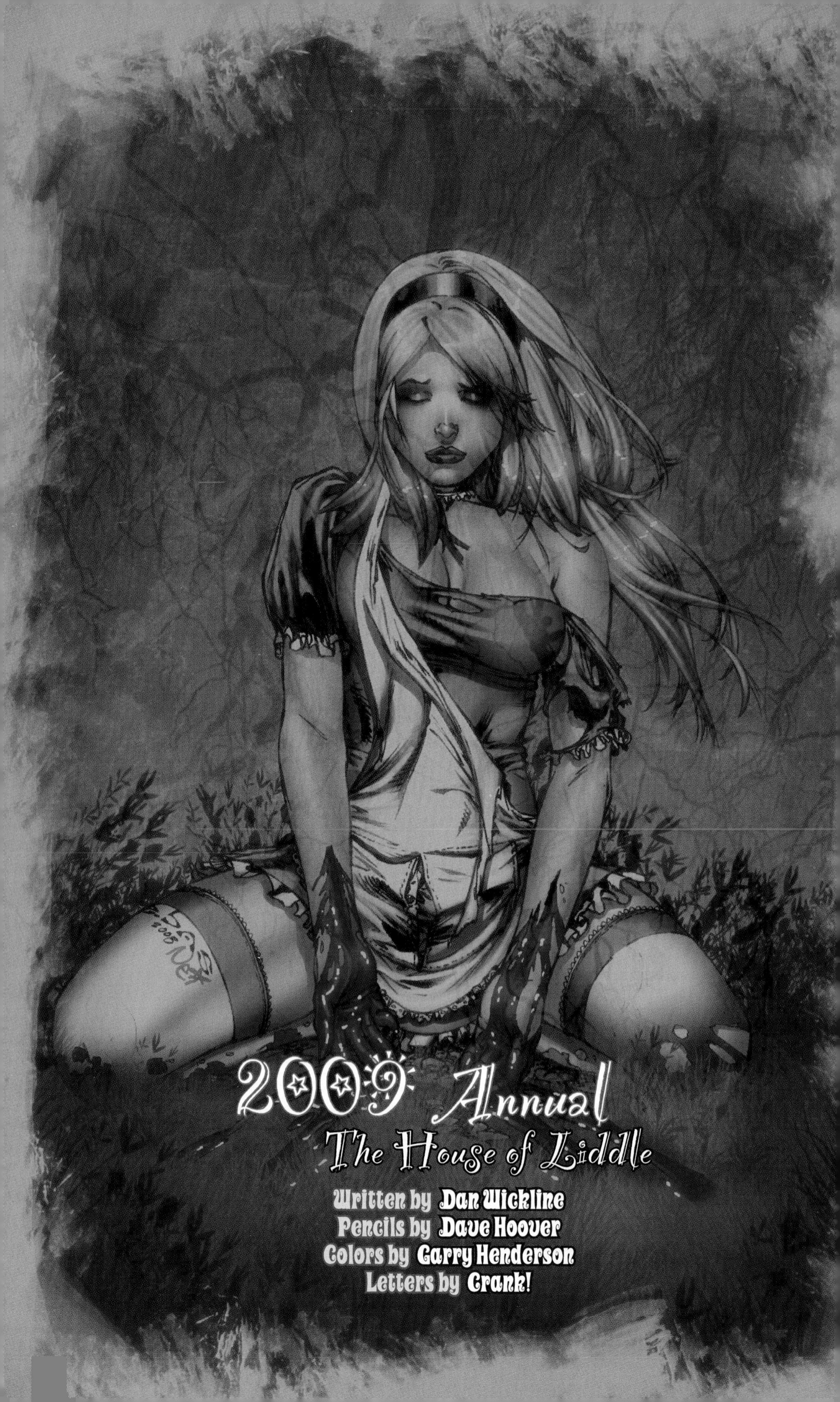

2009 Annual
The House of Liddle

Written by Dan Wickline
Pencils by Dave Hoover
Colors by Garry Henderson
Letters by Crank!

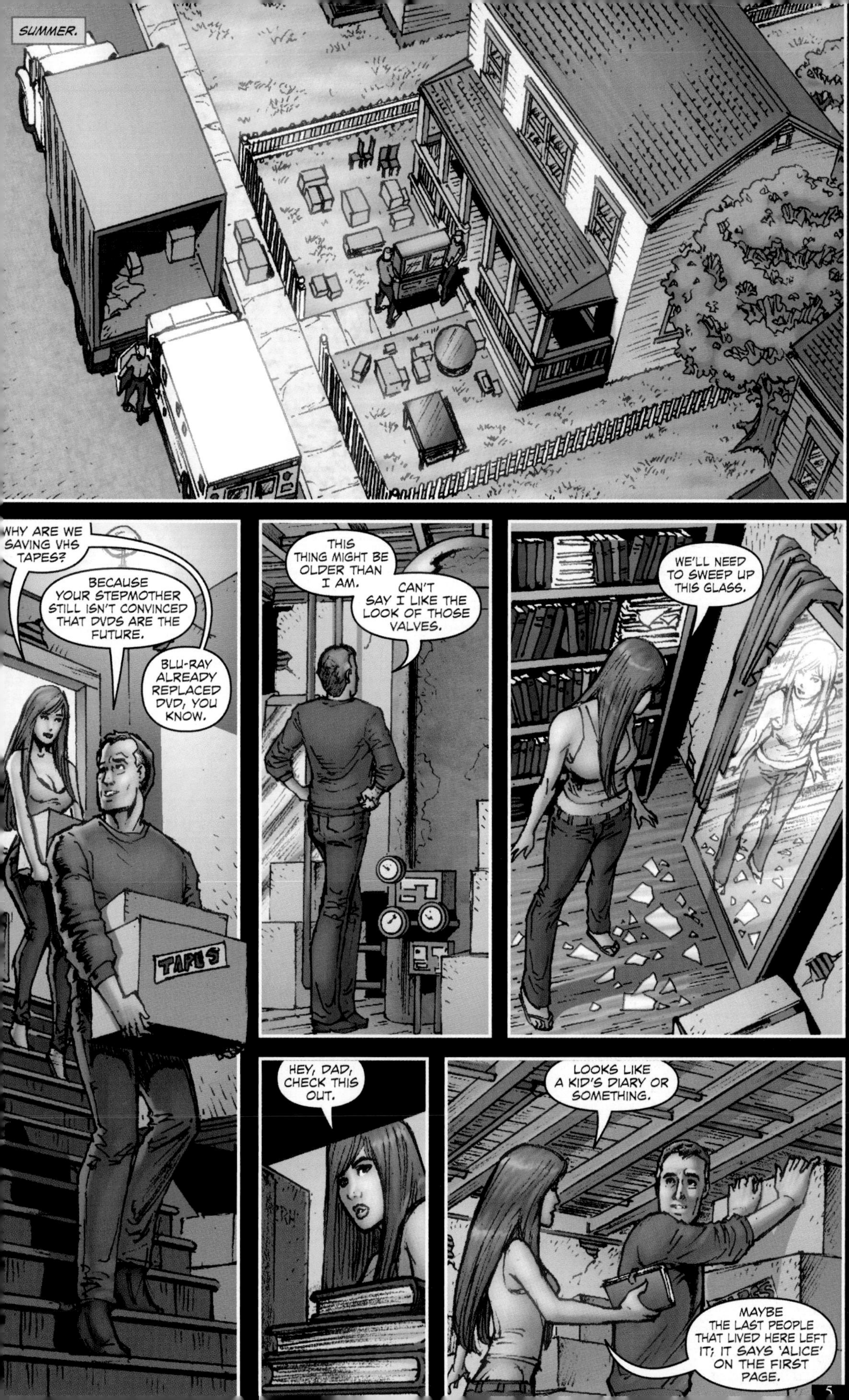
SUMMER.
WHY ARE WE SAVING VHS TAPES?
BECAUSE YOUR STEPMOTHER STILL ISN'T CONVINCED THAT DVDS ARE THE FUTURE.
BLU-RAY ALREADY REPLACED DVD, YOU KNOW.
TAPES
THIS THING MIGHT BE OLDER THAN I AM.
CAN'T SAY I LIKE THE LOOK OF THOSE VALVES.
WE'LL NEED TO SWEEP UP THIS GLASS.
HEY, DAD, CHECK THIS OUT.
LOOKS LIKE A KID'S DIARY OR SOMETHING.
MAYBE THE LAST PEOPLE THAT LIVED HERE LEFT IT; IT SAYS 'ALICE' ON THE FIRST PAGE.

ERIC, THEY'RE BRINGING BEN IN NOW.

DID YOU FINISH YOUR DRAWING?

I STILL NEED TO COLOR IT.

HANG IN THERE, BUDDY. WE'RE ALMOST THERE.

SEE, BEN, I TOLD YOU IT WOULDN'T TAKE TOO LONG.

CAN I HAVE A HOT DOG?

LET'S GET YOU IN YOUR ROOM AND THEN I'LL MAKE YOU ONE.

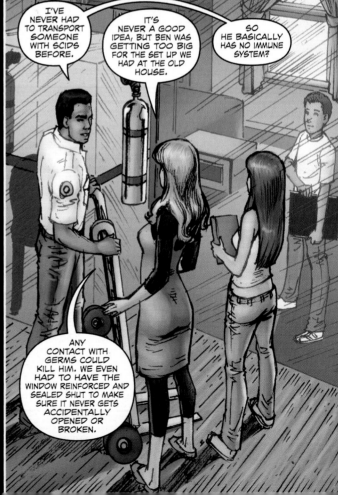

I'VE NEVER HAD TO TRANSPORT SOMEONE WITH SCIDS BEFORE.

IT'S NEVER A GOOD IDEA, BUT BEN WAS GETTING TOO BIG FOR THE SET UP WE HAD AT THE OLD HOUSE.

SO HE BASICALLY HAS NO IMMUNE SYSTEM?

ANY CONTACT WITH GERMS COULD KILL HIM. WE EVEN HAD TO HAVE THE WINDOW REINFORCED AND SEALED SHUT TO MAKE SURE IT NEVER GETS ACCIDENTALLY OPENED OR BROKEN.

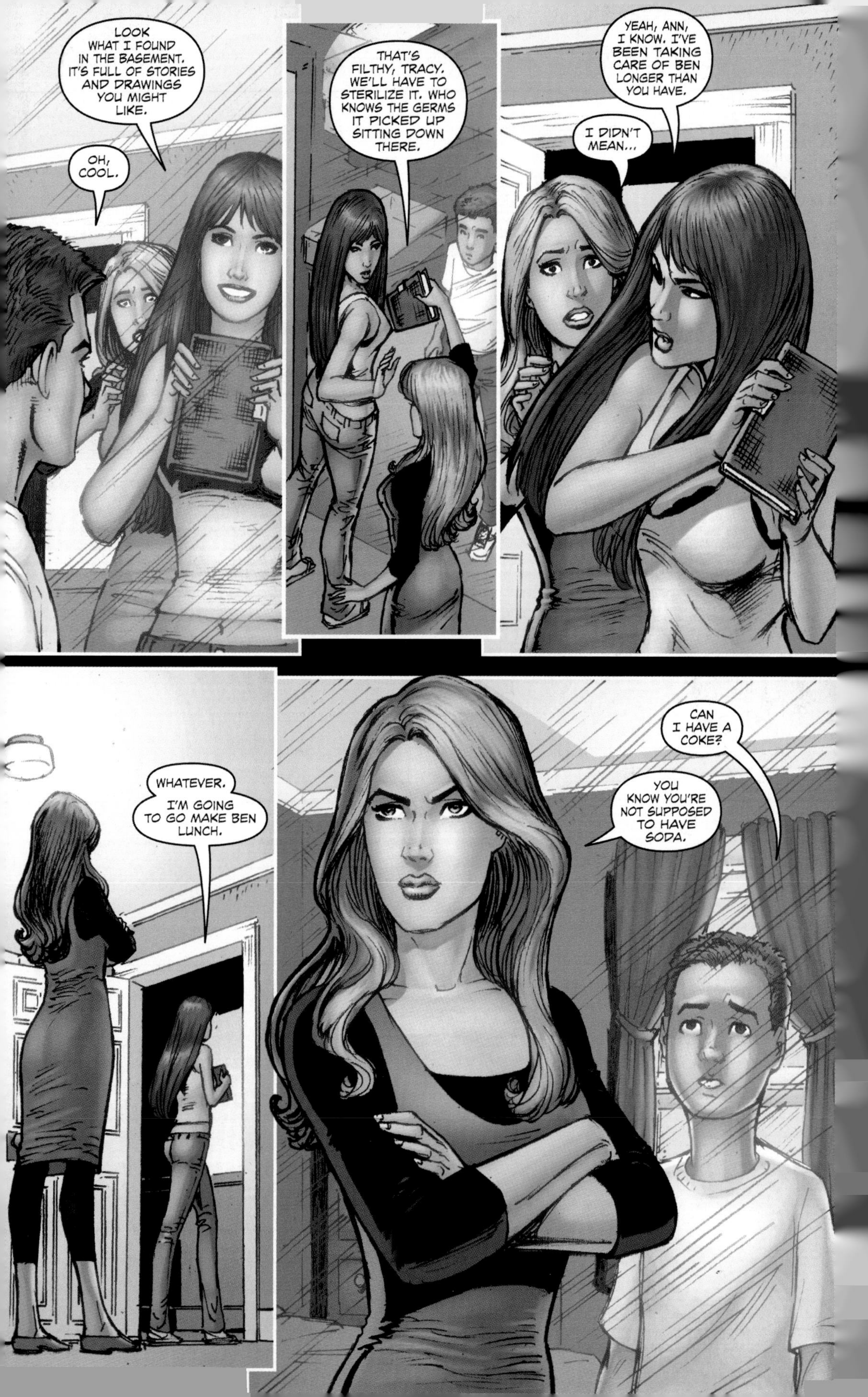
LOOK WHAT I FOUND IN THE BASEMENT. IT'S FULL OF STORIES AND DRAWINGS YOU MIGHT LIKE.
OH, COOL.
THAT'S FILTHY, TRACY. WE'LL HAVE TO STERILIZE IT. WHO KNOWS THE GERMS IT PICKED UP SITTING DOWN THERE.
YEAH, ANN, I KNOW. I'VE BEEN TAKING CARE OF BEN LONGER THAN YOU HAVE.
I DIDN'T MEAN...
WHATEVER.
I'M GOING TO GO MAKE BEN LUNCH.
CAN I HAVE A COKE?
YOU KNOW YOU'RE NOT SUPPOSED TO HAVE SODA.

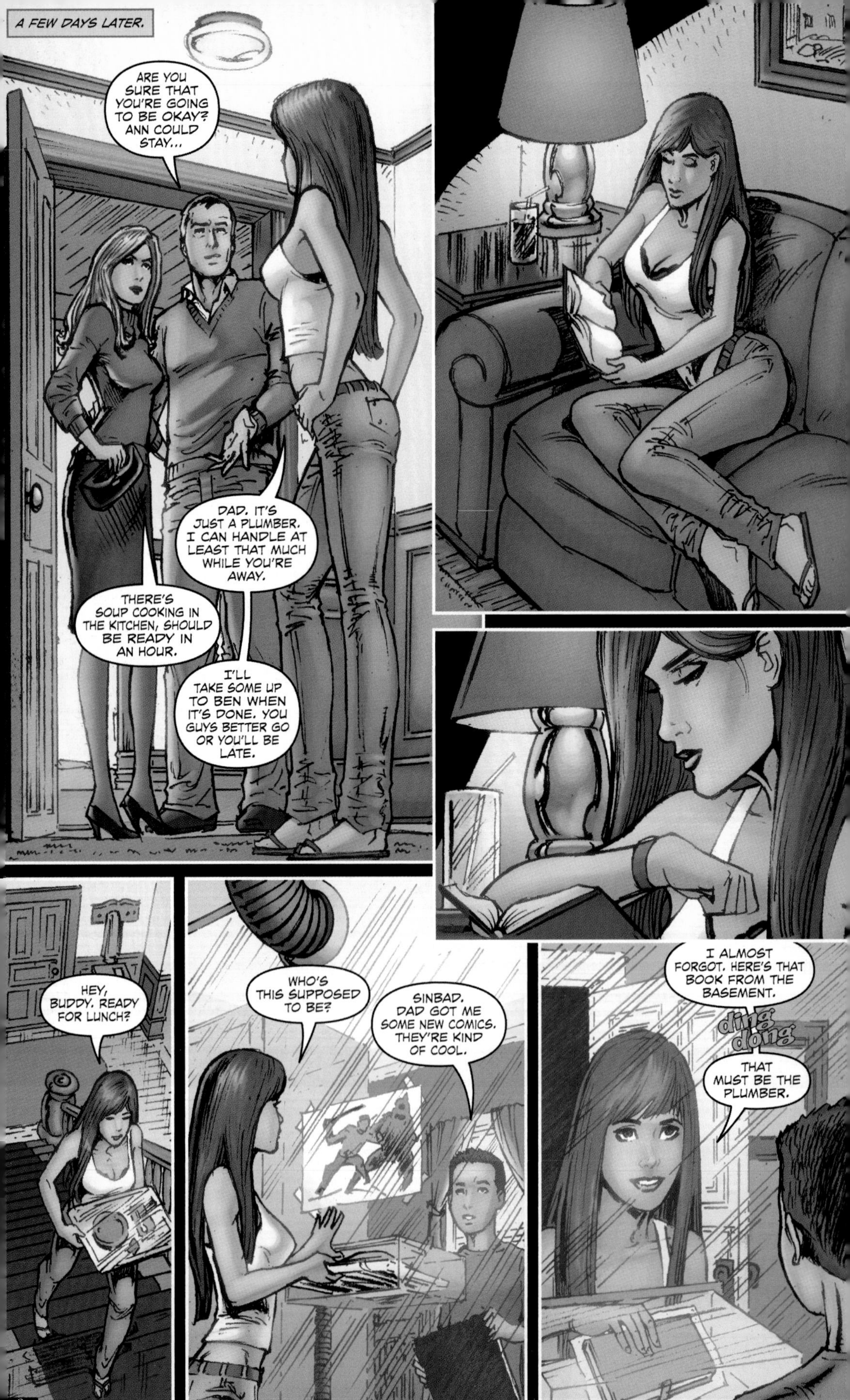
A FEW DAYS LATER.
ARE YOU SURE THAT YOU'RE GOING TO BE OKAY? ANN COULD STAY...
DAD. IT'S JUST A PLUMBER. I CAN HANDLE AT LEAST THAT MUCH WHILE YOU'RE AWAY.
THERE'S SOUP COOKING IN THE KITCHEN, SHOULD BE READY IN AN HOUR.
I'LL TAKE SOME UP TO BEN WHEN IT'S DONE. YOU GUYS BETTER GO OR YOU'LL BE LATE.
HEY, BUDDY. READY FOR LUNCH?
WHO'S THIS SUPPOSED TO BE?
SINBAD. DAD GOT ME SOME NEW COMICS. THEY'RE KIND OF COOL.
I ALMOST FORGOT. HERE'S THAT BOOK FROM THE BASEMENT.
ding dong
THAT MUST BE THE PLUMBER.

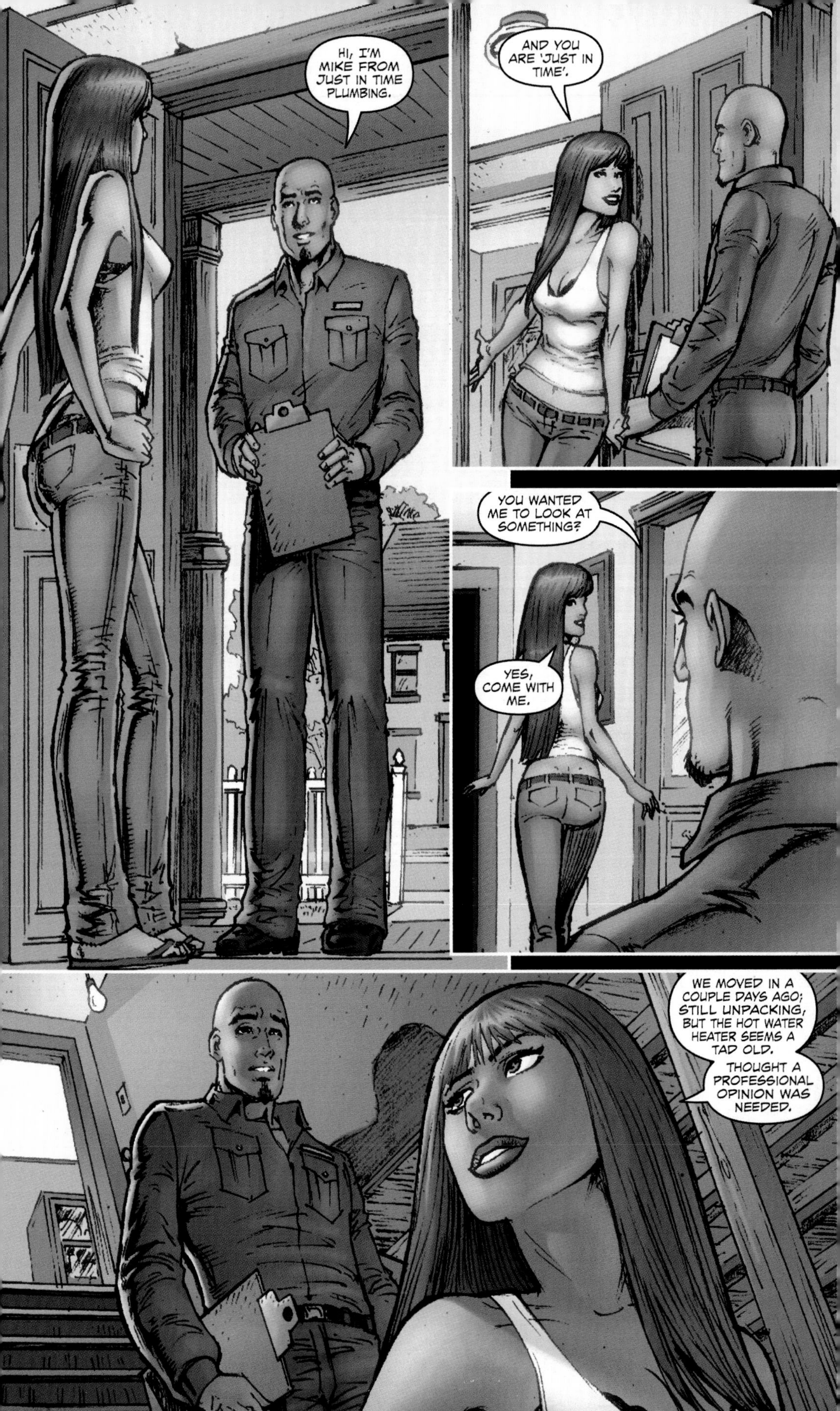
HI, I'M MIKE FROM JUST IN TIME PLUMBING.
AND YOU ARE 'JUST IN TIME'.
YOU WANTED ME TO LOOK AT SOMETHING?
YES, COME WITH ME.
WE MOVED IN A COUPLE DAYS AGO; STILL UNPACKING, BUT THE HOT WATER HEATER SEEMS A TAD OLD.
THOUGHT A PROFESSIONAL OPINION WAS NEEDED.

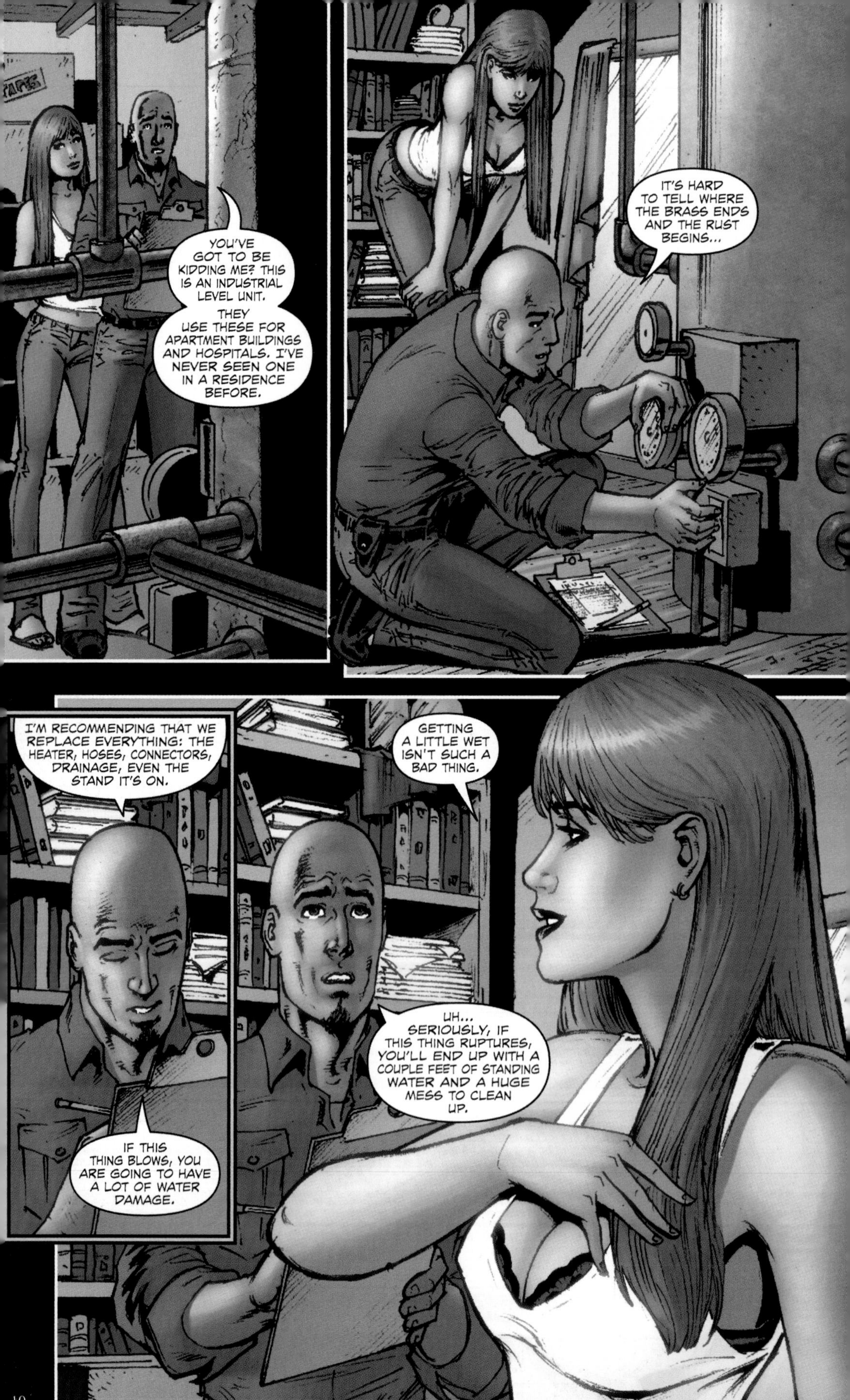
YOU'VE GOT TO BE KIDDING ME? THIS IS AN INDUSTRIAL LEVEL UNIT.
THEY USE THESE FOR APARTMENT BUILDINGS AND HOSPITALS. I'VE NEVER SEEN ONE IN A RESIDENCE BEFORE.
IT'S HARD TO TELL WHERE THE BRASS ENDS AND THE RUST BEGINS...
I'M RECOMMENDING THAT WE REPLACE EVERYTHING: THE HEATER, HOSES, CONNECTORS, DRAINAGE, EVEN THE STAND IT'S ON.
IF THIS THING BLOWS, YOU ARE GOING TO HAVE A LOT OF WATER DAMAGE.
GETTING A LITTLE WET ISN'T SUCH A BAD THING.
UH... SERIOUSLY, IF THIS THING RUPTURES, YOU'LL END UP WITH A COUPLE FEET OF STANDING WATER AND A HUGE MESS TO CLEAN UP.

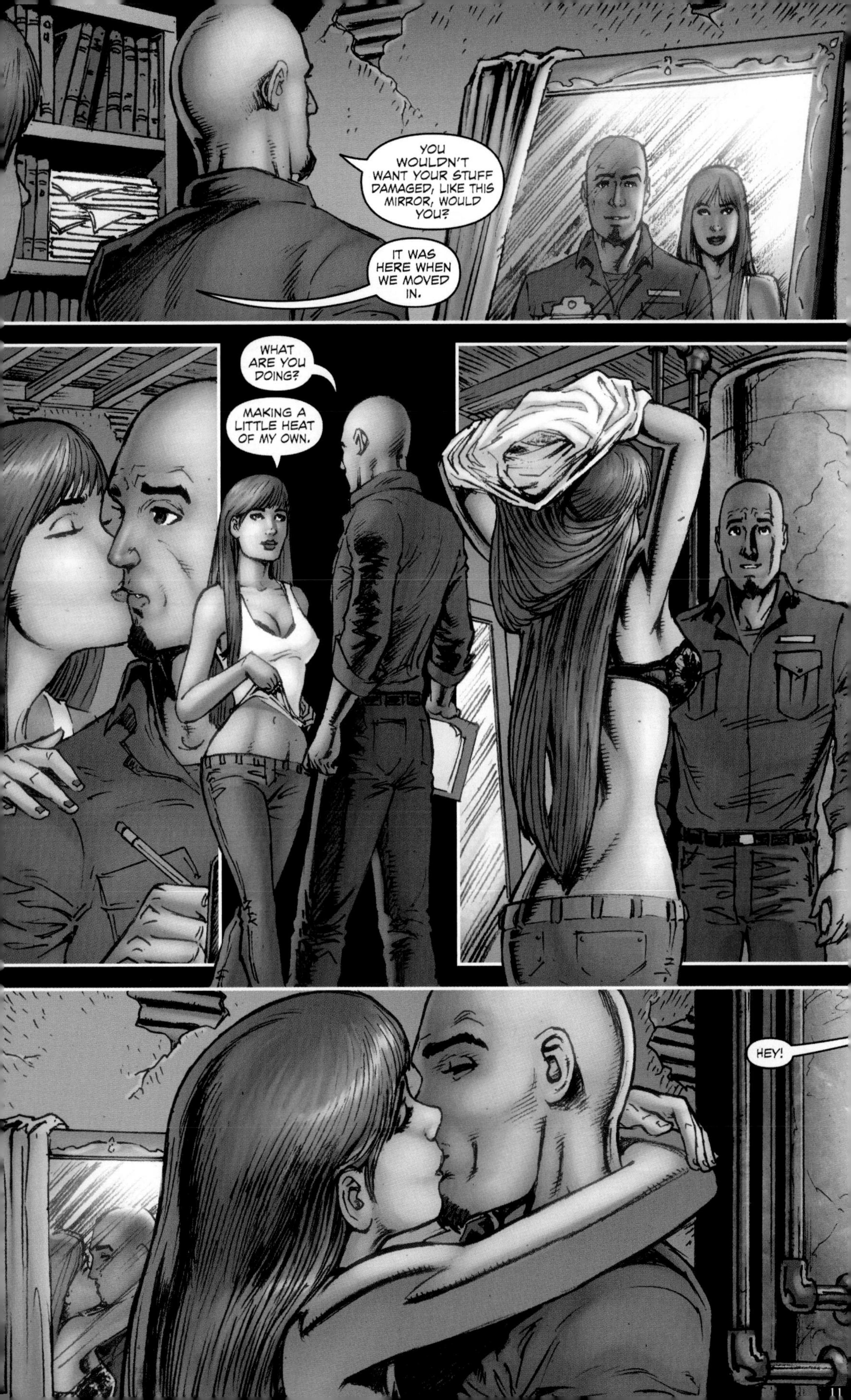
YOU WOULDN'T WANT YOUR STUFF DAMAGED, LIKE THIS MIRROR, WOULD YOU?
IT WAS HERE WHEN WE MOVED IN.
WHAT ARE YOU DOING?
MAKING A LITTLE HEAT OF MY OWN.
HEY!

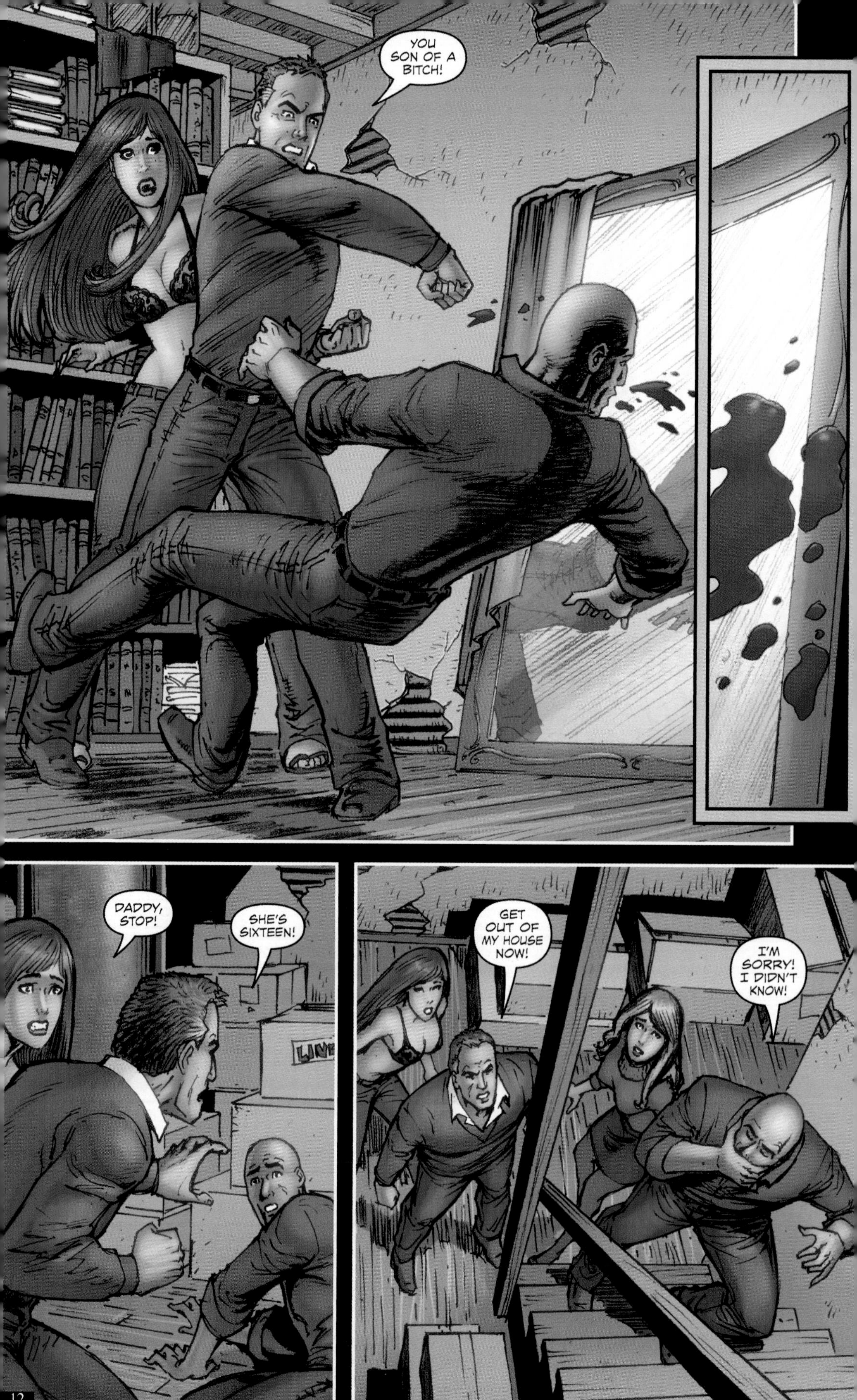
YOU SON OF A BITCH!
DADDY, STOP!
SHE'S SIXTEEN!
GET OUT OF MY HOUSE NOW!
I'M SORRY! I DIDN'T KNOW!

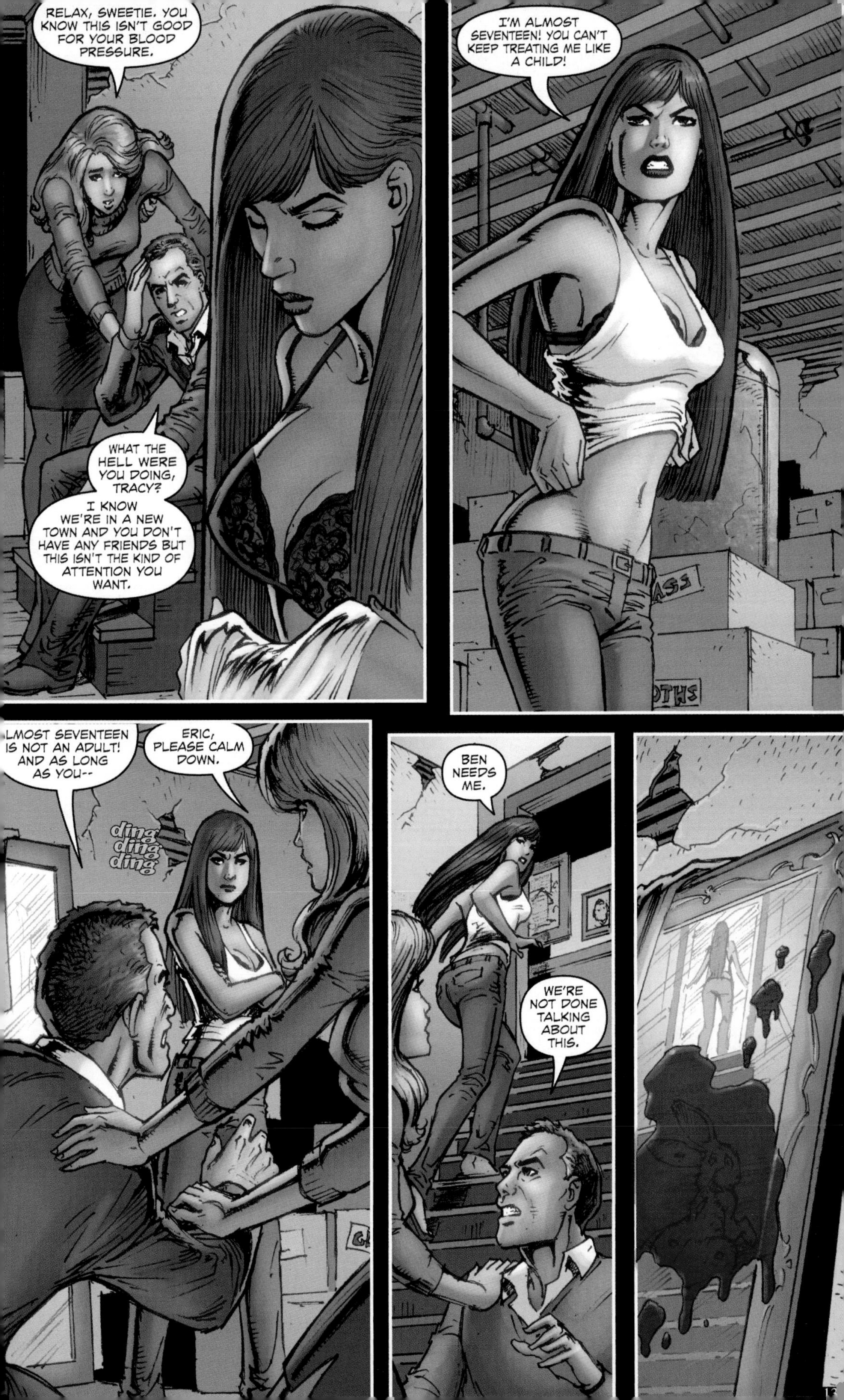
RELAX, SWEETIE. YOU KNOW THIS ISN'T GOOD FOR YOUR BLOOD PRESSURE.
WHAT THE HELL WERE YOU DOING, TRACY?
I KNOW WE'RE IN A NEW TOWN AND YOU DON'T HAVE ANY FRIENDS BUT THIS ISN'T THE KIND OF ATTENTION YOU WANT.
I'M ALMOST SEVENTEEN! YOU CAN'T KEEP TREATING ME LIKE A CHILD!
LMOST SEVENTEEN IS NOT AN ADULT! AND AS LONG AS YOU--
ERIC, PLEASE CALM DOWN.
ding ding ding
BEN NEEDS ME.
WE'RE NOT DONE TALKING ABOUT THIS.

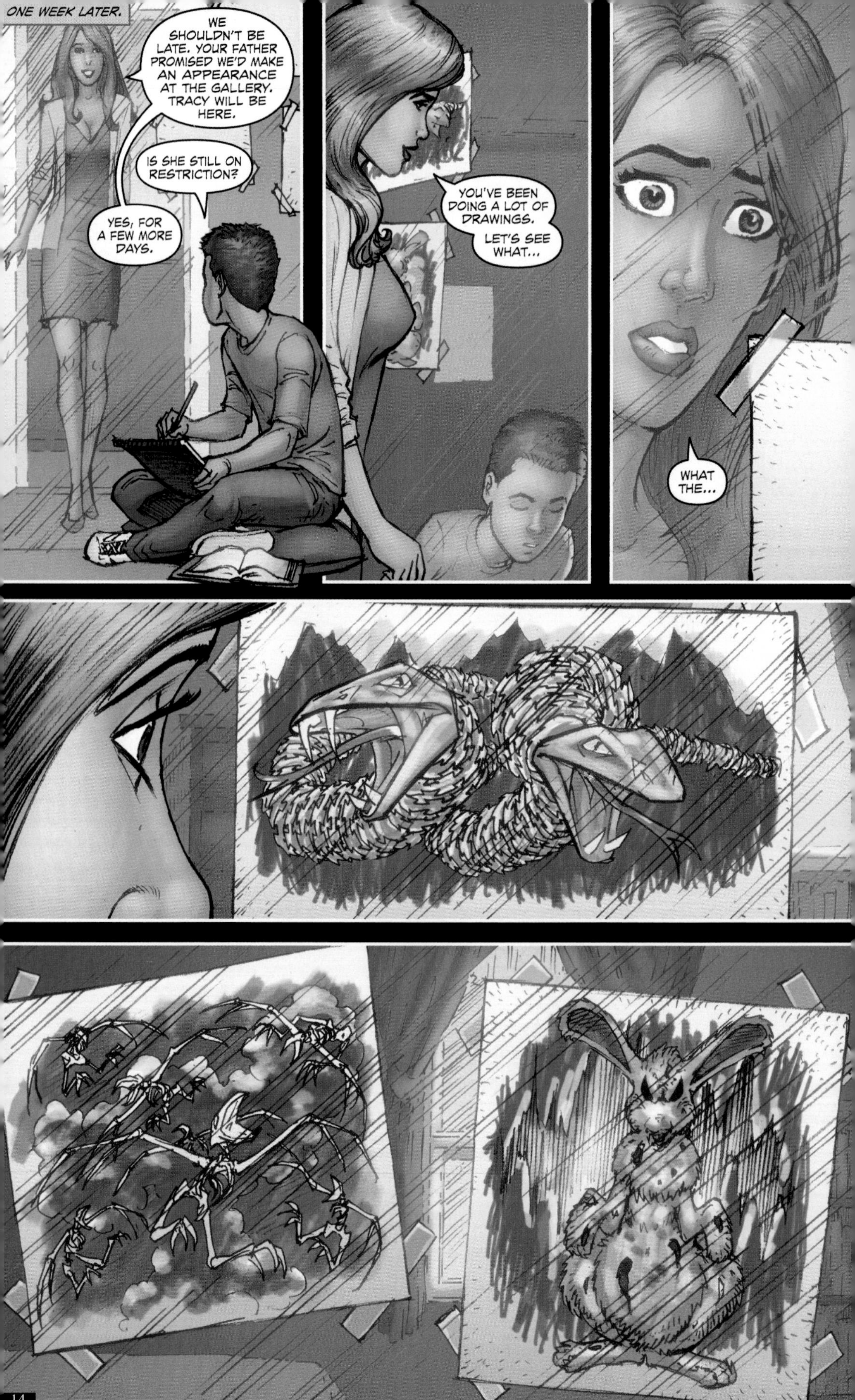
ONE WEEK LATER.
WE SHOULDN'T BE LATE. YOUR FATHER PROMISED WE'D MAKE AN APPEARANCE AT THE GALLERY. TRACY WILL BE HERE.
IS SHE STILL ON RESTRICTION?
YES, FOR A FEW MORE DAYS.
YOU'VE BEEN DOING A LOT OF DRAWINGS.
LET'S SEE WHAT...
WHAT THE...

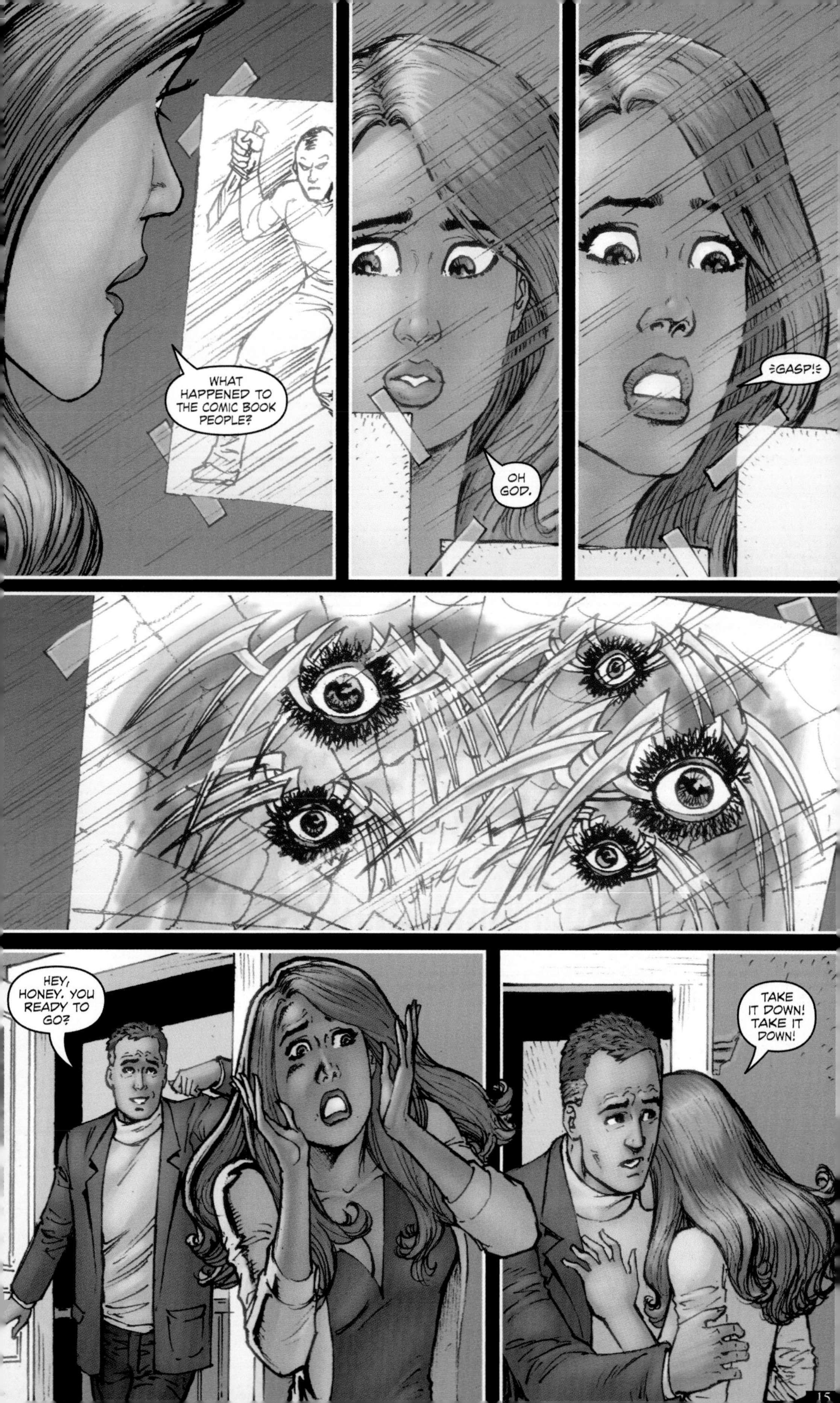
WHAT HAPPENED TO THE COMIC BOOK PEOPLE?
OH GOD.
GASP!
HEY, HONEY. YOU READY TO GO?
TAKE IT DOWN! TAKE IT DOWN!

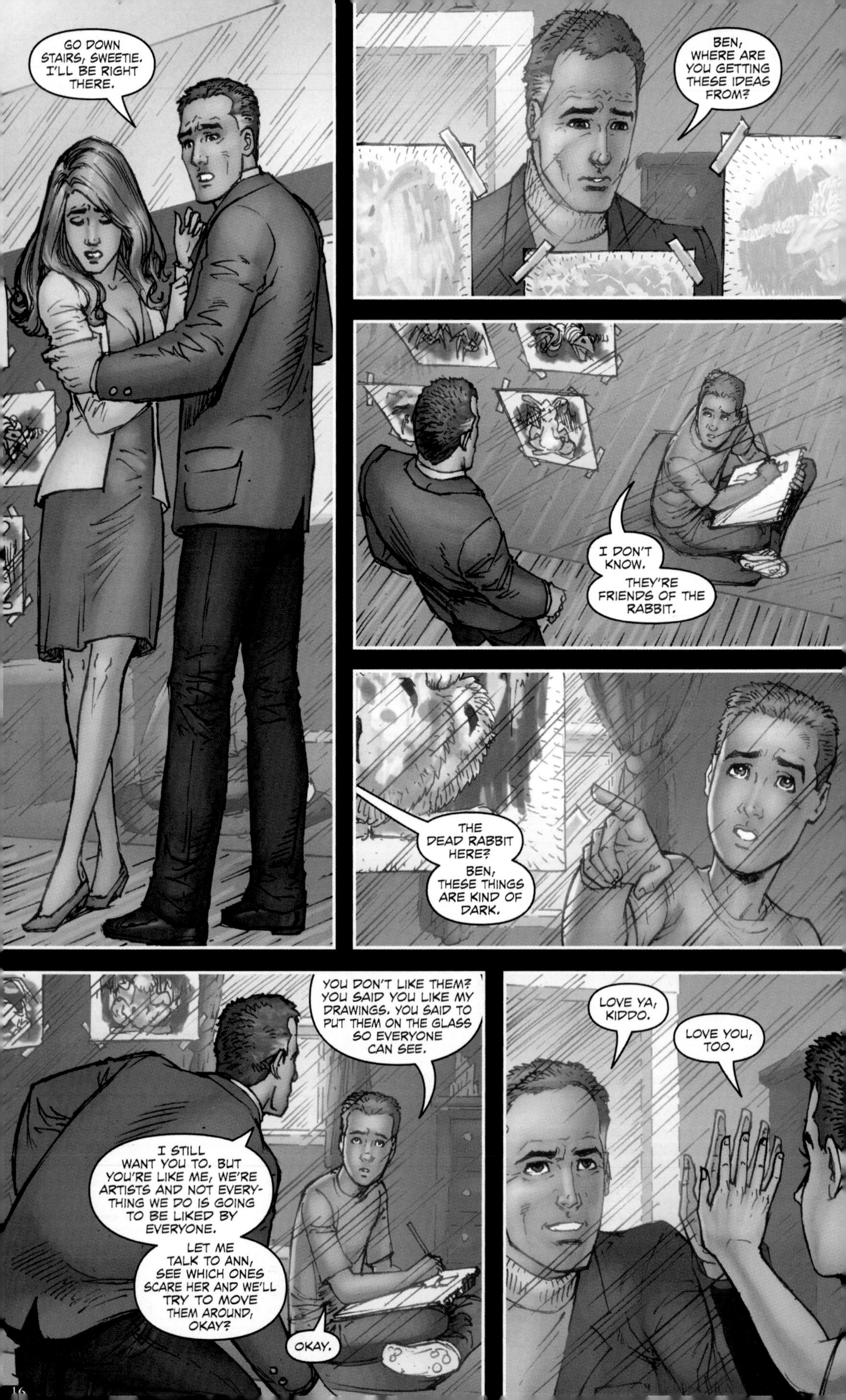
GO DOWN STAIRS, SWEETIE. I'LL BE RIGHT THERE.
BEN, WHERE ARE YOU GETTING THESE IDEAS FROM?
I DON'T KNOW.
THEY'RE FRIENDS OF THE RABBIT.
THE DEAD RABBIT HERE?
BEN, THESE THINGS ARE KIND OF DARK.
YOU DON'T LIKE THEM? YOU SAID YOU LIKE MY DRAWINGS. YOU SAID TO PUT THEM ON THE GLASS SO EVERYONE CAN SEE.
I STILL WANT YOU TO. BUT YOU'RE LIKE ME, WE'RE ARTISTS AND NOT EVERY-THING WE DO IS GOING TO BE LIKED BY EVERYONE.
LET ME TALK TO ANN, SEE WHICH ONES SCARE HER AND WE'LL TRY TO MOVE THEM AROUND, OKAY?
OKAY.
LOVE YA, KIDDO.
LOVE YOU, TOO.

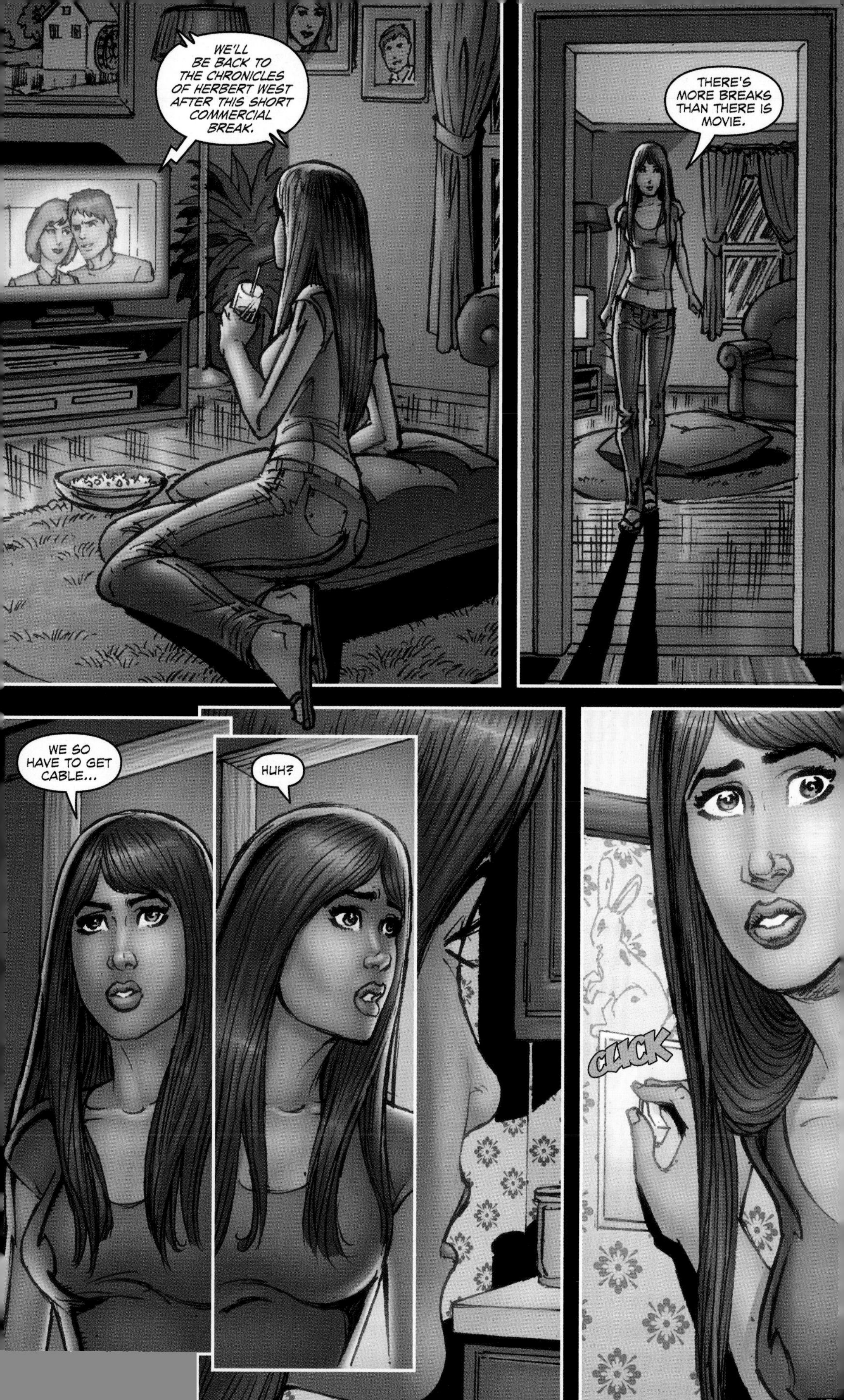
WE'LL BE BACK TO THE CHRONICLES OF HERBERT WEST AFTER THIS SHORT COMMERCIAL BREAK.
THERE'S MORE BREAKS THAN THERE IS MOVIE.
WE SO HAVE TO GET CABLE...
HUH?
CLICK

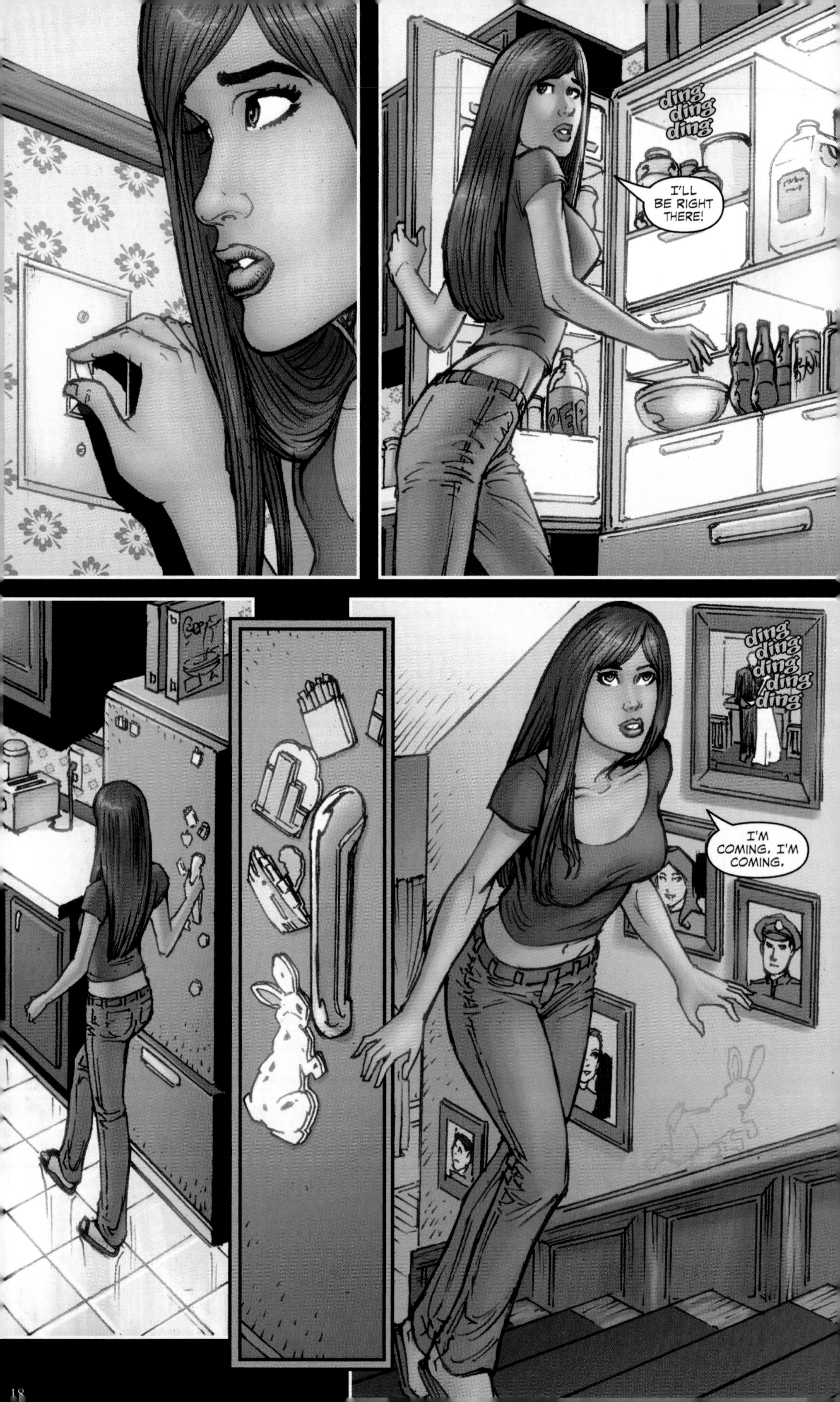
ding
ding
ding
I'LL BE RIGHT THERE!
ding
ding
ding
ding
ding
I'M COMING. I'M COMING.

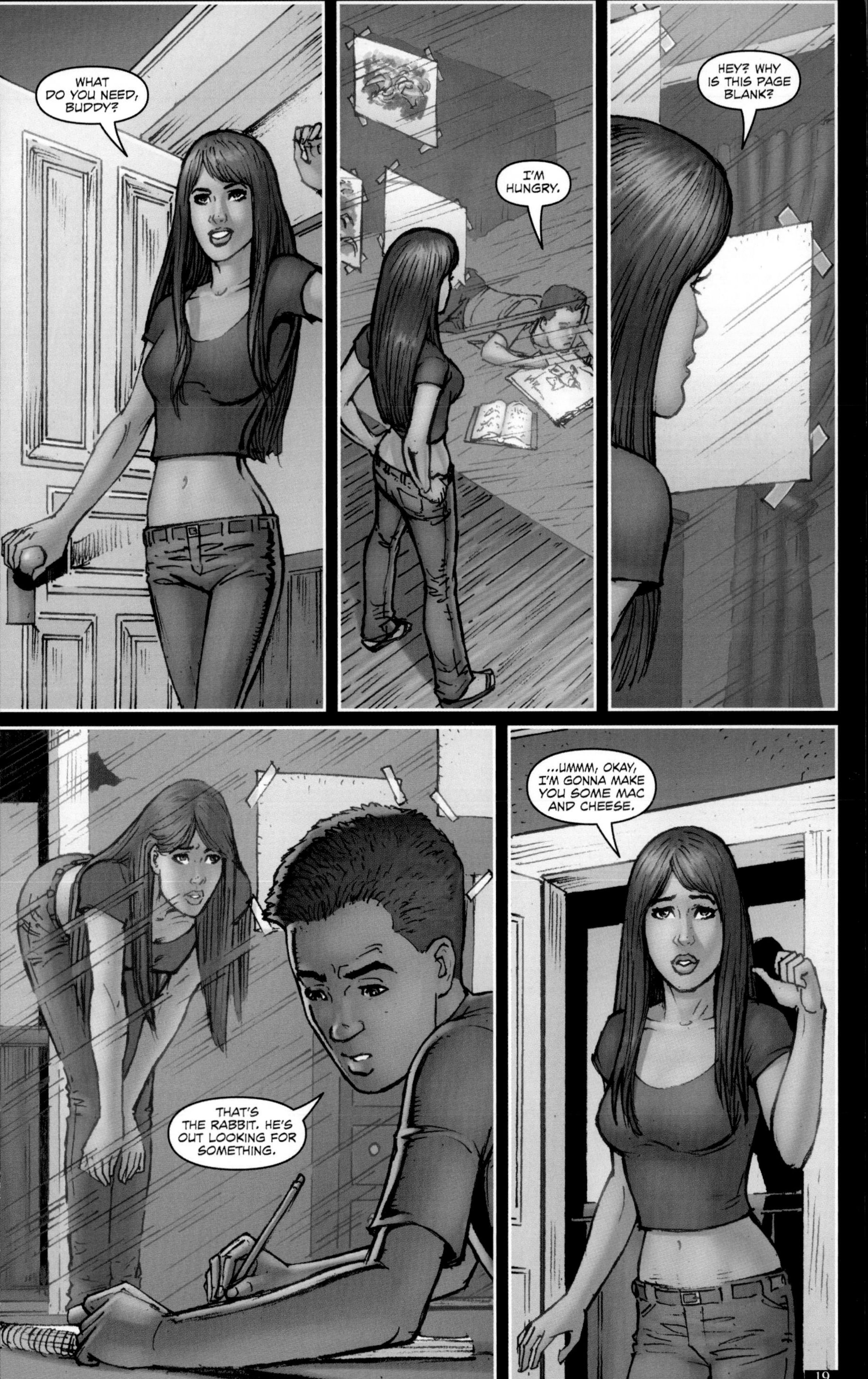
WHAT DO YOU NEED, BUDDY?
I'M HUNGRY.
HEY? WHY IS THIS PAGE BLANK?
THAT'S THE RABBIT. HE'S OUT LOOKING FOR SOMETHING.
...UMMM, OKAY, I'M GONNA MAKE YOU SOME MAC AND CHEESE.

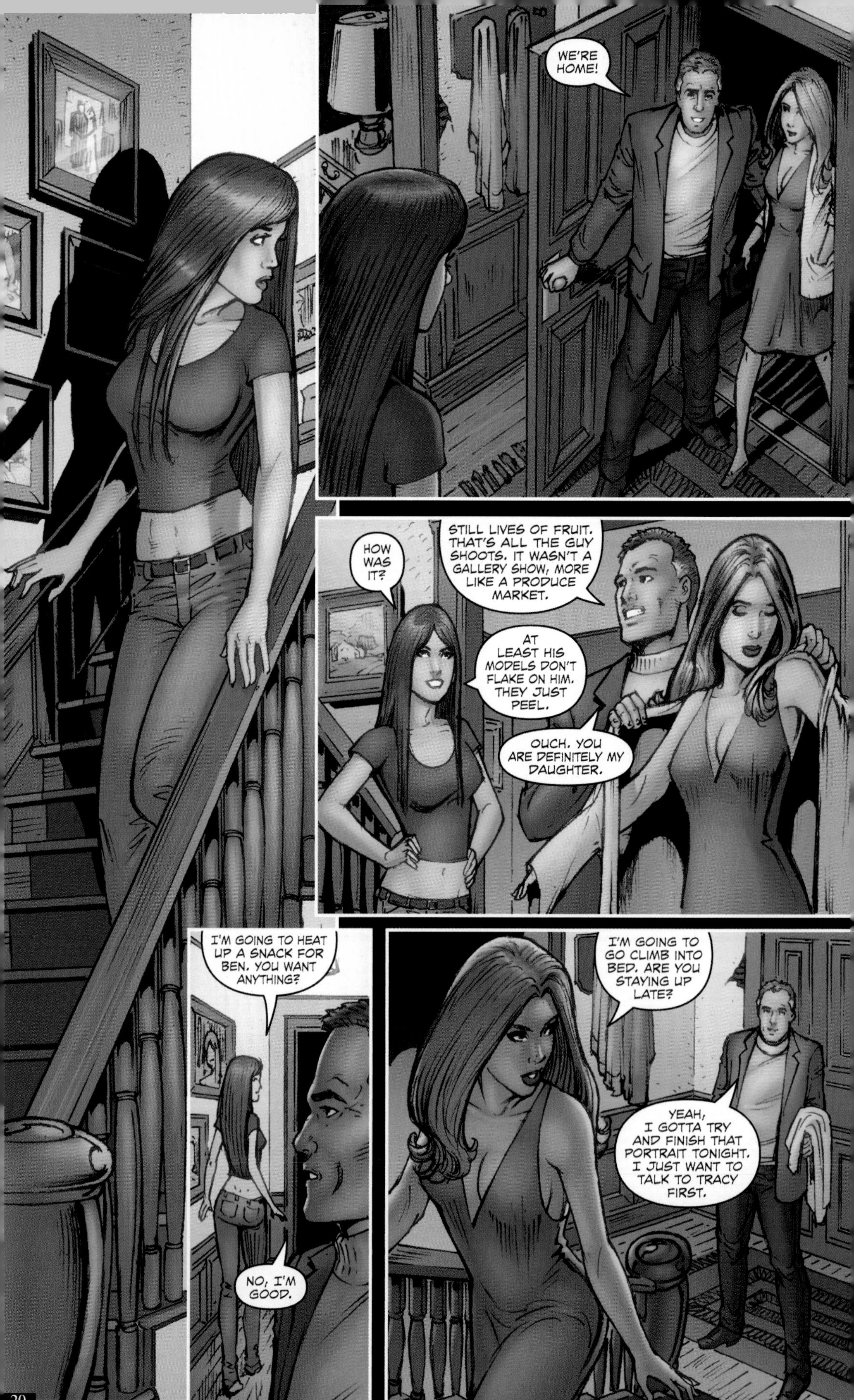
WE'RE HOME!
HOW WAS IT?
STILL LIVES OF FRUIT. THAT'S ALL THE GUY SHOOTS. IT WASN'T A GALLERY SHOW, MORE LIKE A PRODUCE MARKET.
AT LEAST HIS MODELS DON'T FLAKE ON HIM. THEY JUST PEEL.
OUCH. YOU ARE DEFINITELY MY DAUGHTER.
I'M GOING TO HEAT UP A SNACK FOR BEN. YOU WANT ANYTHING?
NO, I'M GOOD.
I'M GOING TO GO CLIMB INTO BED. ARE YOU STAYING UP LATE?
YEAH, I GOTTA TRY AND FINISH THAT PORTRAIT TONIGHT. I JUST WANT TO TALK TO TRACY FIRST.

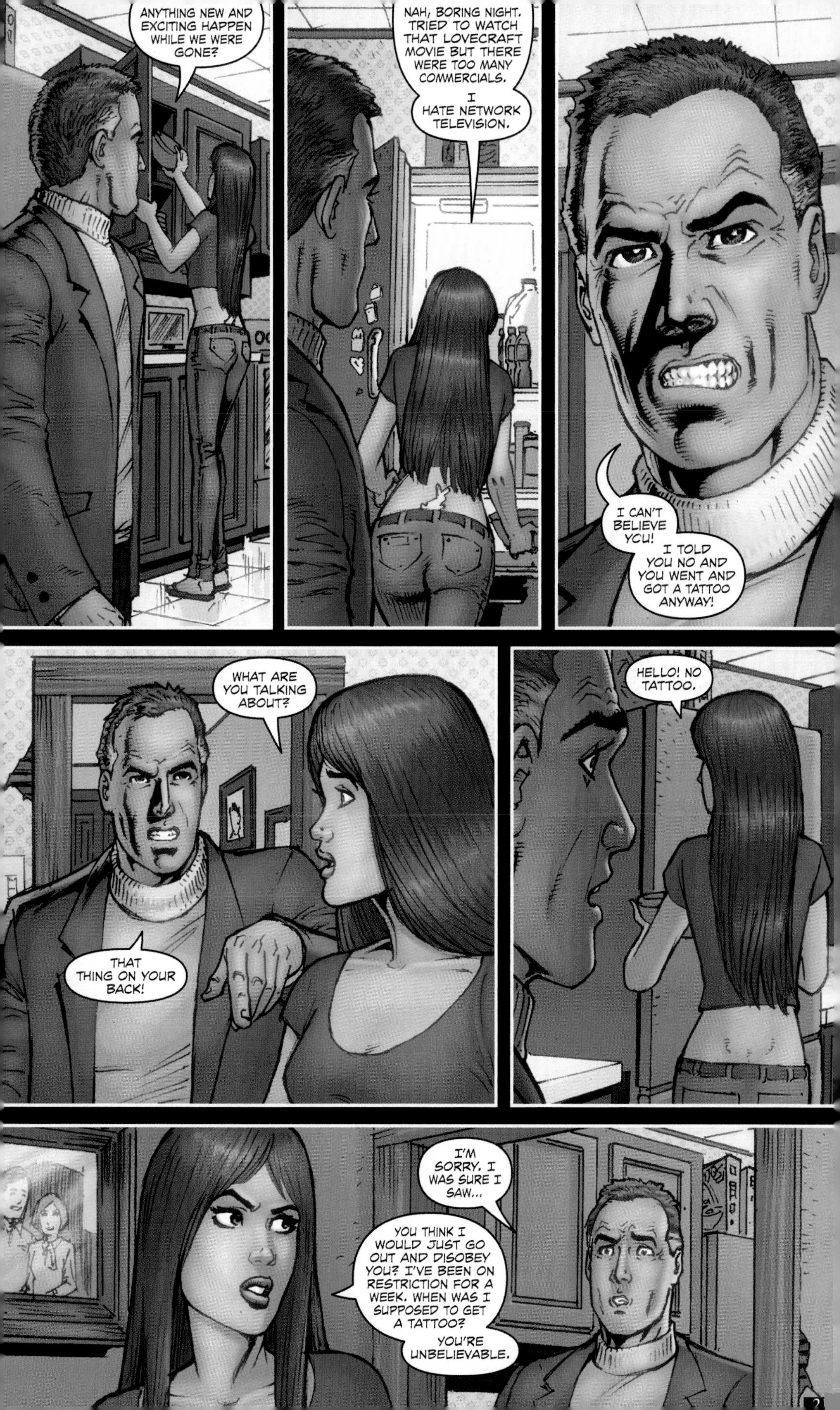
ANYTHING NEW AND EXCITING HAPPEN WHILE WE WERE GONE?
NAH, BORING NIGHT. TRIED TO WATCH THAT LOVECRAFT MOVIE BUT THERE WERE TOO MANY COMMERCIALS.
I HATE NETWORK TELEVISION.
I CAN'T BELIEVE YOU!
I TOLD YOU NO AND YOU WENT AND GOT A TATTOO ANYWAY!
WHAT ARE YOU TALKING ABOUT?
THAT THING ON YOUR BACK!
HELLO! NO TATTOO.
I'M SORRY. I WAS SURE I SAW...
YOU THINK I WOULD JUST GO OUT AND DISOBEY YOU? I'VE BEEN ON RESTRICTION FOR A WEEK. WHEN WAS I SUPPOSED TO GET A TATTOO?
YOU'RE UNBELIEVABLE.

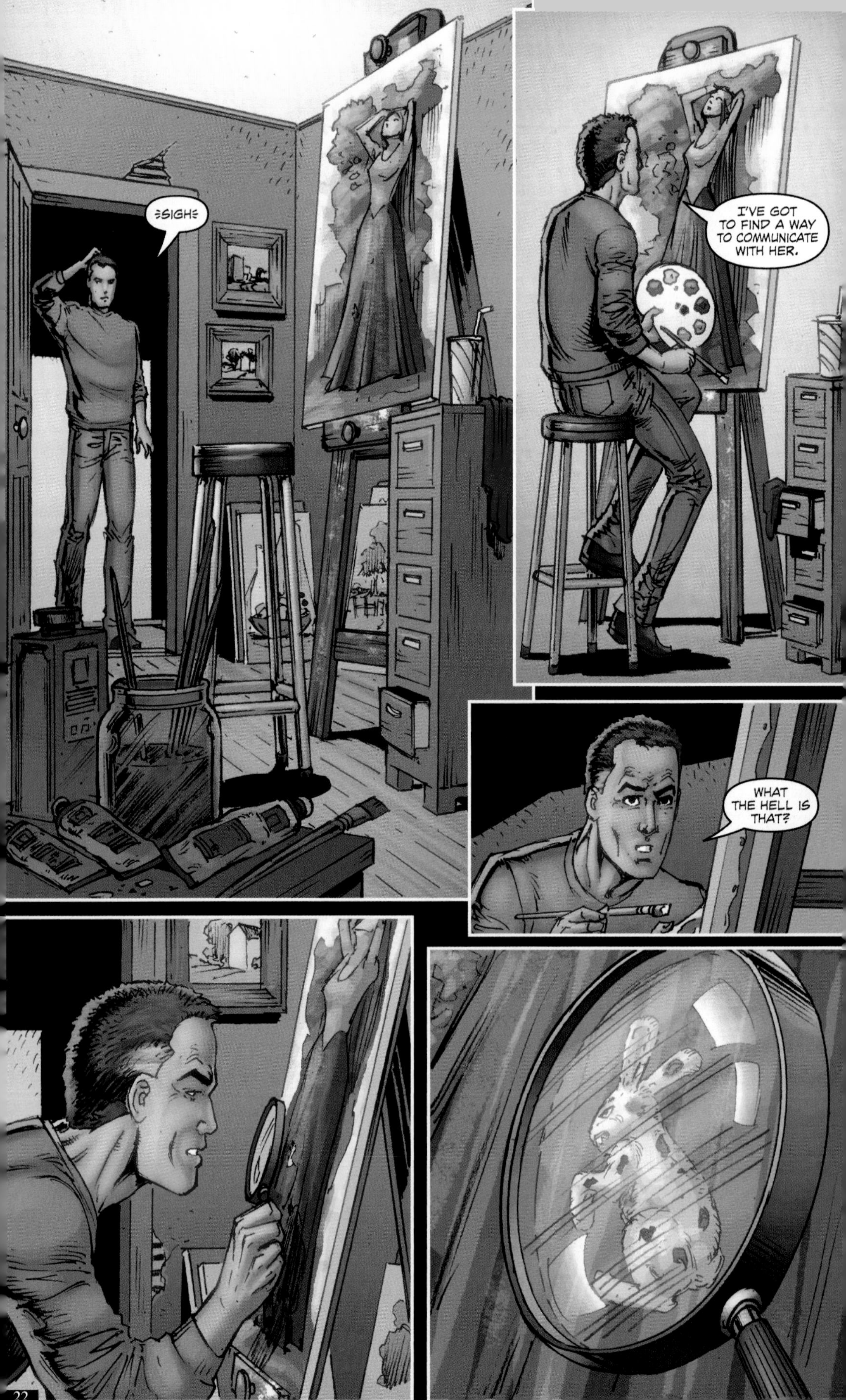

=SIGH=
I'VE GOT TO FIND A WAY TO COMMUNICATE WITH HER.
WHAT THE HELL IS THAT?

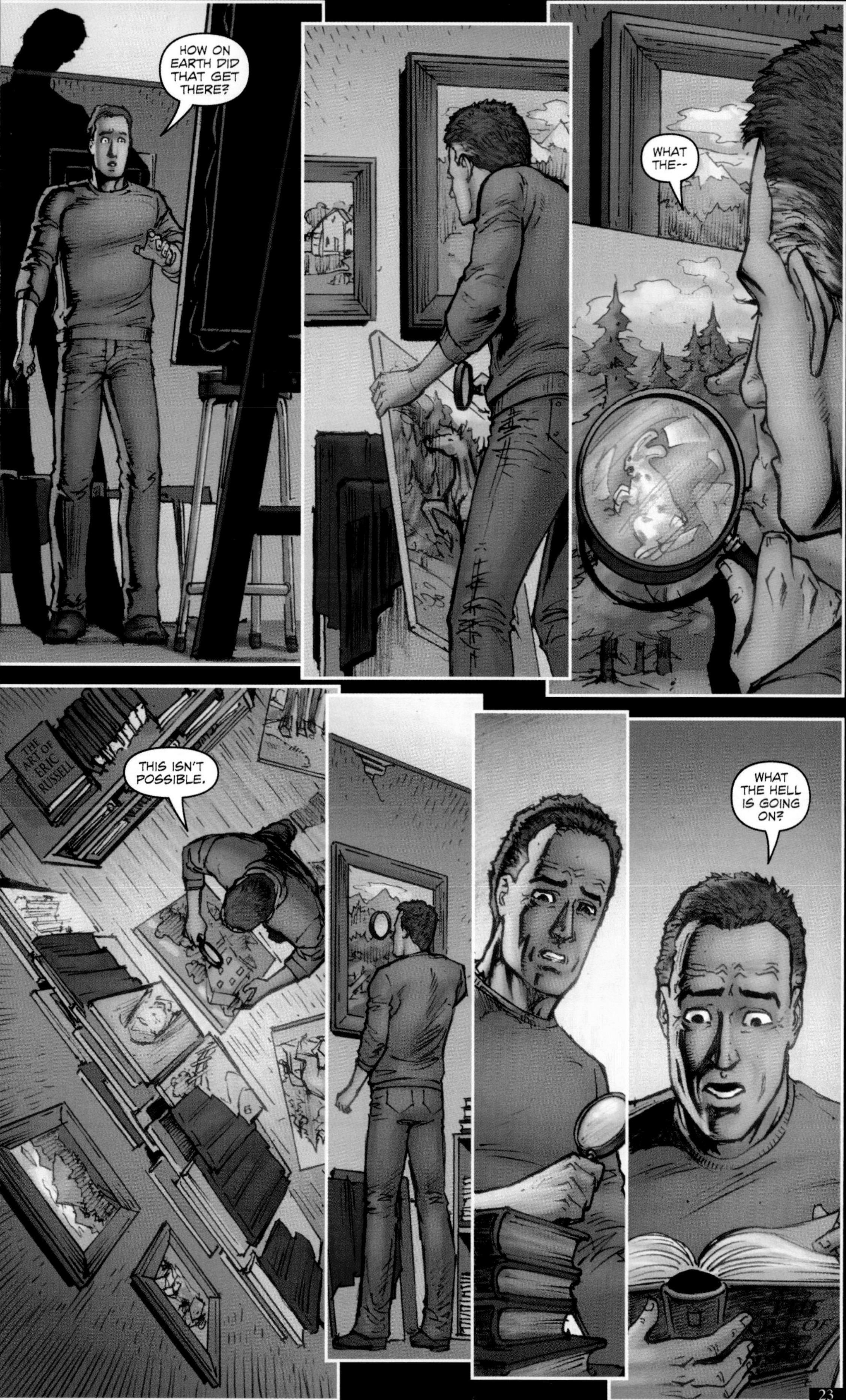
HOW ON EARTH DID THAT GET THERE?
WHAT THE--
THE ART OF ERIC RUSSELL
THIS ISN'T POSSIBLE.
WHAT THE HELL IS GOING ON?

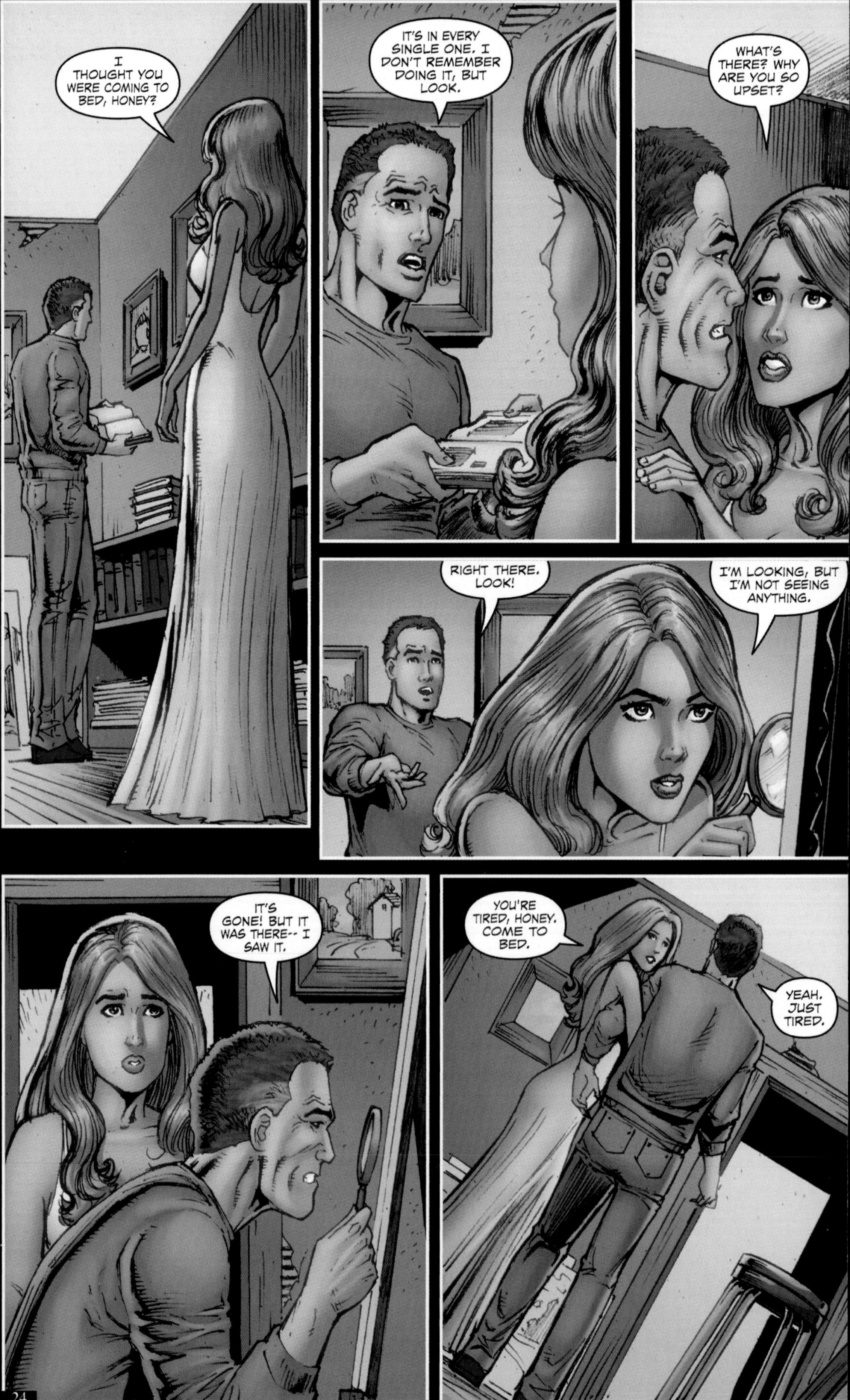
I THOUGHT YOU WERE COMING TO BED, HONEY?
IT'S IN EVERY SINGLE ONE. I DON'T REMEMBER DOING IT, BUT LOOK.
WHAT'S THERE? WHY ARE YOU SO UPSET?
RIGHT THERE. LOOK!
I'M LOOKING, BUT I'M NOT SEEING ANYTHING.
IT'S GONE! BUT IT WAS THERE-- I SAW IT.
YOU'RE TIRED, HONEY. COME TO BED.
YEAH. JUST TIRED.

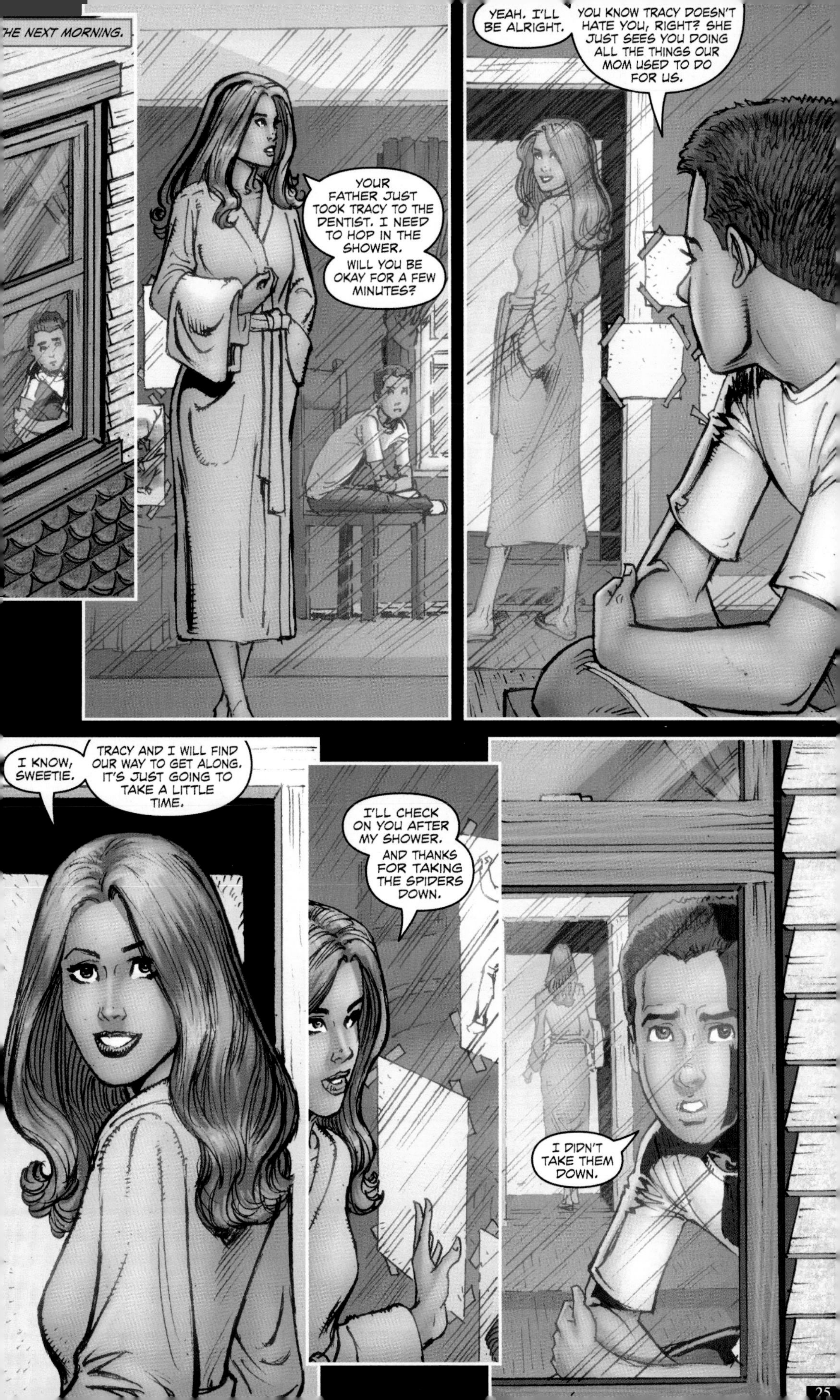
THE NEXT MORNING.
YOUR FATHER JUST TOOK TRACY TO THE DENTIST. I NEED TO HOP IN THE SHOWER.
WILL YOU BE OKAY FOR A FEW MINUTES?
YEAH. I'LL BE ALRIGHT.
YOU KNOW TRACY DOESN'T HATE YOU, RIGHT? SHE JUST SEES YOU DOING ALL THE THINGS OUR MOM USED TO DO FOR US.
I KNOW, SWEETIE.
TRACY AND I WILL FIND OUR WAY TO GET ALONG. IT'S JUST GOING TO TAKE A LITTLE TIME.
I'LL CHECK ON YOU AFTER MY SHOWER.
AND THANKS FOR TAKING THE SPIDERS DOWN.
I DIDN'T TAKE THEM DOWN.

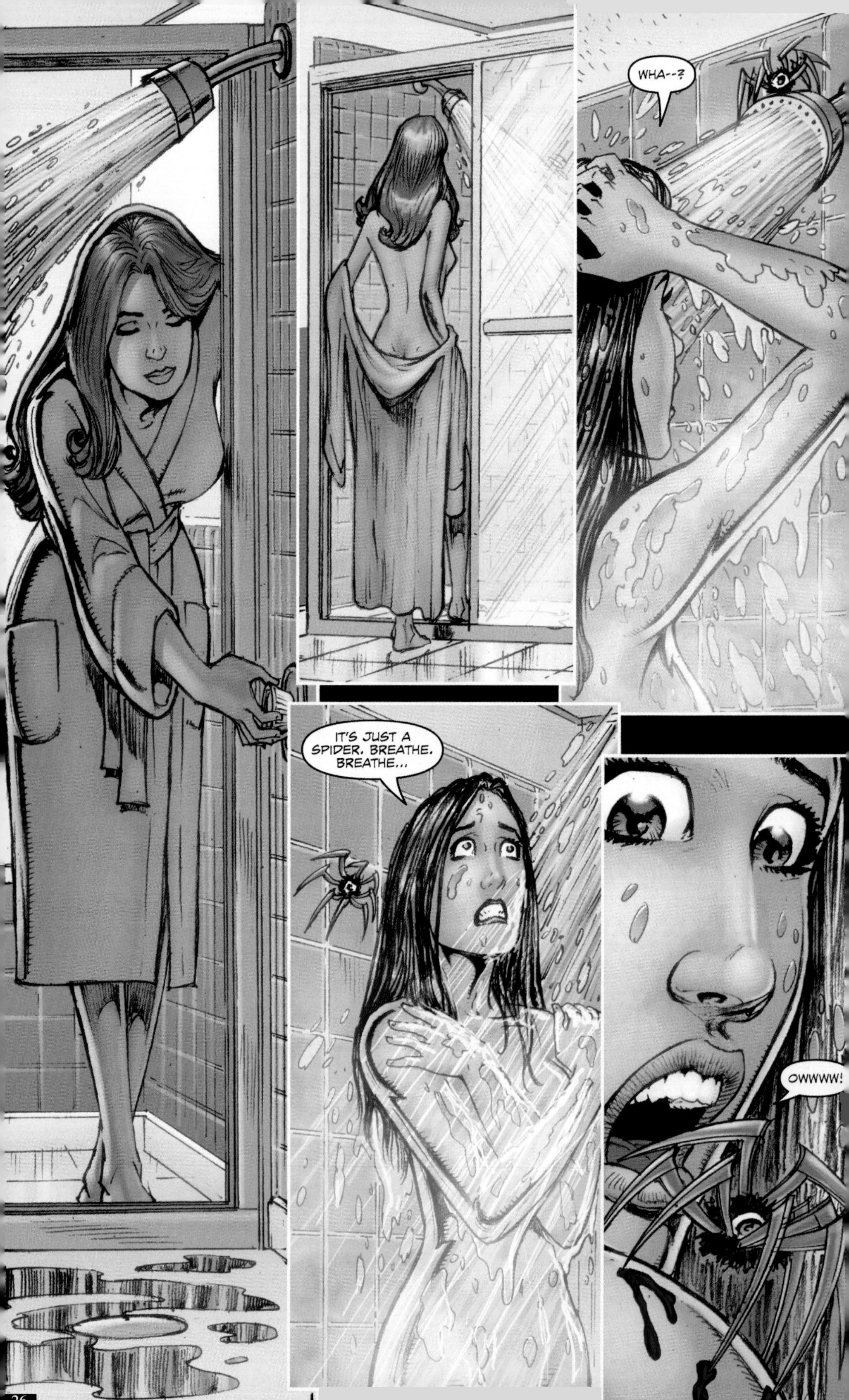
WHA--?
IT'S JUST A SPIDER. BREATHE. BREATHE...
OWWWW!

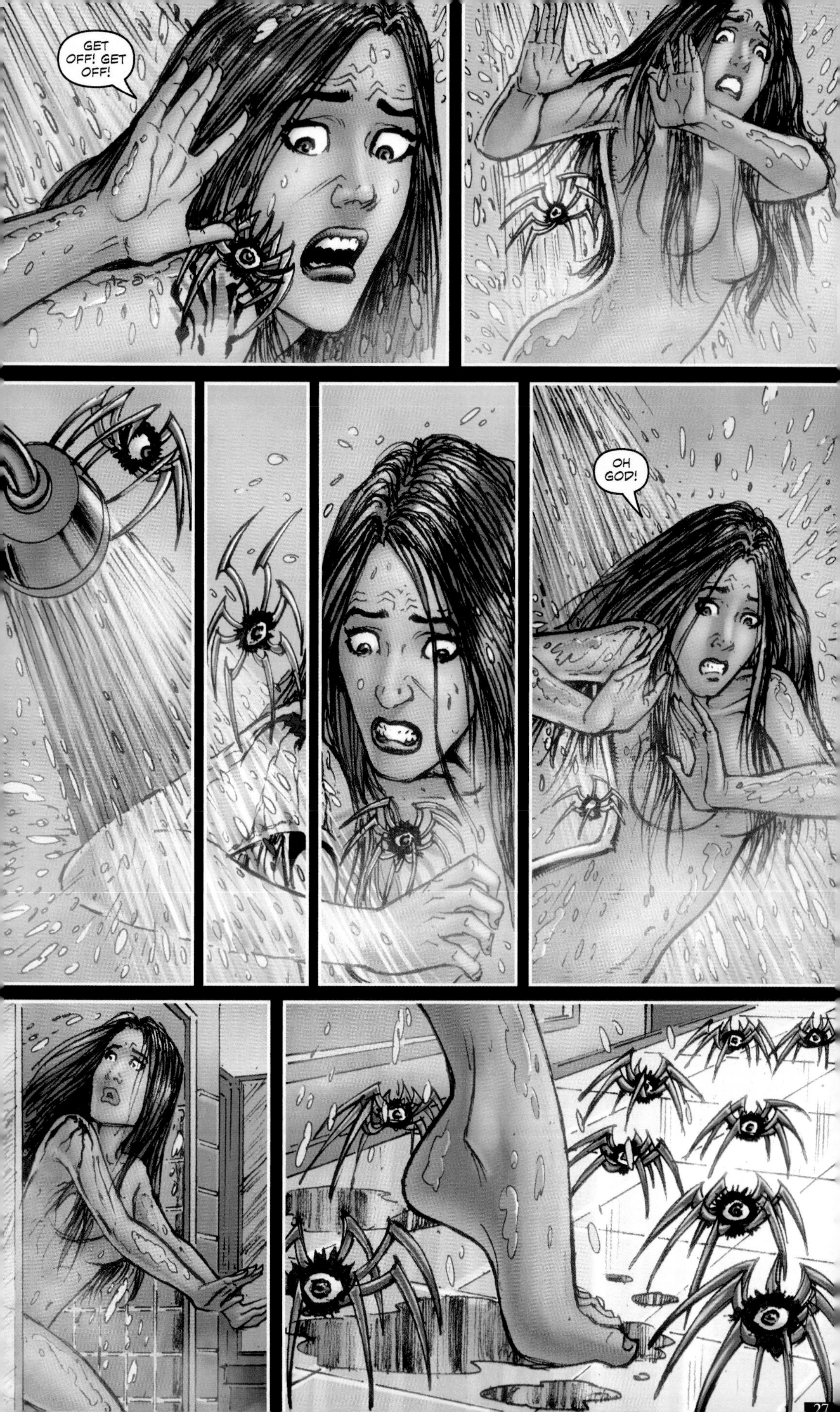
GET OFF! GET OFF!
OH GOD!

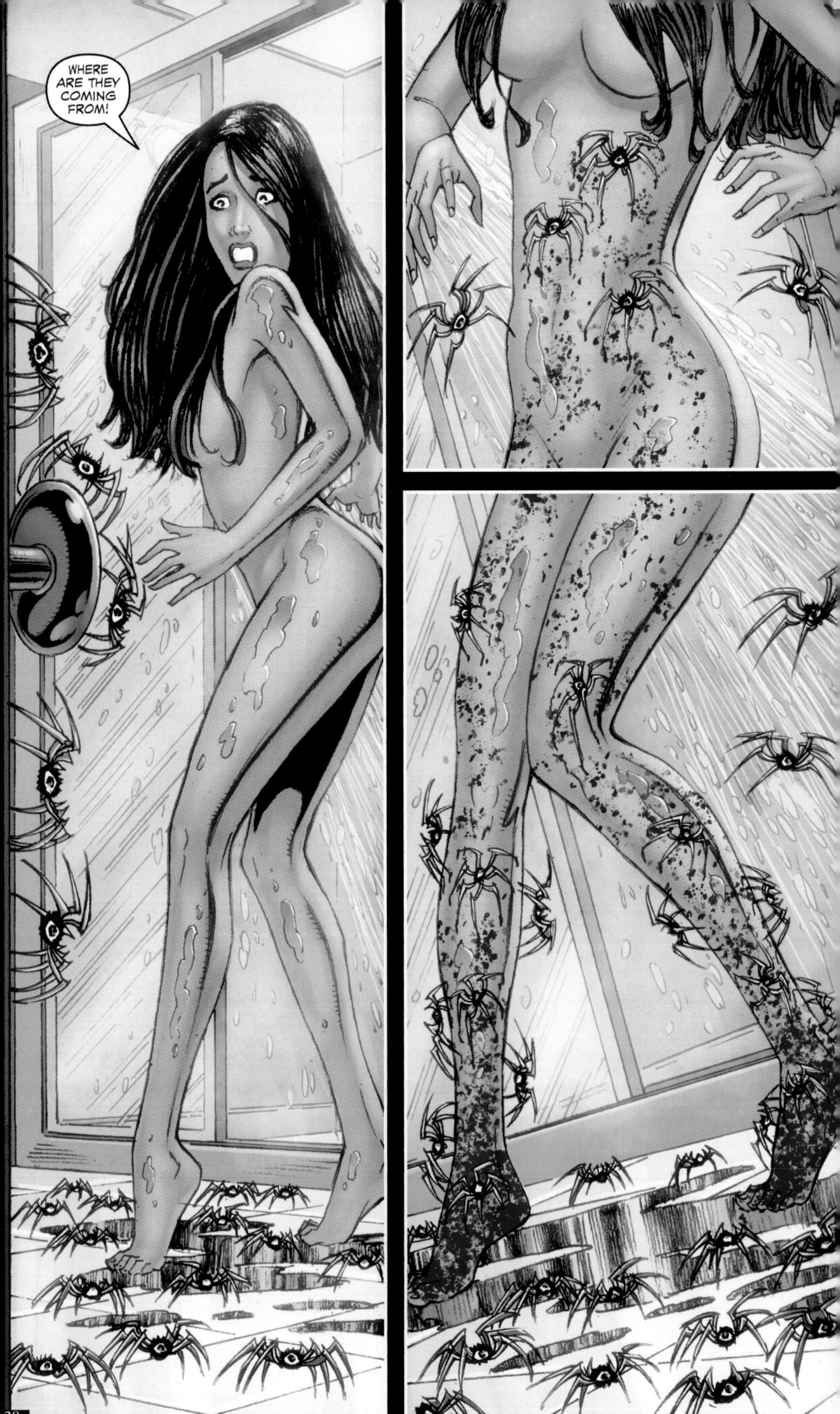
WHERE ARE THEY COMING FROM!

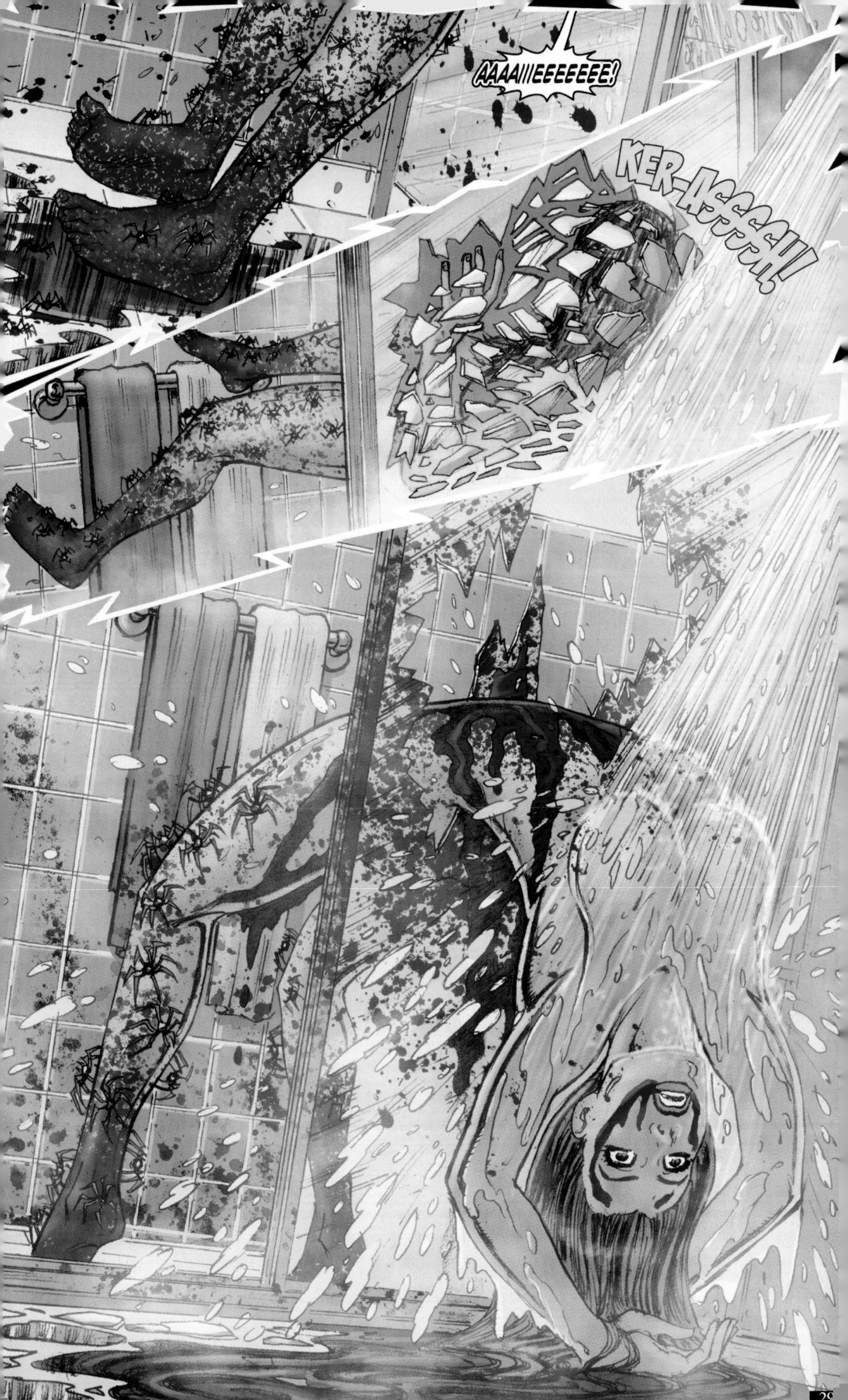
AAAAIIIEEEEEEEE!
KER-ASSSCH!

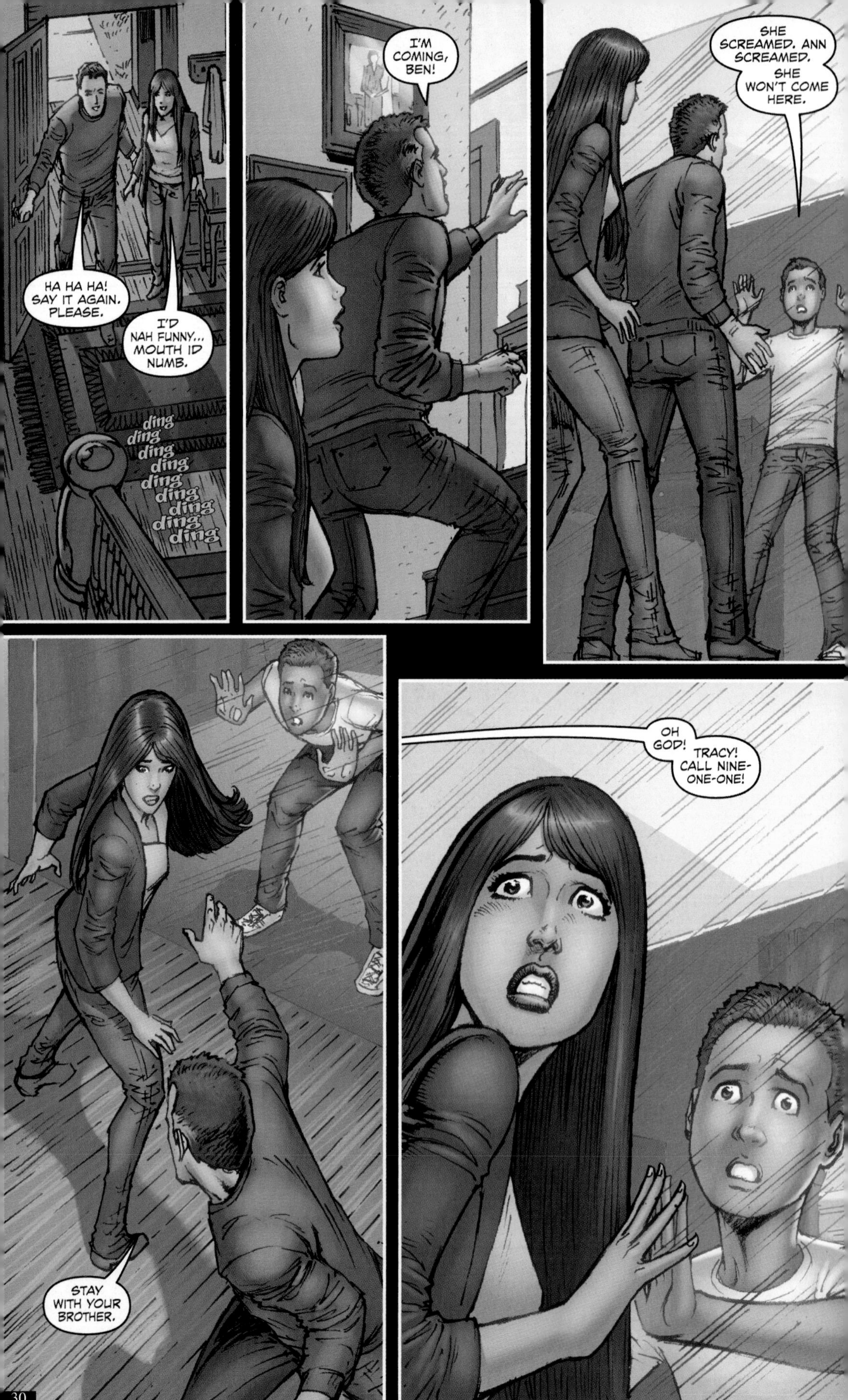
HA HA HA! SAY IT AGAIN. PLEASE.
I'D NAH FUNNY... MOUTH ID NUMB.
ding ding ding ding ding ding ding ding ding
I'M COMING, BEN!
SHE SCREAMED. ANN SCREAMED. SHE WON'T COME HERE.
STAY WITH YOUR BROTHER.
OH GOD! TRACY! CALL NINE-ONE-ONE!

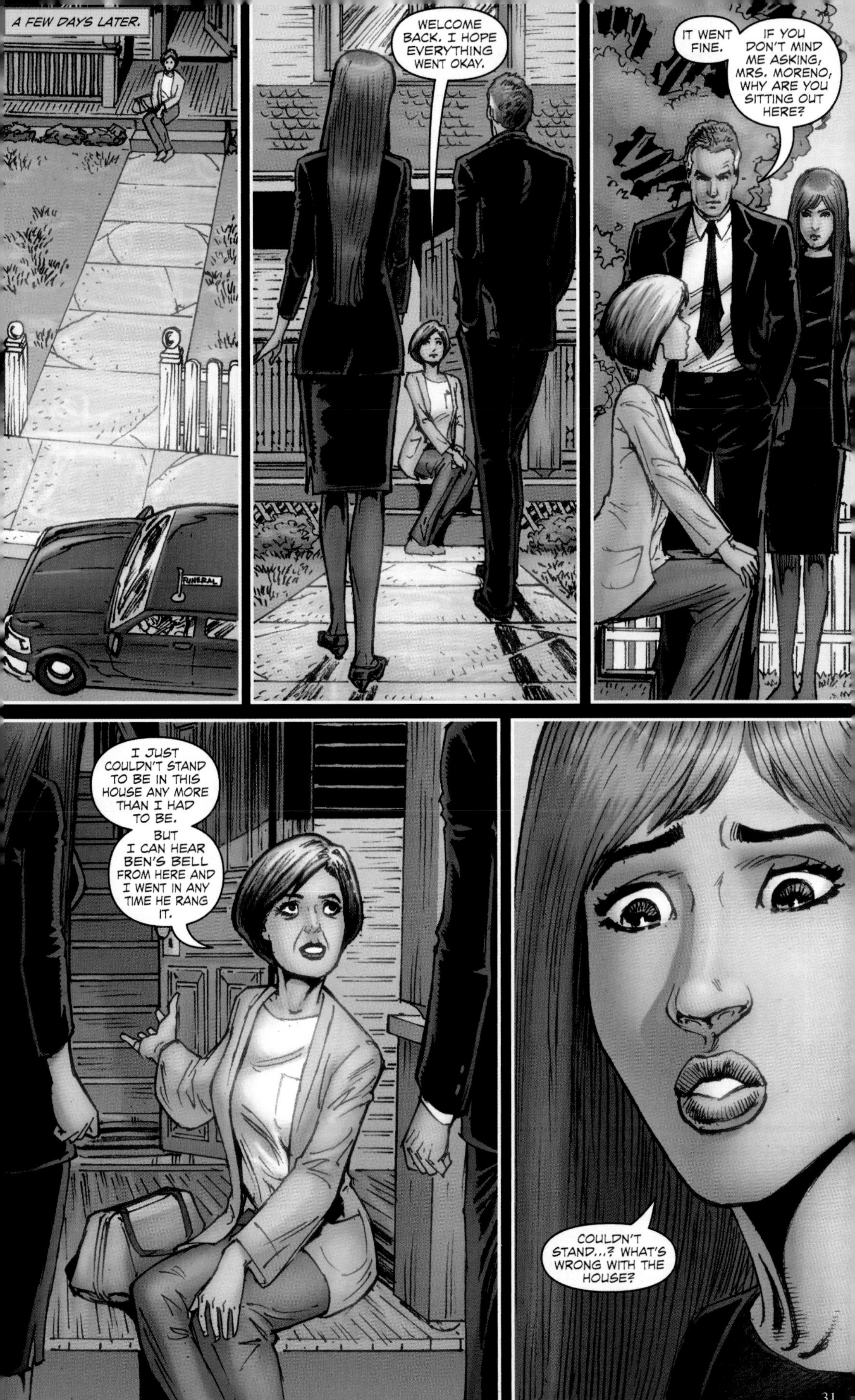
A FEW DAYS LATER.
FUNERAL
WELCOME BACK. I HOPE EVERYTHING WENT OKAY.
IT WENT FINE.
IF YOU DON'T MIND ME ASKING, MRS. MORENO, WHY ARE YOU SITTING OUT HERE?
I JUST COULDN'T STAND TO BE IN THIS HOUSE ANY MORE THAN I HAD TO BE.
BUT I CAN HEAR BEN'S BELL FROM HERE AND I WENT IN ANY TIME HE RANG IT.
COULDN'T STAND...? WHAT'S WRONG WITH THE HOUSE?

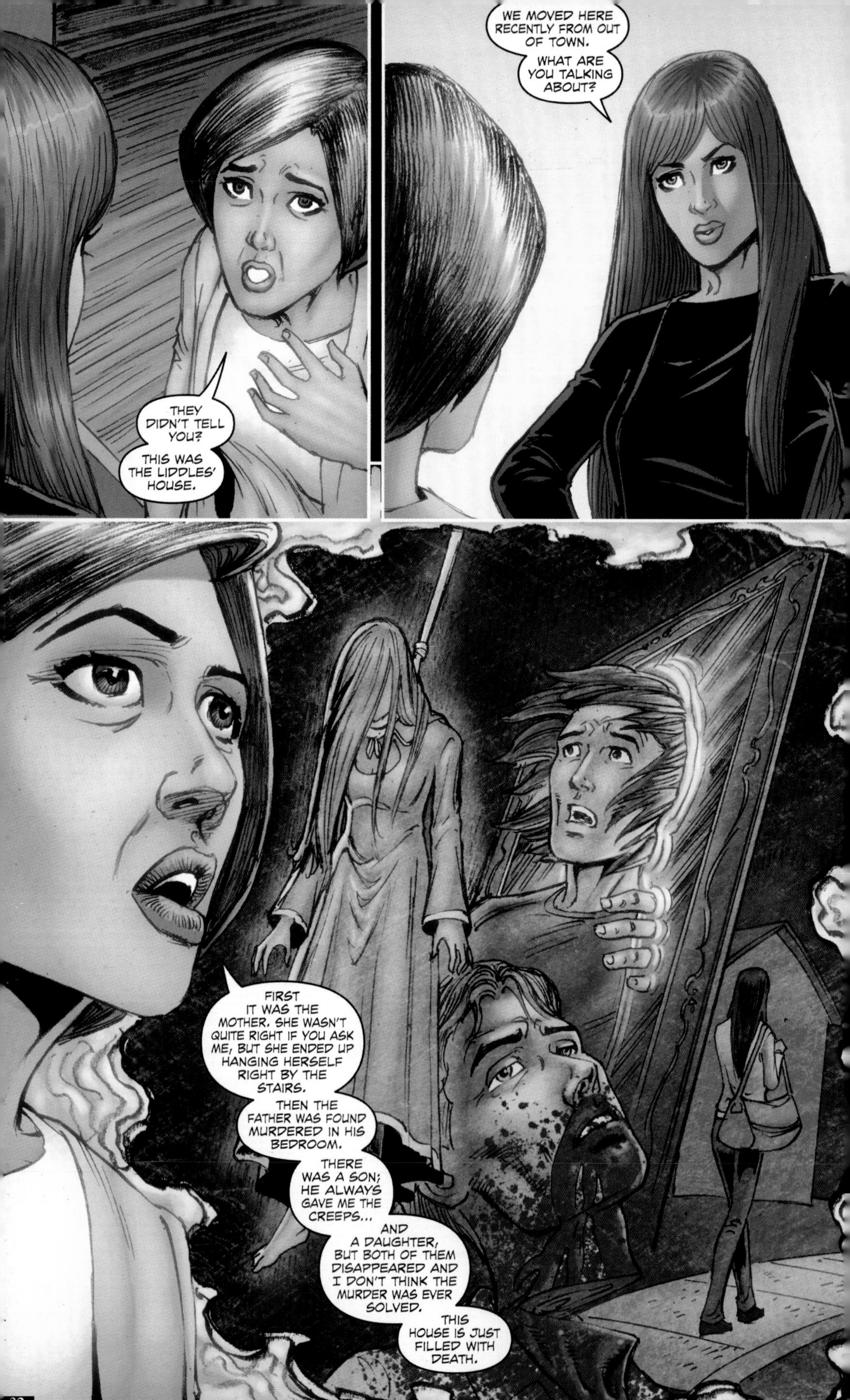
THEY DIDN'T TELL YOU?
THIS WAS THE LIDDLES' HOUSE.
WE MOVED HERE RECENTLY FROM OUT OF TOWN.
WHAT ARE YOU TALKING ABOUT?
FIRST IT WAS THE MOTHER. SHE WASN'T QUITE RIGHT IF YOU ASK ME, BUT SHE ENDED UP HANGING HERSELF RIGHT BY THE STAIRS.
THEN THE FATHER WAS FOUND MURDERED IN HIS BEDROOM.
THERE WAS A SON; HE ALWAYS GAVE ME THE CREEPS...
AND A DAUGHTER, BUT BOTH OF THEM DISAPPEARED AND I DON'T THINK THE MURDER WAS EVER SOLVED.
THIS HOUSE IS JUST FILLED WITH DEATH.

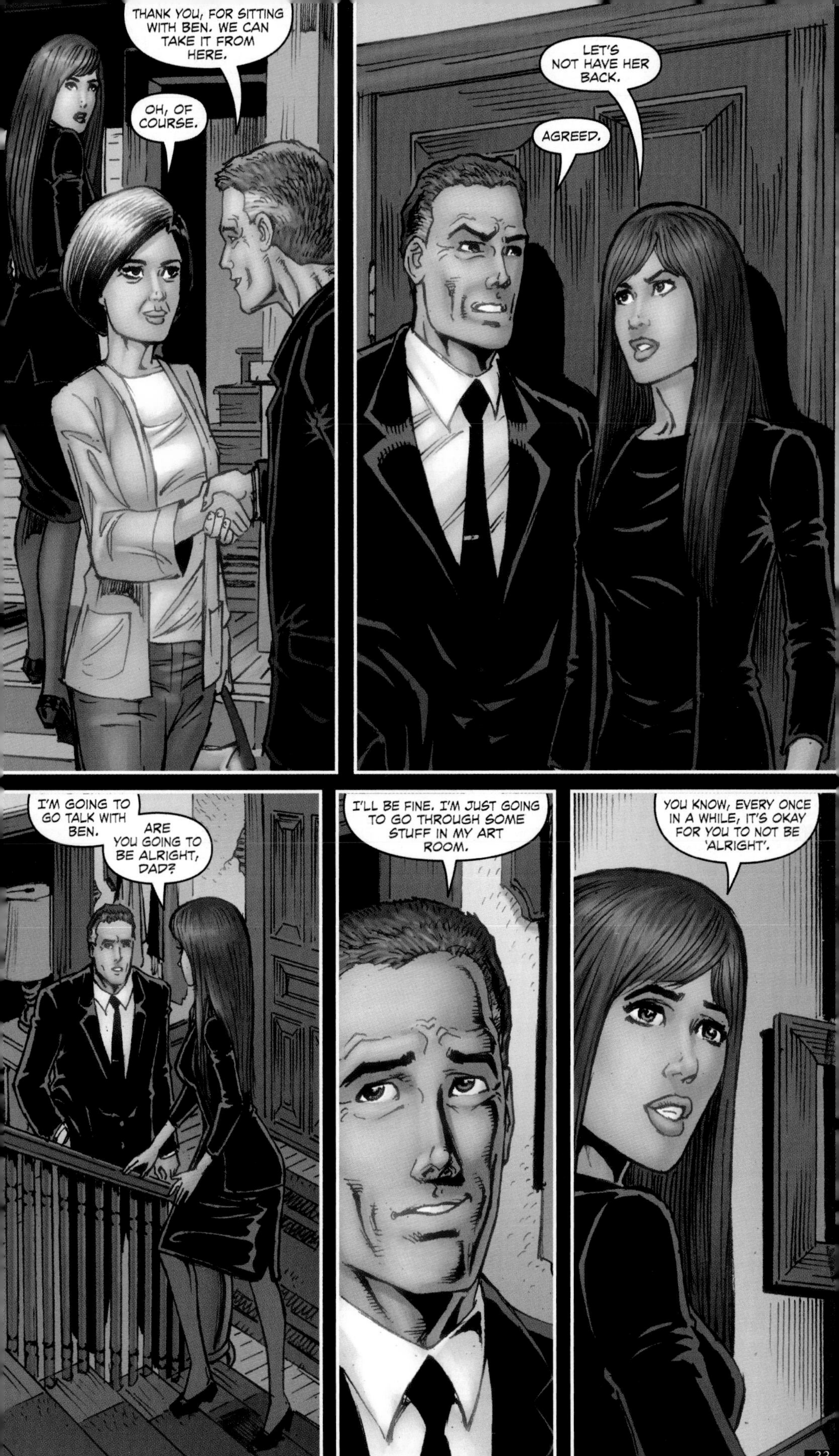
THANK YOU, FOR SITTING WITH BEN. WE CAN TAKE IT FROM HERE.
OH, OF COURSE.
LET'S NOT HAVE HER BACK.
AGREED.
I'M GOING TO GO TALK WITH BEN.
ARE YOU GOING TO BE ALRIGHT, DAD?
I'LL BE FINE. I'M JUST GOING TO GO THROUGH SOME STUFF IN MY ART ROOM.
YOU KNOW, EVERY ONCE IN A WHILE, IT'S OKAY FOR YOU TO NOT BE 'ALRIGHT'.

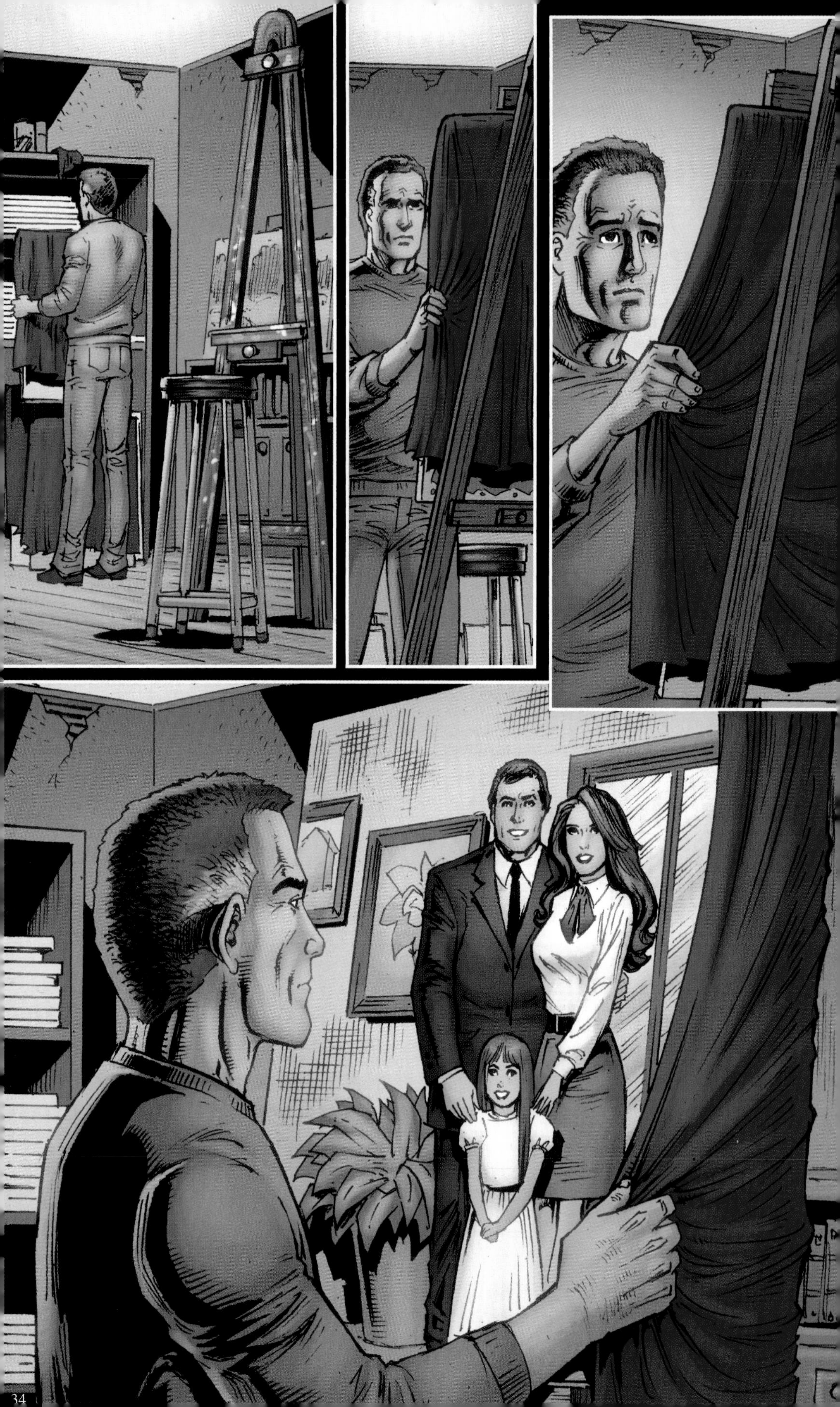

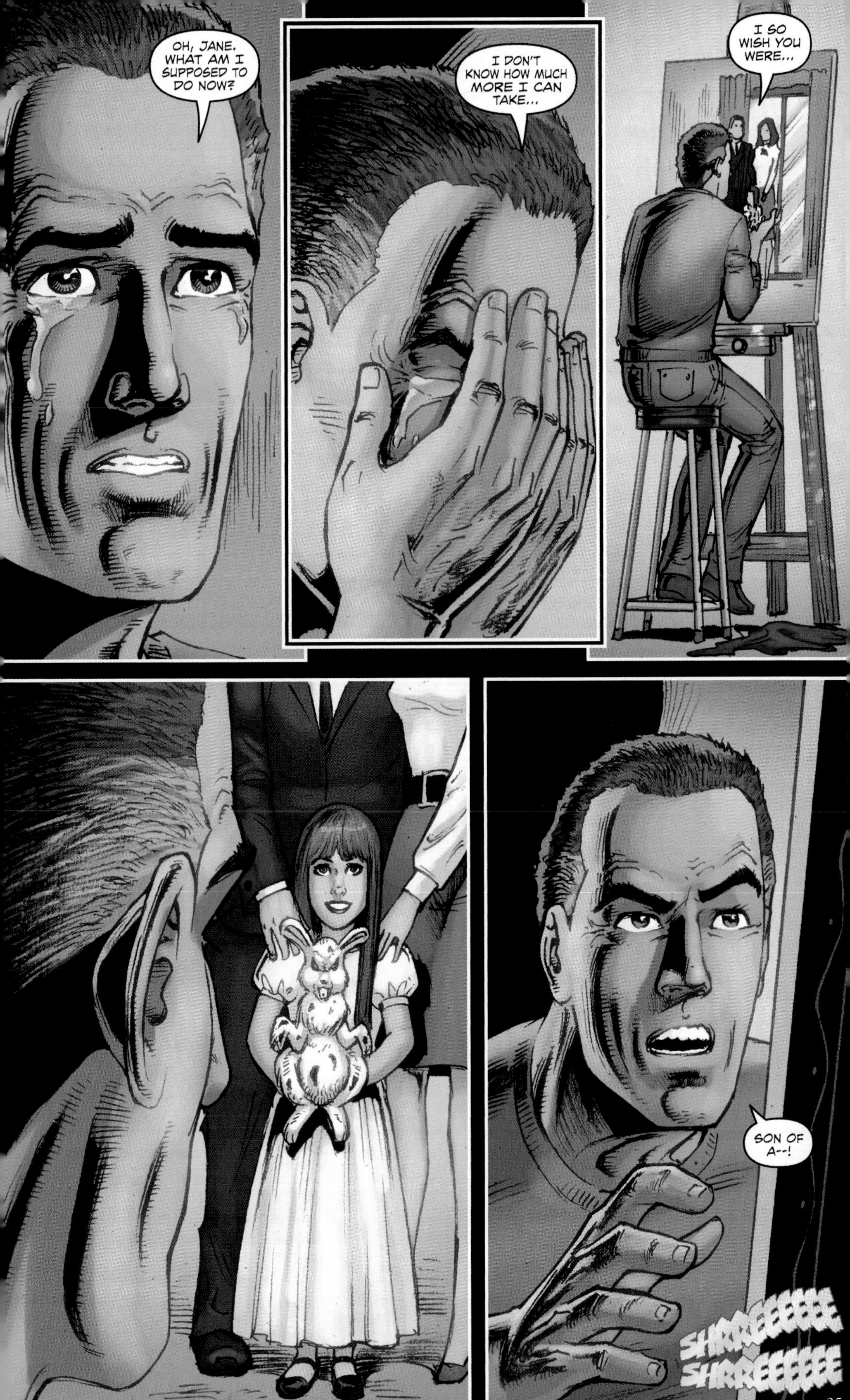
OH, JANE. WHAT AM I SUPPOSED TO DO NOW?
I DON'T KNOW HOW MUCH MORE I CAN TAKE...
I SO WISH YOU WERE...
SON OF A--!
SHRREEEEEE
SHRREEEEEE

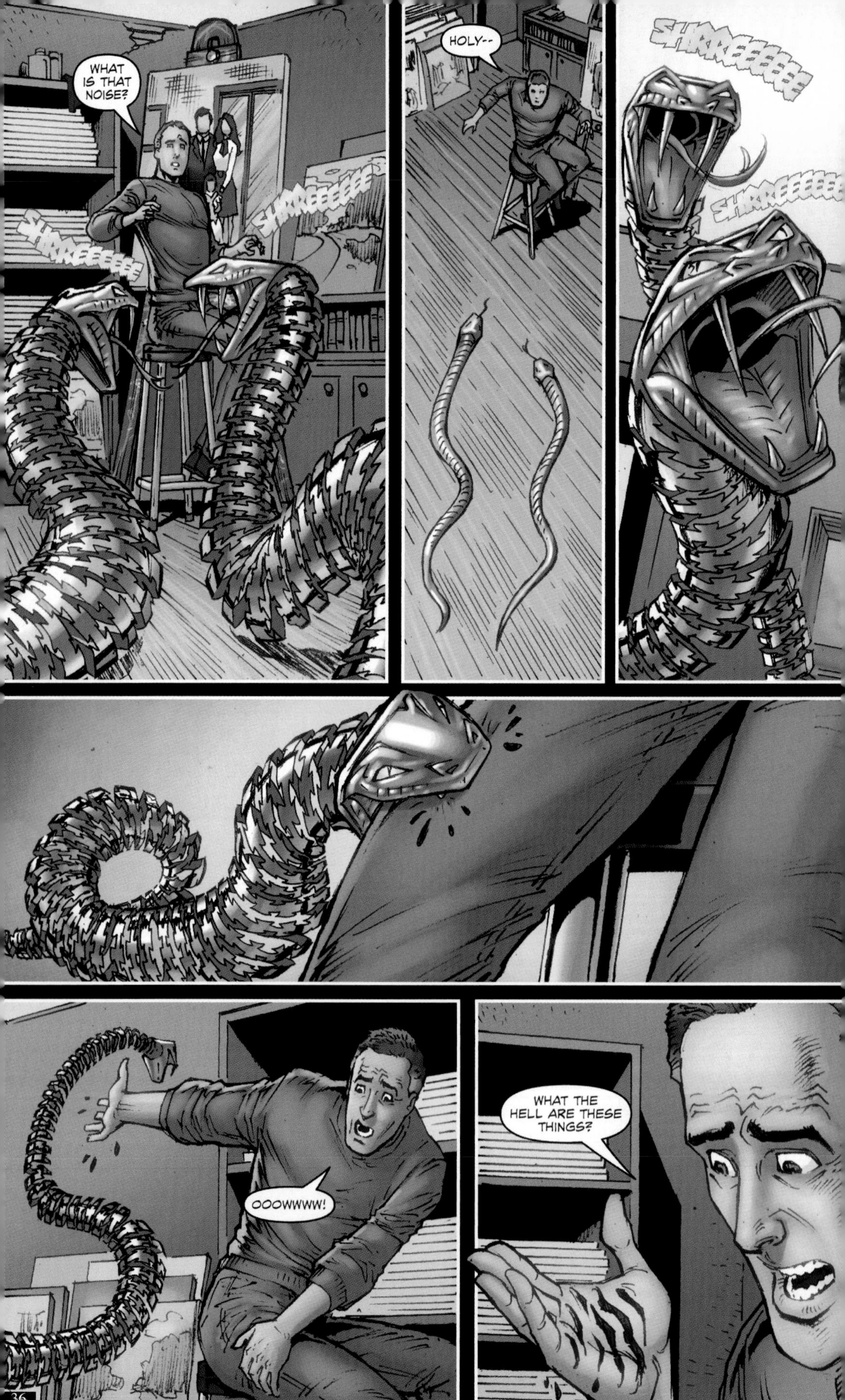
WHAT IS THAT NOISE?
SHRREEEEEE
SHRREEEEEE
HOLY--
SHRREEEEEE
SHRREEEEEE
OOOWWWW!
WHAT THE HELL ARE THESE THINGS?

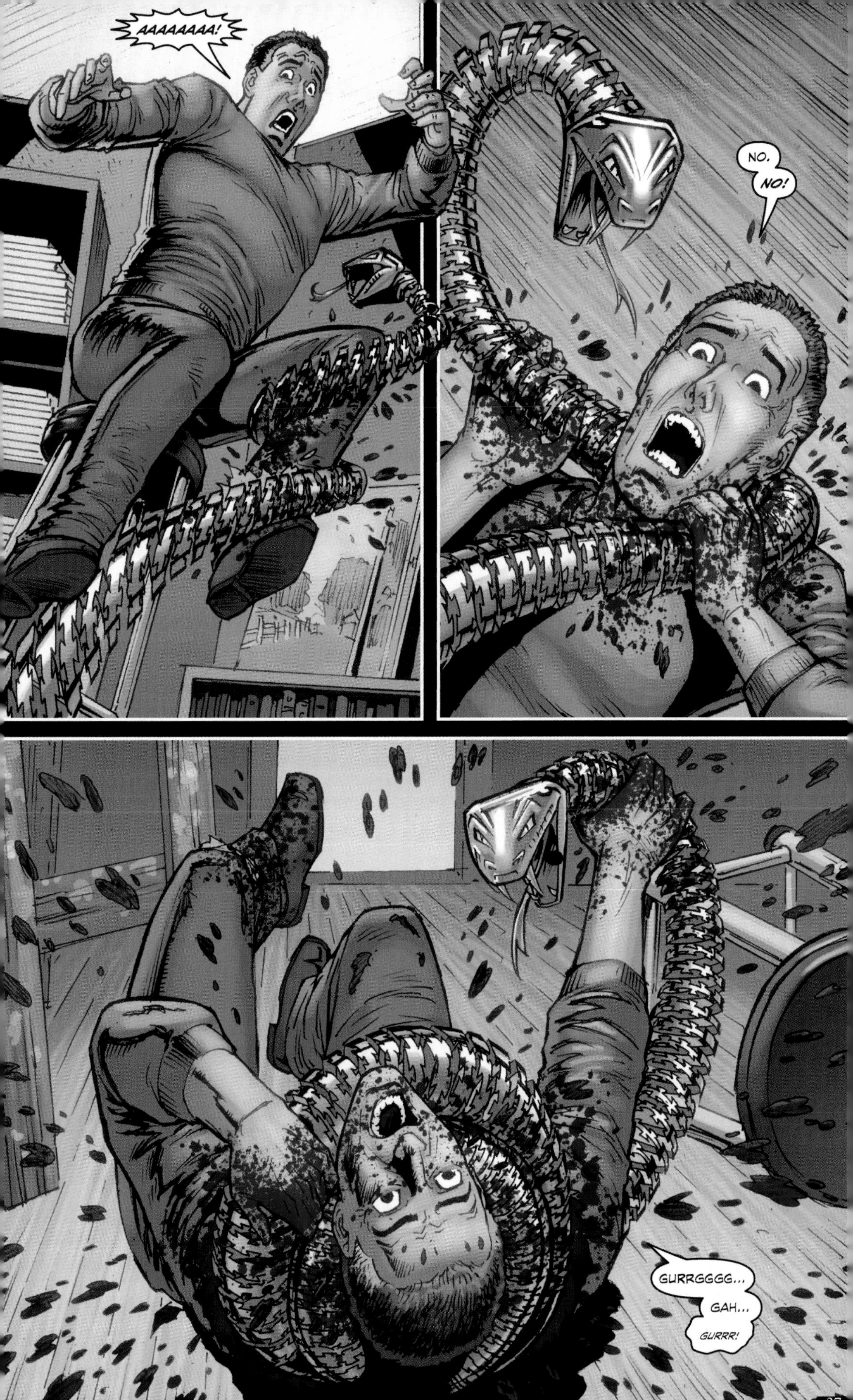
AAAAAAAA!
NO.
NO!
GURRGGGG...
GAH...
GURRR!

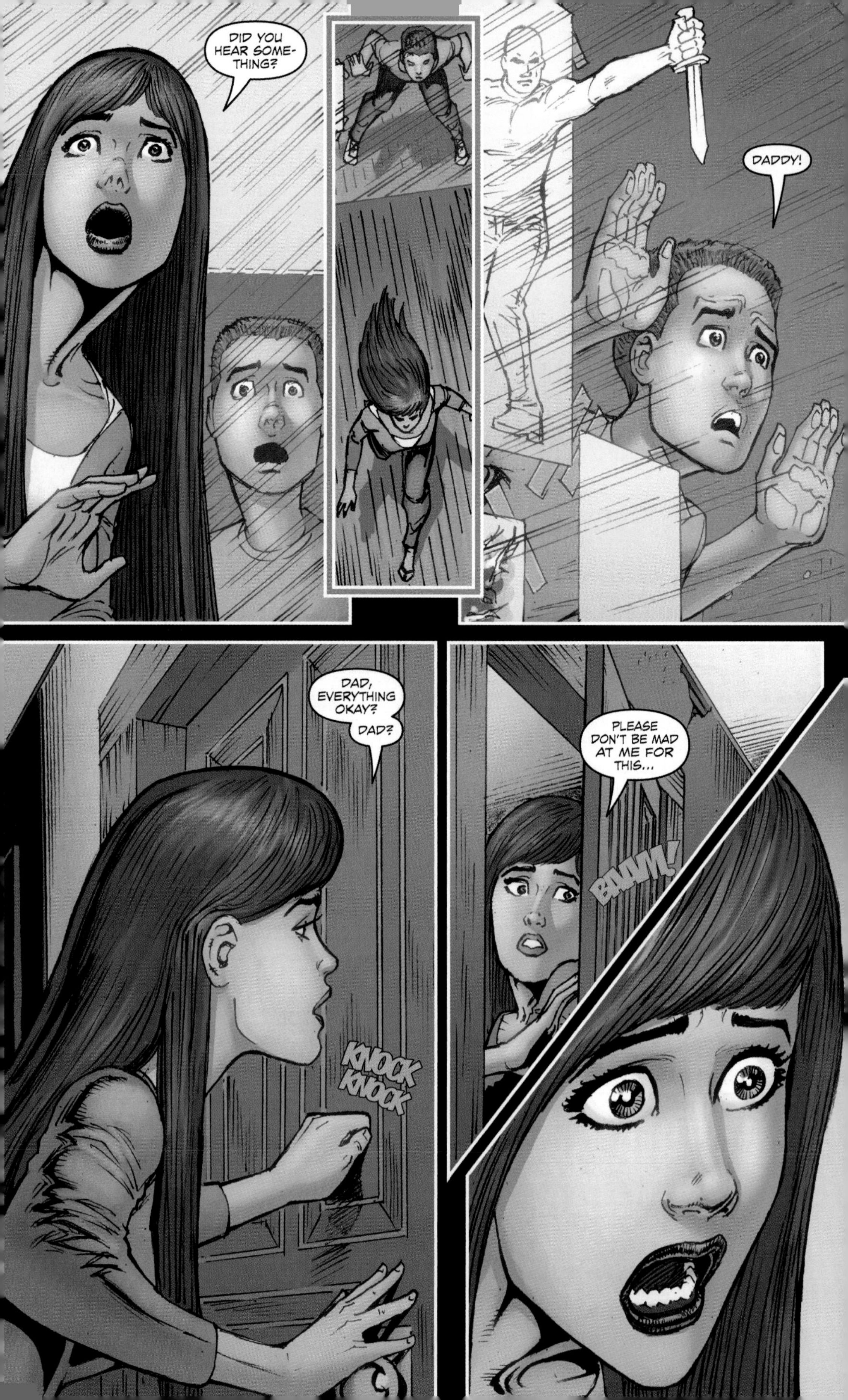
DID YOU HEAR SOME-THING?
DADDY!
DAD, EVERYTHING OKAY?
DAD?
KNOCK KNOCK
PLEASE DON'T BE MAD AT ME FOR THIS...
BAM!

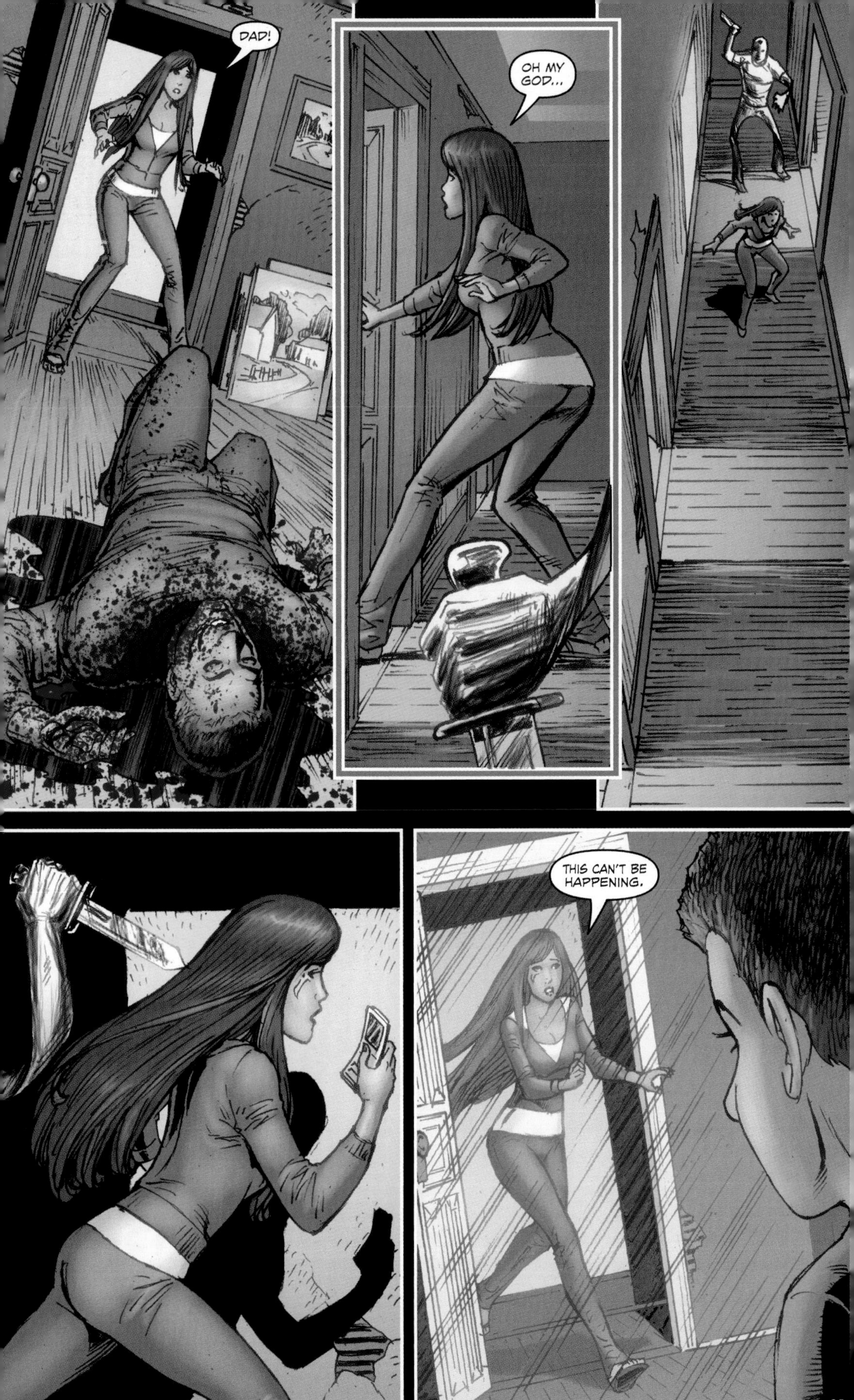
DAD!
OH MY GOD...
THIS CAN'T BE HAPPENING.

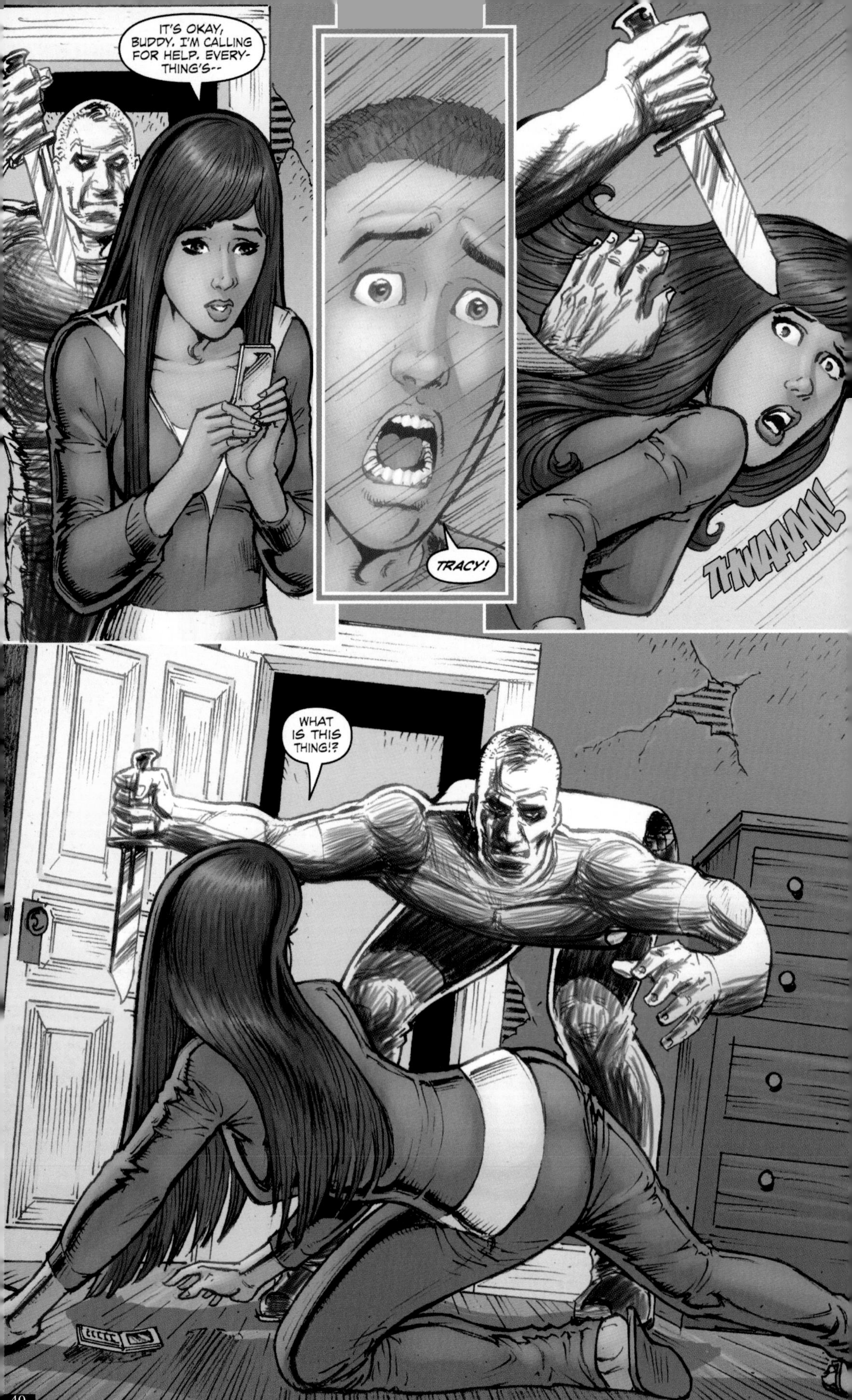
IT'S OKAY, BUDDY. I'M CALLING FOR HELP. EVERY-THING'S--
TRACY!
THWAAAM!
WHAT IS THIS THING!?

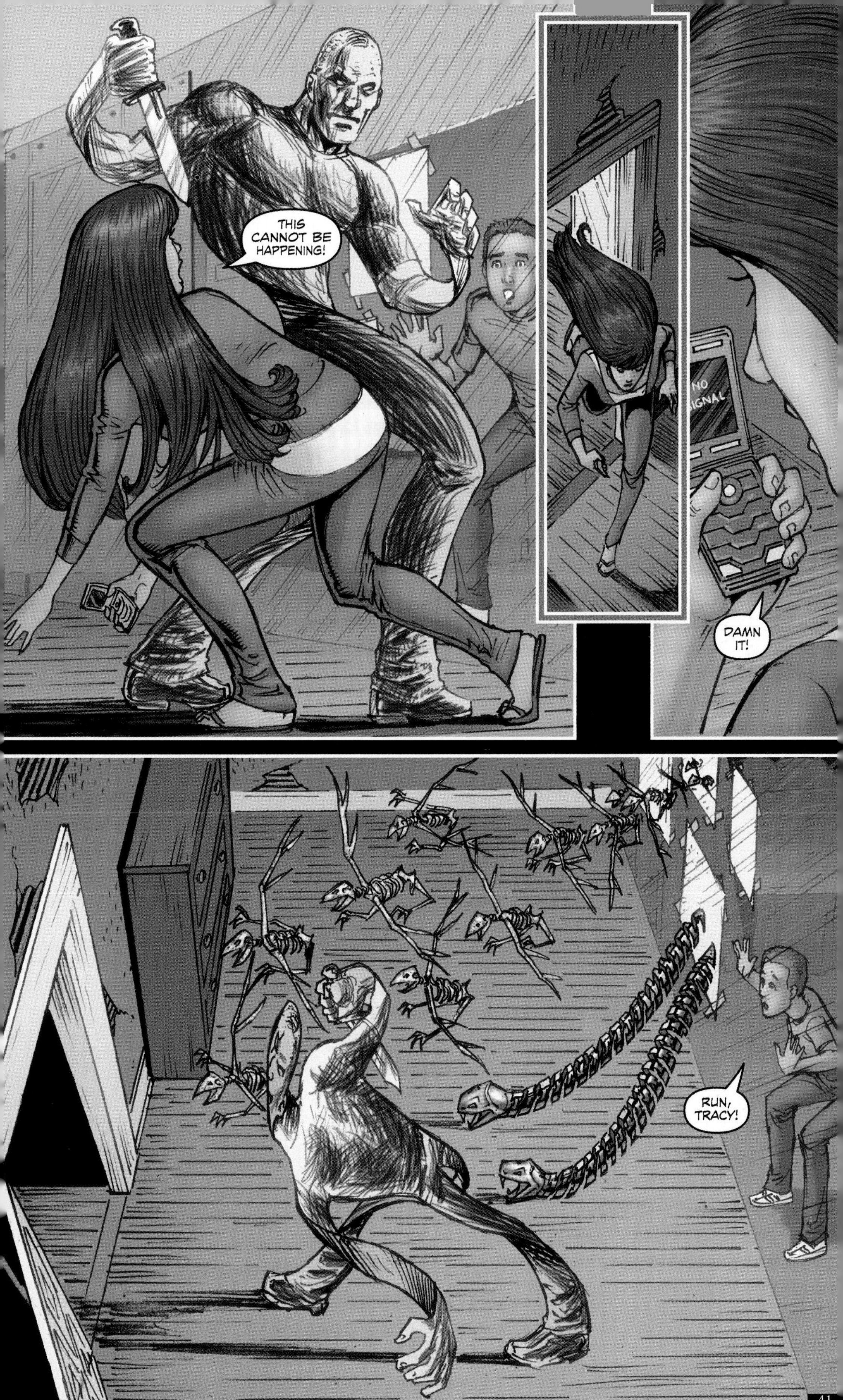

THIS CANNOT BE HAPPENING!
NO SIGNAL
DAMN IT!
RUN, TRACY!

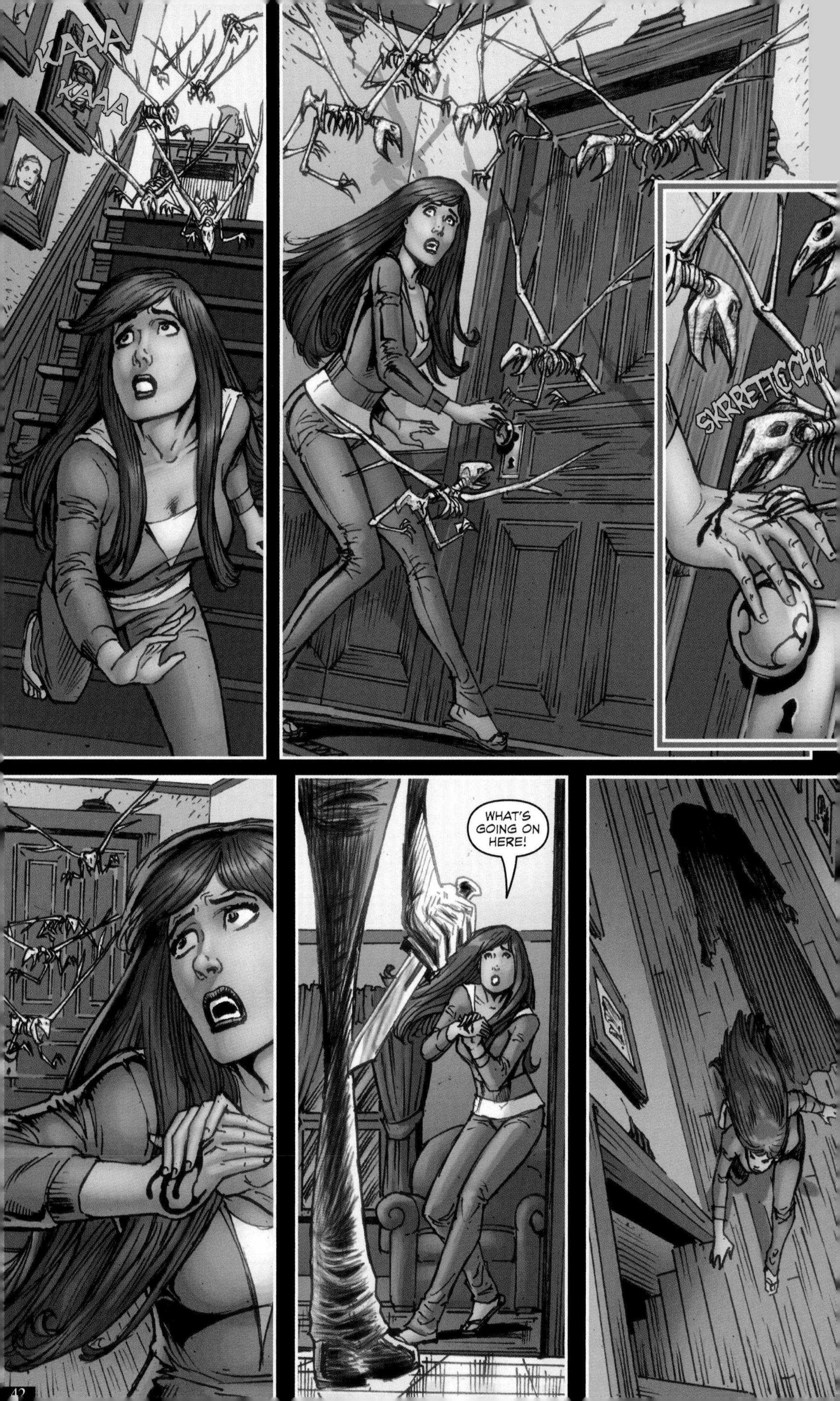
KAAA
KAAAA
SKRRETCCHH
WHAT'S GOING ON HERE!

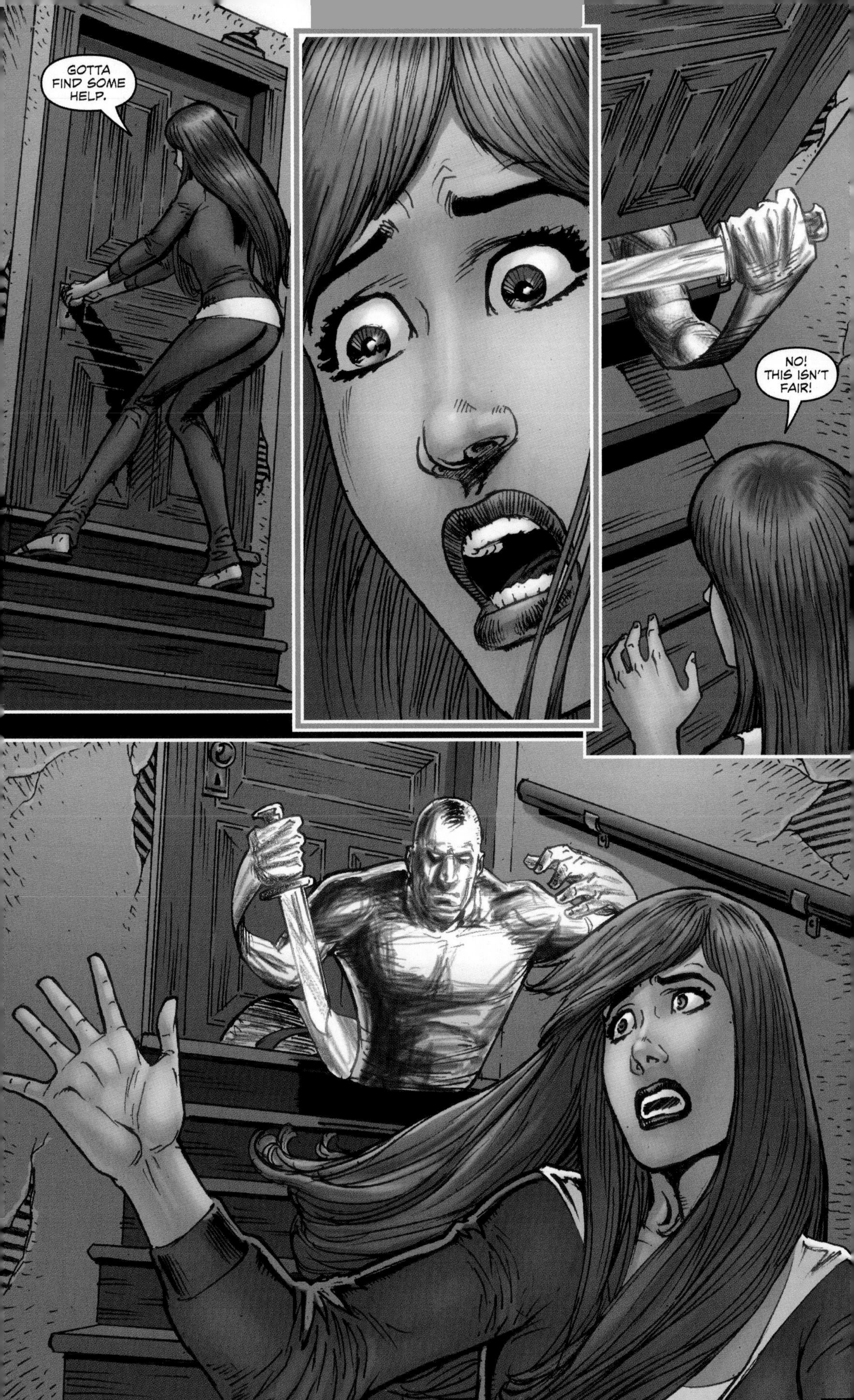
GOTTA FIND SOME HELP.
NO! THIS ISN'T FAIR!

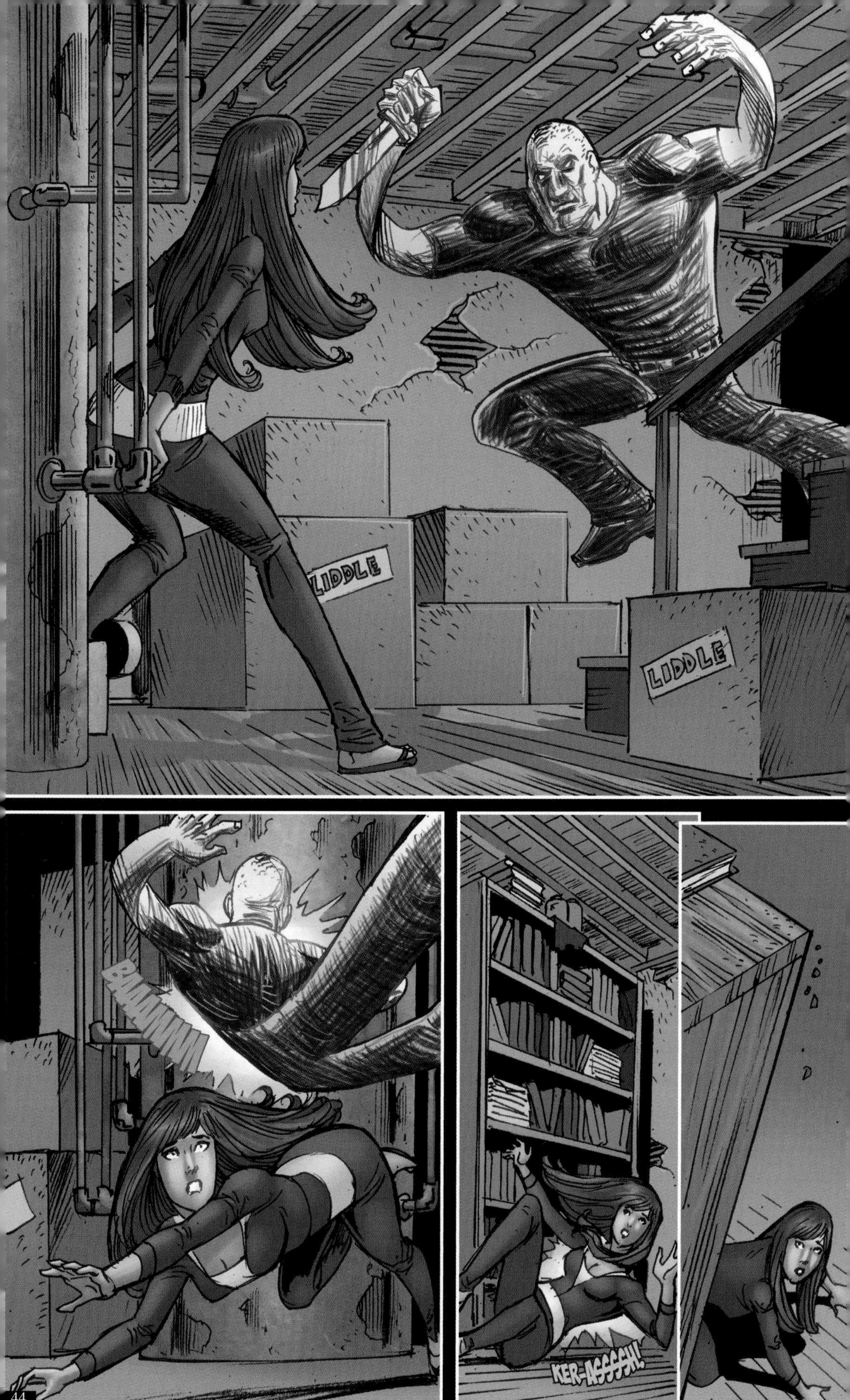
LIDDLE
LIDDLE
KER-ASSSSH!

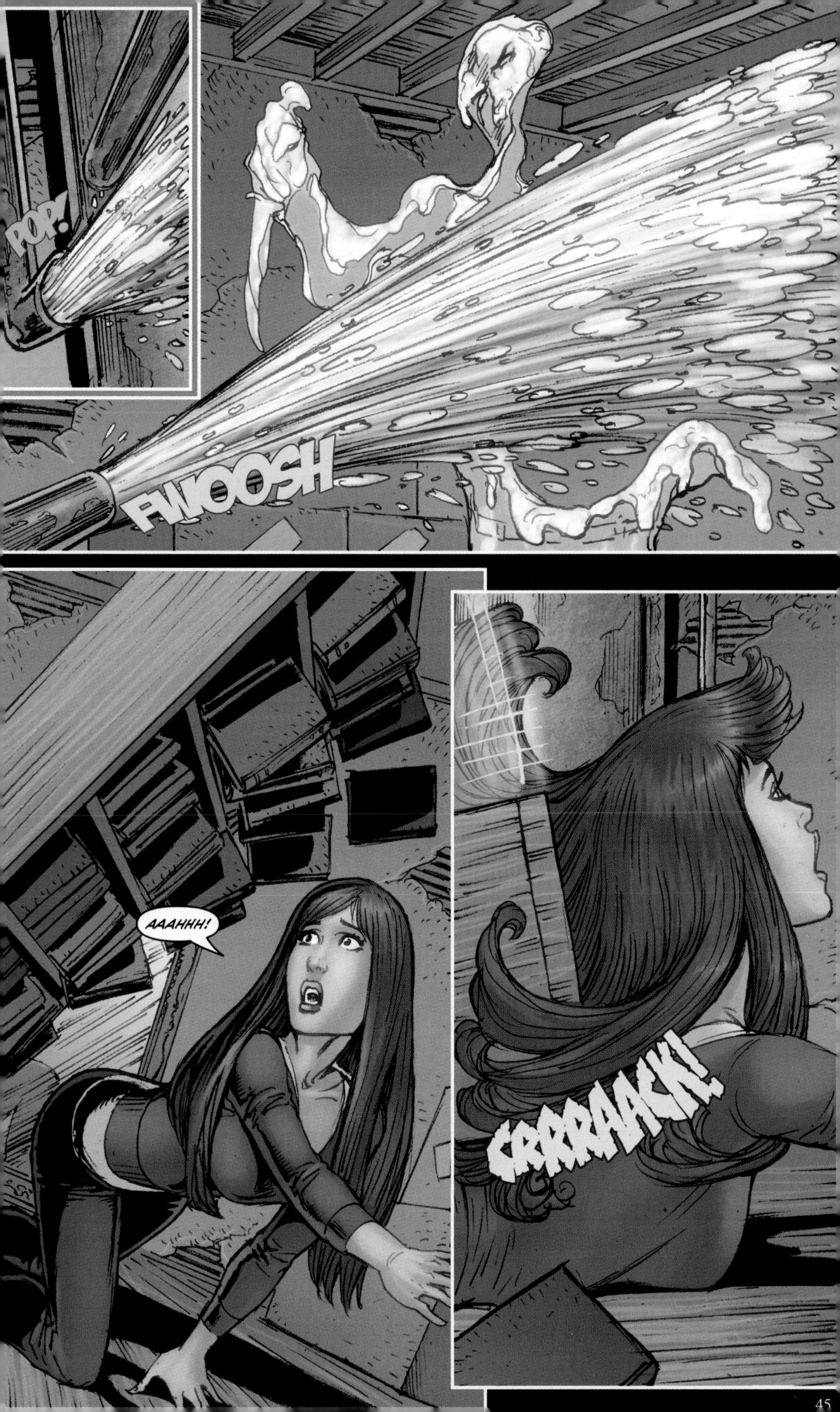
POP!
FWOOSH
AAAHHH!
CRRRAACK!

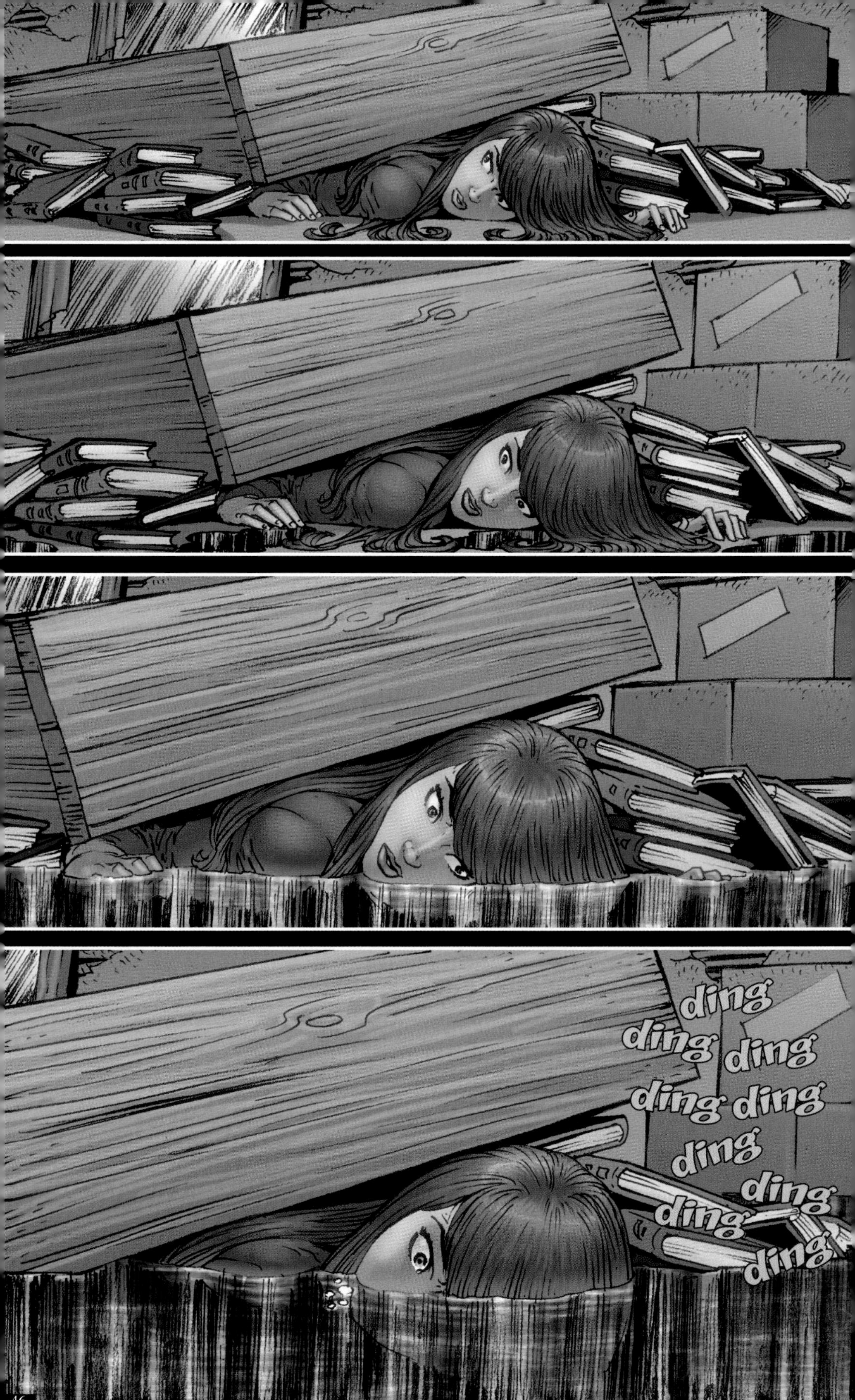
ding
ding ding
ding ding
ding
ding
ding
ding

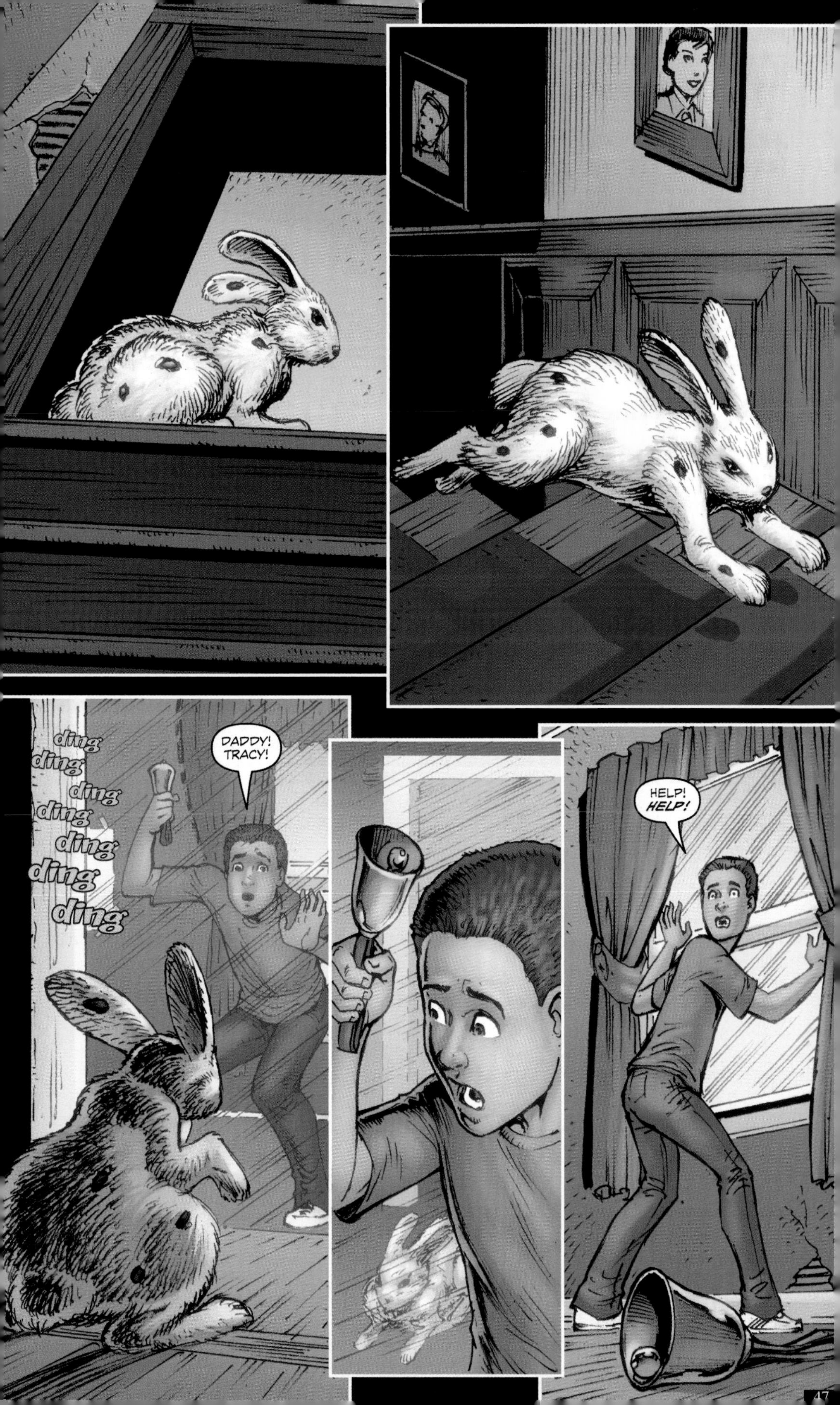
ding
ding
ding
ding
ding
ding
ding
DADDY! TRACY!
HELP! HELP!

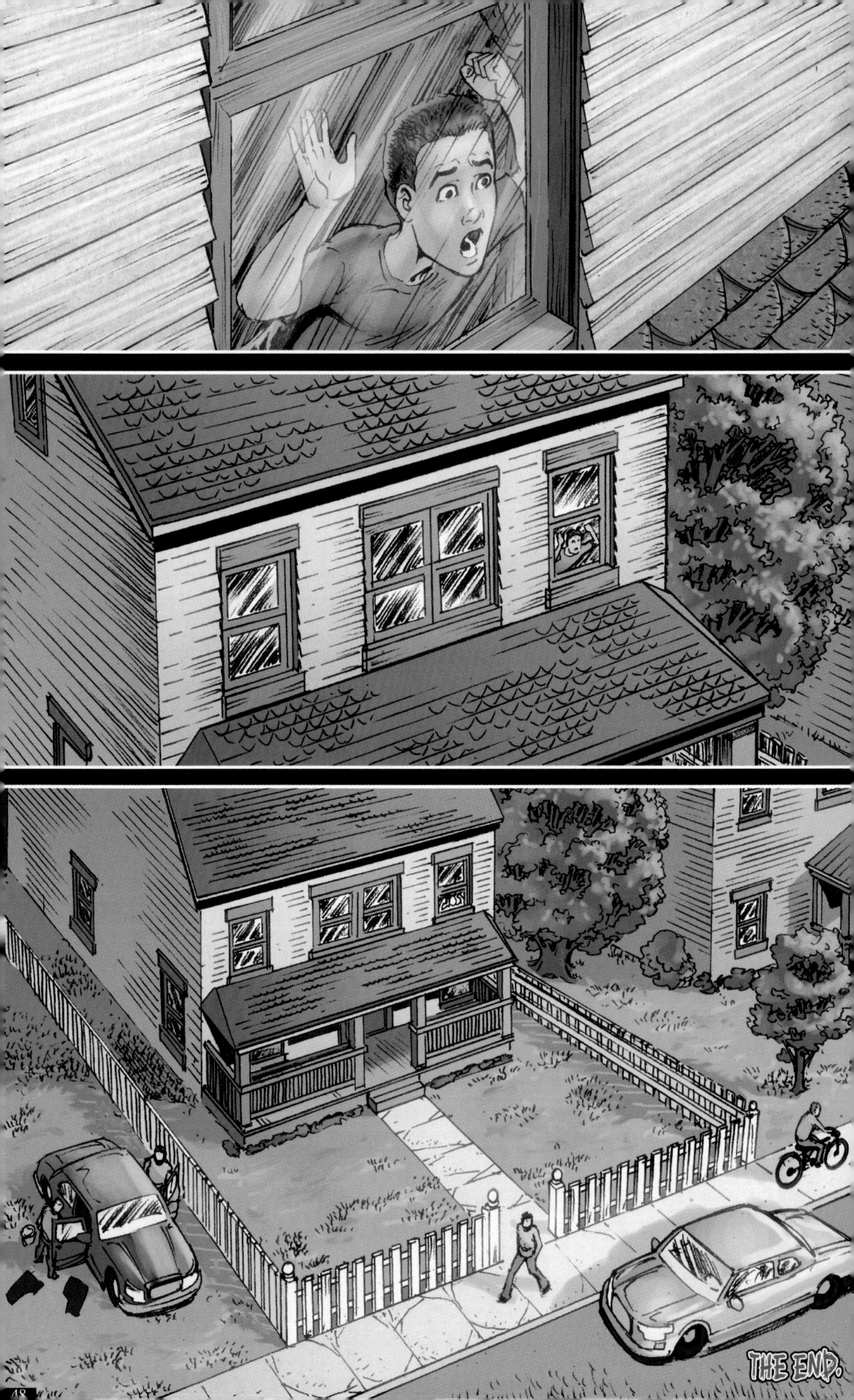
THE END.

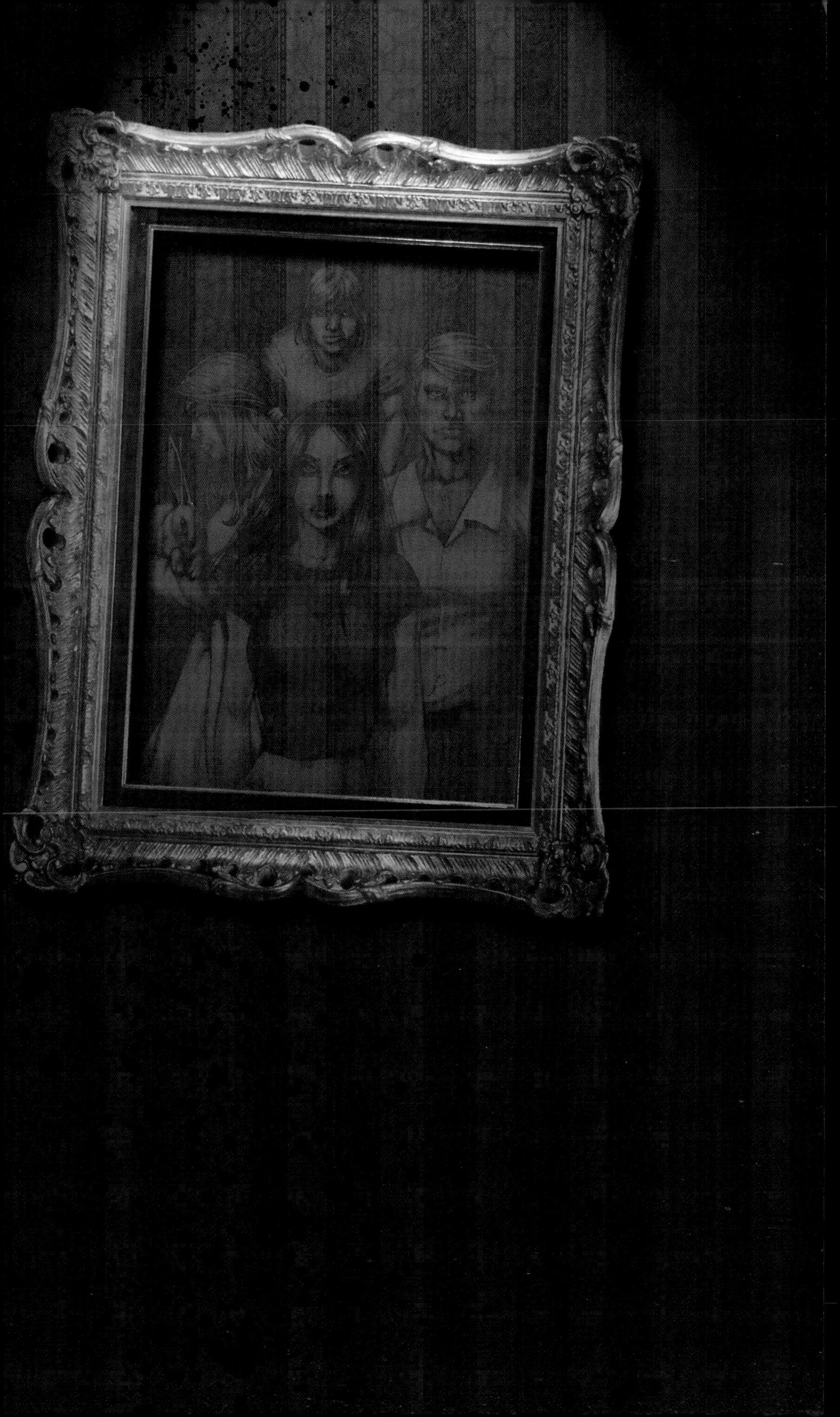

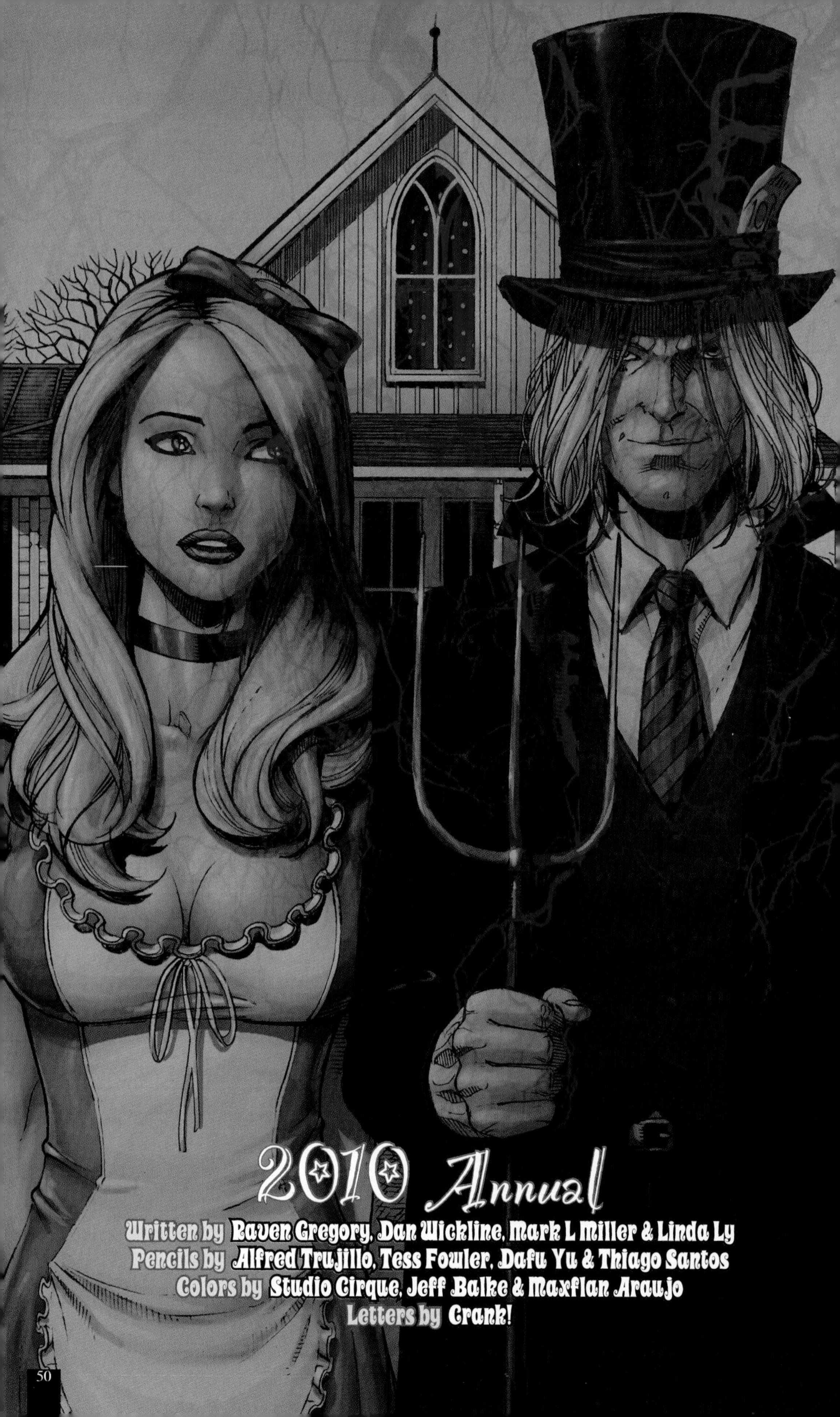
2010 Annual
Written by Raven Gregory, Dan Wickline, Mark L Miller & Linda Ly
Pencils by Alfred Trujillo, Tess Fowler, Dafu Yu & Thiago Santos
Colors by Studio Cirque, Jeff Balke & Maxflan Araujo
Letters by Crank!

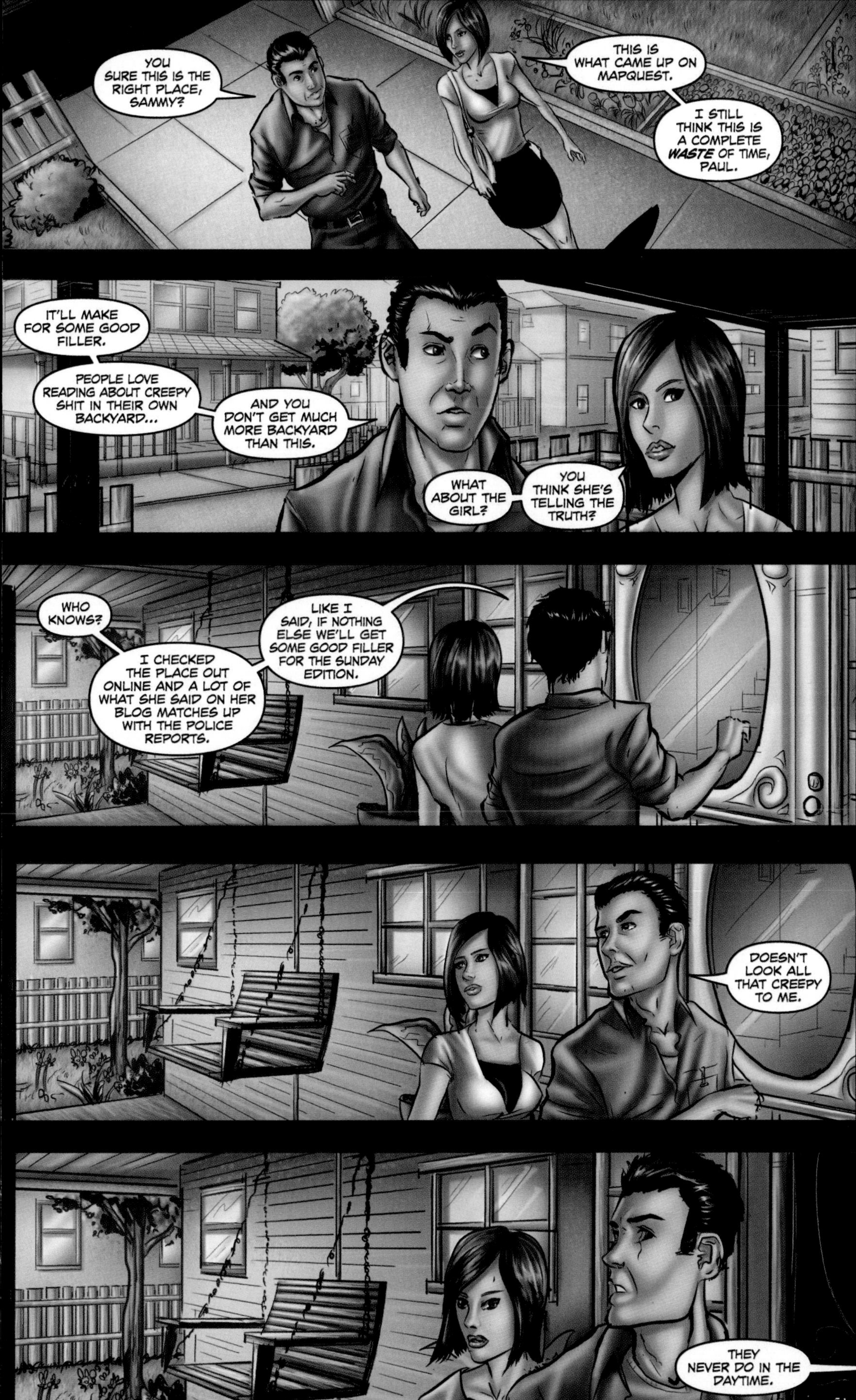
YOU SURE THIS IS THE RIGHT PLACE, SAMMY?
THIS IS WHAT CAME UP ON MAPQUEST.
I STILL THINK THIS IS A COMPLETE WASTE OF TIME, PAUL.
IT'LL MAKE FOR SOME GOOD FILLER.
PEOPLE LOVE READING ABOUT CREEPY SHIT IN THEIR OWN BACKYARD...
AND YOU DON'T GET MUCH MORE BACKYARD THAN THIS.
WHAT ABOUT THE GIRL?
YOU THINK SHE'S TELLING THE TRUTH?
WHO KNOWS?
I CHECKED THE PLACE OUT ONLINE AND A LOT OF WHAT SHE SAID ON HER BLOG MATCHES UP WITH THE POLICE REPORTS.
LIKE I SAID, IF NOTHING ELSE WE'LL GET SOME GOOD FILLER FOR THE SUNDAY EDITION.
DOESN'T LOOK ALL THAT CREEPY TO ME.
THEY NEVER DO IN THE DAYTIME.

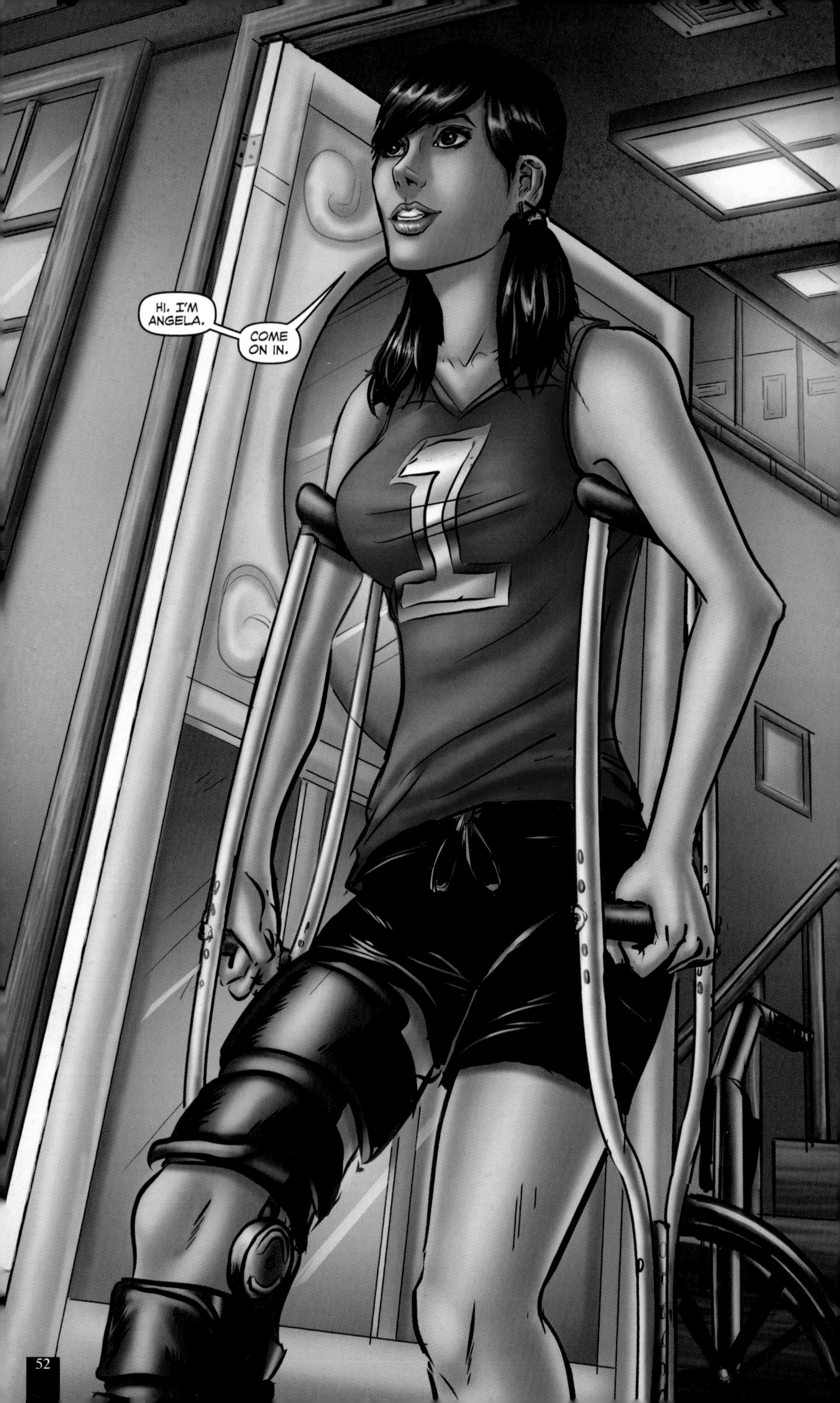
HI. I'M ANGELA.
COME ON IN.

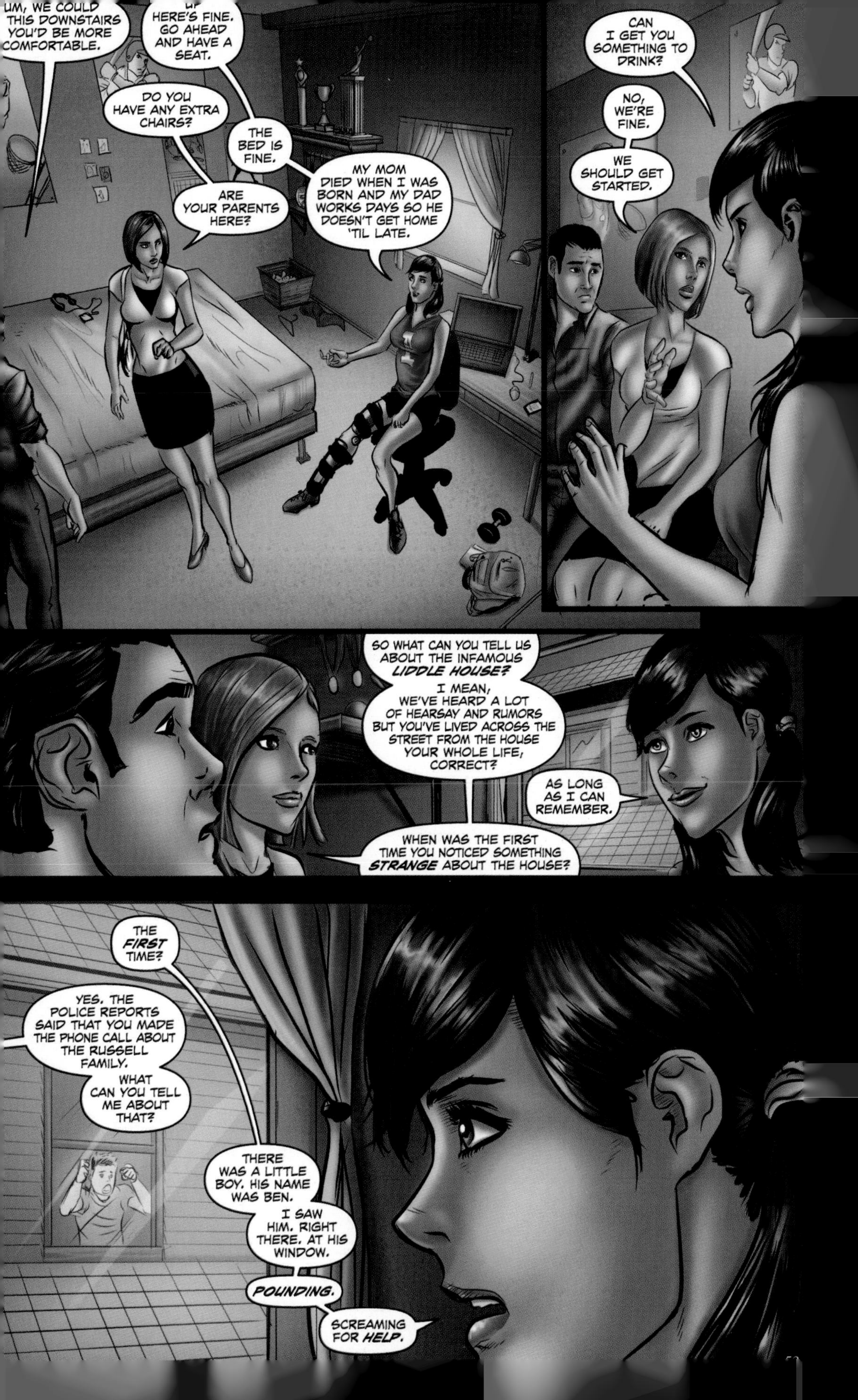
UM, WE COULD THIS DOWNSTAIRS YOU'D BE MORE COMFORTABLE.
HERE'S FINE. GO AHEAD AND HAVE A SEAT.
DO YOU HAVE ANY EXTRA CHAIRS?
THE BED IS FINE.
ARE YOUR PARENTS HERE?
MY MOM DIED WHEN I WAS BORN AND MY DAD WORKS DAYS SO HE DOESN'T GET HOME 'TIL LATE.
CAN I GET YOU SOMETHING TO DRINK?
NO, WE'RE FINE.
WE SHOULD GET STARTED.
SO WHAT CAN YOU TELL US ABOUT THE INFAMOUS *LIDDLE HOUSE?*
I MEAN, WE'VE HEARD A LOT OF HEARSAY AND RUMORS BUT YOU'VE LIVED ACROSS THE STREET FROM THE HOUSE YOUR WHOLE LIFE, CORRECT?
AS LONG AS I CAN REMEMBER.
WHEN WAS THE FIRST TIME YOU NOTICED SOMETHING *STRANGE* ABOUT THE HOUSE?
THE *FIRST* TIME?
YES. THE POLICE REPORTS SAID THAT YOU MADE THE PHONE CALL ABOUT THE RUSSELL FAMILY.
WHAT CAN YOU TELL ME ABOUT THAT?
THERE WAS A LITTLE BOY. HIS NAME WAS BEN.
I SAW HIM. RIGHT THERE. AT HIS WINDOW.
POUNDING.
SCREAMING FOR *HELP.*

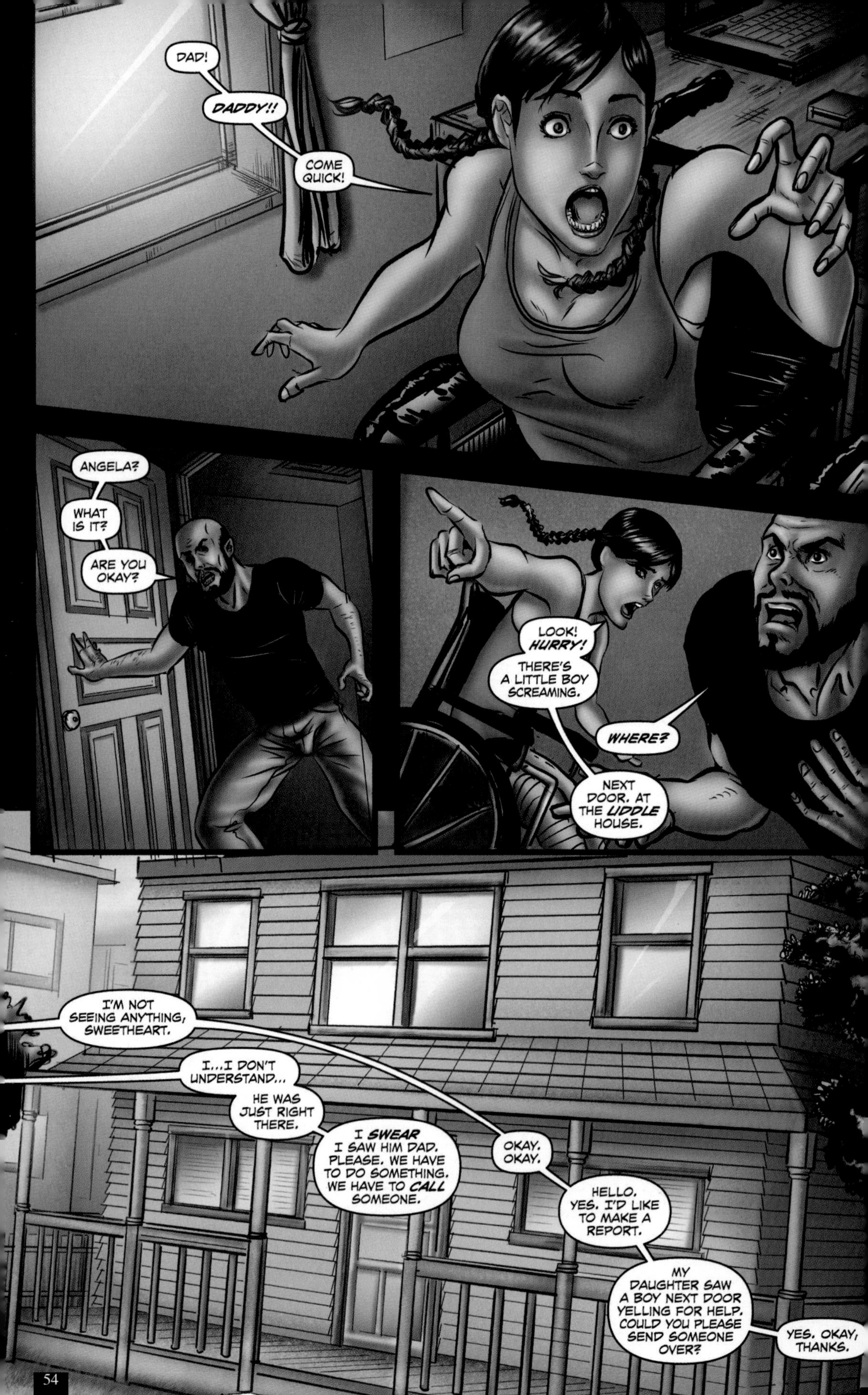
DAD!
DADDY!!
COME QUICK!
ANGELA?
WHAT IS IT?
ARE YOU OKAY?
LOOK! HURRY!
THERE'S A LITTLE BOY SCREAMING.
WHERE?
NEXT DOOR. AT THE LIDDLE HOUSE.
I'M NOT SEEING ANYTHING, SWEETHEART.
I...I DON'T UNDERSTAND...
HE WAS JUST RIGHT THERE.
I SWEAR I SAW HIM DAD. PLEASE. WE HAVE TO DO SOMETHING. WE HAVE TO CALL SOMEONE.
OKAY. OKAY.
HELLO. YES. I'D LIKE TO MAKE A REPORT.
MY DAUGHTER SAW A BOY NEXT DOOR YELLING FOR HELP. COULD YOU PLEASE SEND SOMEONE OVER?
YES. OKAY, THANKS.

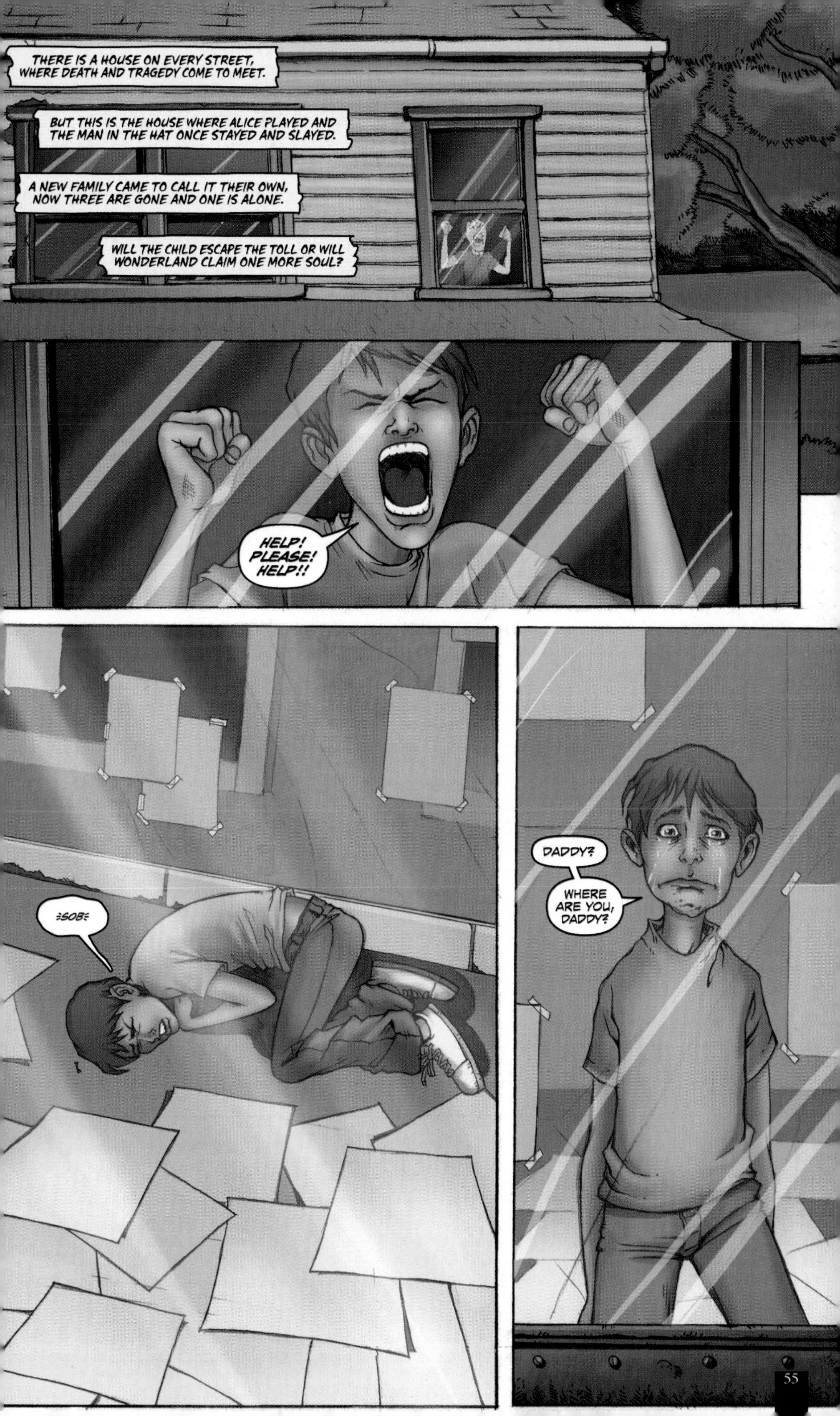
THERE IS A HOUSE ON EVERY STREET, WHERE DEATH AND TRAGEDY COME TO MEET.
BUT THIS IS THE HOUSE WHERE ALICE PLAYED AND THE MAN IN THE HAT ONCE STAYED AND SLAYED.
A NEW FAMILY CAME TO CALL IT THEIR OWN, NOW THREE ARE GONE AND ONE IS ALONE.
WILL THE CHILD ESCAPE THE TOLL OR WILL WONDERLAND CLAIM ONE MORE SOUL?
HELP! PLEASE! HELP!!
SOB
DADDY?
WHERE ARE YOU, DADDY?

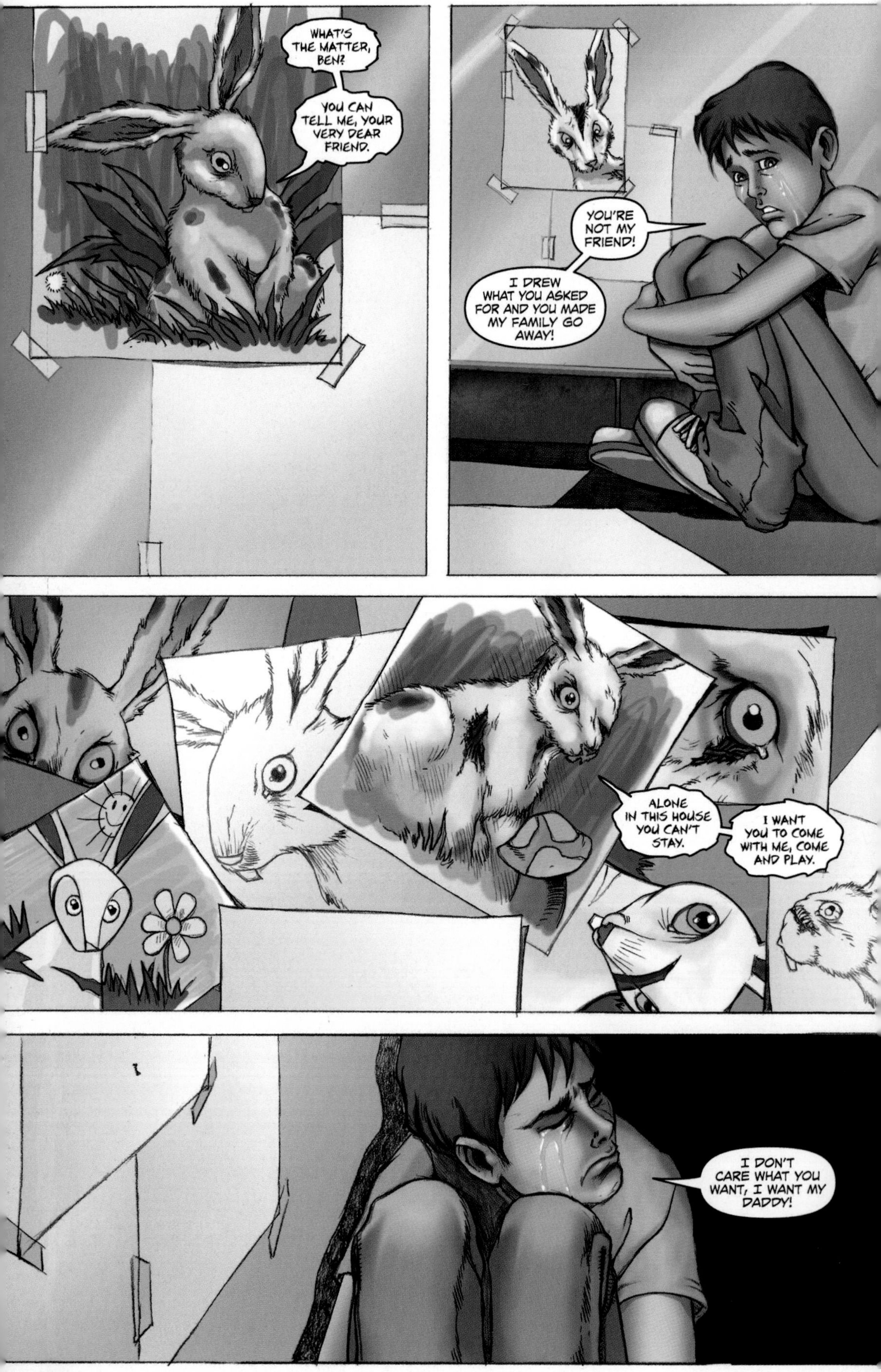
WHAT'S THE MATTER, BEN?
YOU CAN TELL ME, YOUR VERY DEAR FRIEND.
YOU'RE NOT MY FRIEND!
I DREW WHAT YOU ASKED FOR AND YOU MADE MY FAMILY GO AWAY!
ALONE IN THIS HOUSE YOU CAN'T STAY.
I WANT YOU TO COME WITH ME, COME AND PLAY.
I DON'T CARE WHAT YOU WANT, I WANT MY DADDY!

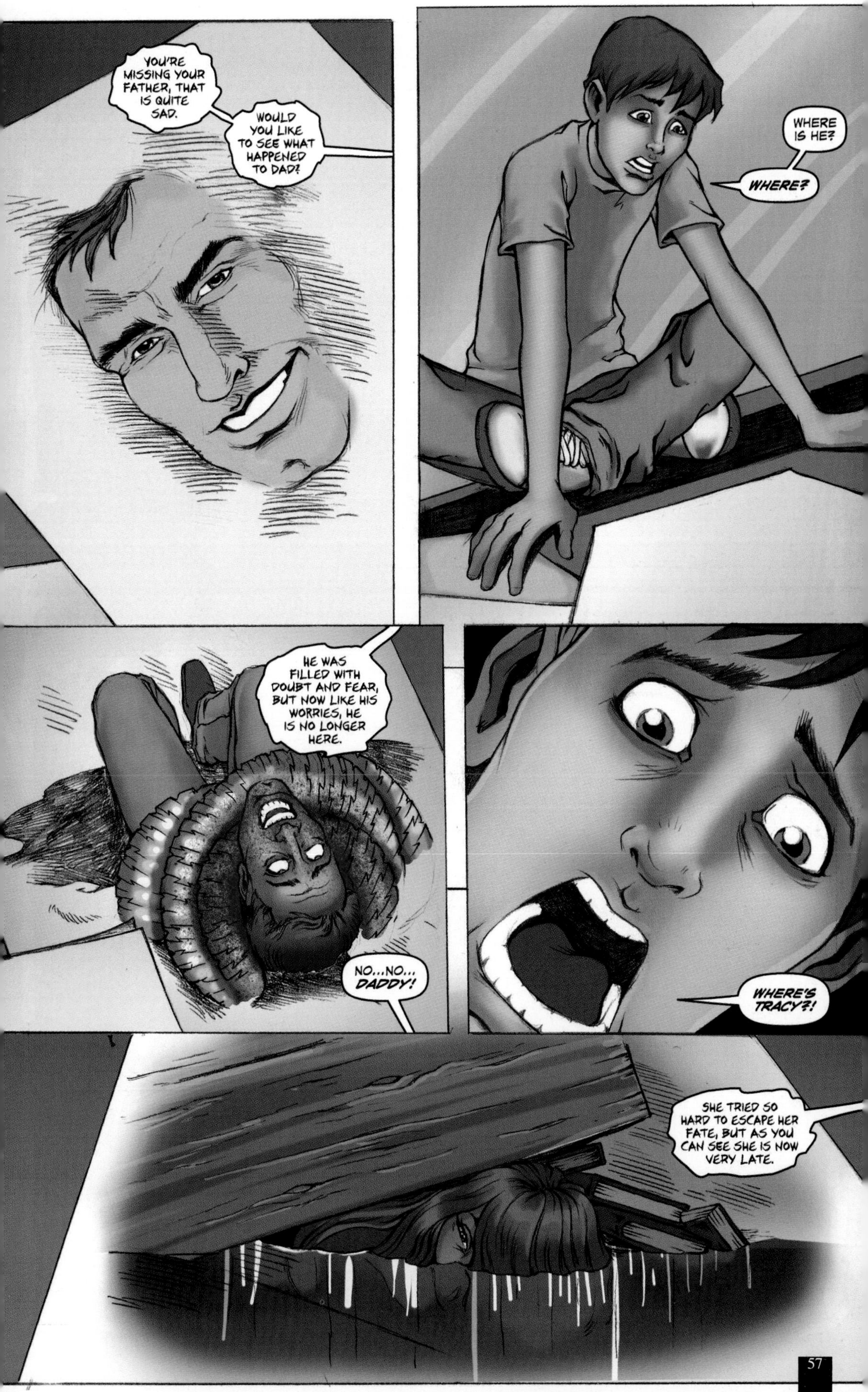
YOU'RE MISSING YOUR FATHER, THAT IS QUITE SAD.
WOULD YOU LIKE TO SEE WHAT HAPPENED TO DAD?
WHERE IS HE?
WHERE?
HE WAS FILLED WITH DOUBT AND FEAR, BUT NOW LIKE HIS WORRIES, HE IS NO LONGER HERE.
NO...NO... DADDY!
WHERE'S TRACY?!
SHE TRIED SO HARD TO ESCAPE HER FATE, BUT AS YOU CAN SEE SHE IS NOW VERY LATE.

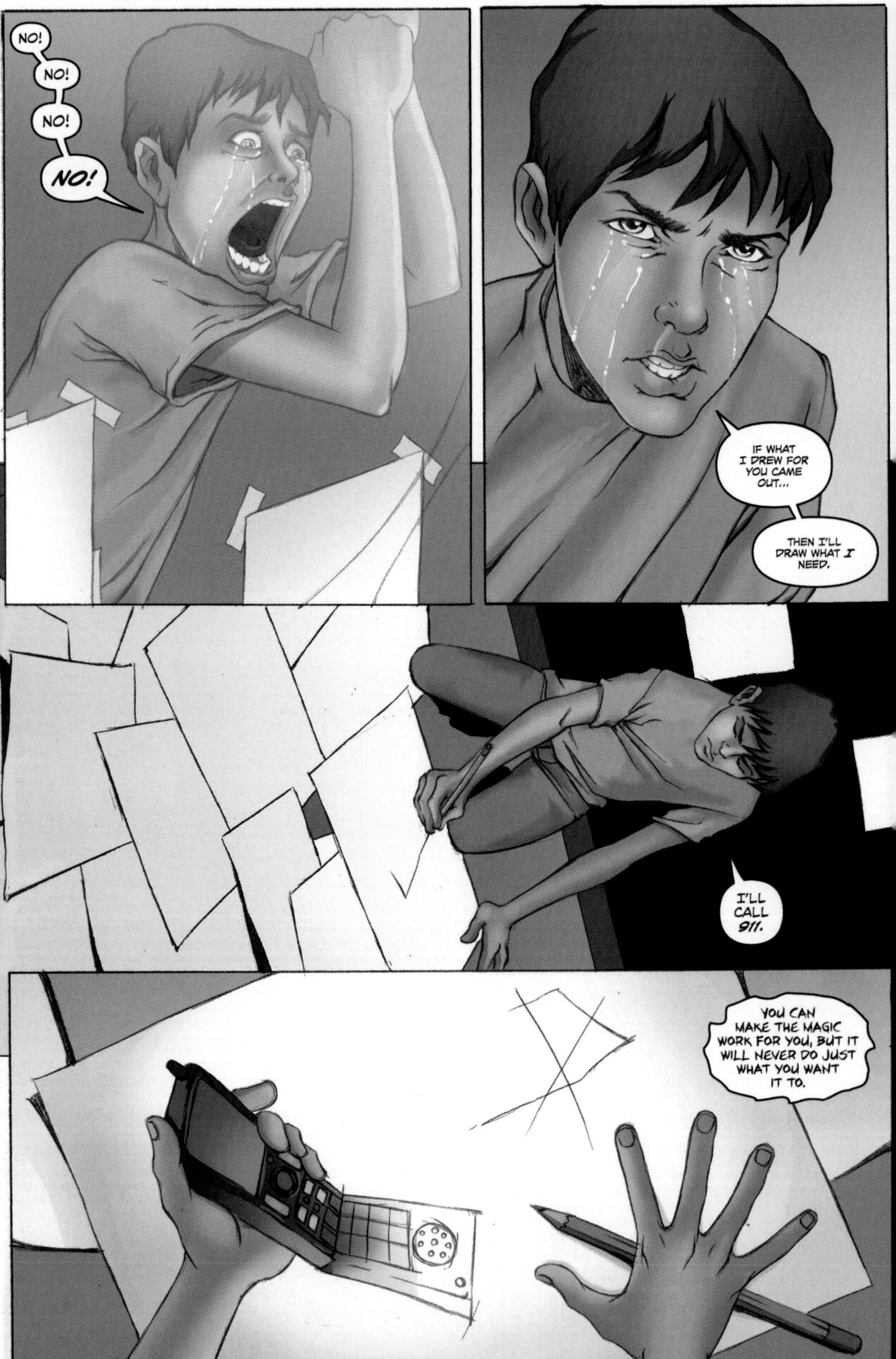
NO!
NO!
NO!
NO!
IF WHAT I DREW FOR YOU CAME OUT...
THEN I'LL DRAW WHAT *I* NEED.
I'LL CALL *911*.
YOU CAN MAKE THE MAGIC WORK FOR YOU, BUT IT WILL NEVER DO JUST WHAT YOU WANT IT TO.

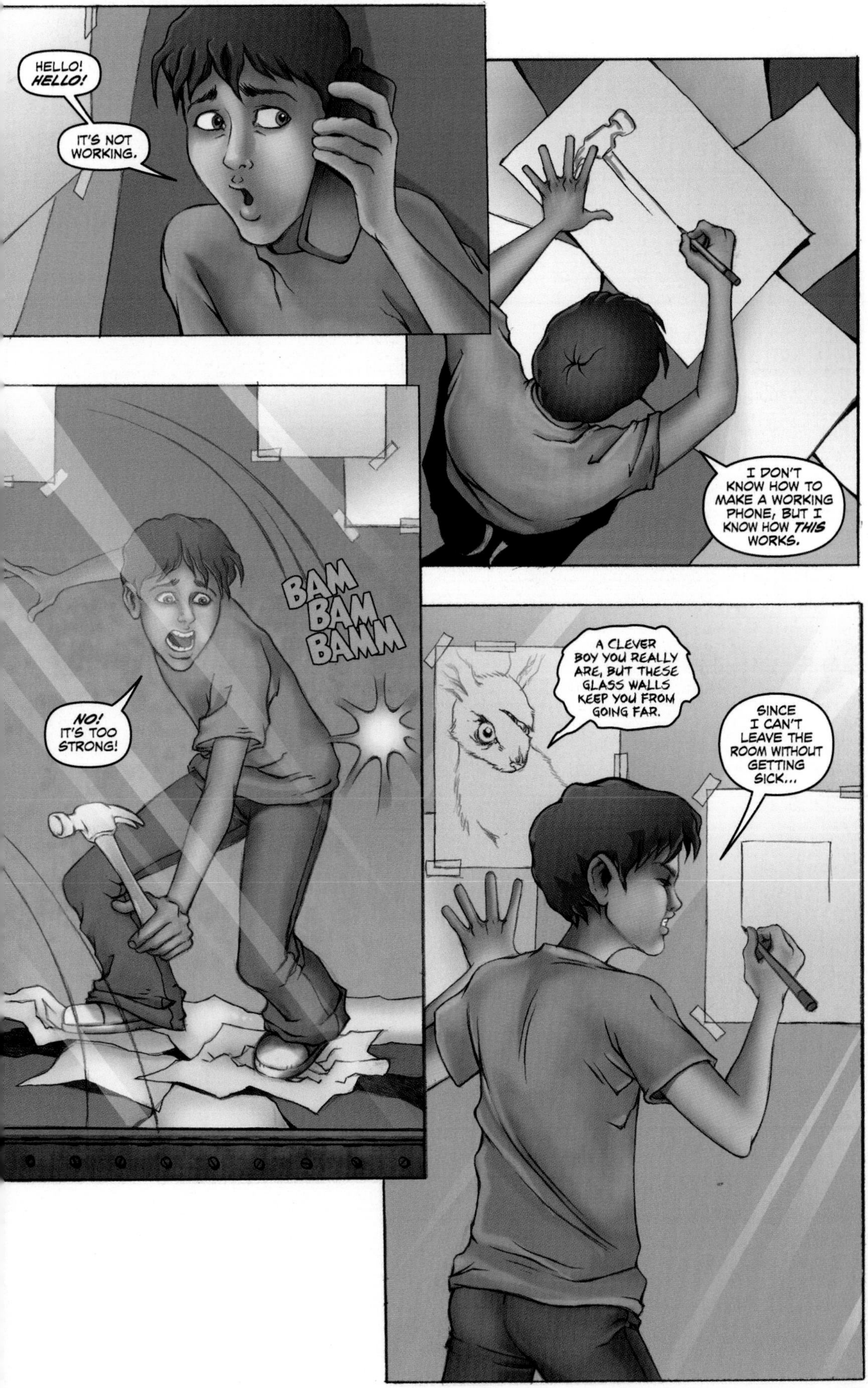
HELLO! HELLO!
IT'S NOT WORKING.
I DON'T KNOW HOW TO MAKE A WORKING PHONE, BUT I KNOW HOW THIS WORKS.
BAM BAM BAMM
NO! IT'S TOO STRONG!
A CLEVER BOY YOU REALLY ARE, BUT THESE GLASS WALLS KEEP YOU FROM GOING FAR.
SINCE I CAN'T LEAVE THE ROOM WITHOUT GETTING SICK...

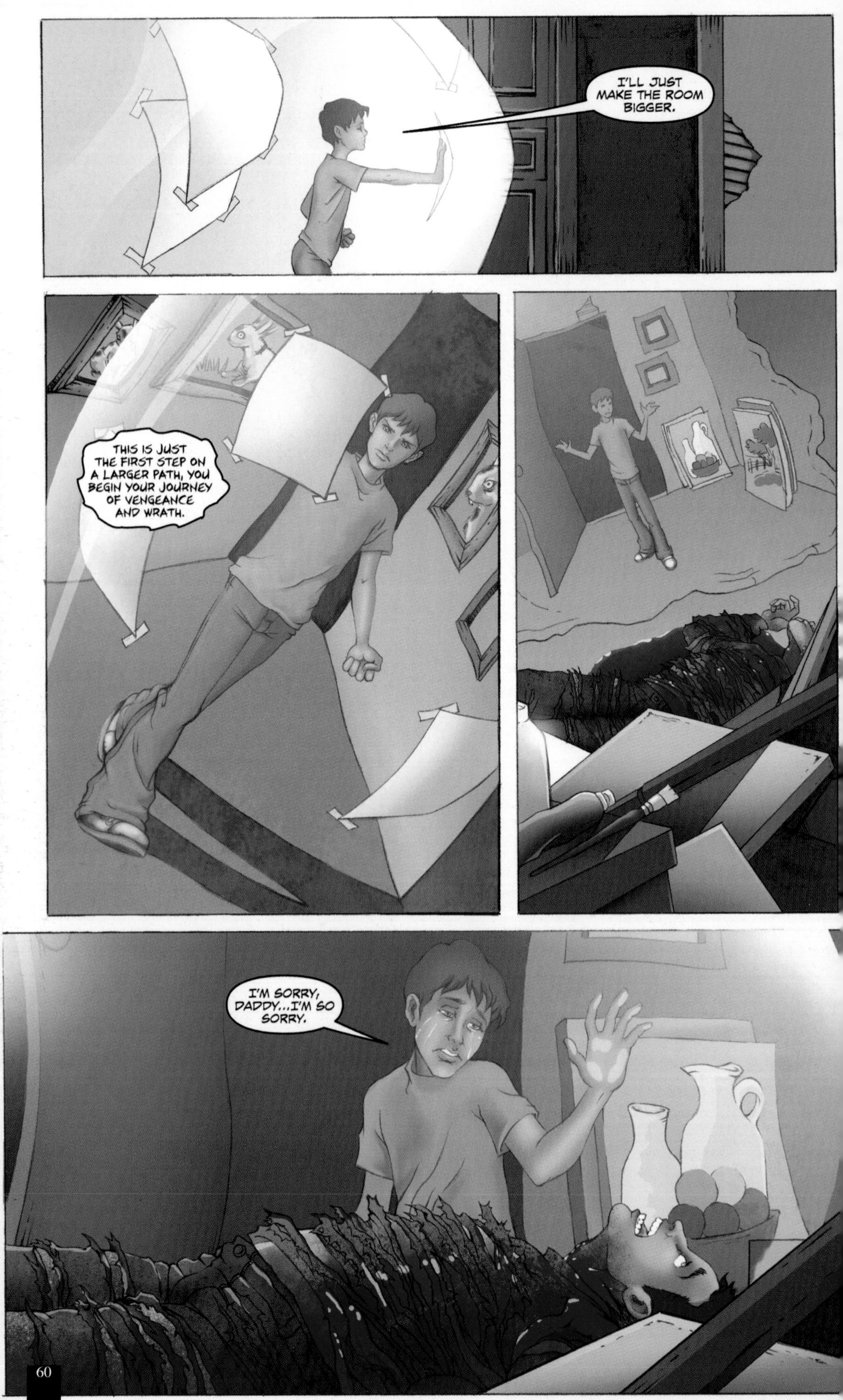
I'LL JUST MAKE THE ROOM BIGGER.
THIS IS JUST THE FIRST STEP ON A LARGER PATH, YOU BEGIN YOUR JOURNEY OF VENGEANCE AND WRATH.
I'M SORRY, DADDY...I'M SO SORRY.

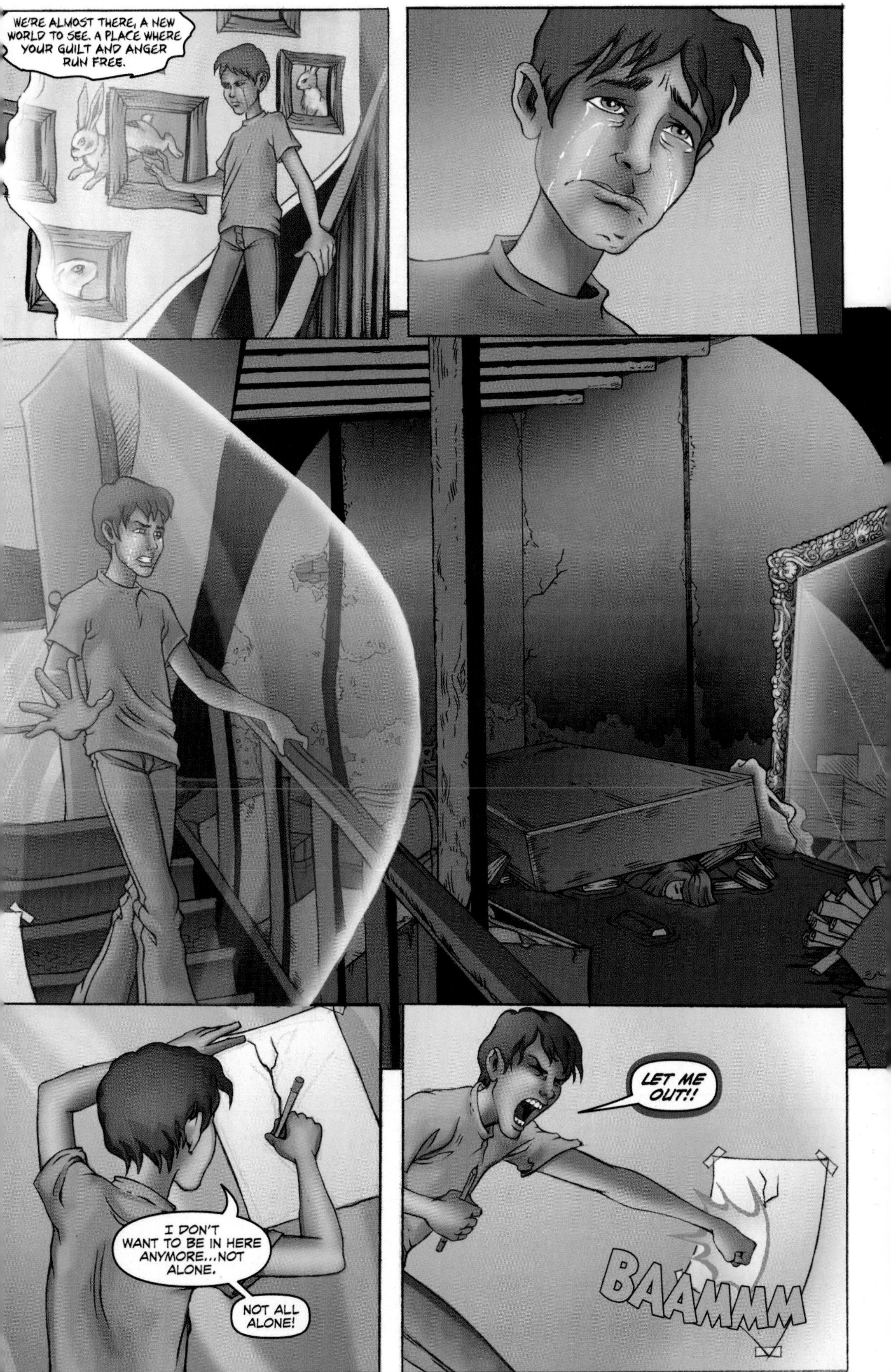
WE'RE ALMOST THERE, A NEW WORLD TO SEE. A PLACE WHERE YOUR GUILT AND ANGER RUN FREE.
I DON'T WANT TO BE IN HERE ANYMORE...NOT ALONE.
NOT ALL ALONE!
LET ME OUT!!
BAAMMM

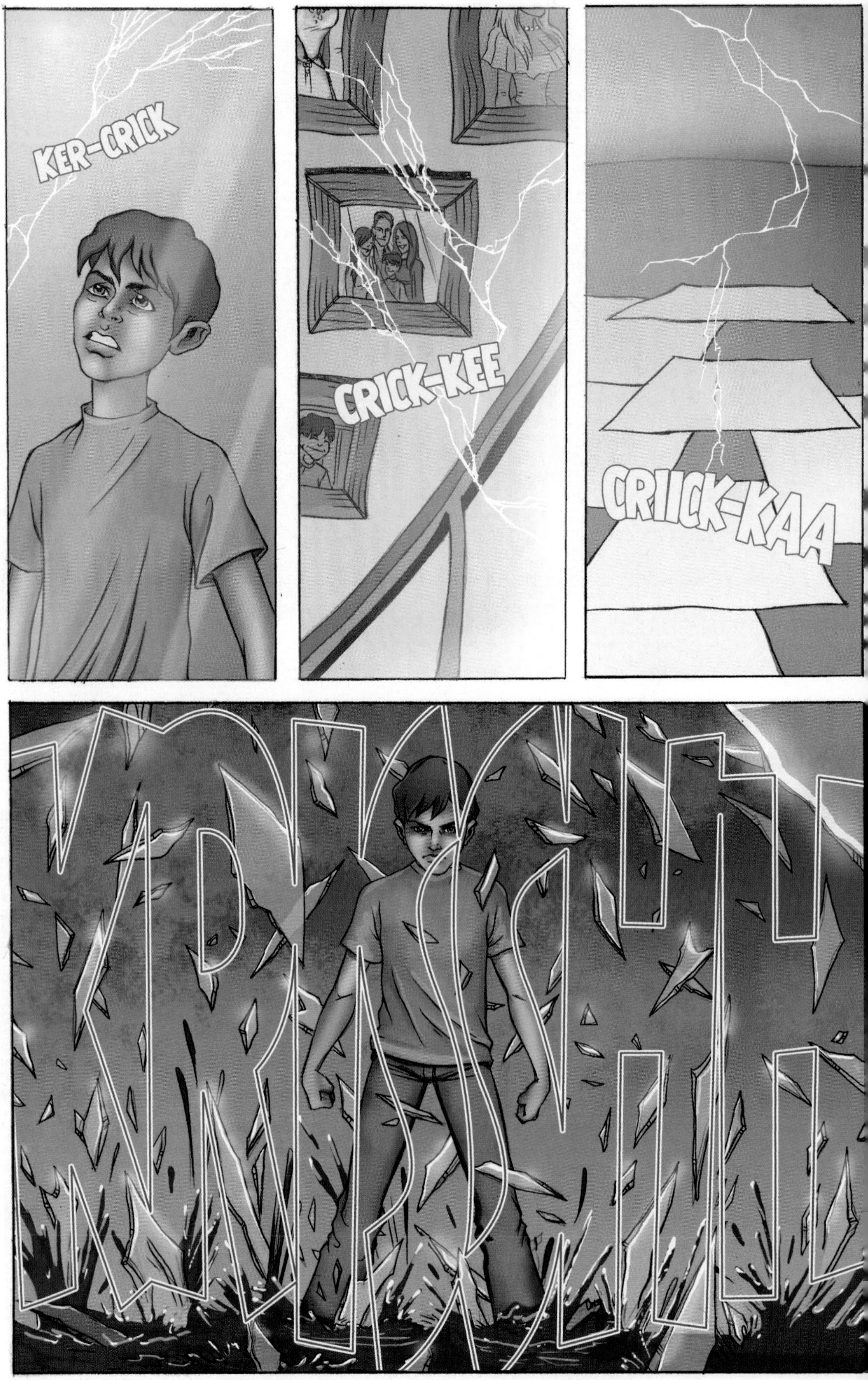
KER-CRICK
CRICK-KEE
CRIICK-KAA

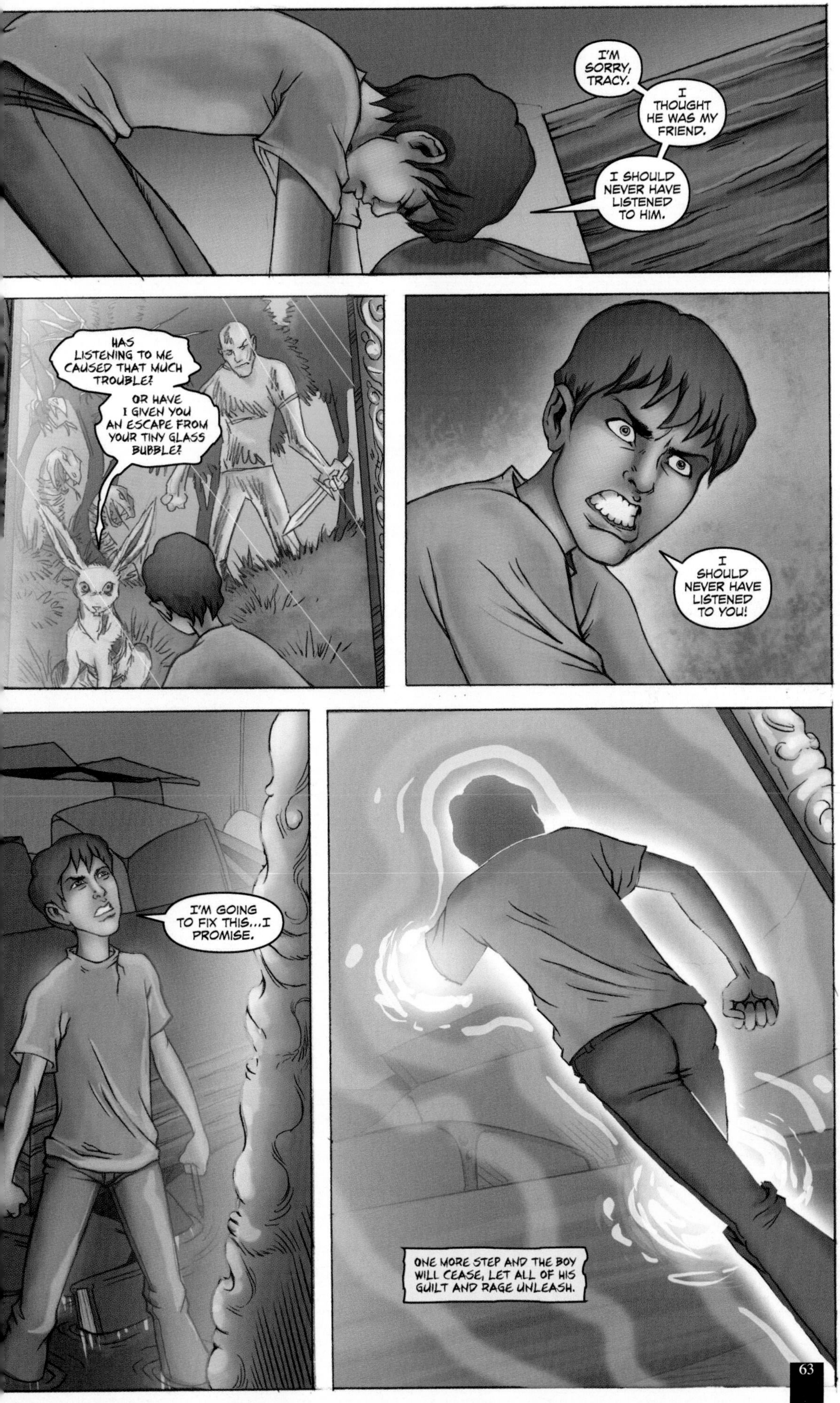
I'M SORRY, TRACY.
I THOUGHT HE WAS MY FRIEND.
I SHOULD NEVER HAVE LISTENED TO HIM.
HAS LISTENING TO ME CAUSED THAT MUCH TROUBLE?
OR HAVE I GIVEN YOU AN ESCAPE FROM YOUR TINY GLASS BUBBLE?
I SHOULD NEVER HAVE LISTENED TO YOU!
I'M GOING TO FIX THIS...I PROMISE.
ONE MORE STEP AND THE BOY WILL CEASE, LET ALL OF HIS GUILT AND RAGE UNLEASH.

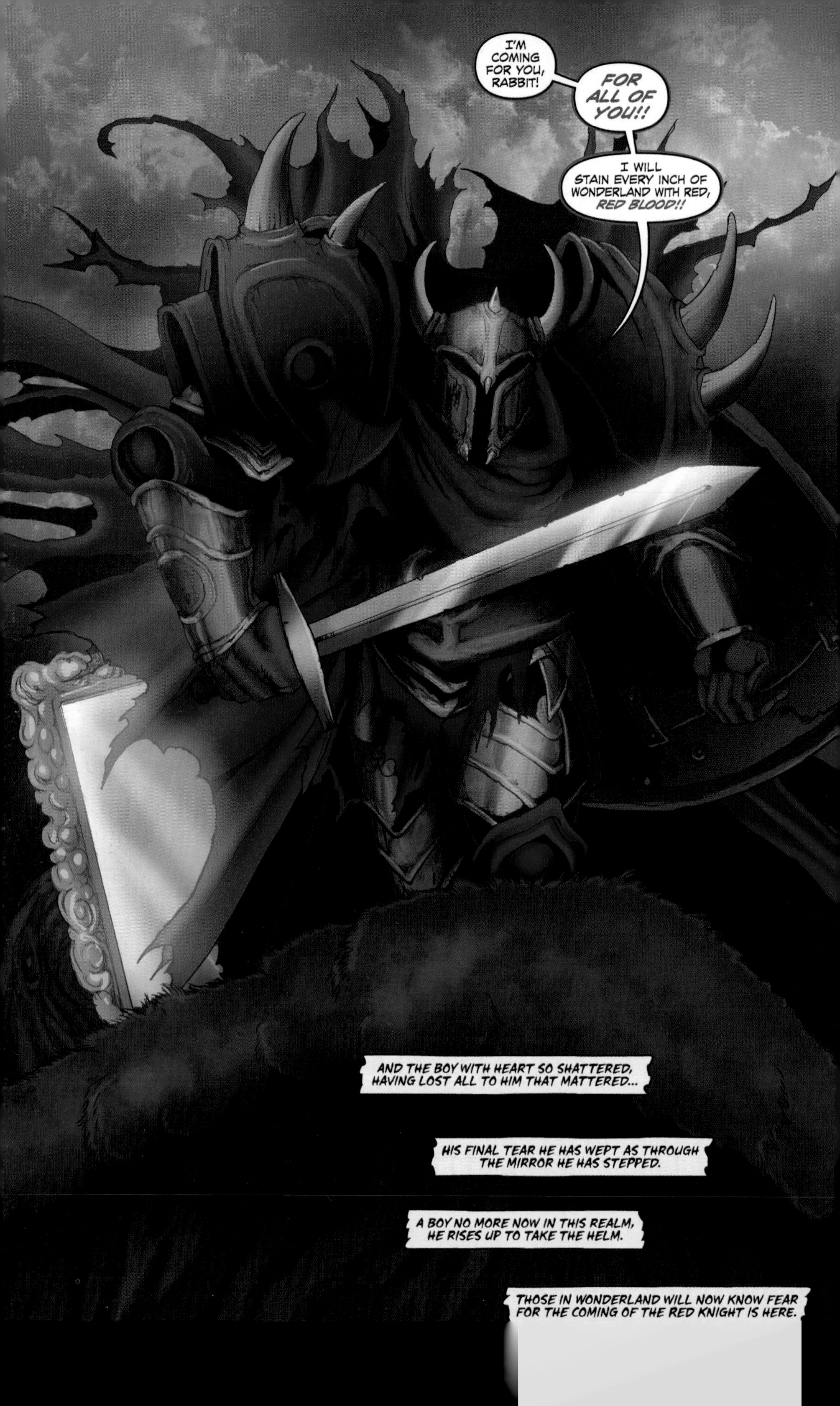

I'M COMING FOR YOU, RABBIT!
FOR ALL OF YOU!!
I WILL STAIN EVERY INCH OF WONDERLAND WITH RED, RED BLOOD!!
AND THE BOY WITH HEART SO SHATTERED, HAVING LOST ALL TO HIM THAT MATTERED...
HIS FINAL TEAR HE HAS WEPT AS THROUGH THE MIRROR HE HAS STEPPED.
A BOY NO MORE NOW IN THIS REALM, HE RISES UP TO TAKE THE HELM.
THOSE IN WONDERLAND WILL NOW KNOW FEAR FOR THE COMING OF THE RED KNIGHT IS HERE.

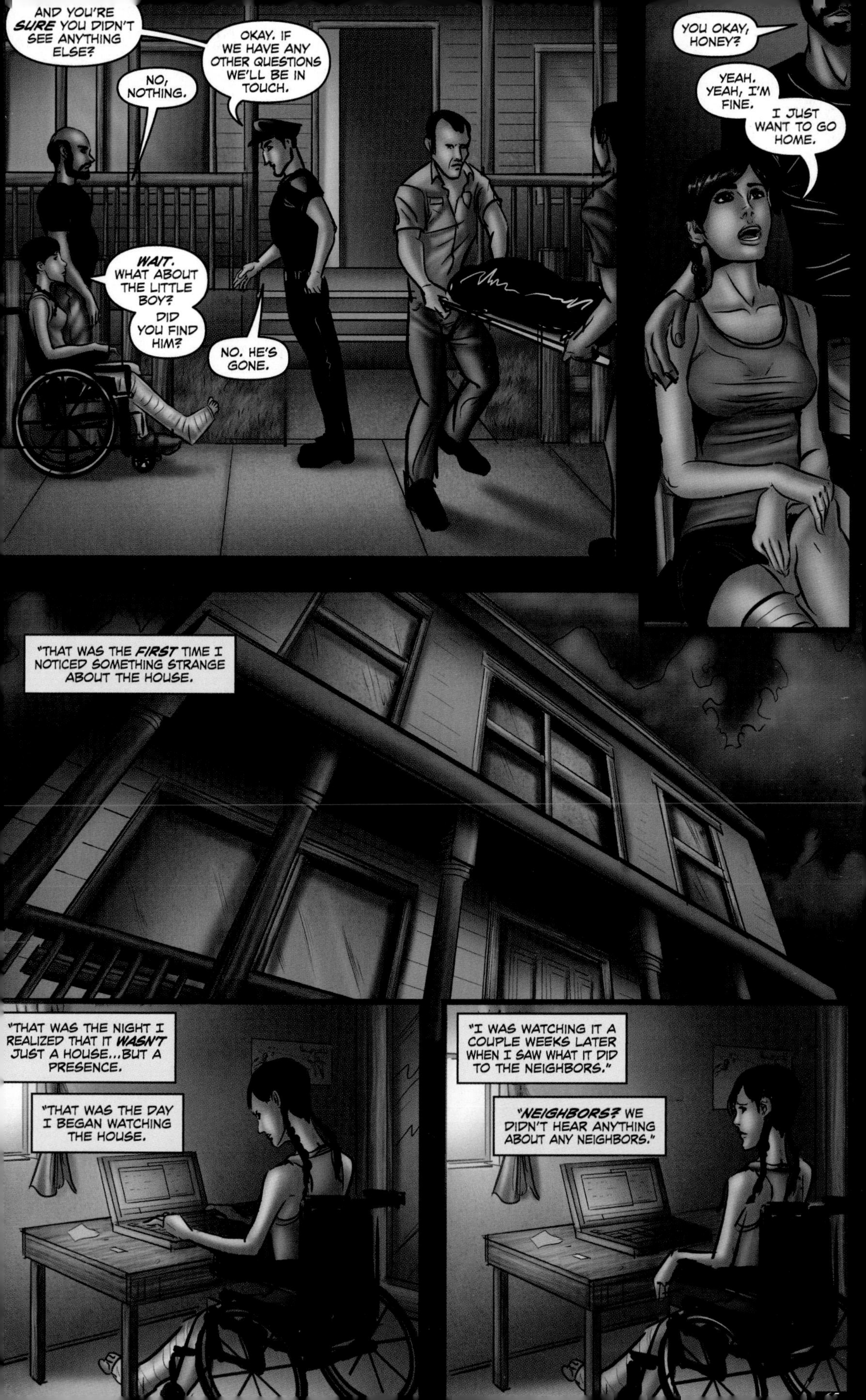
AND YOU'RE *SURE* YOU DIDN'T SEE ANYTHING ELSE?
NO, NOTHING.
OKAY. IF WE HAVE ANY OTHER QUESTIONS WE'LL BE IN TOUCH.
WAIT. WHAT ABOUT THE LITTLE BOY?
DID YOU FIND HIM?
NO. HE'S GONE.
YOU OKAY, HONEY?
YEAH. YEAH, I'M FINE.
I JUST WANT TO GO HOME.
"THAT WAS THE *FIRST* TIME I NOTICED SOMETHING STRANGE ABOUT THE HOUSE.
"THAT WAS THE NIGHT I REALIZED THAT IT *WASN'T* JUST A HOUSE...BUT A PRESENCE.
"THAT WAS THE DAY I BEGAN WATCHING THE HOUSE.
"I WAS WATCHING IT A COUPLE WEEKS LATER WHEN I SAW WHAT IT DID TO THE NEIGHBORS."
"*NEIGHBORS?* WE DIDN'T HEAR ANYTHING ABOUT ANY NEIGHBORS."

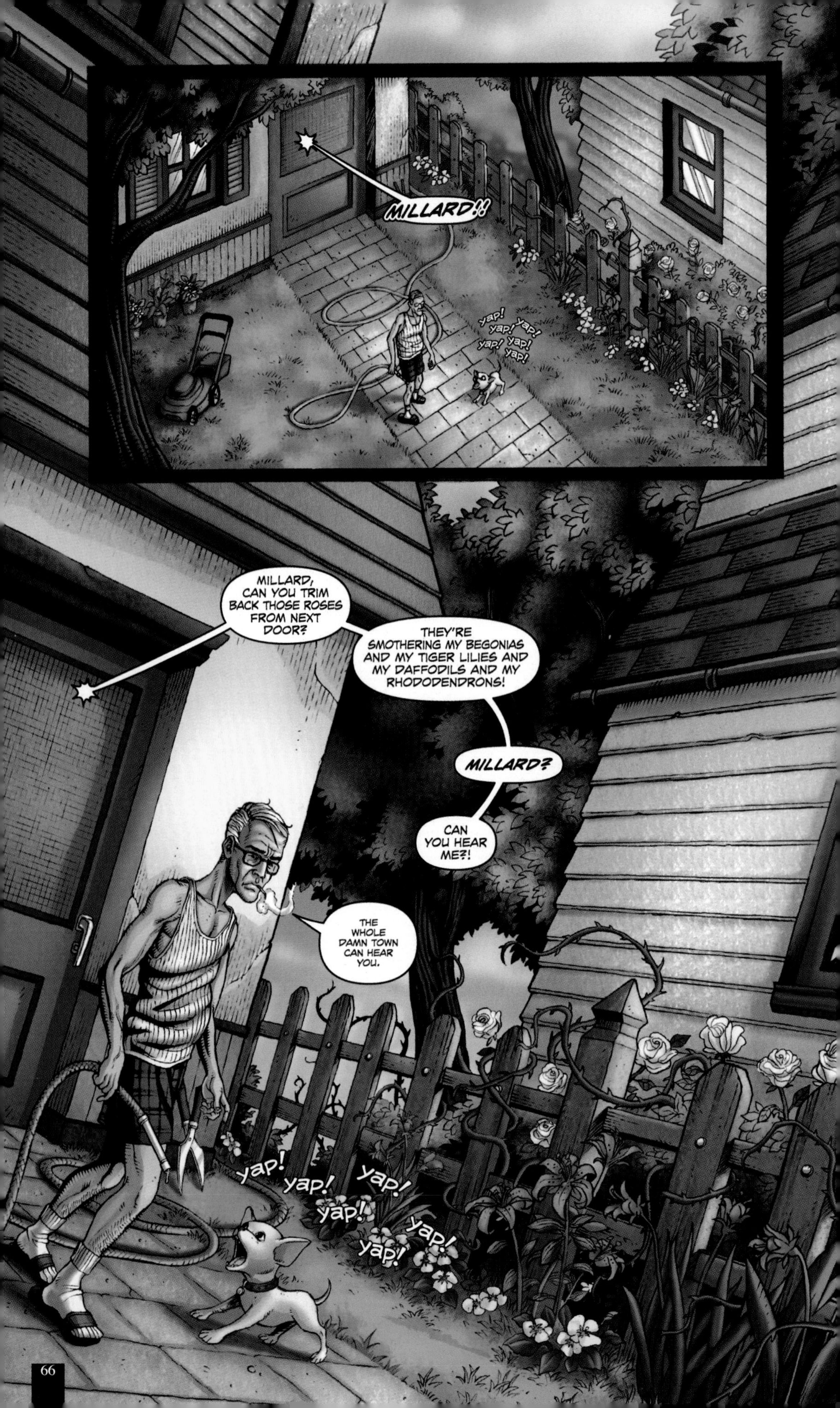

MILLARD!!
yap! yap! yap! yap! yap! yap!
MILLARD, CAN YOU TRIM BACK THOSE ROSES FROM NEXT DOOR?
THEY'RE SMOTHERING MY BEGONIAS AND MY TIGER LILIES AND MY DAFFODILS AND MY RHODODENDRONS!
MILLARD?
CAN YOU HEAR ME?!
THE WHOLE DAMN TOWN CAN HEAR YOU.
yap! yap! yap! yap! yap! yap!

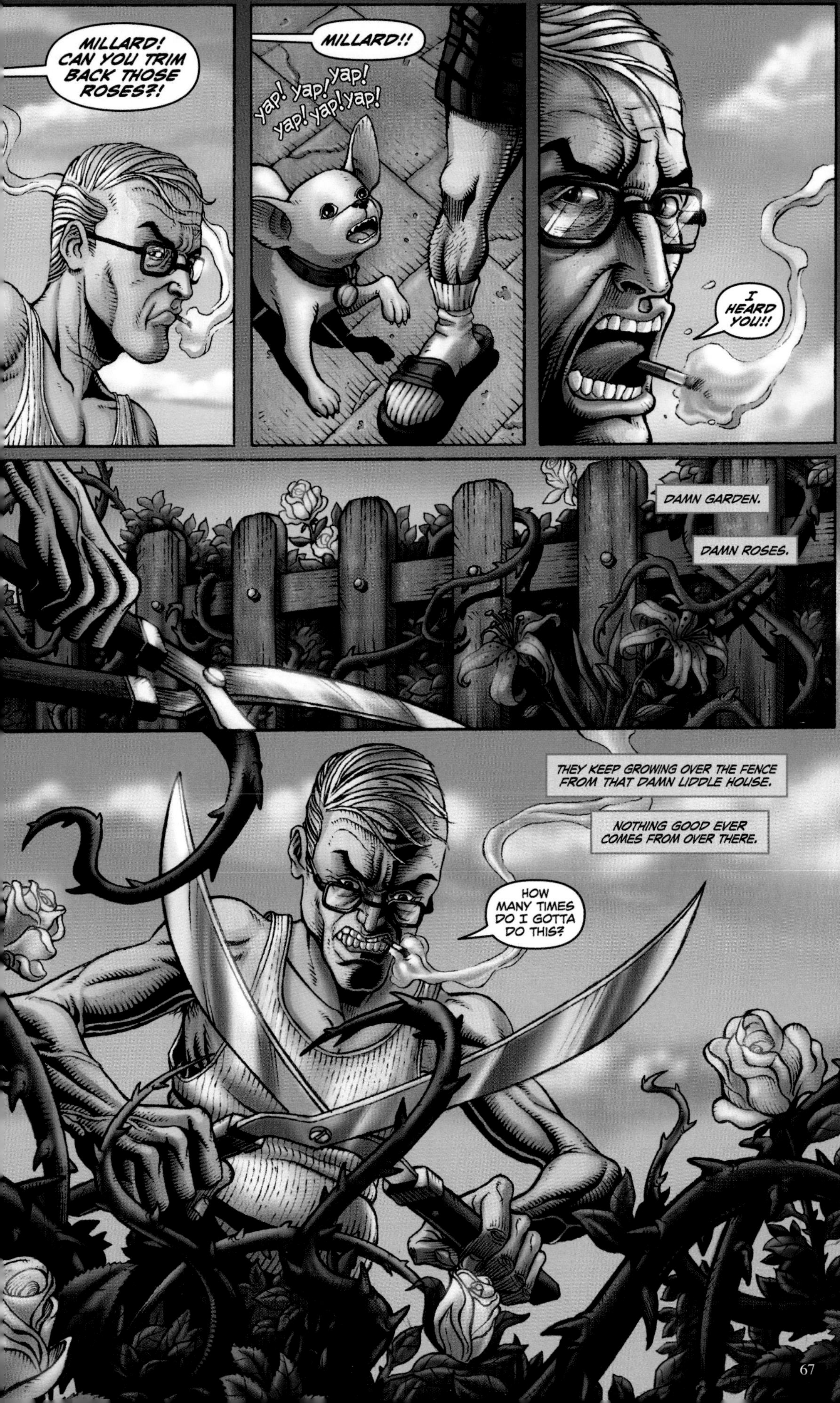
MILLARD! CAN YOU TRIM BACK THOSE ROSES?!
MILLARD!!
yap! yap! yap! yap! yap! yap!
I HEARD YOU!!
DAMN GARDEN.
DAMN ROSES.
THEY KEEP GROWING OVER THE FENCE FROM THAT DAMN LIDDLE HOUSE.
NOTHING GOOD EVER COMES FROM OVER THERE.
HOW MANY TIMES DO I GOTTA DO THIS?

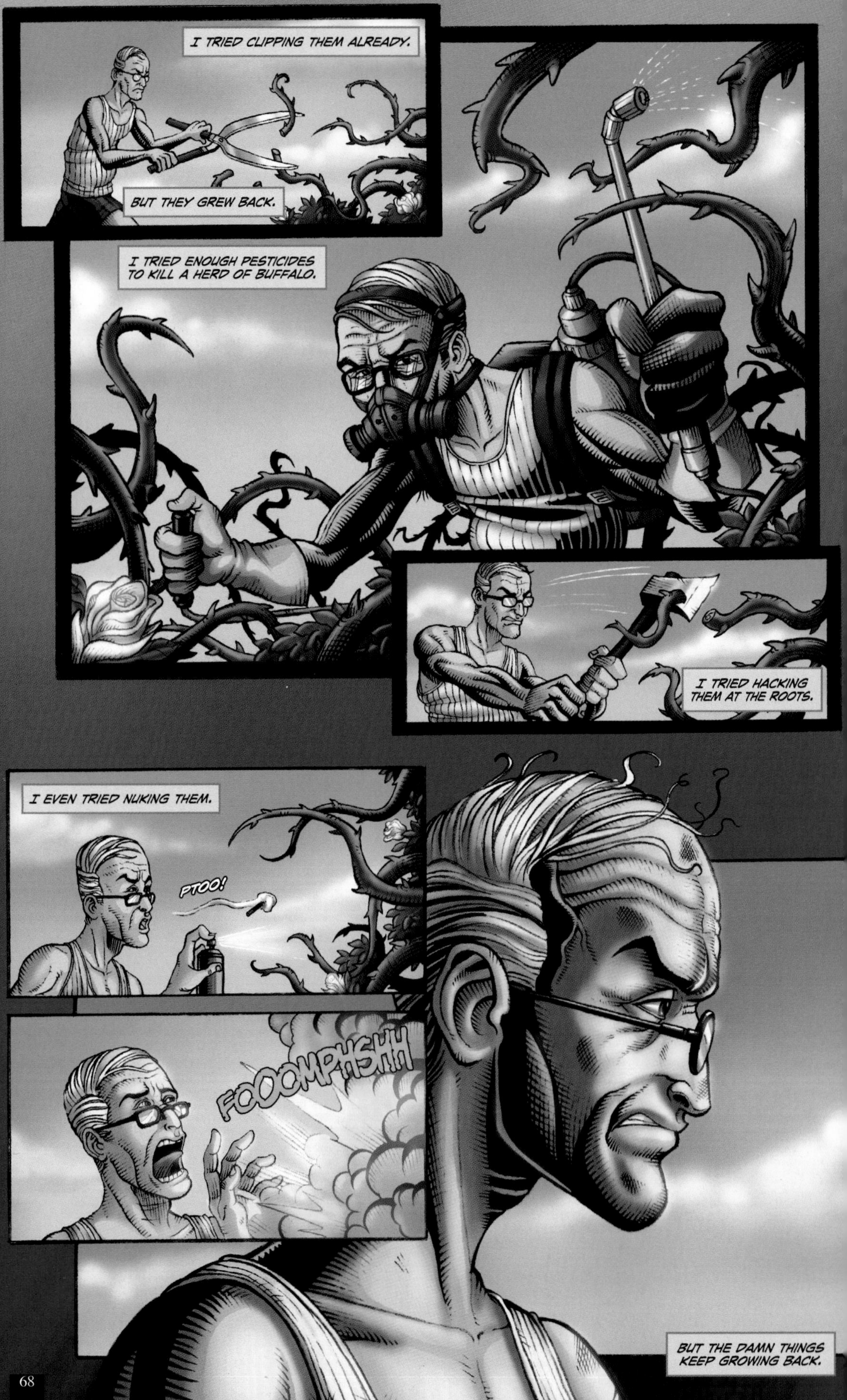
I TRIED CLIPPING THEM ALREADY.
BUT THEY GREW BACK.
I TRIED ENOUGH PESTICIDES TO KILL A HERD OF BUFFALO.
I TRIED HACKING THEM AT THE ROOTS.
I EVEN TRIED NUKING THEM.
PTOO!
FOOOMPHSHH
BUT THE DAMN THINGS KEEP GROWING BACK.

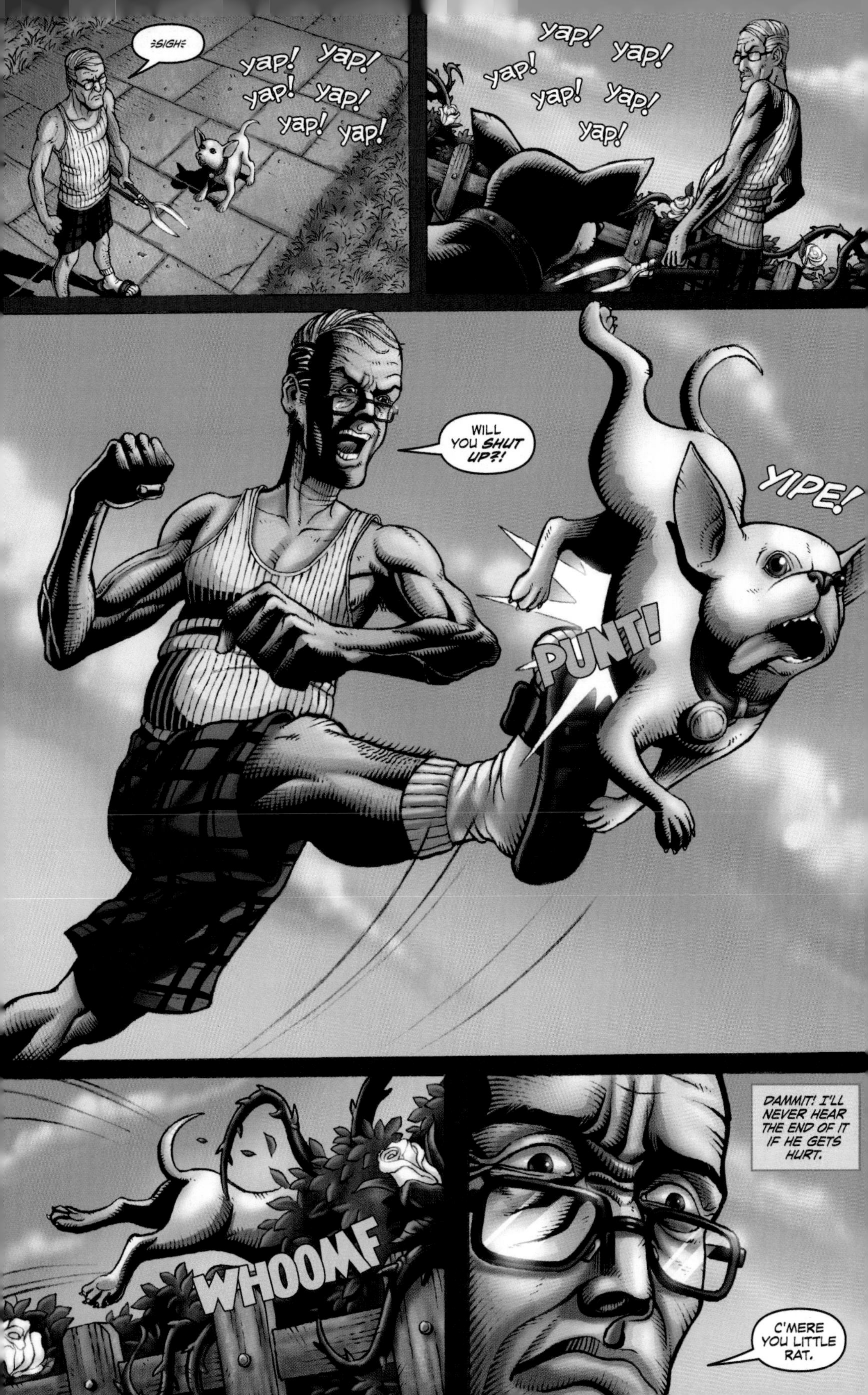

=SIGH=
yap! yap! yap! yap! yap! yap!
yap! yap! yap! yap! yap!
WILL YOU SHUT UP?!
YIPE!
PUNT!
WHOOMF
DAMMIT! I'LL NEVER HEAR THE END OF IT IF HE GETS HURT.
C'MERE YOU LITTLE RAT.

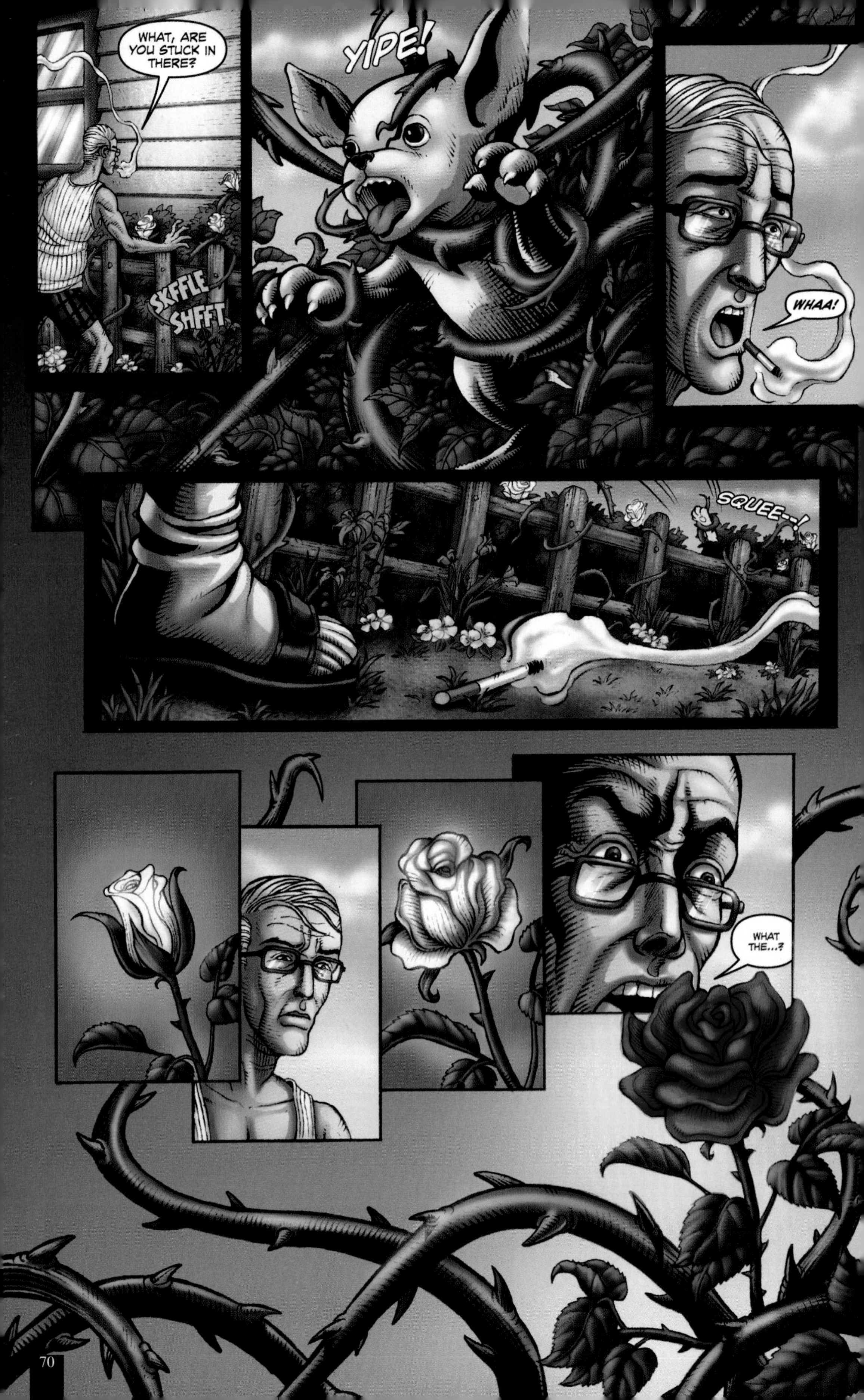
WHAT, ARE YOU STUCK IN THERE?
SKFFLE
SHFFT
YIPE!
WHAA!
SQUEE--!
WHAT THE...?

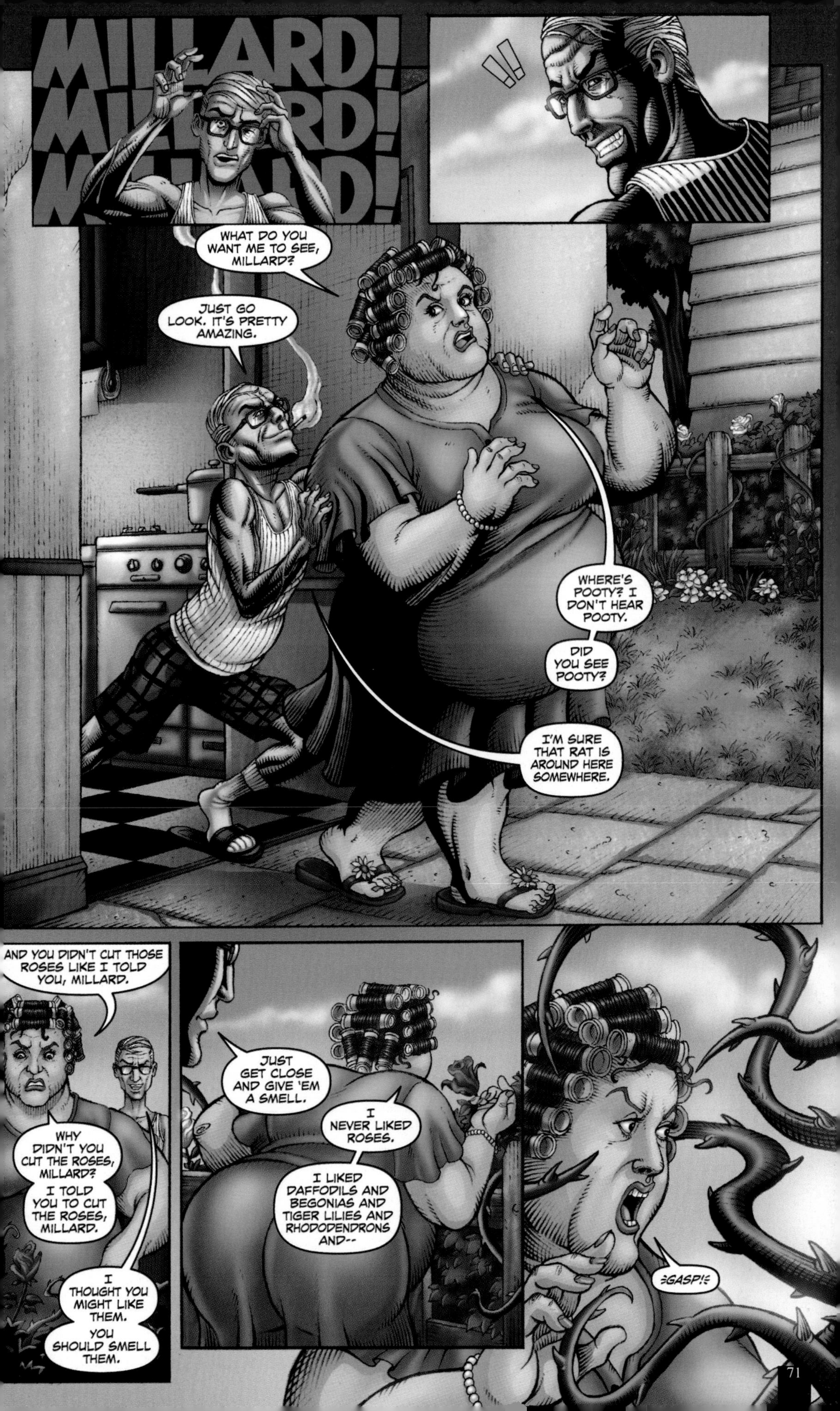

MILLARD! MILLARD! MILLARD!
!!
WHAT DO YOU WANT ME TO SEE, MILLARD?
JUST GO LOOK. IT'S PRETTY AMAZING.
WHERE'S POOTY? I DON'T HEAR POOTY.
DID YOU SEE POOTY?
I'M SURE THAT RAT IS AROUND HERE SOMEWHERE.
AND YOU DIDN'T CUT THOSE ROSES LIKE I TOLD YOU, MILLARD.
WHY DIDN'T YOU CUT THE ROSES, MILLARD?
I TOLD YOU TO CUT THE ROSES, MILLARD.
I THOUGHT YOU MIGHT LIKE THEM.
YOU SHOULD SMELL THEM.
JUST GET CLOSE AND GIVE 'EM A SMELL.
I NEVER LIKED ROSES.
I LIKED DAFFODILS AND BEGONIAS AND TIGER LILIES AND RHODODENDRONS AND--
GASP!

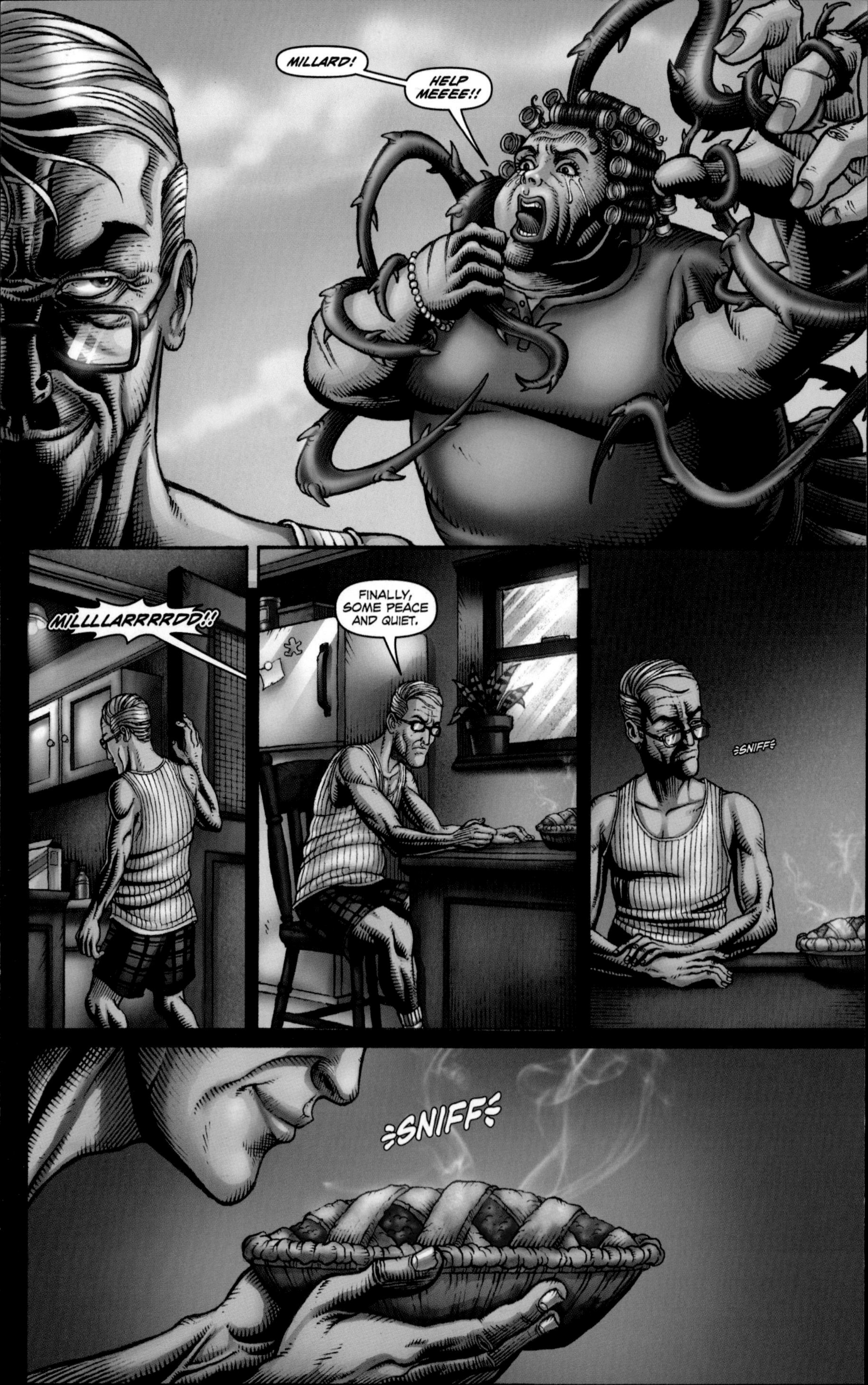
MILLARD!
HELP MEEEE!!
MILLLLARRRRDD!!
FINALLY, SOME PEACE AND QUIET.
SNIFF
SNIFF

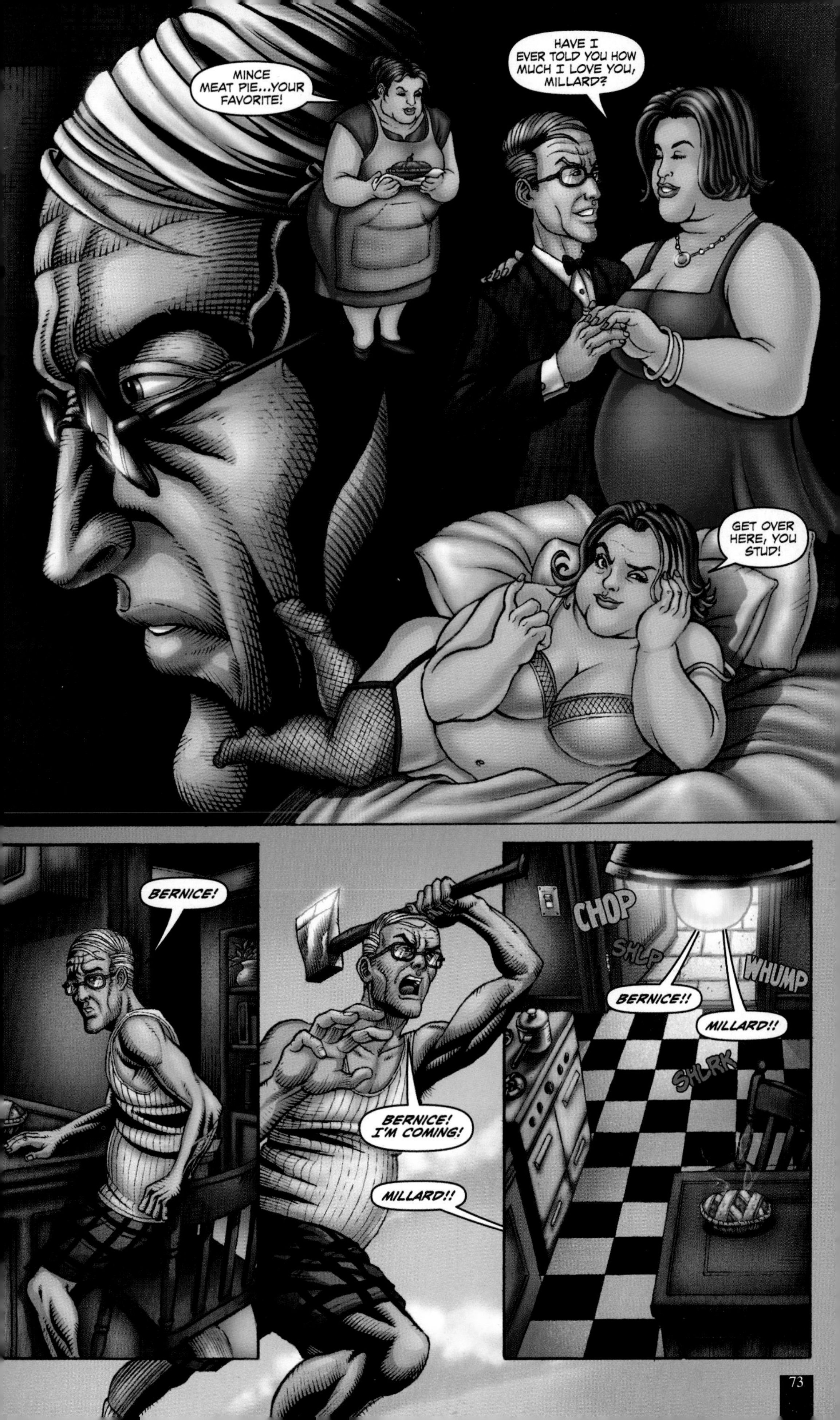

MINCE MEAT PIE...YOUR FAVORITE!
HAVE I EVER TOLD YOU HOW MUCH I LOVE YOU, MILLARD?
GET OVER HERE, YOU STUD!
BERNICE!
BERNICE! I'M COMING!
MILLARD!!
CHOP
SHLP
WHUMP
BERNICE!!
MILLARD!!
SHLRK

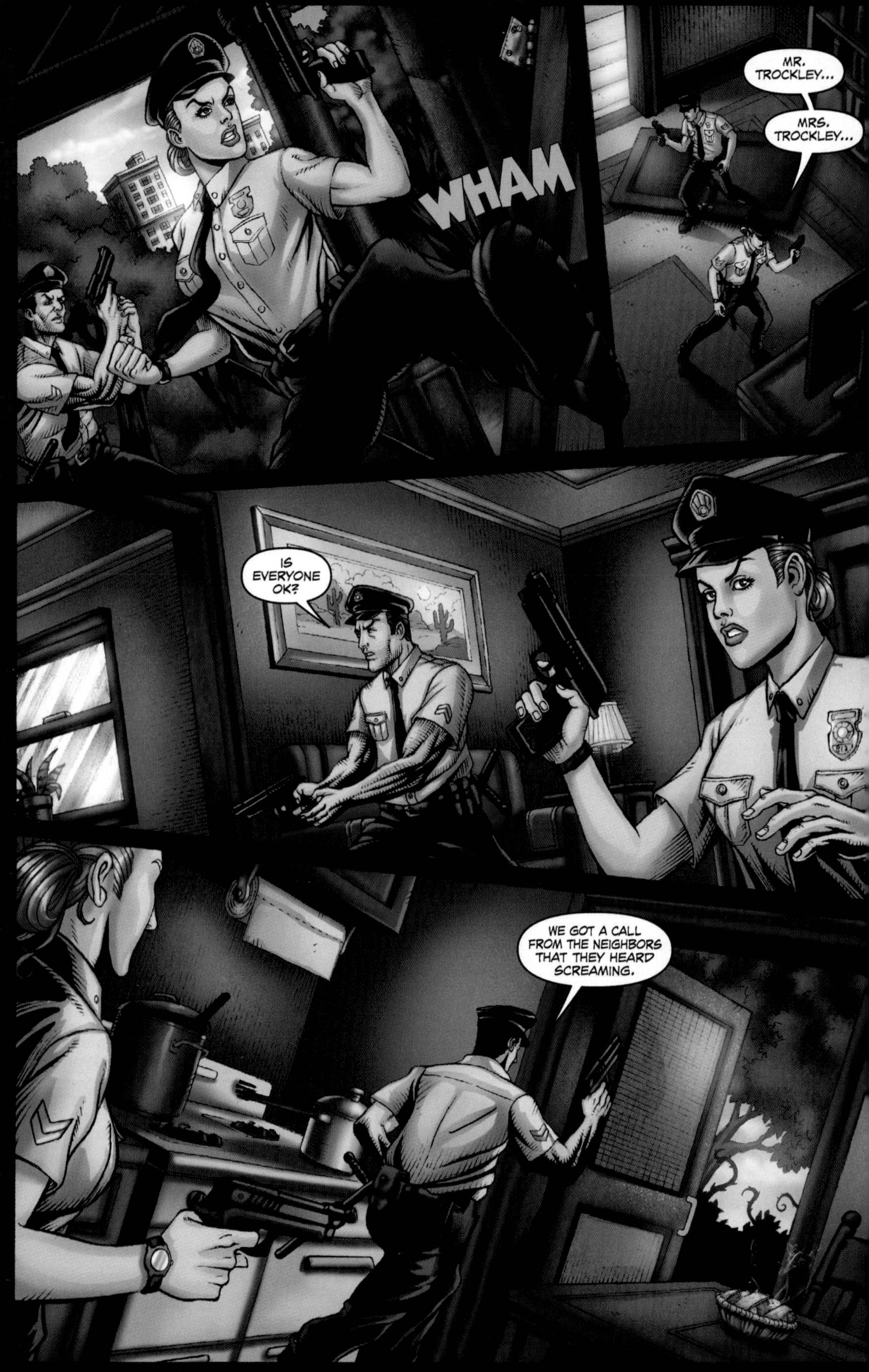
WHAM
MR. TROCKLEY...
MRS. TROCKLEY...
IS EVERYONE OK?
WE GOT A CALL FROM THE NEIGHBORS THAT THEY HEARD SCREAMING.

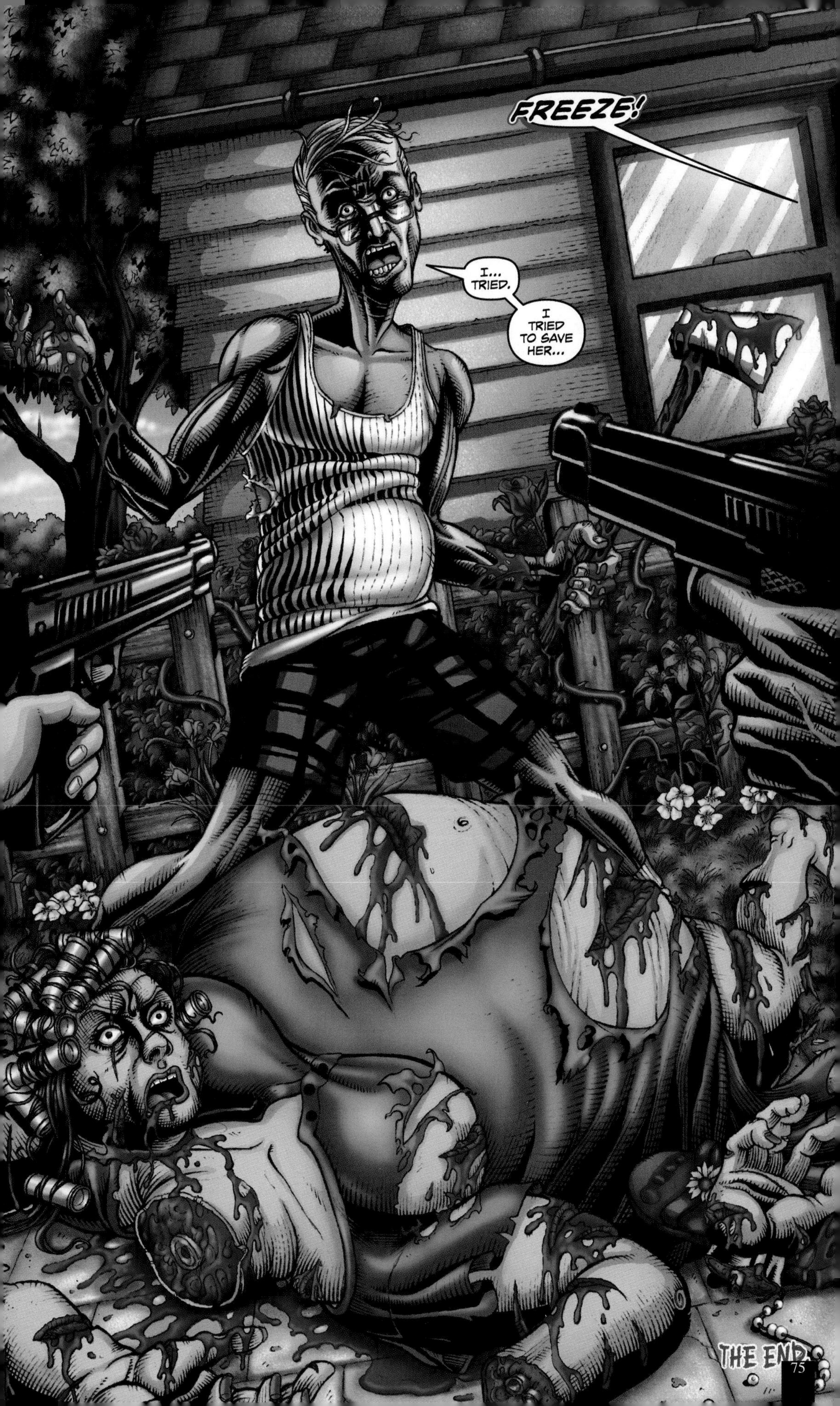
FREEZE!
I... TRIED.
I TRIED TO SAVE HER...
THE END

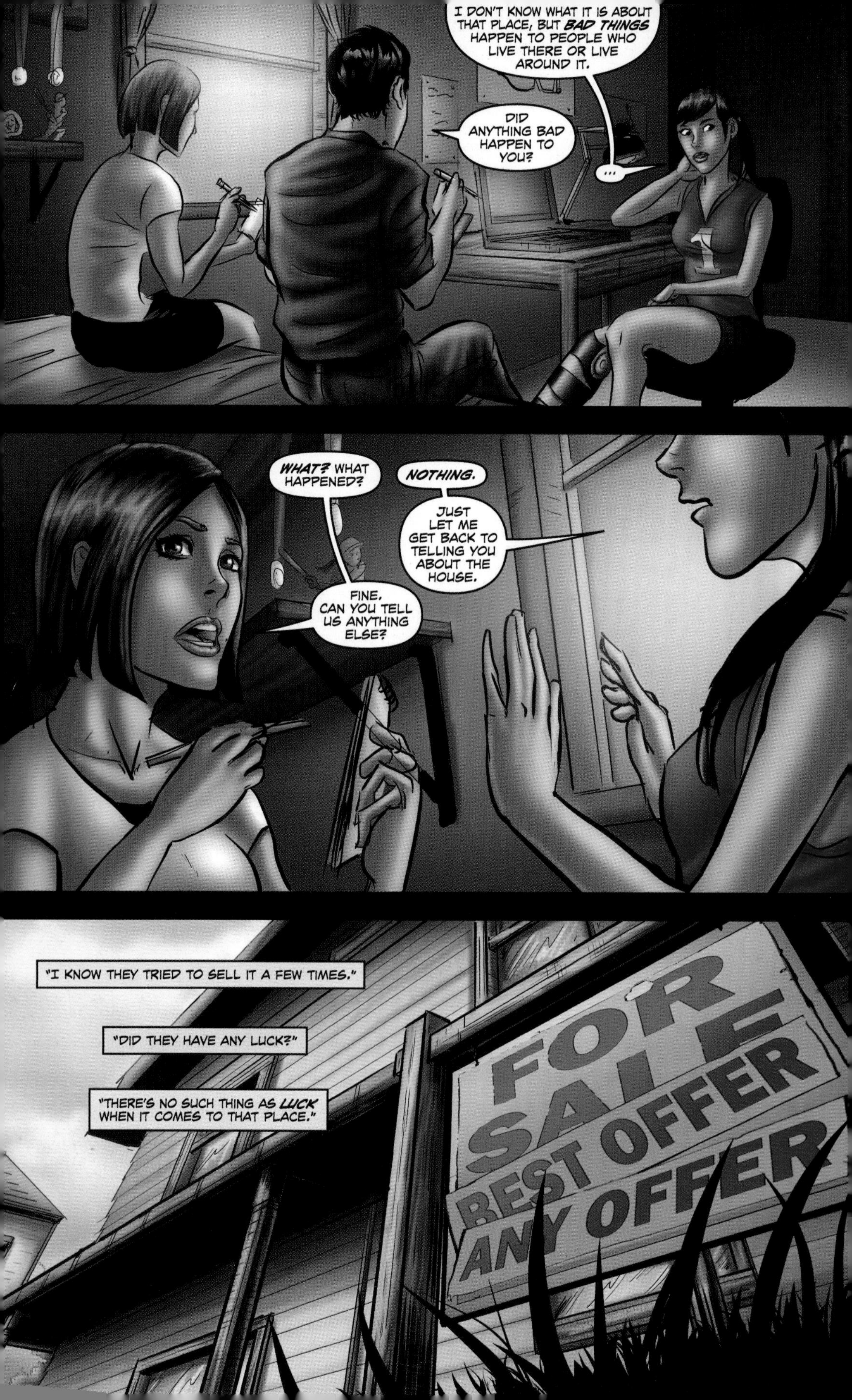
I DON'T KNOW WHAT IT IS ABOUT THAT PLACE, BUT BAD THINGS HAPPEN TO PEOPLE WHO LIVE THERE OR LIVE AROUND IT.
DID ANYTHING BAD HAPPEN TO YOU?
...
WHAT? WHAT HAPPENED?
NOTHING.
JUST LET ME GET BACK TO TELLING YOU ABOUT THE HOUSE.
FINE. CAN YOU TELL US ANYTHING ELSE?
"I KNOW THEY TRIED TO SELL IT A FEW TIMES."
"DID THEY HAVE ANY LUCK?"
"THERE'S NO SUCH THING AS LUCK WHEN IT COMES TO THAT PLACE."
FOR SALE
BEST OFFER
ANY OFFER

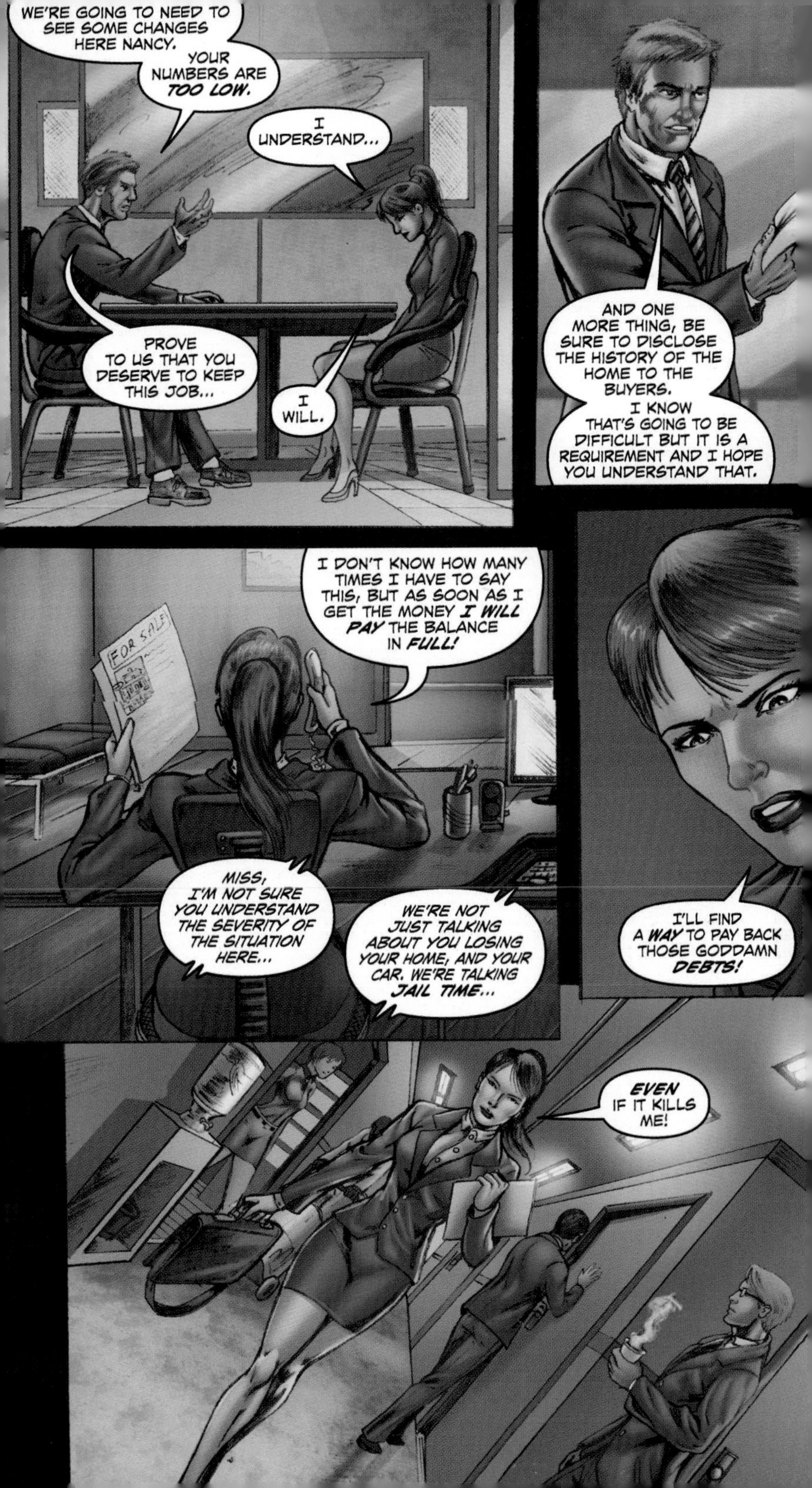
WE'RE GOING TO NEED TO SEE SOME CHANGES HERE NANCY.
YOUR NUMBERS ARE TOO LOW.
I UNDERSTAND...
PROVE TO US THAT YOU DESERVE TO KEEP THIS JOB...
I WILL.
AND ONE MORE THING, BE SURE TO DISCLOSE THE HISTORY OF THE HOME TO THE BUYERS.
I KNOW THAT'S GOING TO BE DIFFICULT BUT IT IS A REQUIREMENT AND I HOPE YOU UNDERSTAND THAT.
I DON'T KNOW HOW MANY TIMES I HAVE TO SAY THIS, BUT AS SOON AS I GET THE MONEY I WILL PAY THE BALANCE IN FULL!
FOR SALE
MISS, I'M NOT SURE YOU UNDERSTAND THE SEVERITY OF THE SITUATION HERE...
WE'RE NOT JUST TALKING ABOUT YOU LOSING YOUR HOME, AND YOUR CAR. WE'RE TALKING JAIL TIME...
I'LL FIND A WAY TO PAY BACK THOSE GODDAMN DEBTS!
EVEN IF IT KILLS ME!

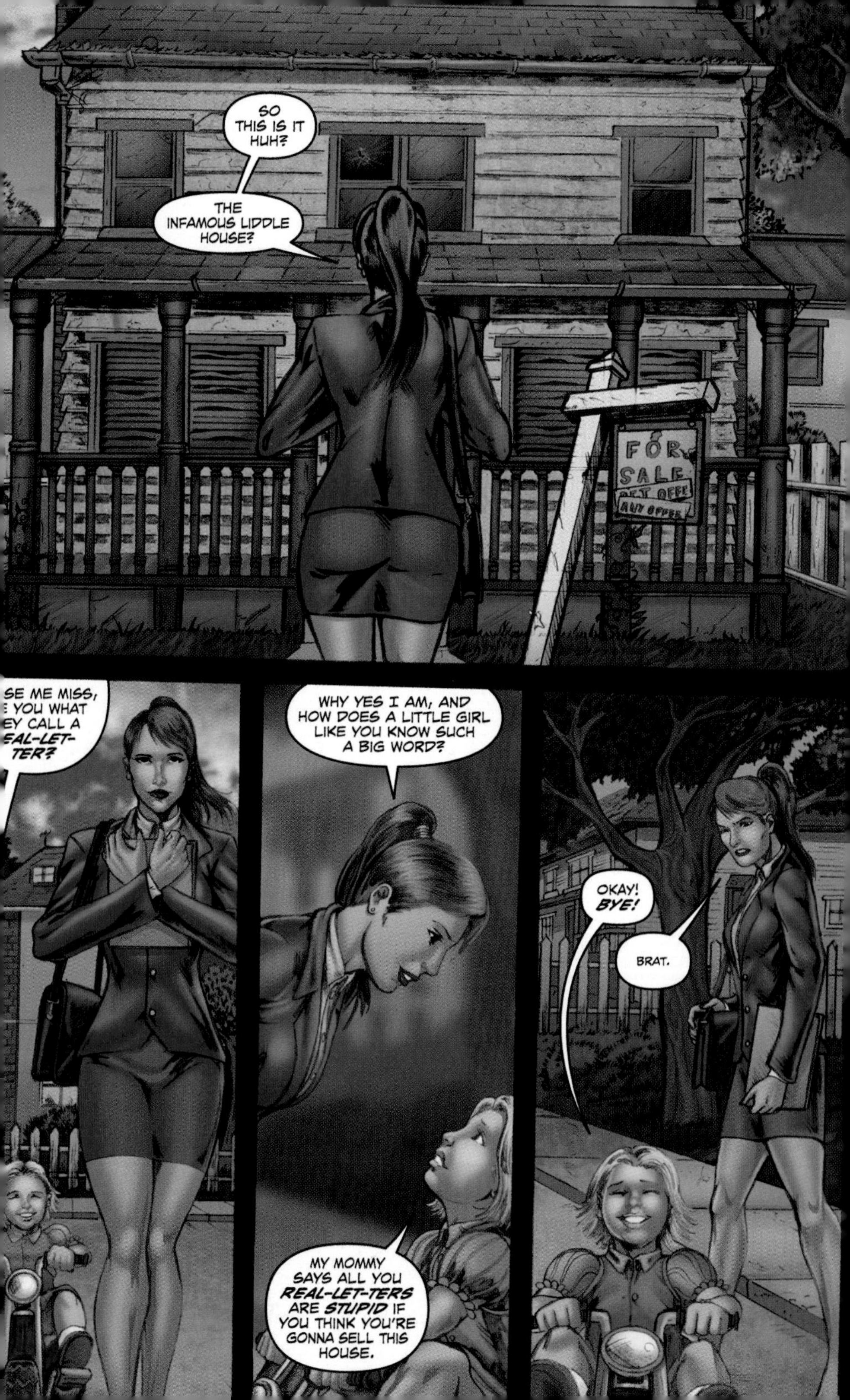
SO THIS IS IT HUH?
THE INFAMOUS LIDDLE HOUSE?
FOR SALE
SE ME MISS, YOU WHAT EY CALL A EAL-LET-TER?
WHY YES I AM, AND HOW DOES A LITTLE GIRL LIKE YOU KNOW SUCH A BIG WORD?
MY MOMMY SAYS ALL YOU REAL-LET-TERS ARE STUPID IF YOU THINK YOU'RE GONNA SELL THIS HOUSE.
OKAY! BYE!
BRAT.

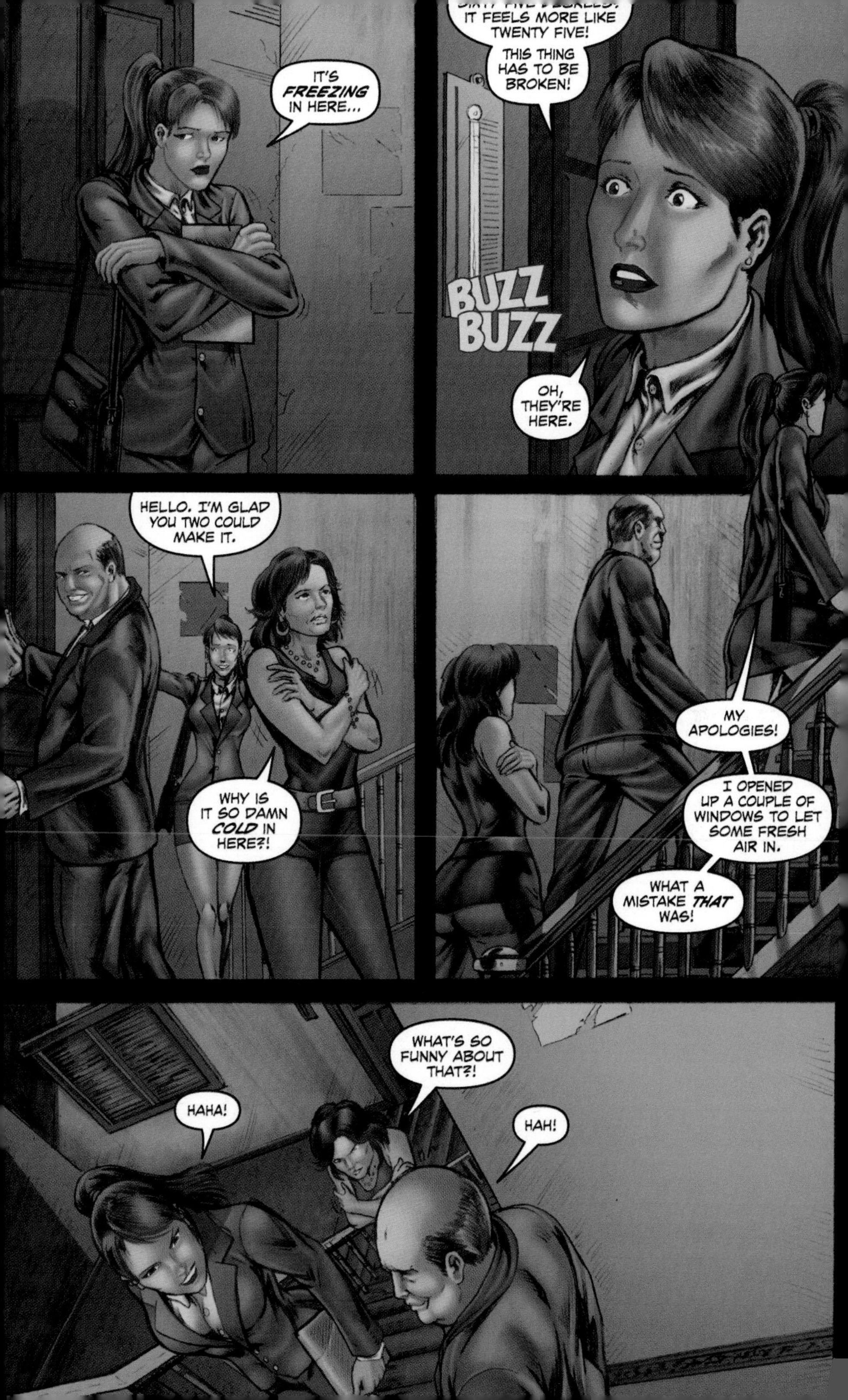
IT'S *FREEZING* IN HERE...
IT FEELS MORE LIKE TWENTY FIVE!
THIS THING HAS TO BE BROKEN!
BUZZ BUZZ
OH, THEY'RE HERE.
HELLO. I'M GLAD YOU TWO COULD MAKE IT.
WHY IS IT SO DAMN *COLD* IN HERE?!
MY APOLOGIES!
I OPENED UP A COUPLE OF WINDOWS TO LET SOME FRESH AIR IN.
WHAT A MISTAKE *THAT* WAS!
WHAT'S SO FUNNY ABOUT THAT?!
HAHA!
HAH!

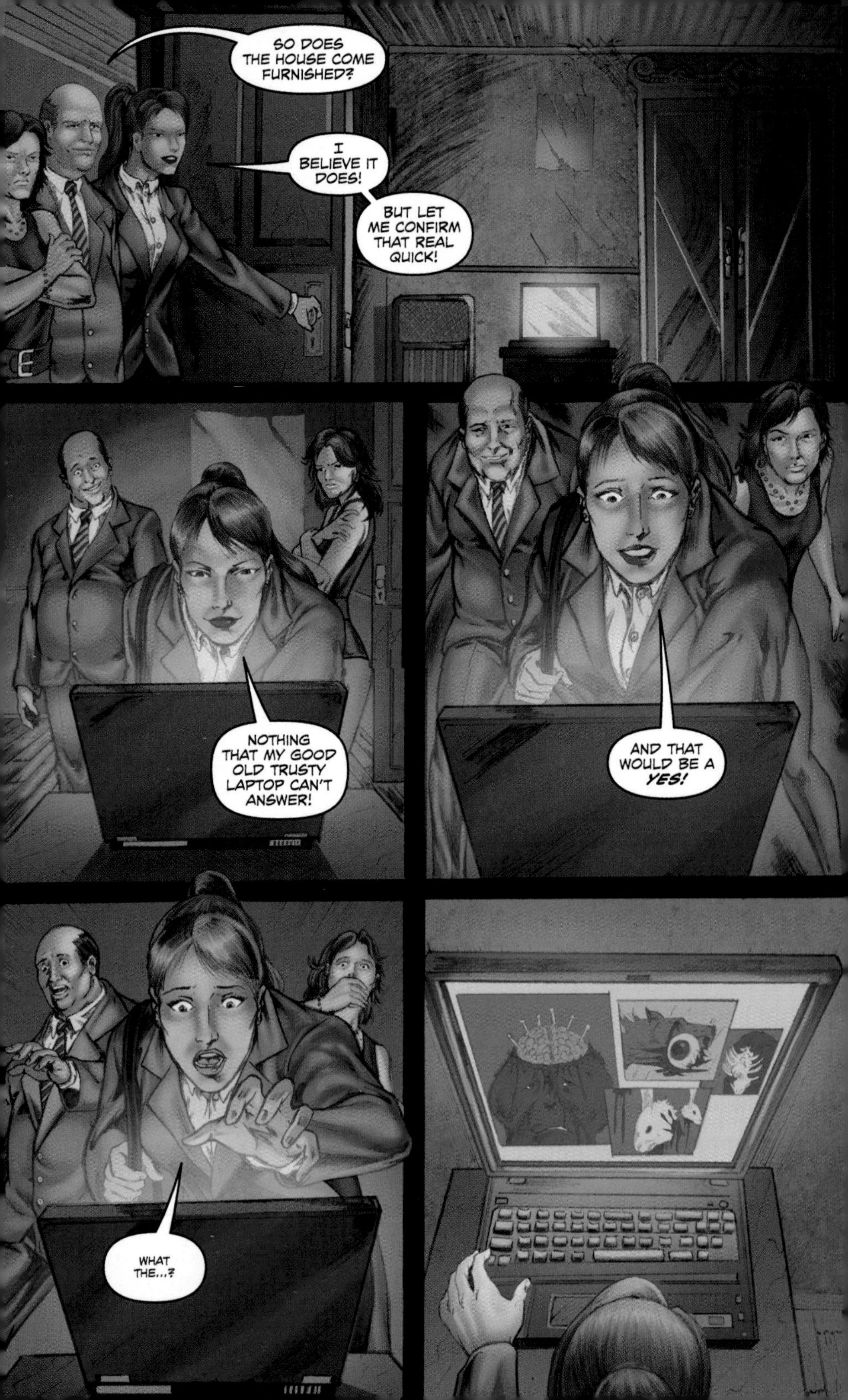

SO DOES THE HOUSE COME FURNISHED?
I BELIEVE IT DOES!
BUT LET ME CONFIRM THAT REAL QUICK!
NOTHING THAT MY GOOD OLD TRUSTY LAPTOP CAN'T ANSWER!
AND THAT WOULD BE A *YES!*
WHAT THE...?

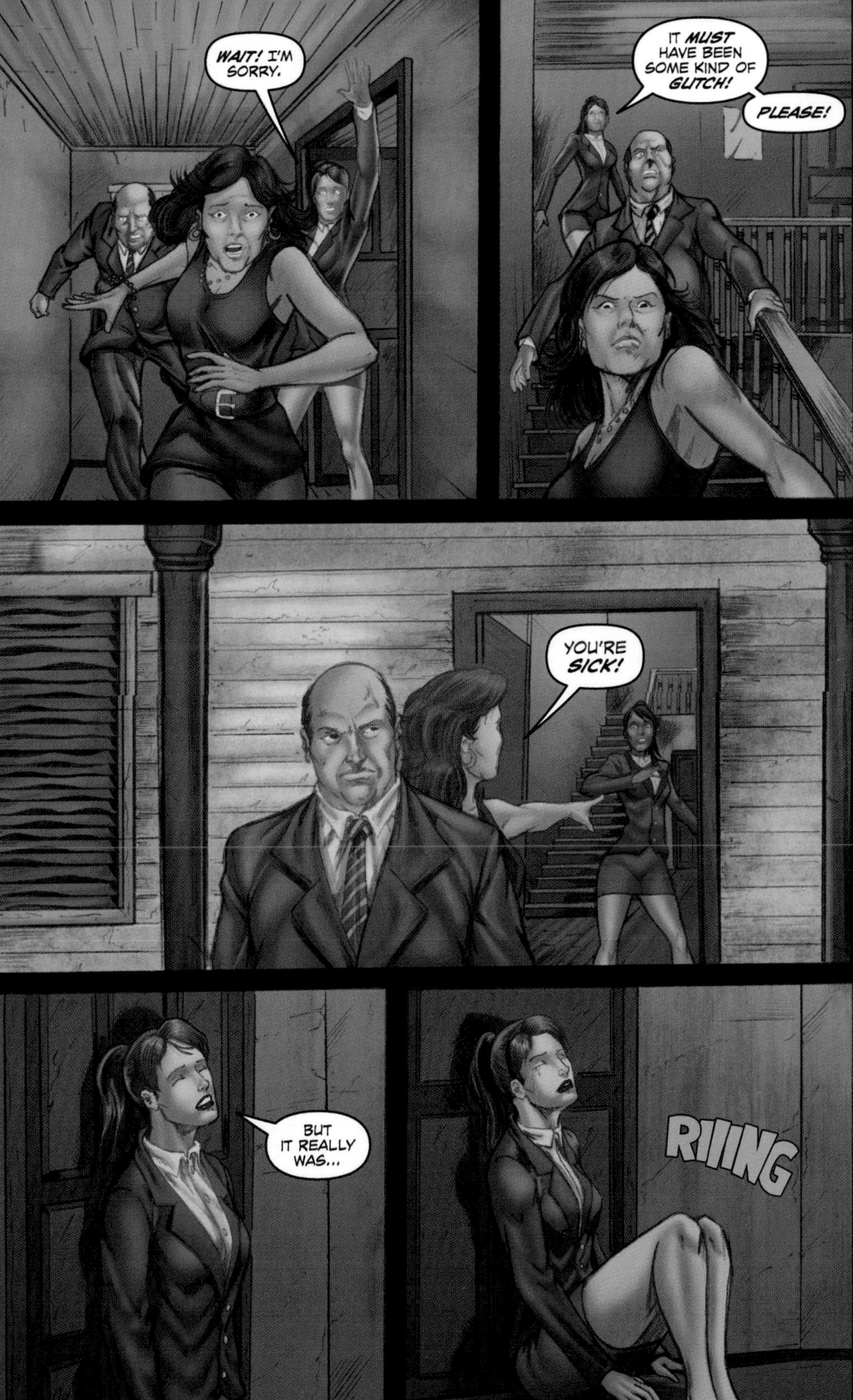
WAIT! I'M SORRY.
IT MUST HAVE BEEN SOME KIND OF GLITCH!
PLEASE!
YOU'RE SICK!
BUT IT REALLY WAS...
RIIING

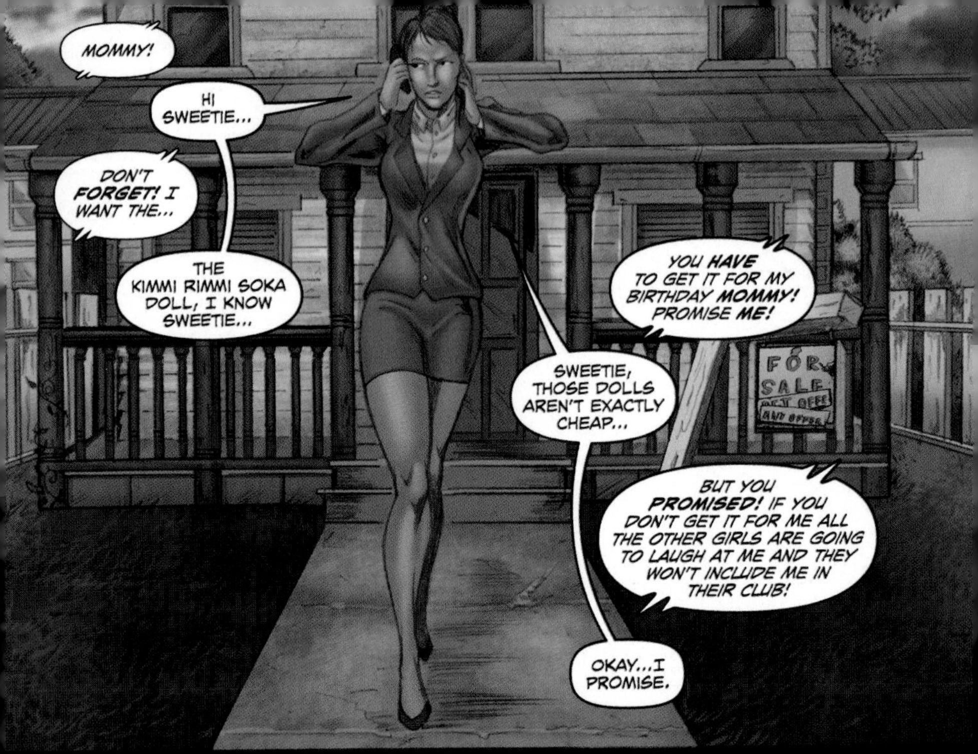
MOMMY!
HI SWEETIE...
DON'T FORGET! I WANT THE...
THE KIMMI RIMMI SOKA DOLL, I KNOW SWEETIE...
YOU HAVE TO GET IT FOR MY BIRTHDAY MOMMY! PROMISE ME!
SWEETIE, THOSE DOLLS AREN'T EXACTLY CHEAP...
FOR SALE
BUT YOU PROMISED! IF YOU DON'T GET IT FOR ME ALL THE OTHER GIRLS ARE GOING TO LAUGH AT ME AND THEY WON'T INCLUDE ME IN THEIR CLUB!
OKAY...I PROMISE.

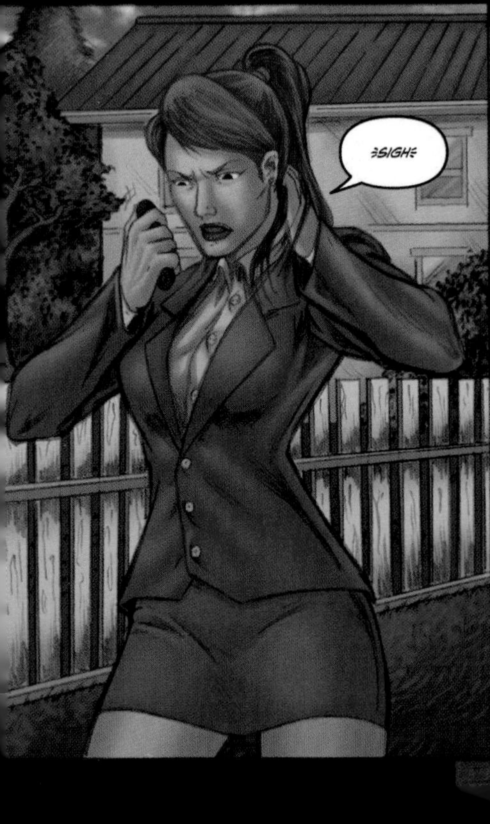
SIGH

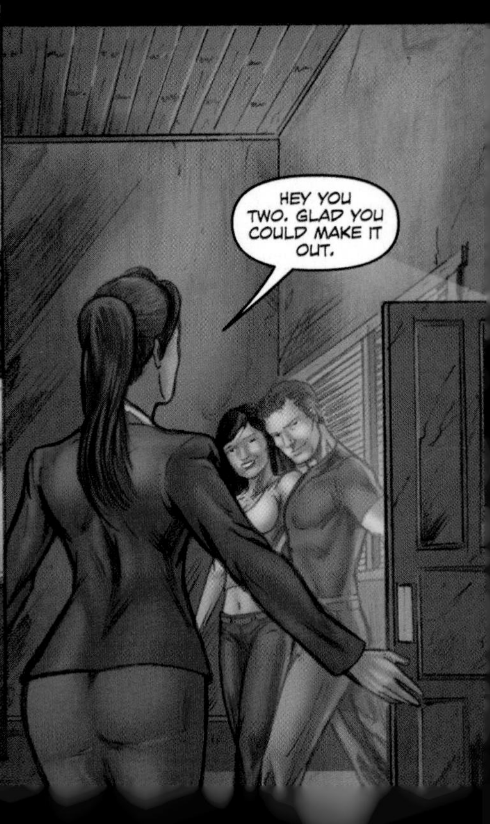
HEY YOU TWO. GLAD YOU COULD MAKE IT OUT.

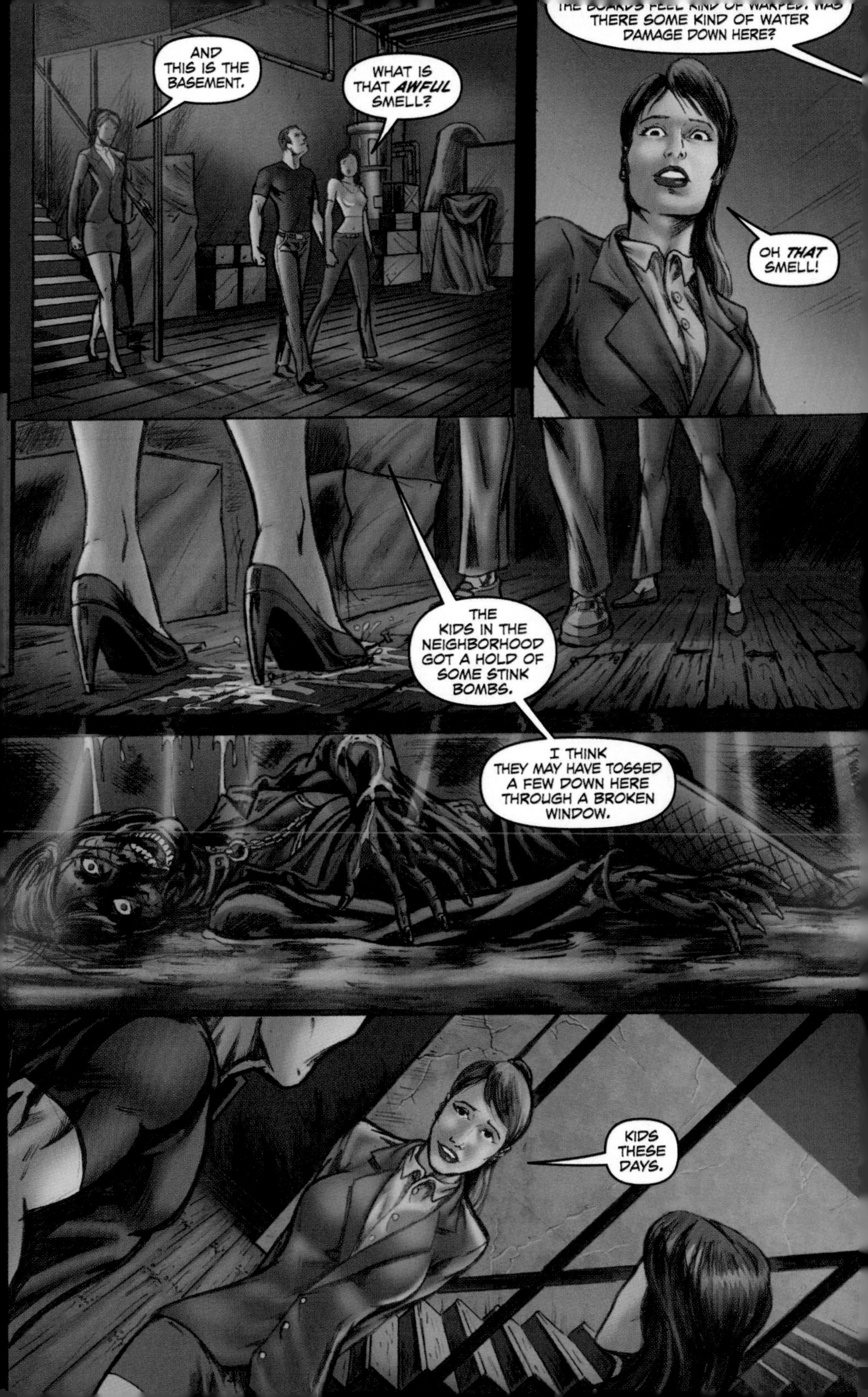
AND THIS IS THE BASEMENT.
WHAT IS THAT AWFUL SMELL?
THE BOARDS FEEL KIND OF WARPED. WAS THERE SOME KIND OF WATER DAMAGE DOWN HERE?
OH THAT SMELL!
THE KIDS IN THE NEIGHBORHOOD GOT A HOLD OF SOME STINK BOMBS.
I THINK THEY MAY HAVE TOSSED A FEW DOWN HERE THROUGH A BROKEN WINDOW.
KIDS THESE DAYS.

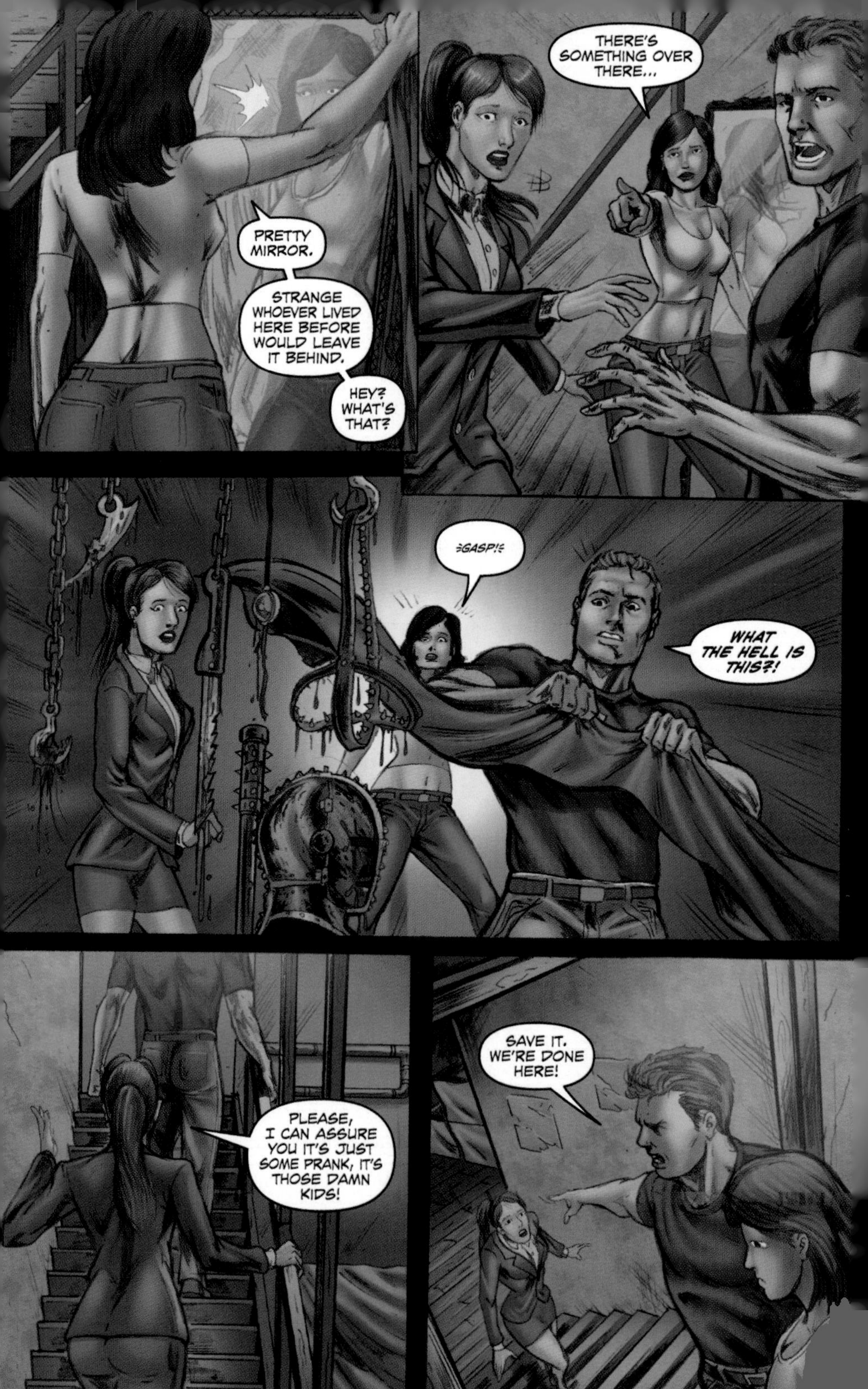
PRETTY MIRROR.
STRANGE WHOEVER LIVED HERE BEFORE WOULD LEAVE IT BEHIND.
HEY? WHAT'S THAT?
THERE'S SOMETHING OVER THERE...
=GASP!=
WHAT THE HELL IS THIS?!
PLEASE, I CAN ASSURE YOU IT'S JUST SOME PRANK, IT'S THOSE DAMN KIDS!
SAVE IT. WE'RE DONE HERE!

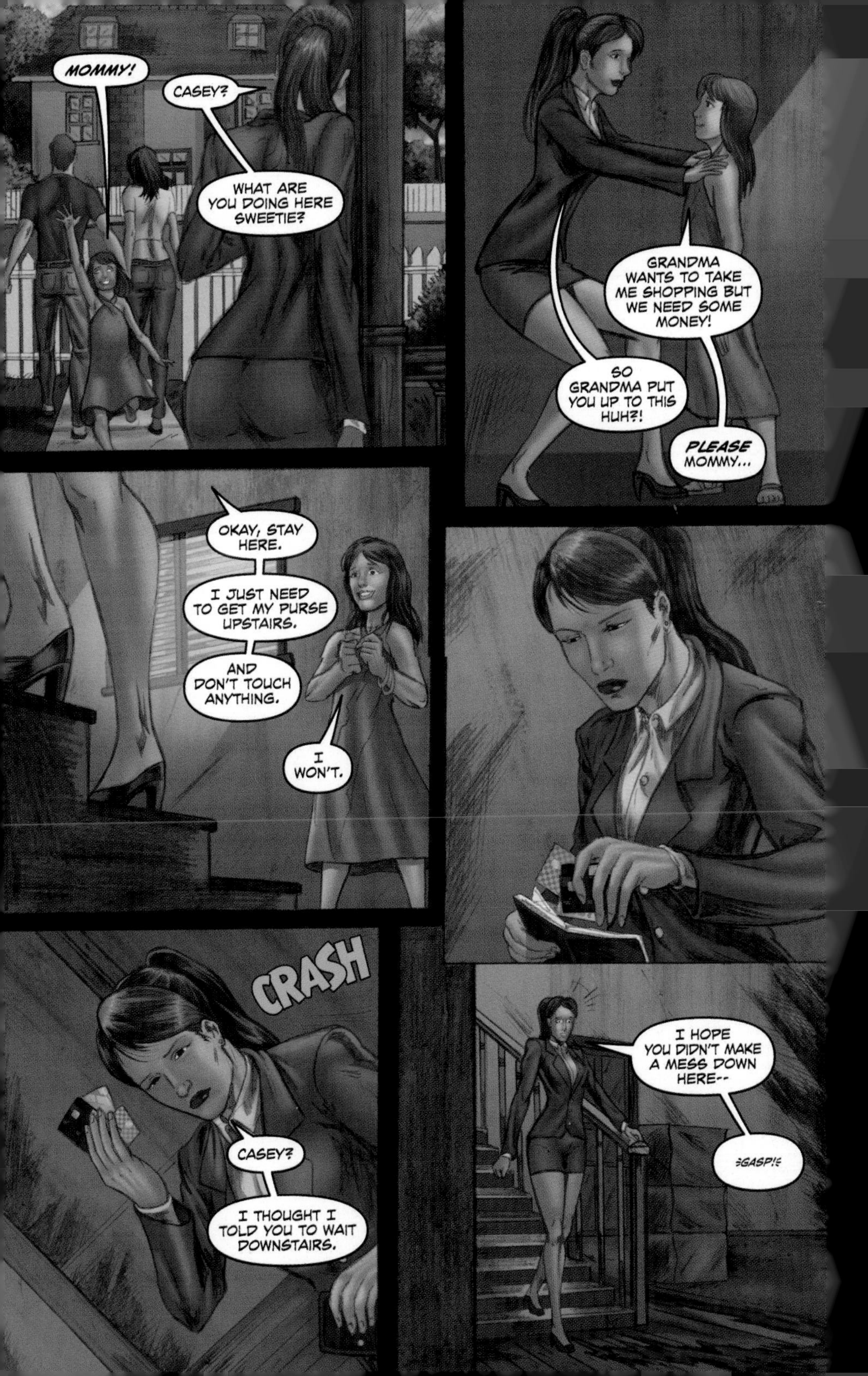
MOMMY!
CASEY?
WHAT ARE YOU DOING HERE SWEETIE?
GRANDMA WANTS TO TAKE ME SHOPPING BUT WE NEED SOME MONEY!
SO GRANDMA PUT YOU UP TO THIS HUH?!
PLEASE MOMMY...
OKAY, STAY HERE.
I JUST NEED TO GET MY PURSE UPSTAIRS.
AND DON'T TOUCH ANYTHING.
I WON'T.
CRASH
CASEY?
I THOUGHT I TOLD YOU TO WAIT DOWNSTAIRS.
I HOPE YOU DIDN'T MAKE A MESS DOWN HERE--
GASP!

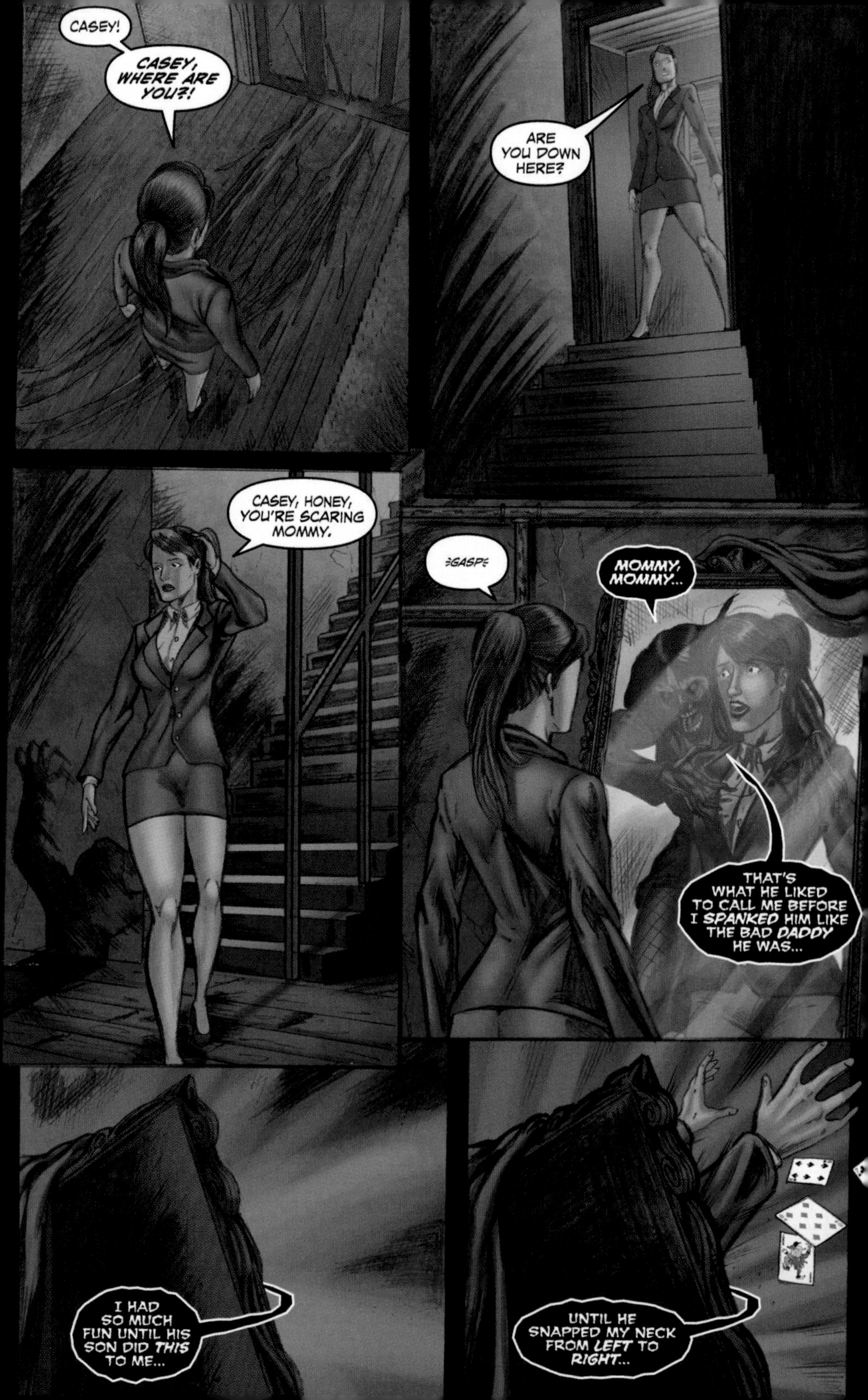
CASEY!
CASEY, WHERE ARE YOU?!
ARE YOU DOWN HERE?
CASEY, HONEY, YOU'RE SCARING MOMMY.
GASP
MOMMY, MOMMY...
THAT'S WHAT HE LIKED TO CALL ME BEFORE I SPANKED HIM LIKE THE BAD DADDY HE WAS...
I HAD SO MUCH FUN UNTIL HIS SON DID THIS TO ME...
UNTIL HE SNAPPED MY NECK FROM LEFT TO RIGHT...

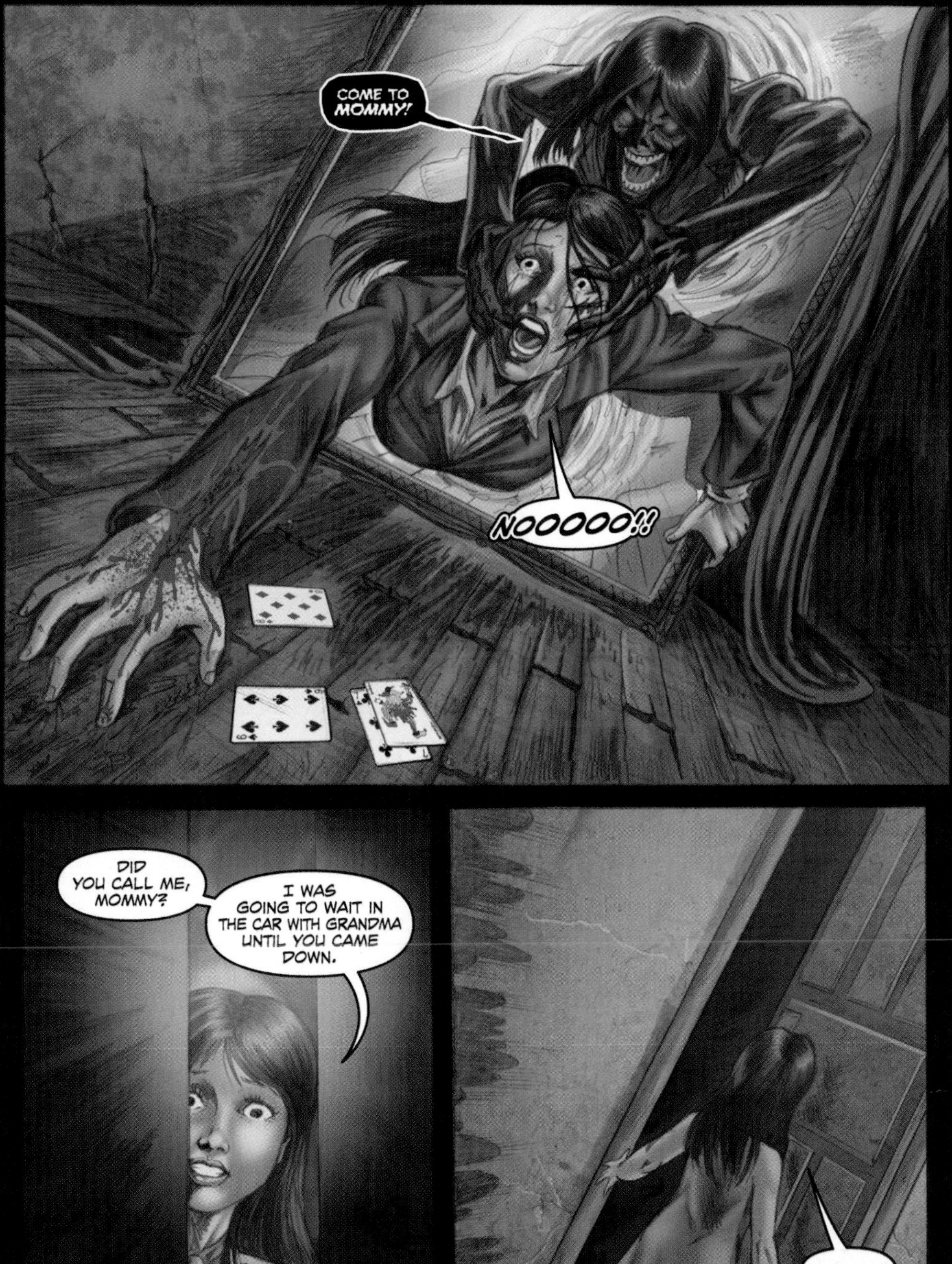
COME TO MOMMY!
NOOOOO!!
DID YOU CALL ME, MOMMY?
I WAS GOING TO WAIT IN THE CAR WITH GRANDMA UNTIL YOU CAME DOWN.
I'M DOWN IN THE BASEMENT, HONEY.
COME HERE. I HAVE A SURPRISE FOR YOU.
MOMMY?

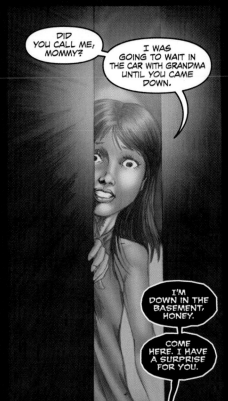

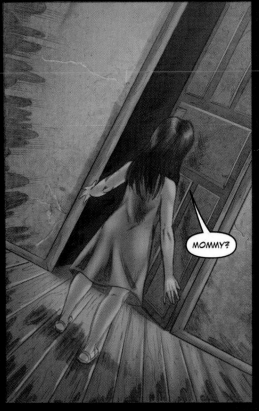

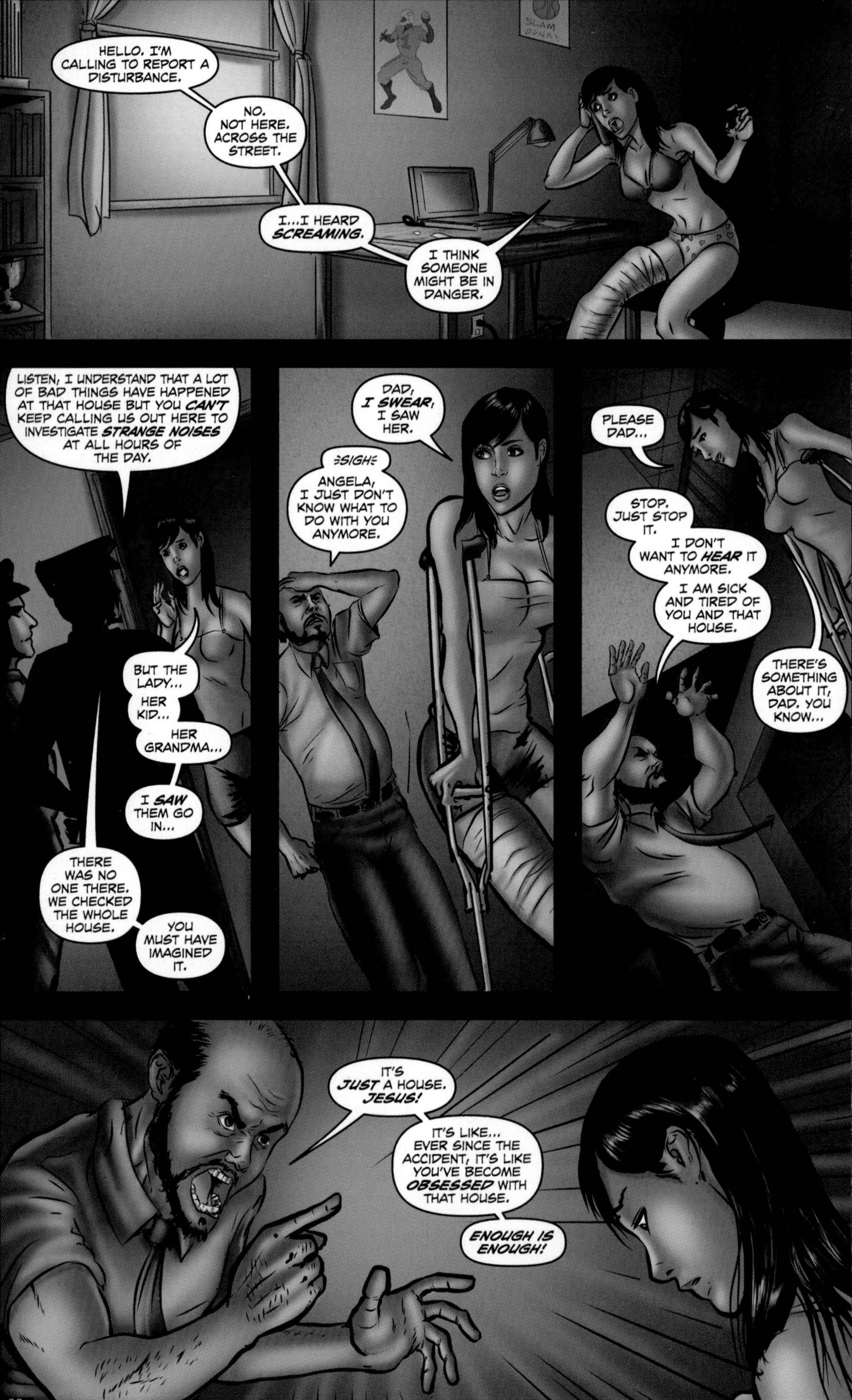
HELLO. I'M CALLING TO REPORT A DISTURBANCE.
NO. NOT HERE. ACROSS THE STREET.
I...I HEARD *SCREAMING*.
I THINK SOMEONE MIGHT BE IN DANGER.
LISTEN, I UNDERSTAND THAT A LOT OF BAD THINGS HAVE HAPPENED AT THAT HOUSE BUT YOU *CAN'T* KEEP CALLING US OUT HERE TO INVESTIGATE *STRANGE NOISES* AT ALL HOURS OF THE DAY.
BUT THE LADY...
HER KID...
HER GRANDMA...
I *SAW* THEM GO IN...
THERE WAS NO ONE THERE. WE CHECKED THE WHOLE HOUSE.
YOU MUST HAVE IMAGINED IT.
DAD, *I SWEAR*, I SAW HER.
SIGH
ANGELA, I JUST DON'T KNOW WHAT TO DO WITH YOU ANYMORE.
PLEASE DAD...
STOP. JUST STOP IT.
I DON'T WANT TO *HEAR* IT ANYMORE.
I AM SICK AND TIRED OF YOU AND THAT HOUSE.
THERE'S SOMETHING ABOUT IT, DAD. YOU KNOW...
IT'S *JUST* A HOUSE. *JESUS!*
IT'S LIKE... EVER SINCE THE ACCIDENT, IT'S LIKE YOU'VE BECOME *OBSESSED* WITH THAT HOUSE.
ENOUGH IS ENOUGH!

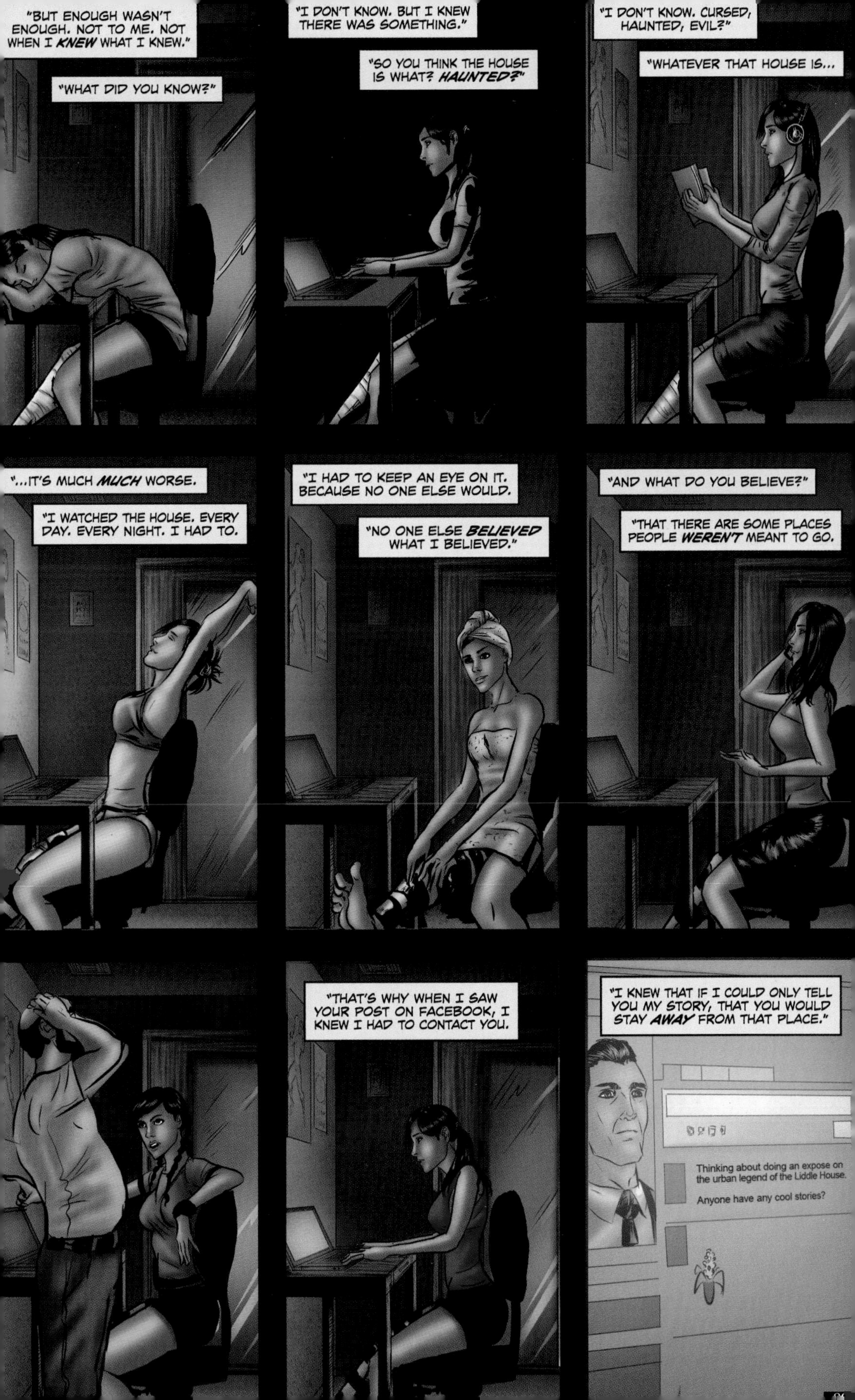
"BUT ENOUGH WASN'T ENOUGH. NOT TO ME. NOT WHEN I *KNEW* WHAT I KNEW."
"WHAT DID YOU KNOW?"
"I DON'T KNOW. BUT I KNEW THERE WAS SOMETHING."
"SO YOU THINK THE HOUSE IS WHAT? *HAUNTED?*"
"I DON'T KNOW. CURSED, HAUNTED, EVIL?"
"WHATEVER THAT HOUSE IS...
"...IT'S MUCH *MUCH* WORSE.
"I WATCHED THE HOUSE. EVERY DAY. EVERY NIGHT. I HAD TO.
"I HAD TO KEEP AN EYE ON IT. BECAUSE NO ONE ELSE WOULD.
"NO ONE ELSE *BELIEVED* WHAT I BELIEVED."
"AND WHAT DO YOU BELIEVE?"
"THAT THERE ARE SOME PLACES PEOPLE *WEREN'T* MEANT TO GO.
"THAT'S WHY WHEN I SAW YOUR POST ON FACEBOOK, I KNEW I HAD TO CONTACT YOU.
"I KNEW THAT IF I COULD ONLY TELL YOU MY STORY, THAT YOU WOULD STAY *AWAY* FROM THAT PLACE."
Thinking about doing an expose on the urban legend of the Liddle House.
Anyone have any cool stories?

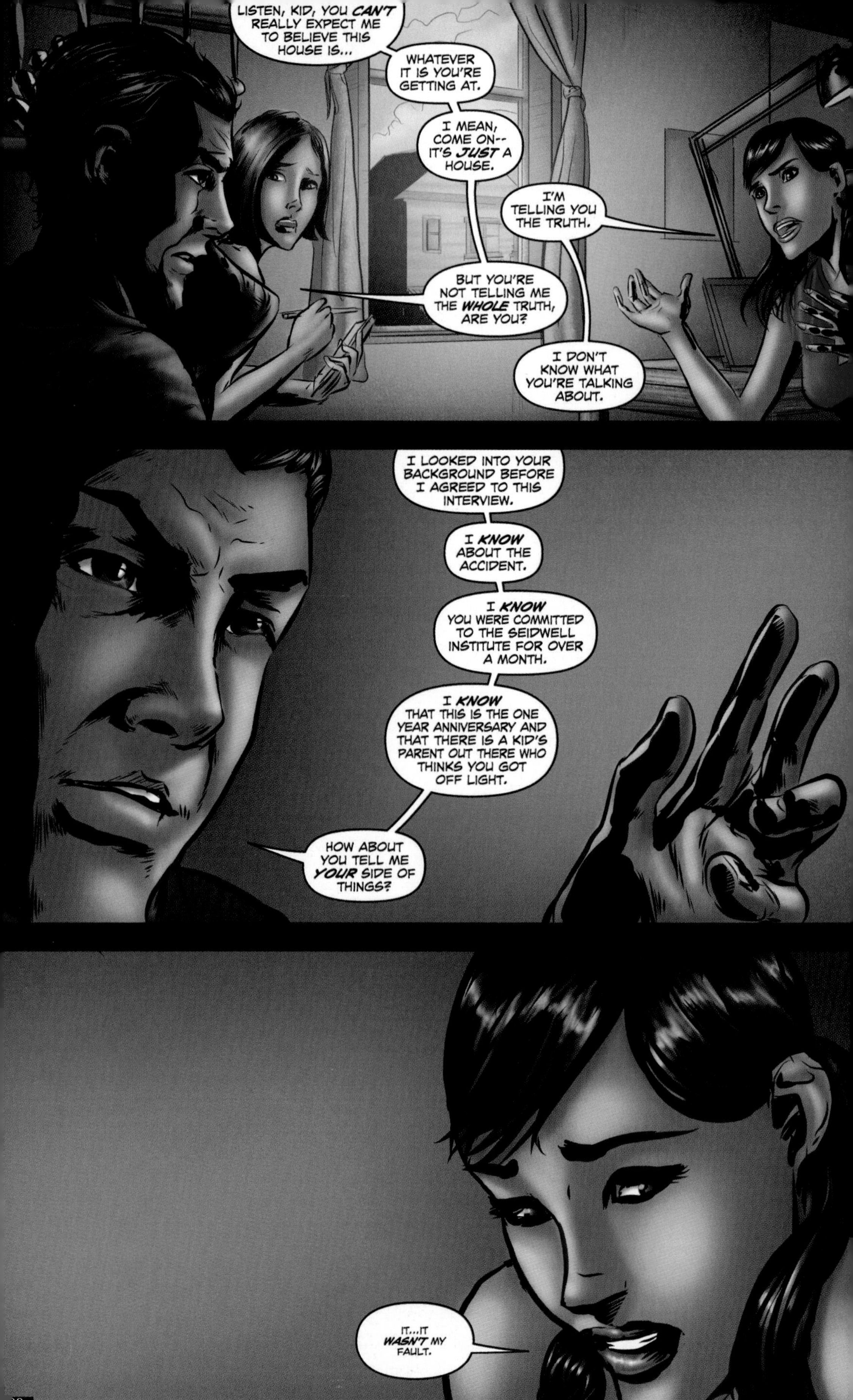
LISTEN, KID, YOU *CAN'T* REALLY EXPECT ME TO BELIEVE THIS HOUSE IS...
WHATEVER IT IS YOU'RE GETTING AT.
I MEAN, COME ON-- IT'S *JUST* A HOUSE.
I'M TELLING YOU THE TRUTH.
BUT YOU'RE NOT TELLING ME THE *WHOLE* TRUTH, ARE YOU?
I DON'T KNOW WHAT YOU'RE TALKING ABOUT.
I LOOKED INTO YOUR BACKGROUND BEFORE I AGREED TO THIS INTERVIEW.
I *KNOW* ABOUT THE ACCIDENT.
I *KNOW* YOU WERE COMMITTED TO THE SEIDWELL INSTITUTE FOR OVER A MONTH.
I *KNOW* THAT THIS IS THE ONE YEAR ANNIVERSARY AND THAT THERE IS A KID'S PARENT OUT THERE WHO THINKS YOU GOT OFF LIGHT.
HOW ABOUT YOU TELL ME *YOUR* SIDE OF THINGS?
IT...IT *WASN'T* MY FAULT.

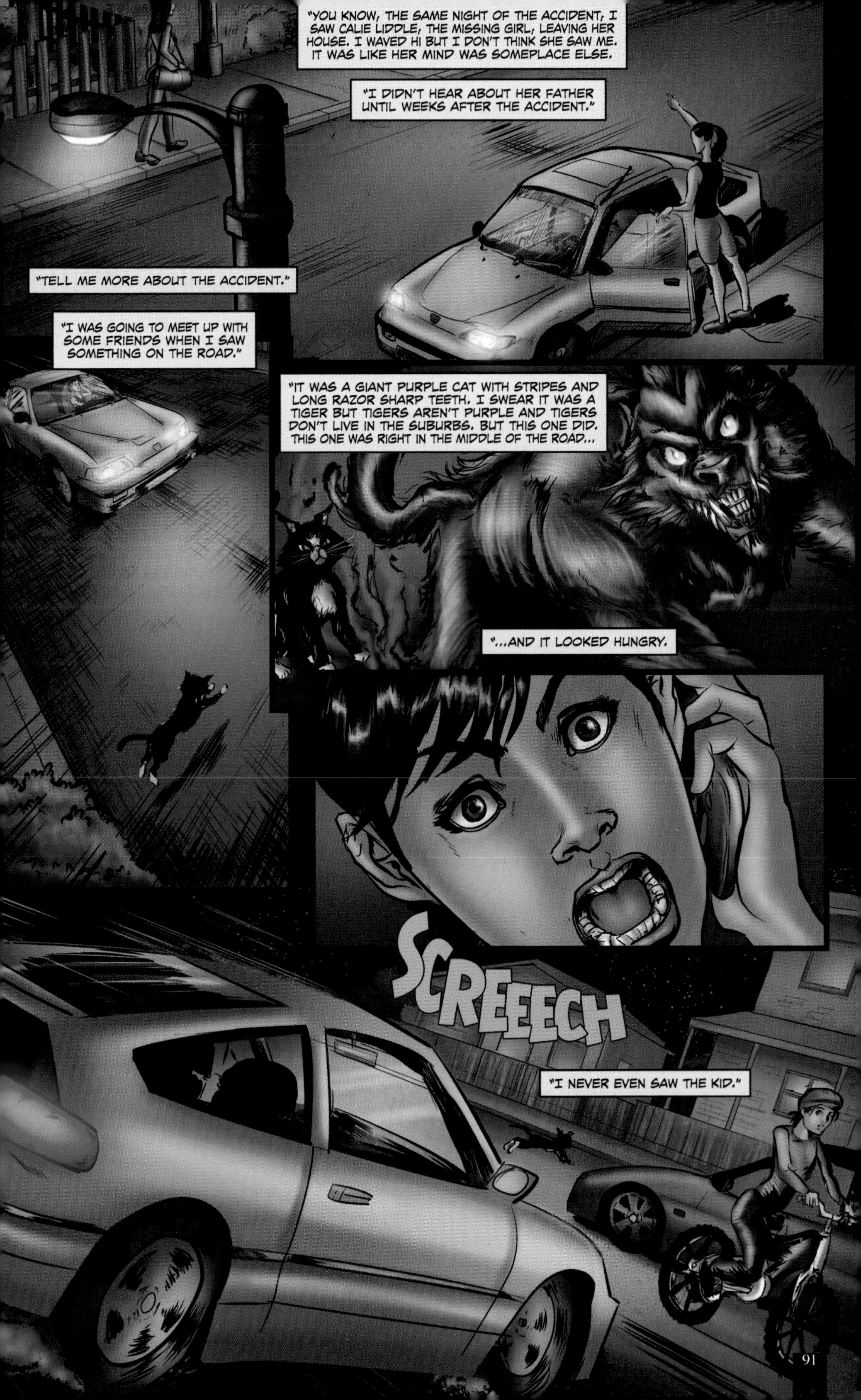
"YOU KNOW, THE SAME NIGHT OF THE ACCIDENT, I SAW CALIE LIDDLE, THE MISSING GIRL, LEAVING HER HOUSE. I WAVED HI BUT I DON'T THINK SHE SAW ME. IT WAS LIKE HER MIND WAS SOMEPLACE ELSE.
"I DIDN'T HEAR ABOUT HER FATHER UNTIL WEEKS AFTER THE ACCIDENT."
"TELL ME MORE ABOUT THE ACCIDENT."
"I WAS GOING TO MEET UP WITH SOME FRIENDS WHEN I SAW SOMETHING ON THE ROAD."
"IT WAS A GIANT PURPLE CAT WITH STRIPES AND LONG RAZOR SHARP TEETH. I SWEAR IT WAS A TIGER BUT TIGERS AREN'T PURPLE AND TIGERS DON'T LIVE IN THE SUBURBS. BUT THIS ONE DID. THIS ONE WAS RIGHT IN THE MIDDLE OF THE ROAD...
"...AND IT LOOKED HUNGRY.
SCREEECH
"I NEVER EVEN SAW THE KID."

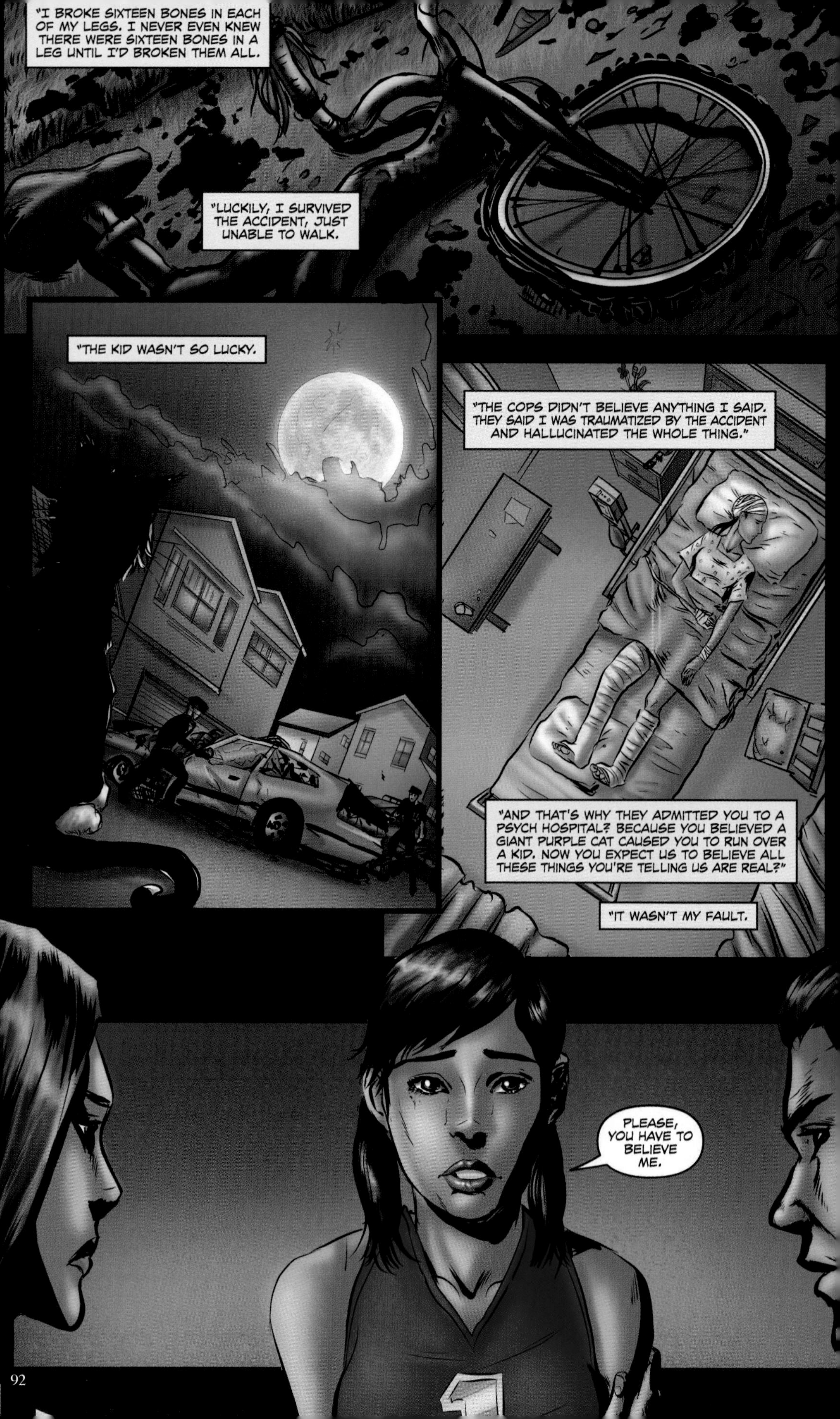
"I BROKE SIXTEEN BONES IN EACH OF MY LEGS. I NEVER EVEN KNEW THERE WERE SIXTEEN BONES IN A LEG UNTIL I'D BROKEN THEM ALL.
"LUCKILY, I SURVIVED THE ACCIDENT, JUST UNABLE TO WALK.
"THE KID WASN'T SO LUCKY.
"THE COPS DIDN'T BELIEVE ANYTHING I SAID. THEY SAID I WAS TRAUMATIZED BY THE ACCIDENT AND HALLUCINATED THE WHOLE THING."
"AND THAT'S WHY THEY ADMITTED YOU TO A PSYCH HOSPITAL? BECAUSE YOU BELIEVED A GIANT PURPLE CAT CAUSED YOU TO RUN OVER A KID. NOW YOU EXPECT US TO BELIEVE ALL THESE THINGS YOU'RE TELLING US ARE REAL?"
"IT WASN'T MY FAULT.
PLEASE, YOU HAVE TO BELIEVE ME.

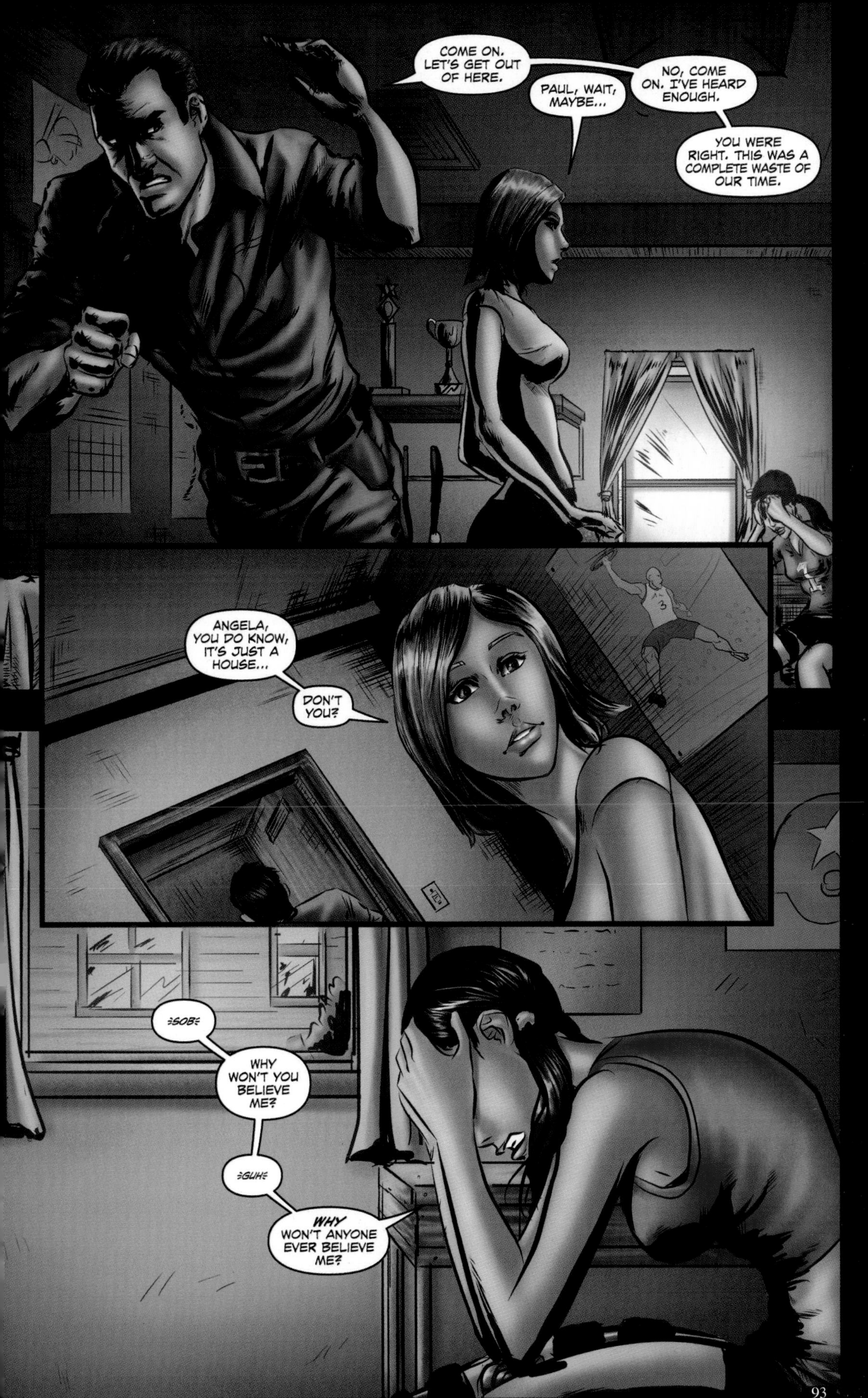

COME ON. LET'S GET OUT OF HERE.
PAUL, WAIT, MAYBE...
NO, COME ON. I'VE HEARD ENOUGH.
YOU WERE RIGHT. THIS WAS A COMPLETE WASTE OF OUR TIME.
ANGELA, YOU DO KNOW, IT'S JUST A HOUSE...
DON'T YOU?
≈SOB≈
WHY WON'T YOU BELIEVE ME?
≈GUH≈
WHY WON'T ANYONE EVER BELIEVE ME?

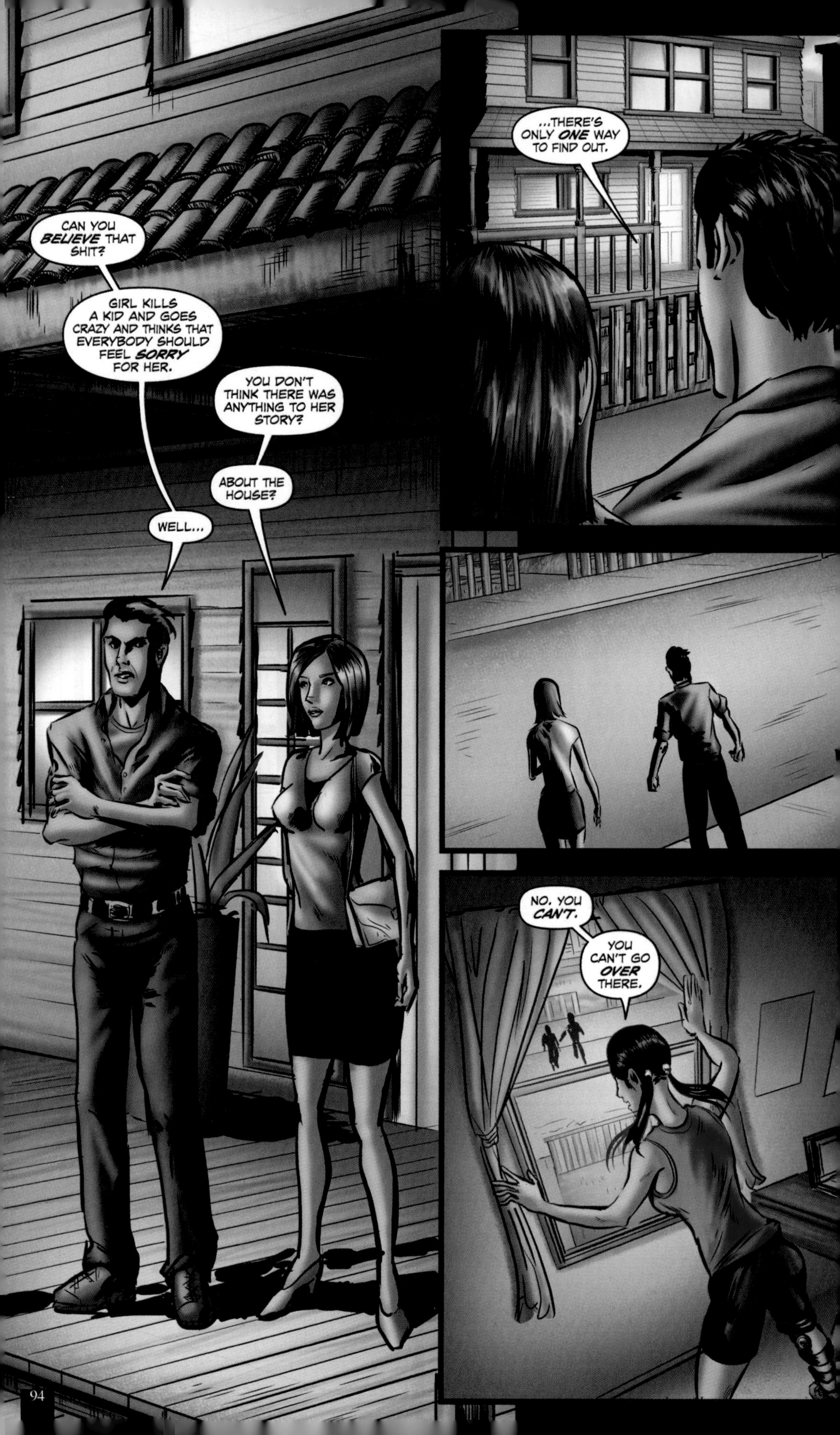
CAN YOU *BELIEVE* THAT SHIT?
GIRL KILLS A KID AND GOES CRAZY AND THINKS THAT EVERYBODY SHOULD FEEL *SORRY* FOR HER.
YOU DON'T THINK THERE WAS ANYTHING TO HER STORY?
ABOUT THE HOUSE?
WELL...
...THERE'S ONLY *ONE* WAY TO FIND OUT.
NO. YOU *CAN'T*.
YOU CAN'T GO *OVER* THERE.

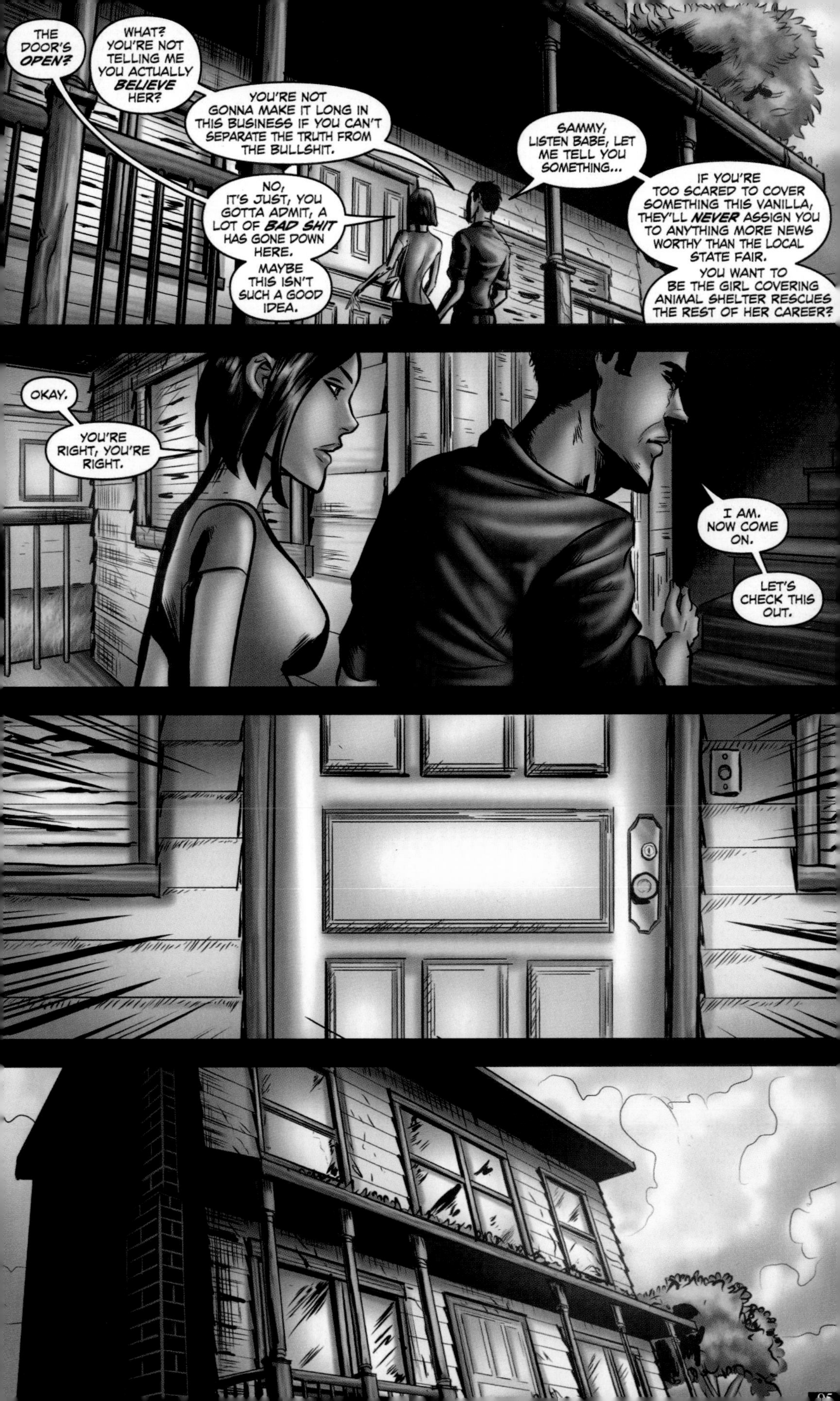

THE DOOR'S *OPEN?*
WHAT? YOU'RE NOT TELLING ME YOU ACTUALLY *BELIEVE* HER?
YOU'RE NOT GONNA MAKE IT LONG IN THIS BUSINESS IF YOU CAN'T SEPARATE THE TRUTH FROM THE BULLSHIT.
NO, IT'S JUST, YOU GOTTA ADMIT, A LOT OF *BAD SHIT* HAS GONE DOWN HERE.
MAYBE THIS ISN'T SUCH A GOOD IDEA.
SAMMY, LISTEN BABE, LET ME TELL YOU SOMETHING...
IF YOU'RE TOO SCARED TO COVER SOMETHING THIS VANILLA, THEY'LL *NEVER* ASSIGN YOU TO ANYTHING MORE NEWS WORTHY THAN THE LOCAL STATE FAIR.
YOU WANT TO BE THE GIRL COVERING ANIMAL SHELTER RESCUES THE REST OF HER CAREER?
OKAY.
YOU'RE RIGHT, YOU'RE RIGHT.
I AM. NOW COME ON.
LET'S CHECK THIS OUT.

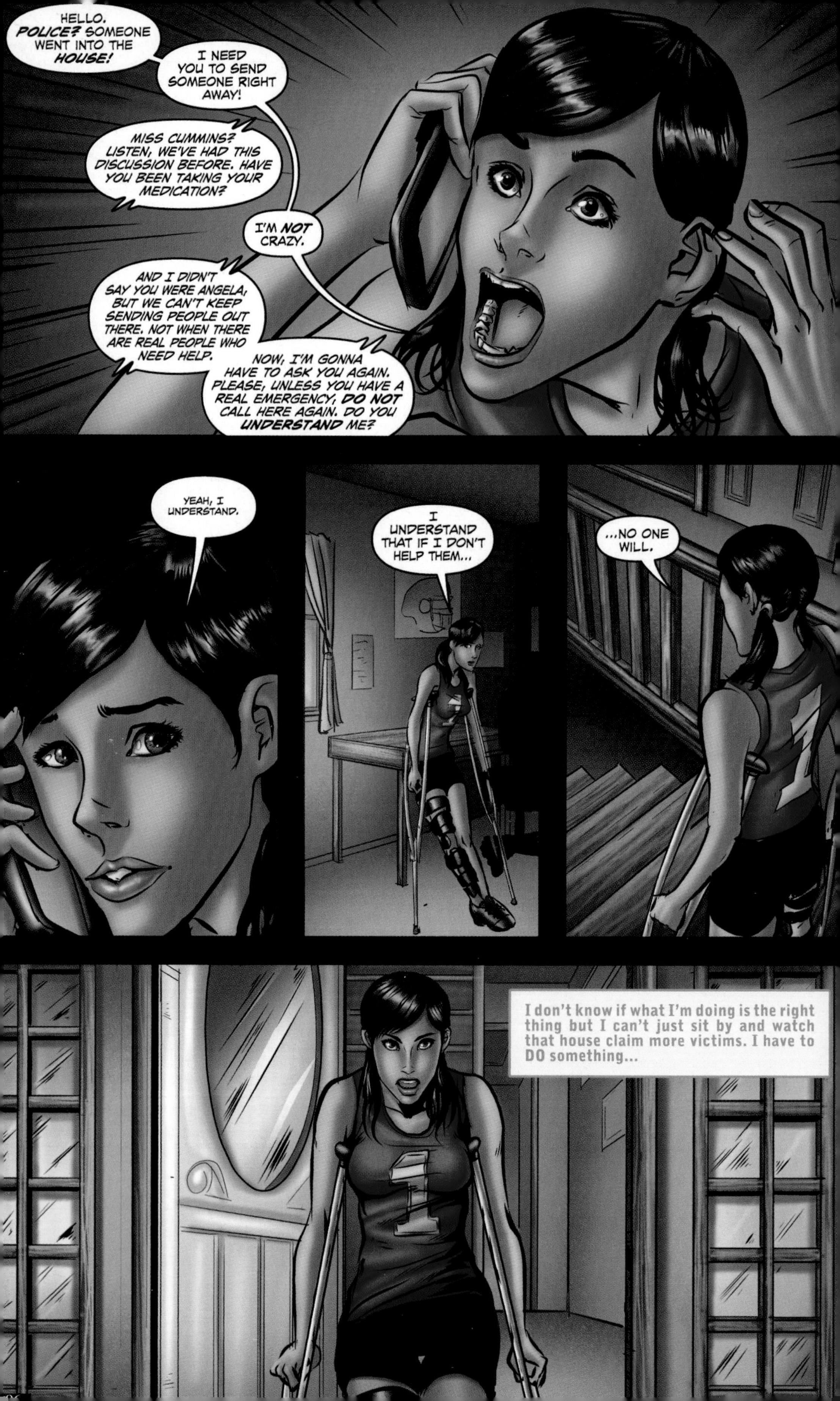
HELLO. POLICE? SOMEONE WENT INTO THE HOUSE!
I NEED YOU TO SEND SOMEONE RIGHT AWAY!
MISS CUMMINS? LISTEN, WE'VE HAD THIS DISCUSSION BEFORE. HAVE YOU BEEN TAKING YOUR MEDICATION?
I'M NOT CRAZY.
AND I DIDN'T SAY YOU WERE ANGELA, BUT WE CAN'T KEEP SENDING PEOPLE OUT THERE. NOT WHEN THERE ARE REAL PEOPLE WHO NEED HELP.
NOW, I'M GONNA HAVE TO ASK YOU AGAIN. PLEASE, UNLESS YOU HAVE A REAL EMERGENCY, DO NOT CALL HERE AGAIN. DO YOU UNDERSTAND ME?
YEAH, I UNDERSTAND.
I UNDERSTAND THAT IF I DON'T HELP THEM...
...NO ONE WILL.
I don't know if what I'm doing is the right thing but I can't just sit by and watch that house claim more victims. I have to DO something...

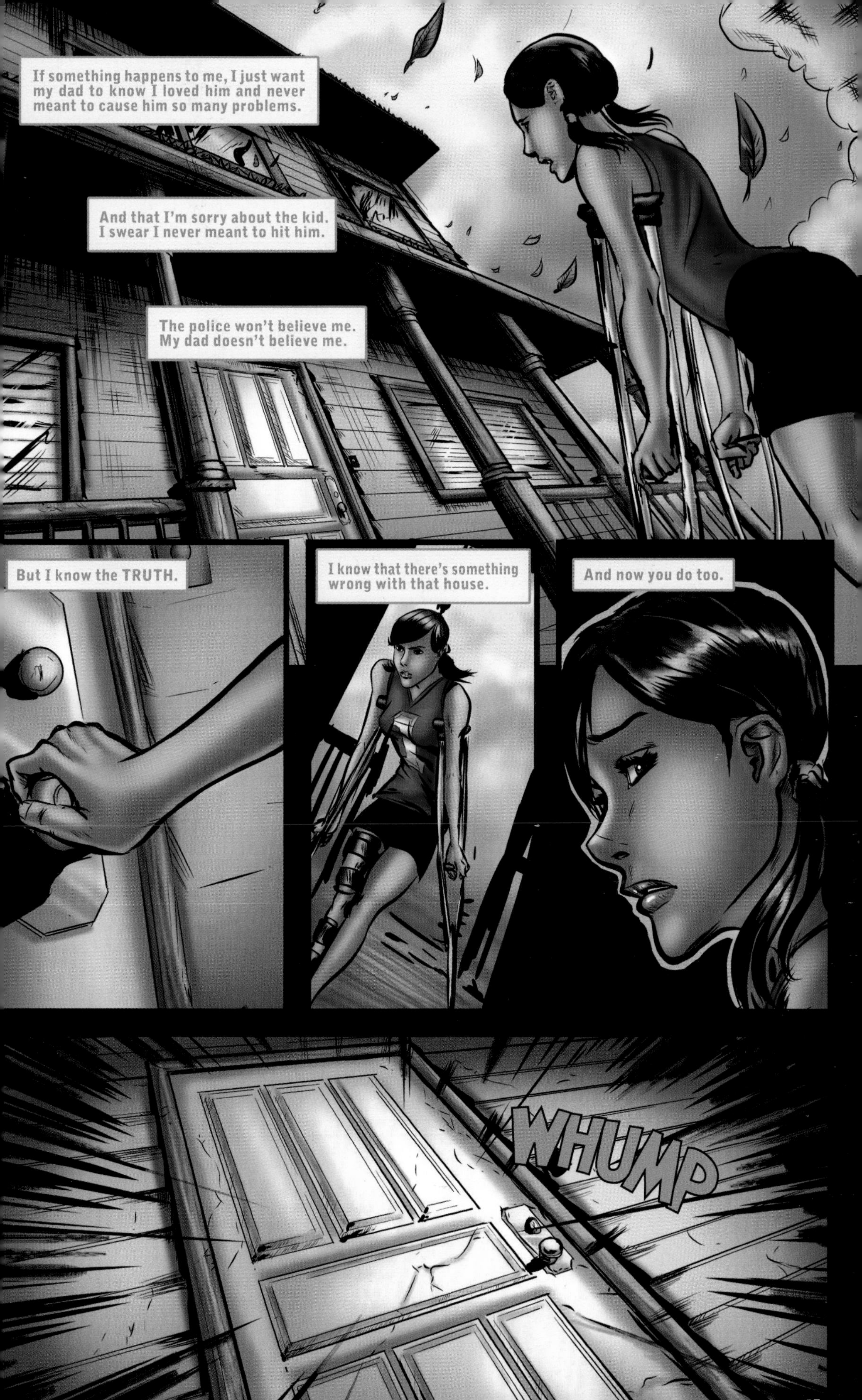
If something happens to me, I just want my dad to know I loved him and never meant to cause him so many problems.
And that I'm sorry about the kid. I swear I never meant to hit him.
The police won't believe me. My dad doesn't believe me.
But I know the TRUTH.
I know that there's something wrong with that house.
And now you do too.
WHUMP

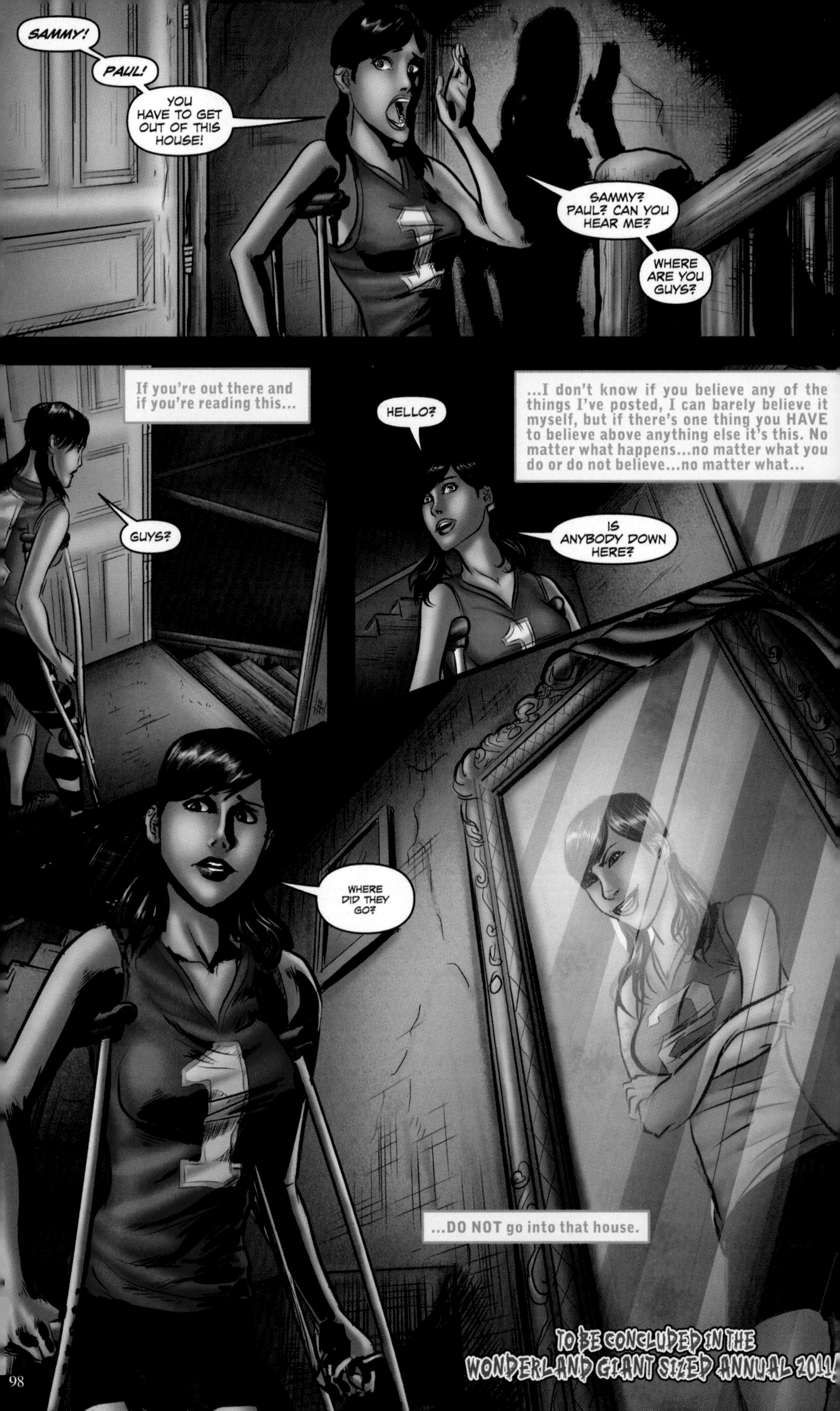
SAMMY!
PAUL!
YOU HAVE TO GET OUT OF THIS HOUSE!
SAMMY? PAUL? CAN YOU HEAR ME?
WHERE ARE YOU GUYS?
If you're out there and if you're reading this...
GUYS?
HELLO?
...I don't know if you believe any of the things I've posted, I can barely believe it myself, but if there's one thing you HAVE to believe above anything else it's this. No matter what happens...no matter what you do or do not believe...no matter what...
IS ANYBODY DOWN HERE?
WHERE DID THEY GO?
...DO NOT go into that house.
TO BE CONCLUDED IN THE WONDERLAND GIANT SIZED ANNUAL 2011!

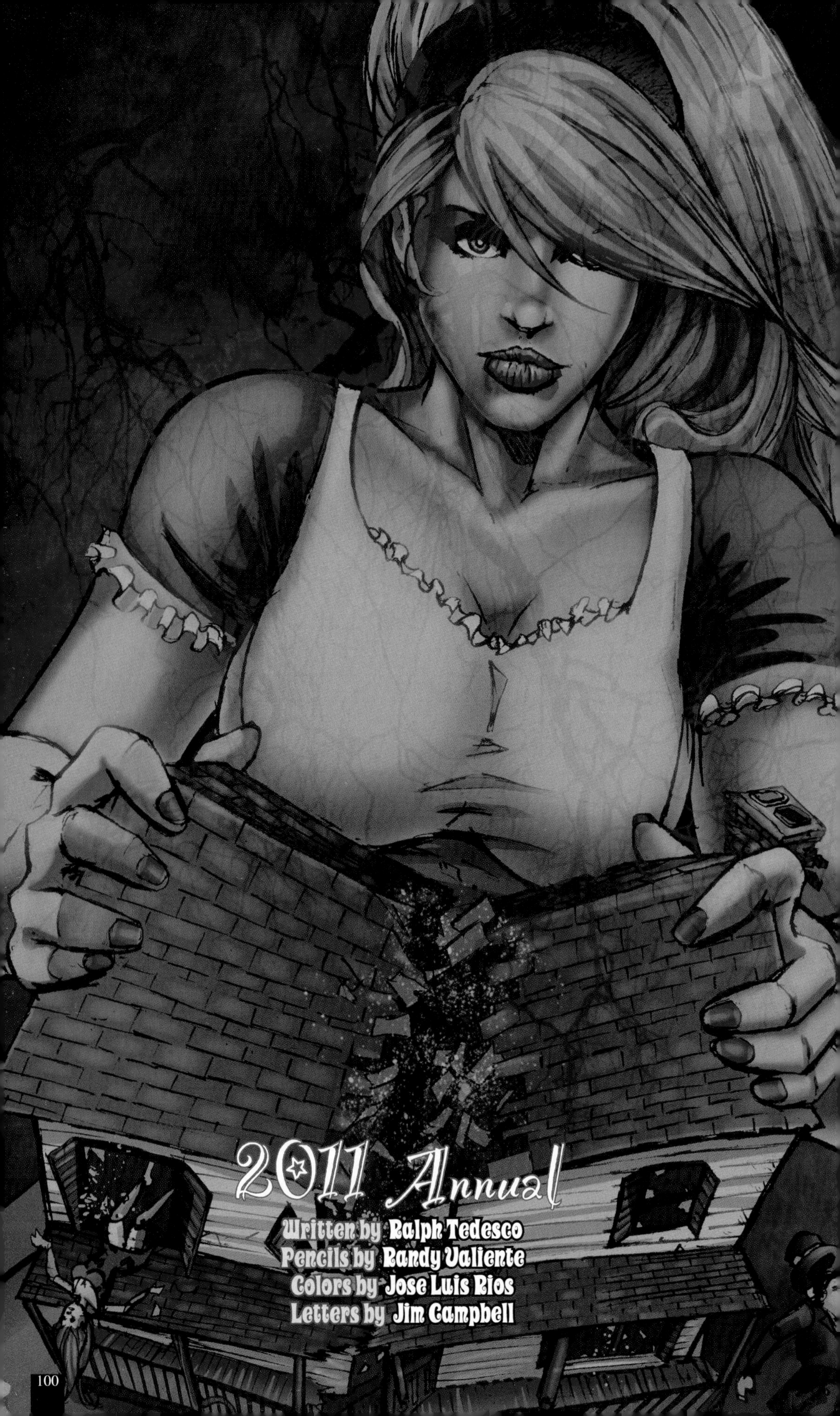
2011 Annual
Written by Ralph Tedesco
Pencils by Randy Valiente
Colors by Jose Luis Rios
Letters by Jim Campbell

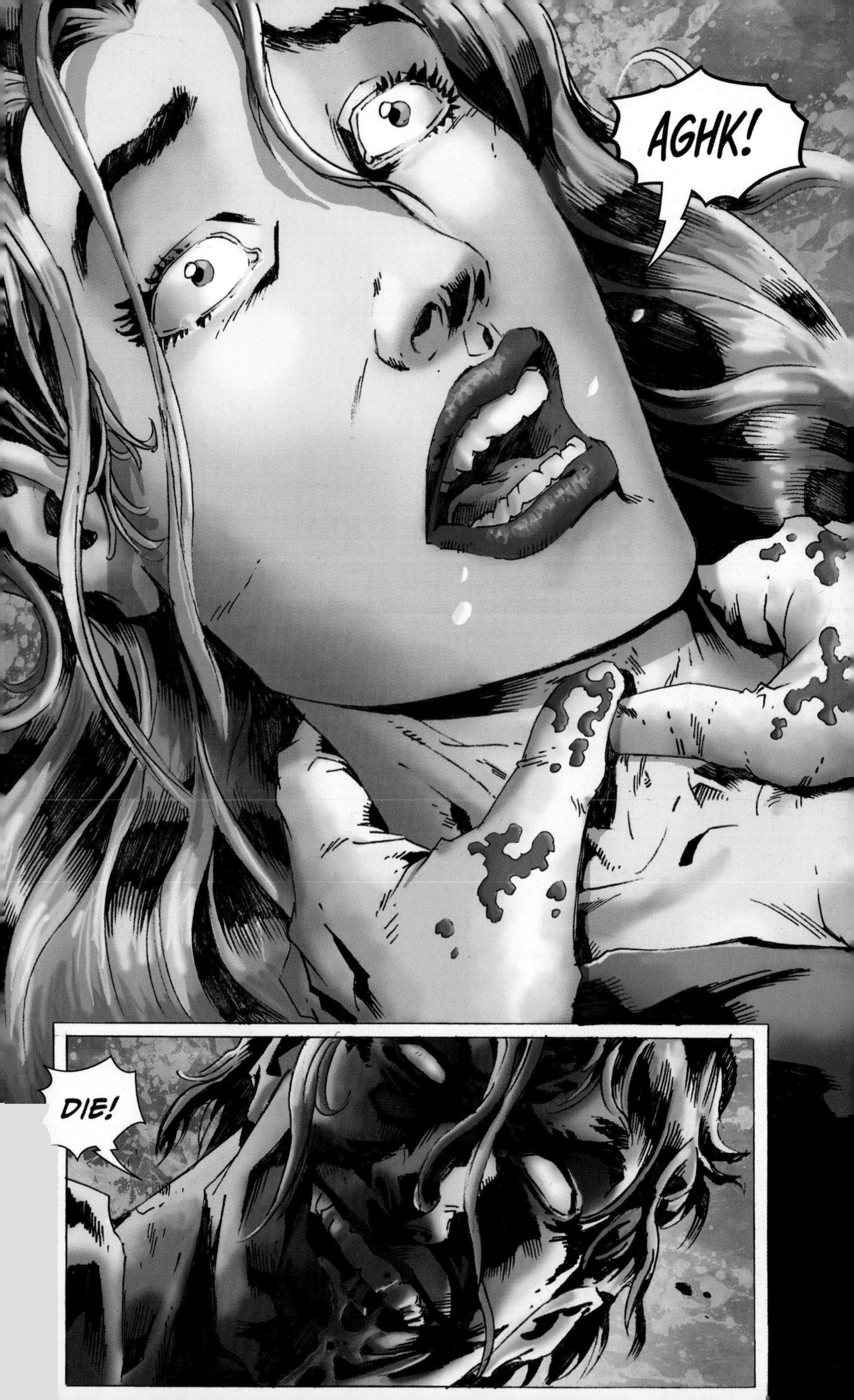
AGHK!
DIE!

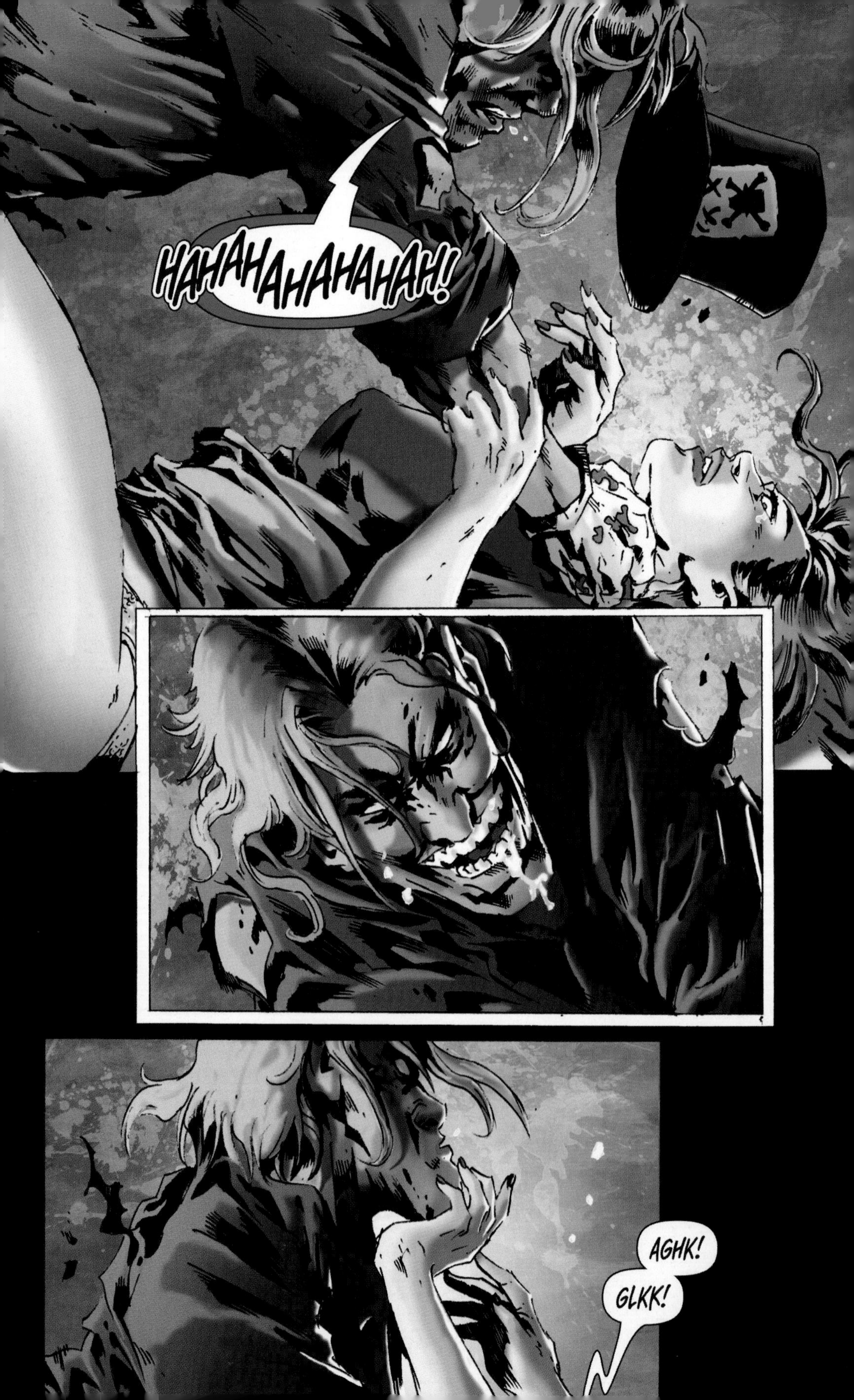
HAHAHAHAHAHAH!
AGHK!
GLKK!

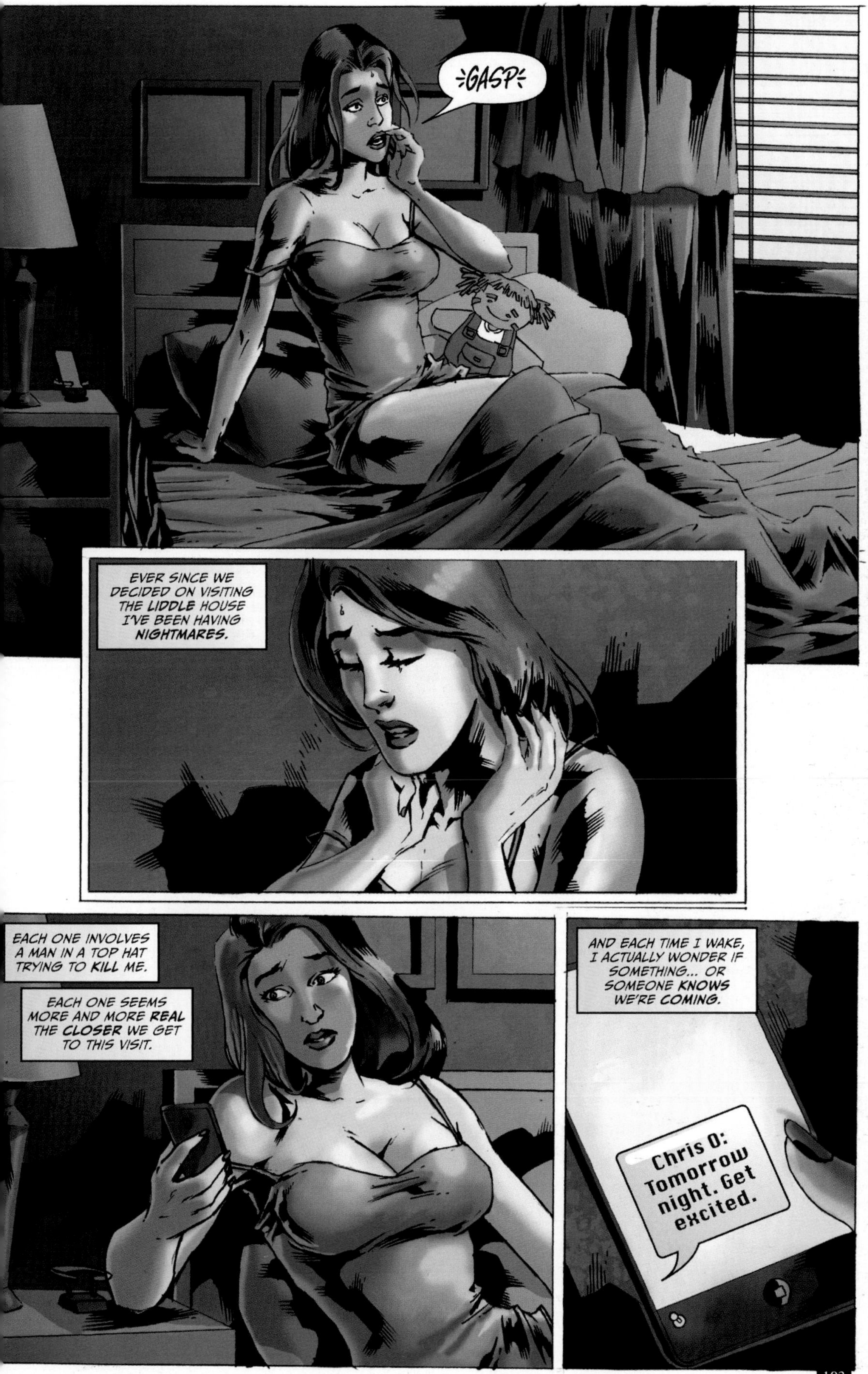
GASP
EVER SINCE WE DECIDED ON VISITING THE LIDDLE HOUSE I'VE BEEN HAVING NIGHTMARES.
EACH ONE INVOLVES A MAN IN A TOP HAT TRYING TO KILL ME.
EACH ONE SEEMS MORE AND MORE REAL THE CLOSER WE GET TO THIS VISIT.
AND EACH TIME I WAKE, I ACTUALLY WONDER IF SOMETHING... OR SOMEONE KNOWS WE'RE COMING.
Chris O: Tomorrow night. Get excited.

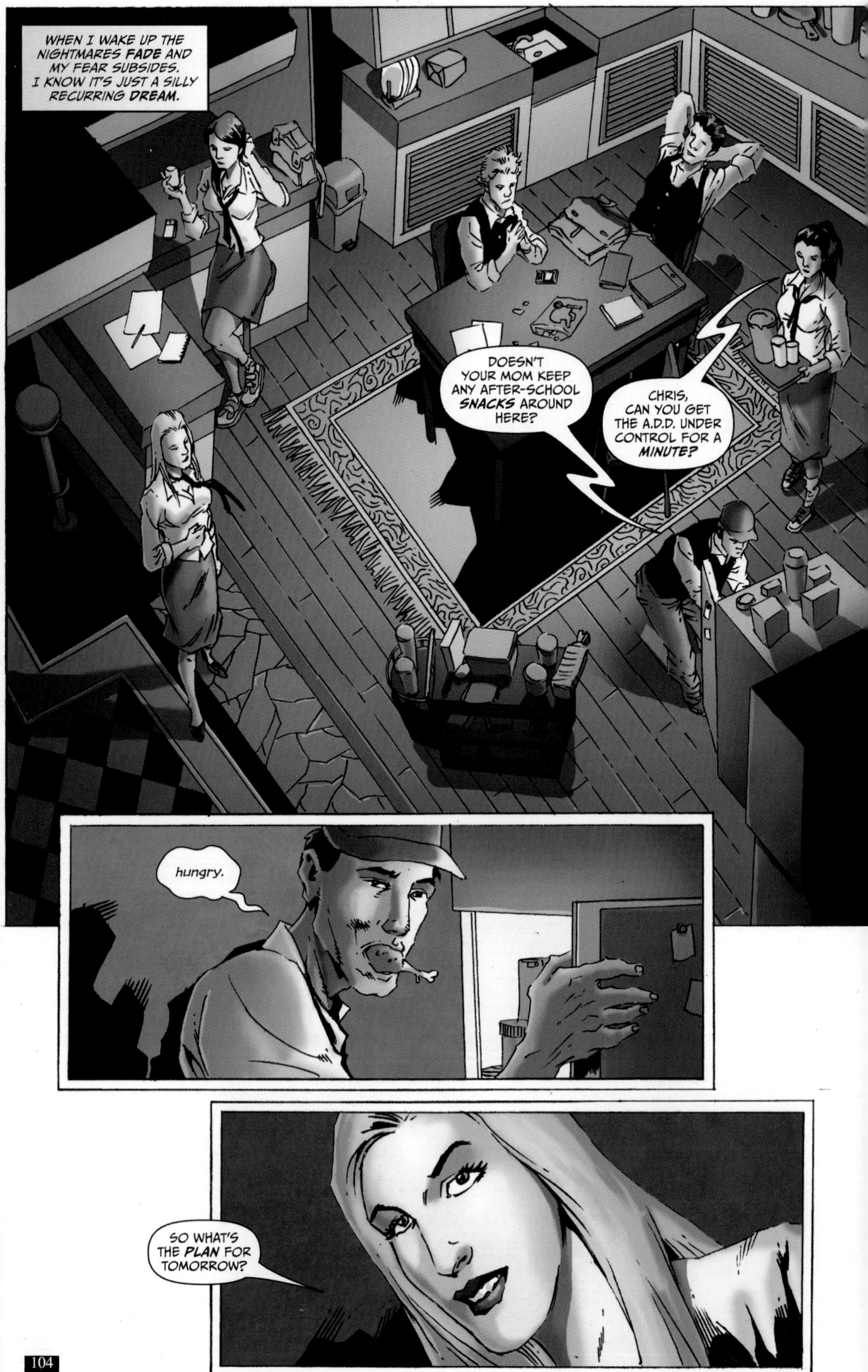
WHEN I WAKE UP THE NIGHTMARES FADE AND MY FEAR SUBSIDES. I KNOW IT'S JUST A SILLY RECURRING DREAM.
DOESN'T YOUR MOM KEEP ANY AFTER-SCHOOL SNACKS AROUND HERE?
CHRIS, CAN YOU GET THE A.D.D. UNDER CONTROL FOR A MINUTE?
hungry.
SO WHAT'S THE PLAN FOR TOMORROW?

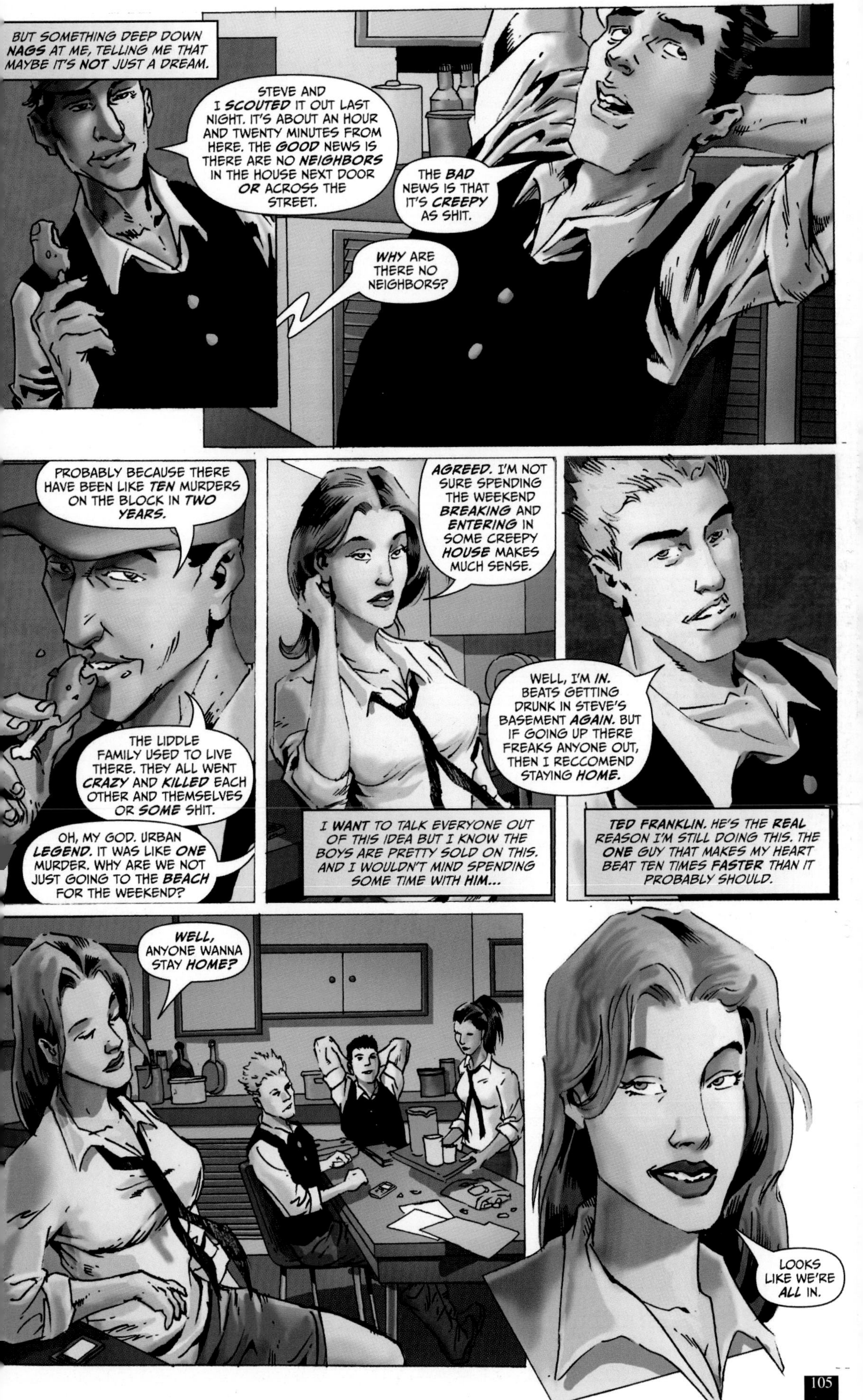

BUT SOMETHING DEEP DOWN NAGS AT ME, TELLING ME THAT MAYBE IT'S NOT JUST A DREAM.
STEVE AND I SCOUTED IT OUT LAST NIGHT. IT'S ABOUT AN HOUR AND TWENTY MINUTES FROM HERE. THE GOOD NEWS IS THERE ARE NO NEIGHBORS IN THE HOUSE NEXT DOOR OR ACROSS THE STREET.
THE BAD NEWS IS THAT IT'S CREEPY AS SHIT.
WHY ARE THERE NO NEIGHBORS?
PROBABLY BECAUSE THERE HAVE BEEN LIKE TEN MURDERS ON THE BLOCK IN TWO YEARS.
THE LIDDLE FAMILY USED TO LIVE THERE. THEY ALL WENT CRAZY AND KILLED EACH OTHER AND THEMSELVES OR SOME SHIT.
OH, MY GOD. URBAN LEGEND. IT WAS LIKE ONE MURDER. WHY ARE WE NOT JUST GOING TO THE BEACH FOR THE WEEKEND?
AGREED. I'M NOT SURE SPENDING THE WEEKEND BREAKING AND ENTERING IN SOME CREEPY HOUSE MAKES MUCH SENSE.
I WANT TO TALK EVERYONE OUT OF THIS IDEA BUT I KNOW THE BOYS ARE PRETTY SOLD ON THIS. AND I WOULDN'T MIND SPENDING SOME TIME WITH HIM...
WELL, I'M IN. BEATS GETTING DRUNK IN STEVE'S BASEMENT AGAIN. BUT IF GOING UP THERE FREAKS ANYONE OUT, THEN I RECCOMEND STAYING HOME.
TED FRANKLIN. HE'S THE REAL REASON I'M STILL DOING THIS. THE ONE GUY THAT MAKES MY HEART BEAT TEN TIMES FASTER THAN IT PROBABLY SHOULD.
WELL, ANYONE WANNA STAY HOME?
LOOKS LIKE WE'RE ALL IN.

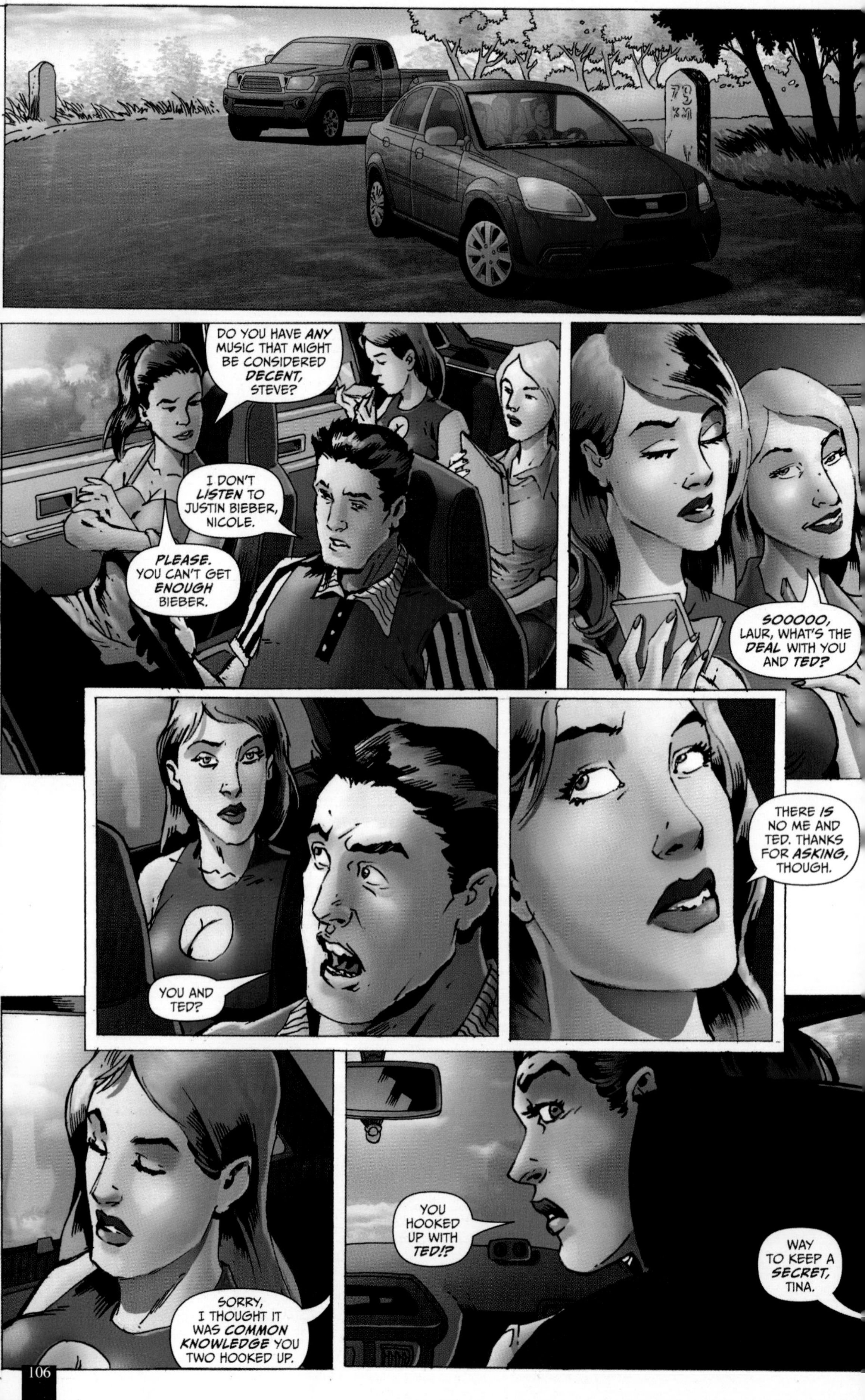

DO YOU HAVE ANY MUSIC THAT MIGHT BE CONSIDERED DECENT, STEVE?
I DON'T LISTEN TO JUSTIN BIEBER, NICOLE.
PLEASE. YOU CAN'T GET ENOUGH BIEBER.
SOOOOO, LAUR, WHAT'S THE DEAL WITH YOU AND TED?
YOU AND TED?
THERE IS NO ME AND TED. THANKS FOR ASKING, THOUGH.
SORRY, I THOUGHT IT WAS COMMON KNOWLEDGE YOU TWO HOOKED UP.
YOU HOOKED UP WITH TED!?
WAY TO KEEP A SECRET, TINA.

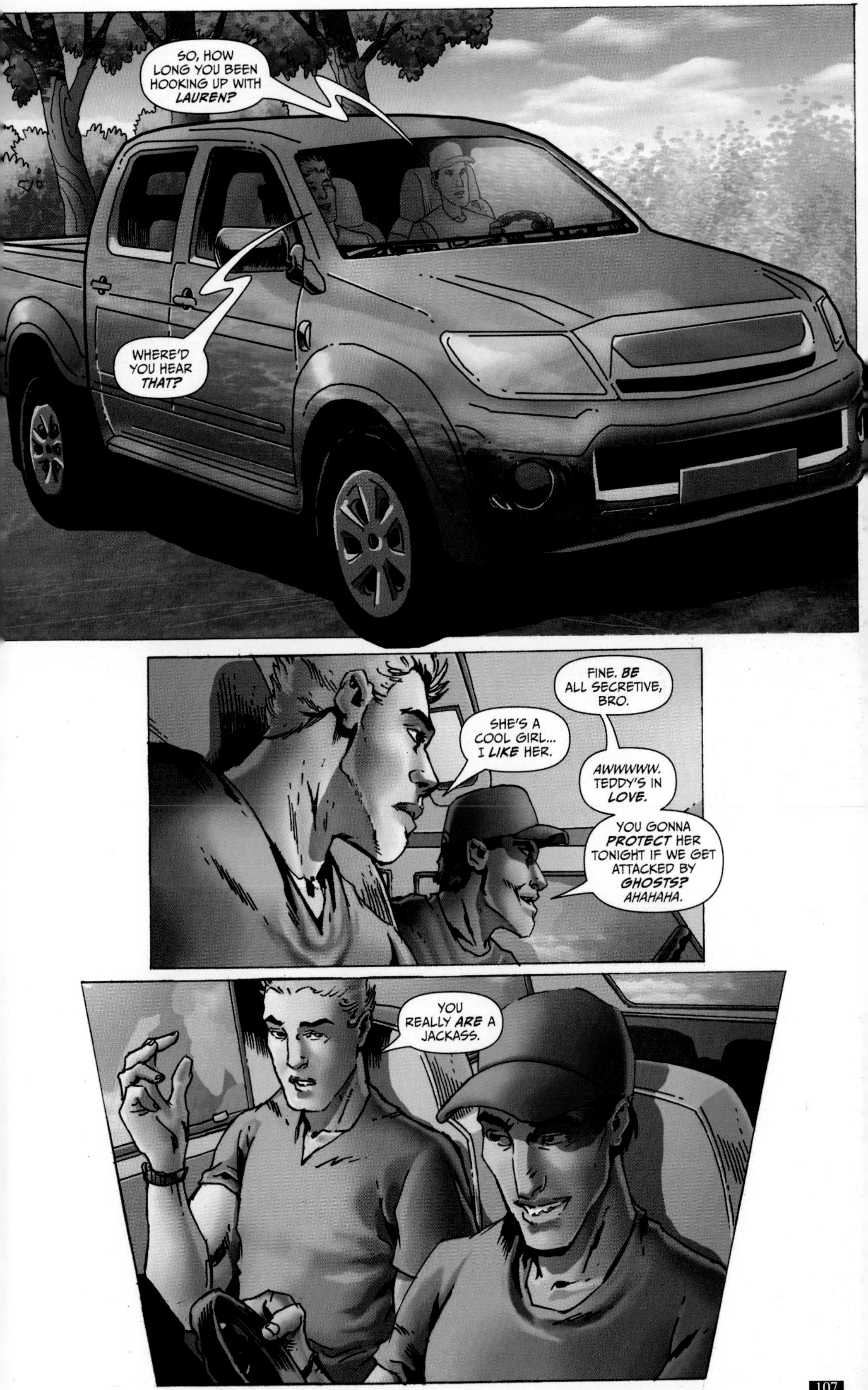
SO, HOW LONG YOU BEEN HOOKING UP WITH *LAUREN?*
WHERE'D YOU HEAR *THAT?*
SHE'S A COOL GIRL... I *LIKE* HER.
FINE. *BE* ALL SECRETIVE, BRO.
AWWWWW. TEDDY'S IN *LOVE.*
YOU GONNA *PROTECT* HER TONIGHT IF WE GET ATTACKED BY *GHOSTS?* *AHAHAHA.*
YOU REALLY *ARE* A JACKASS.

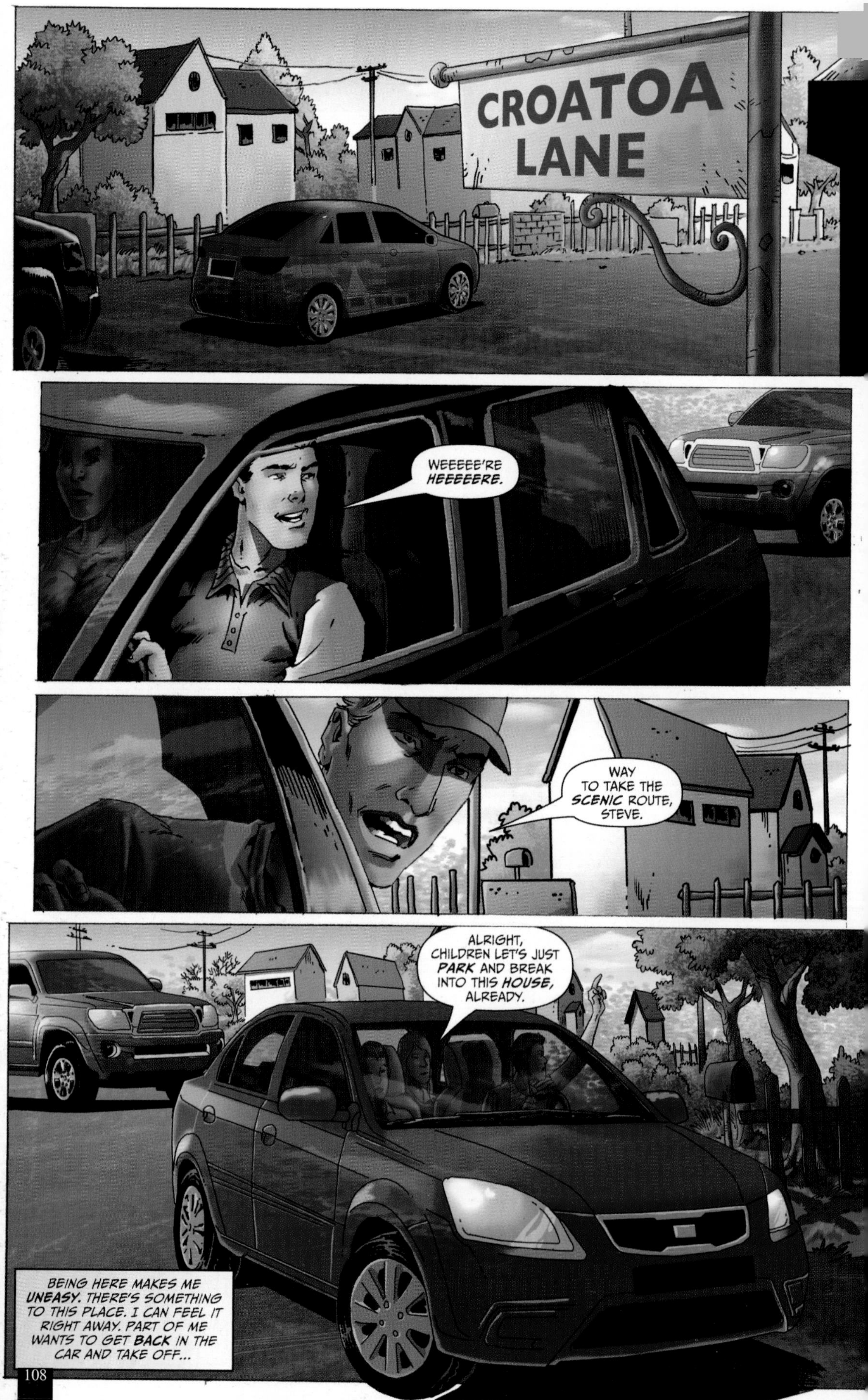
CROATOA LANE
WEEEEEE'RE HEEEEEERE.
WAY TO TAKE THE SCENIC ROUTE, STEVE.
ALRIGHT, CHILDREN LET'S JUST PARK AND BREAK INTO THIS HOUSE, ALREADY.
BEING HERE MAKES ME UNEASY. THERE'S SOMETHING TO THIS PLACE. I CAN FEEL IT RIGHT AWAY. PART OF ME WANTS TO GET BACK IN THE CAR AND TAKE OFF...

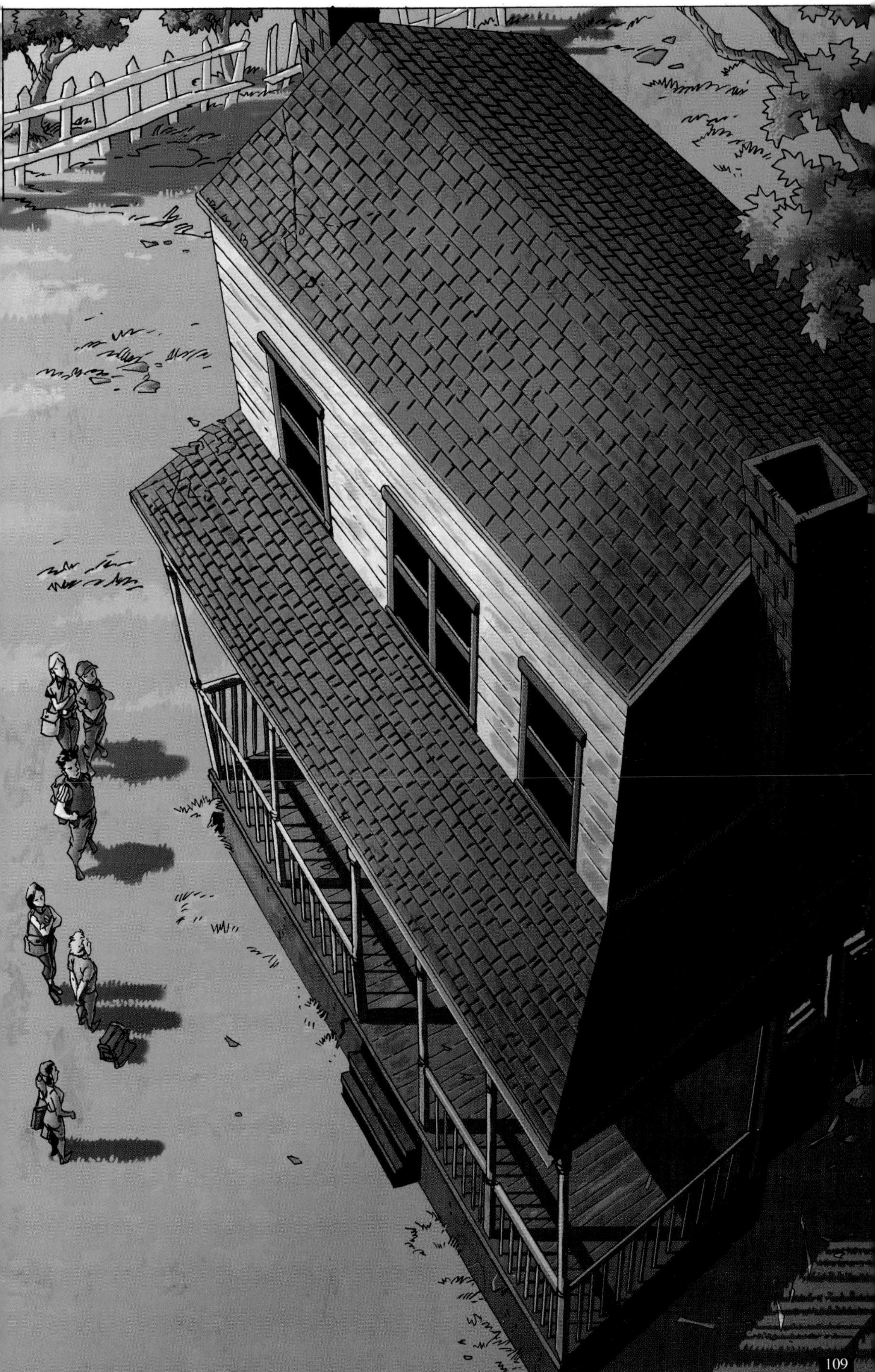

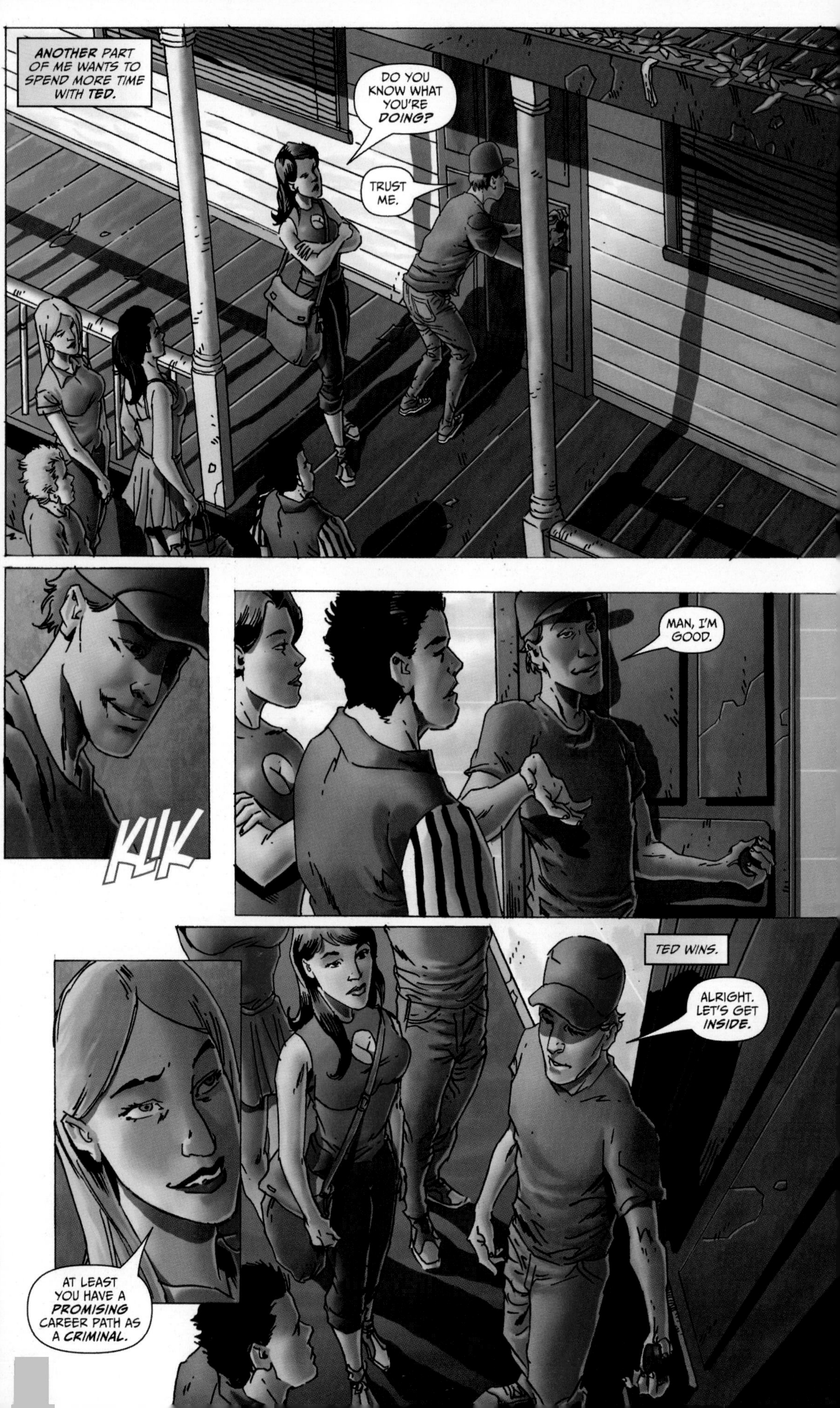
ANOTHER PART OF ME WANTS TO SPEND MORE TIME WITH TED.
DO YOU KNOW WHAT YOU'RE DOING?
TRUST ME.
KLIK
MAN, I'M GOOD.
TED WINS.
ALRIGHT. LET'S GET INSIDE.
AT LEAST YOU HAVE A PROMISING CAREER PATH AS A CRIMINAL.

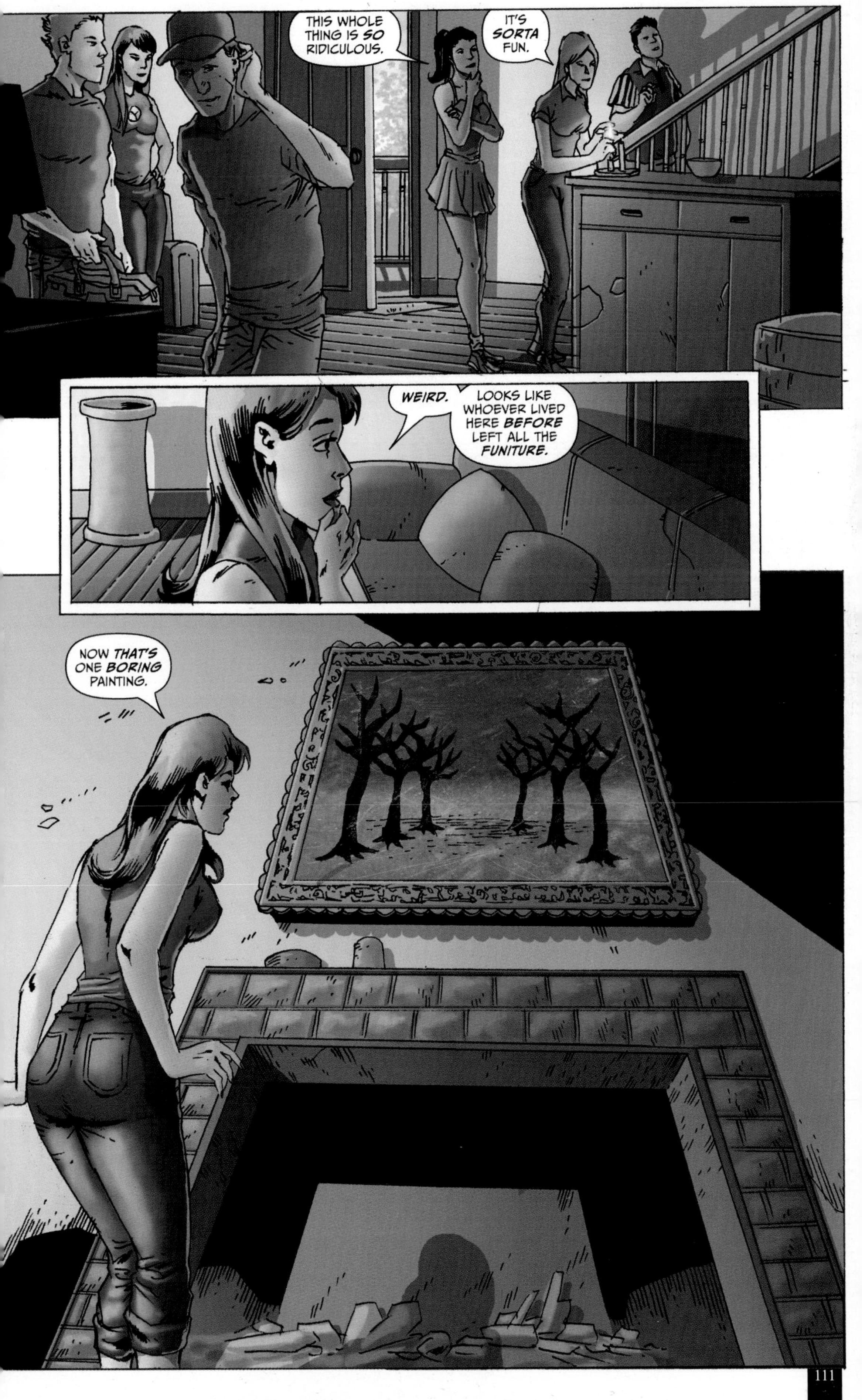
THIS WHOLE THING IS SO RIDICULOUS.
IT'S SORTA FUN.
WEIRD.
LOOKS LIKE WHOEVER LIVED HERE BEFORE LEFT ALL THE FUNITURE.
NOW THAT'S ONE BORING PAINTING.

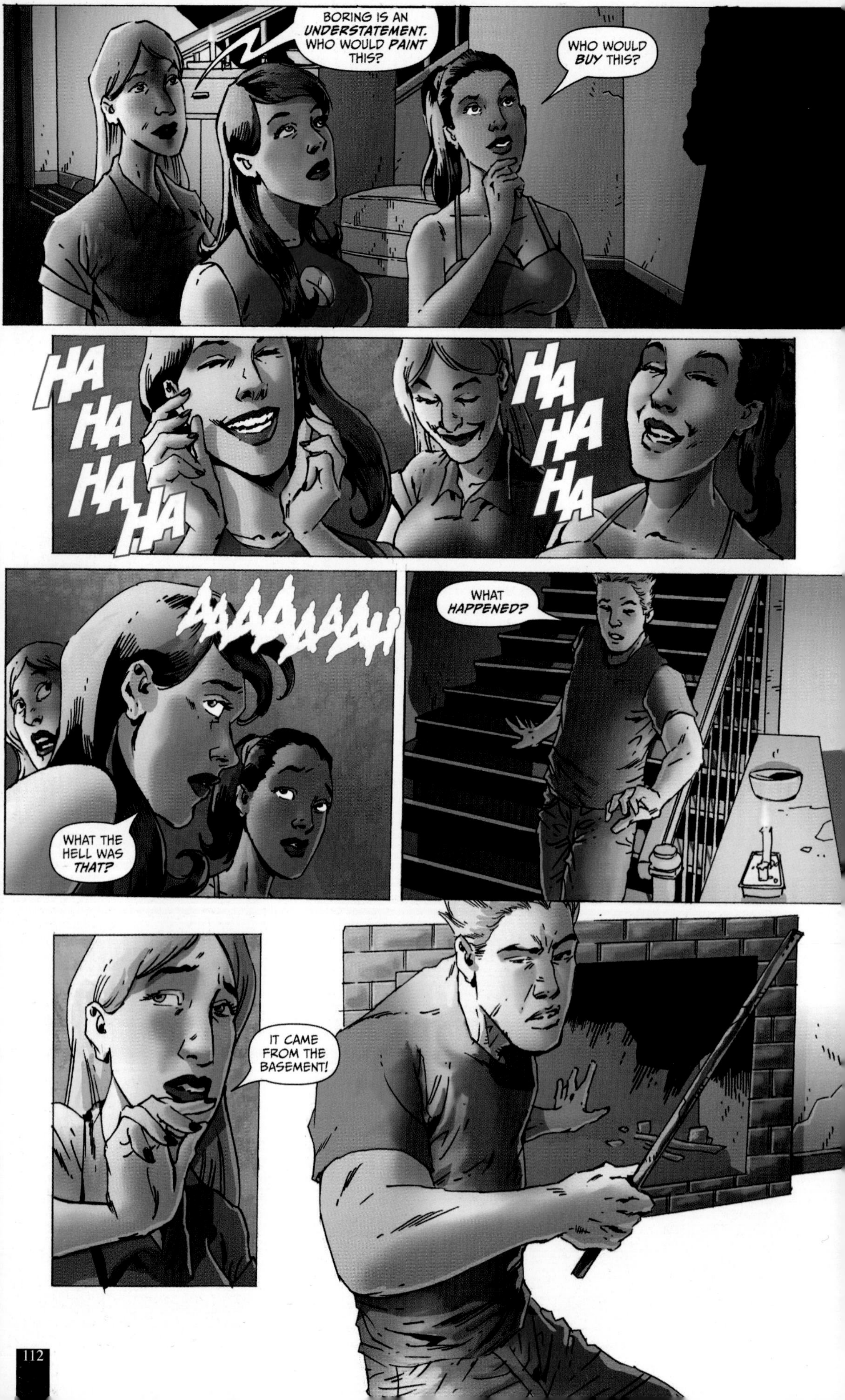
BORING IS AN UNDERSTATEMENT. WHO WOULD PAINT THIS?
WHO WOULD BUY THIS?
HA HA HA HA
HA HA HA
AAAAAAAH
WHAT THE HELL WAS THAT?
WHAT HAPPENED?
IT CAME FROM THE BASEMENT!

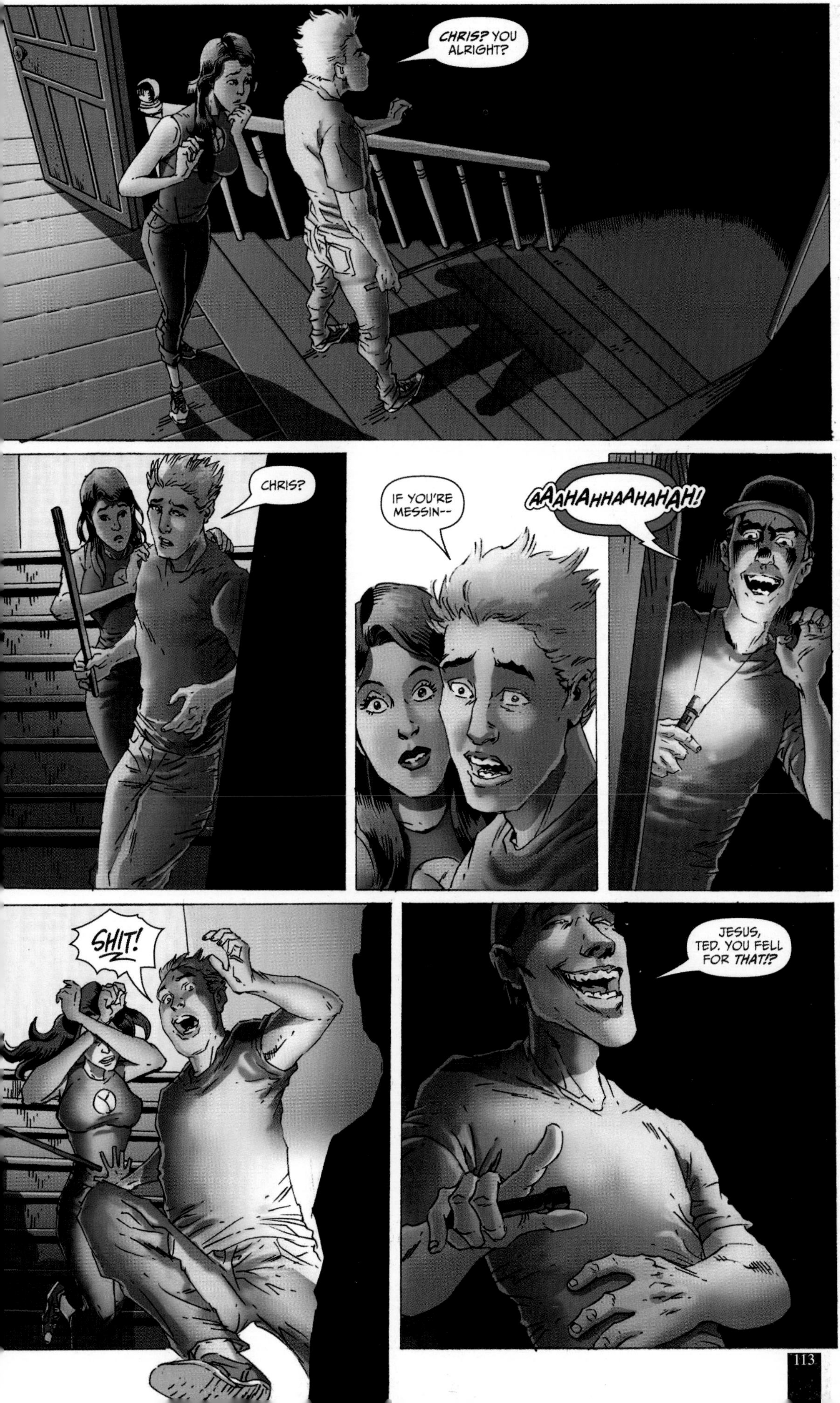
CHRIS? YOU ALRIGHT?
CHRIS?
IF YOU'RE MESSIN--
AAAHAHHAAHAHAH!
SHIT!
JESUS, TED. YOU FELL FOR THAT!?

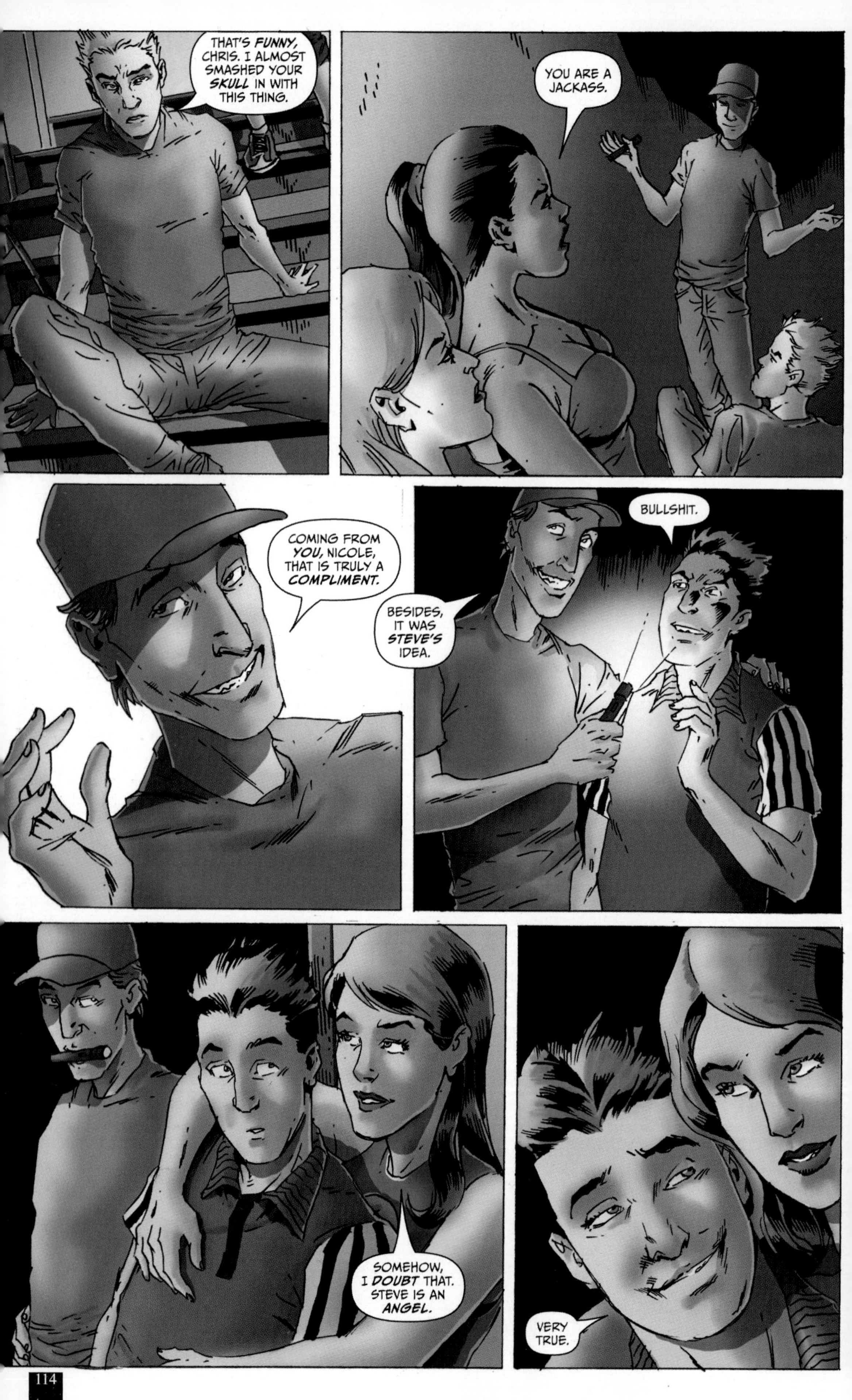
THAT'S FUNNY, CHRIS. I ALMOST SMASHED YOUR SKULL IN WITH THIS THING.
YOU ARE A JACKASS.
COMING FROM YOU, NICOLE, THAT IS TRULY A COMPLIMENT.
BULLSHIT.
BESIDES, IT WAS STEVE'S IDEA.
SOMEHOW, I DOUBT THAT. STEVE IS AN ANGEL.
VERY TRUE.

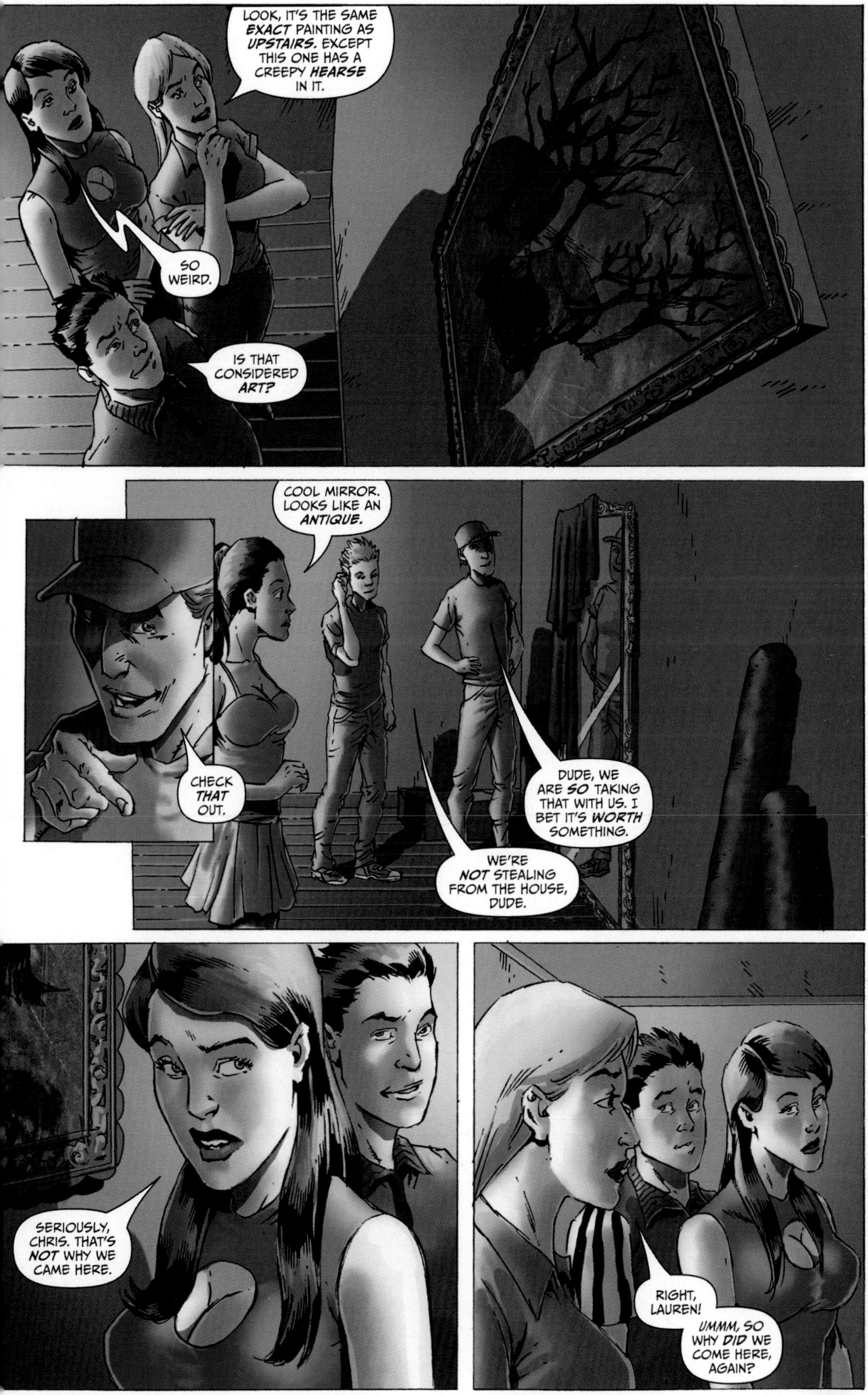
LOOK, IT'S THE SAME EXACT PAINTING AS UPSTAIRS. EXCEPT THIS ONE HAS A CREEPY HEARSE IN IT.
SO WEIRD.
IS THAT CONSIDERED ART?
COOL MIRROR. LOOKS LIKE AN ANTIQUE.
CHECK THAT OUT.
DUDE, WE ARE SO TAKING THAT WITH US. I BET IT'S WORTH SOMETHING.
WE'RE NOT STEALING FROM THE HOUSE, DUDE.
SERIOUSLY, CHRIS. THAT'S NOT WHY WE CAME HERE.
RIGHT, LAUREN!
UMMM, SO WHY DID WE COME HERE, AGAIN?

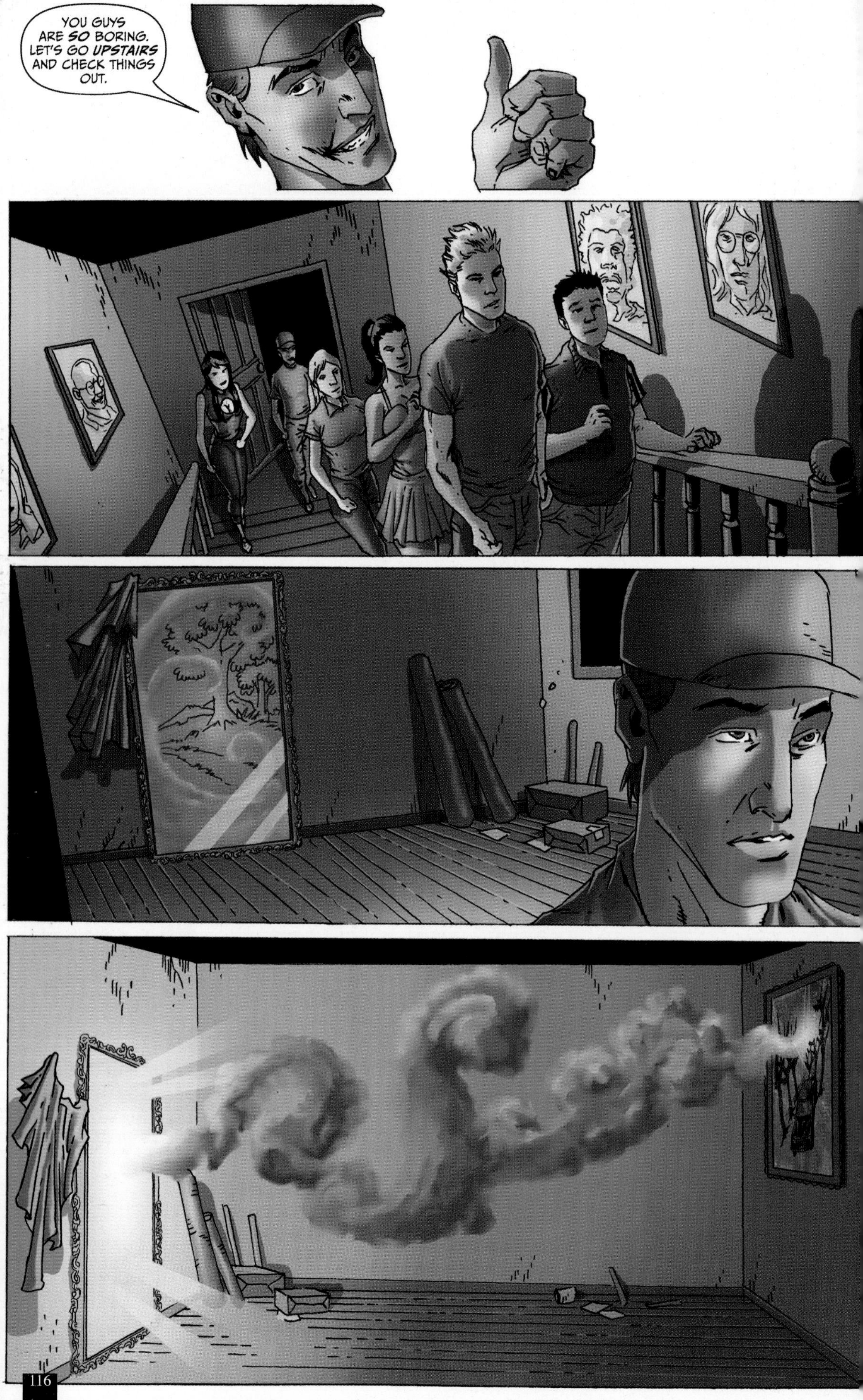
YOU GUYS ARE *SO* BORING. LET'S GO *UPSTAIRS* AND CHECK THINGS OUT.

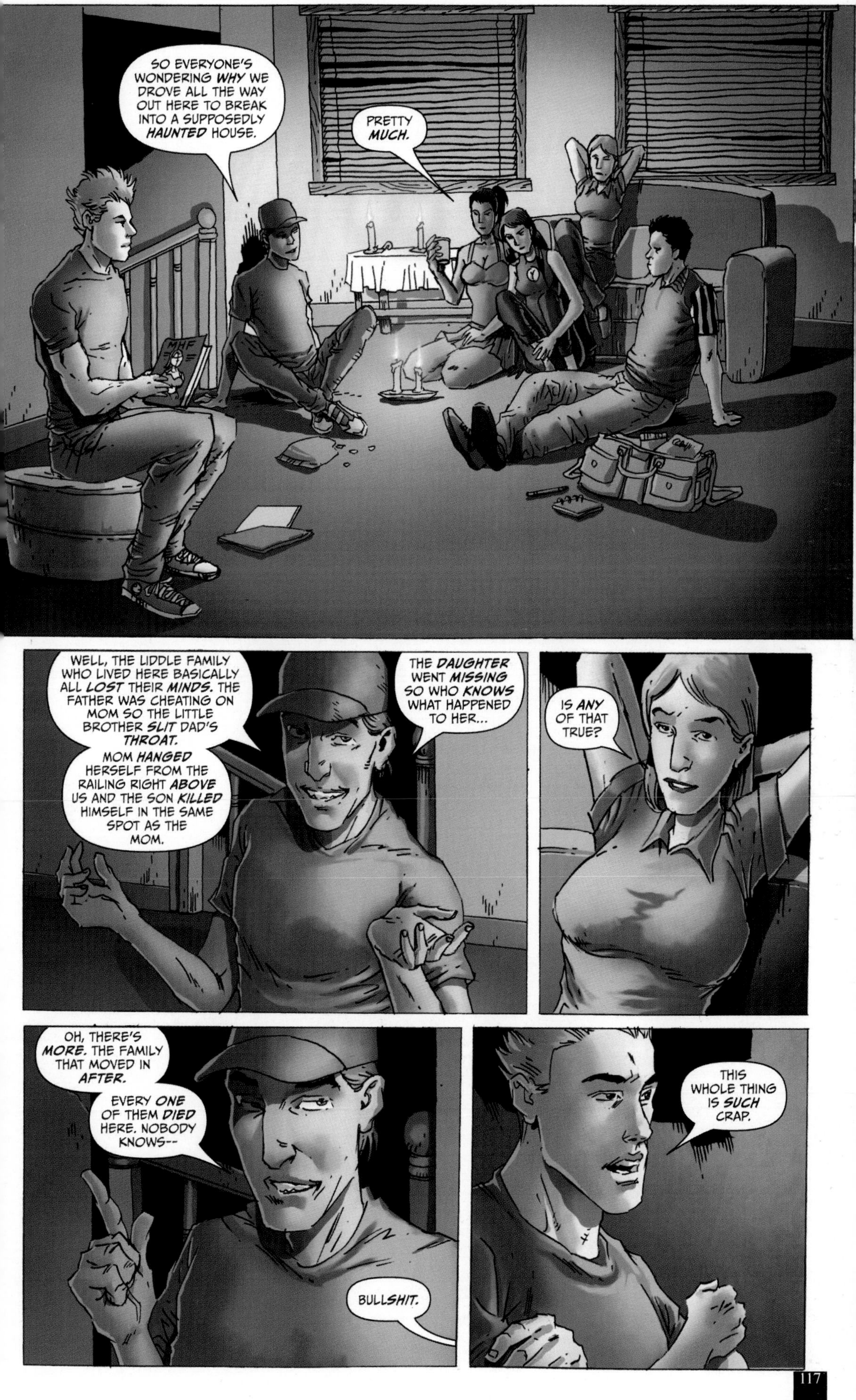

SO EVERYONE'S WONDERING WHY WE DROVE ALL THE WAY OUT HERE TO BREAK INTO A SUPPOSEDLY HAUNTED HOUSE.
PRETTY MUCH.
MHF
WELL, THE LIDDLE FAMILY WHO LIVED HERE BASICALLY ALL LOST THEIR MINDS. THE FATHER WAS CHEATING ON MOM SO THE LITTLE BROTHER SLIT DAD'S THROAT.
MOM HANGED HERSELF FROM THE RAILING RIGHT ABOVE US AND THE SON KILLED HIMSELF IN THE SAME SPOT AS THE MOM.
THE DAUGHTER WENT MISSING SO WHO KNOWS WHAT HAPPENED TO HER...
IS ANY OF THAT TRUE?
OH, THERE'S MORE. THE FAMILY THAT MOVED IN AFTER.
EVERY ONE OF THEM DIED HERE. NOBODY KNOWS--
BULLSHIT.
THIS WHOLE THING IS SUCH CRAP.

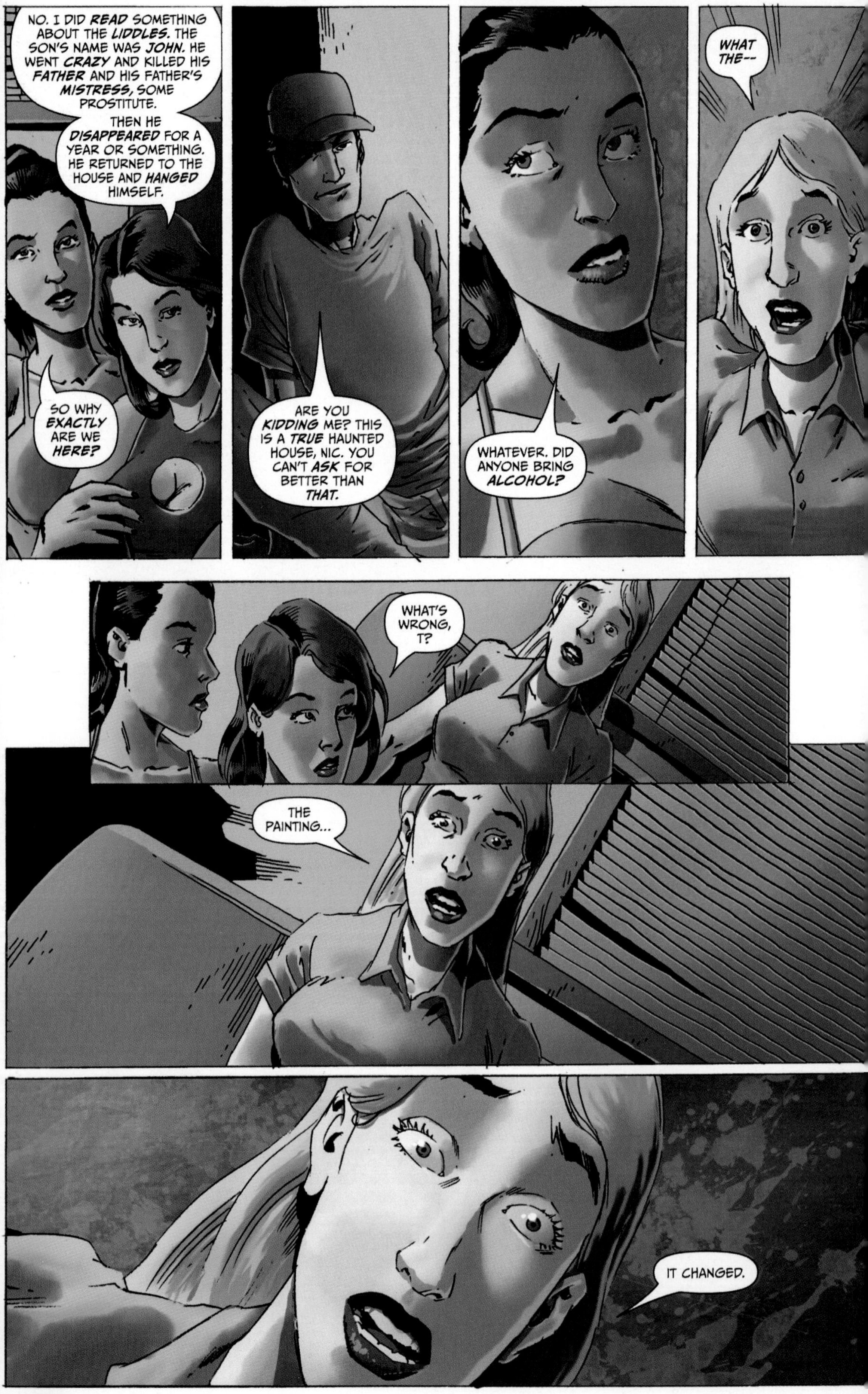
NO. I DID READ SOMETHING ABOUT THE LIDDLES. THE SON'S NAME WAS JOHN. HE WENT CRAZY AND KILLED HIS FATHER AND HIS FATHER'S MISTRESS, SOME PROSTITUTE.
THEN HE DISAPPEARED FOR A YEAR OR SOMETHING. HE RETURNED TO THE HOUSE AND HANGED HIMSELF.
SO WHY EXACTLY ARE WE HERE?
ARE YOU KIDDING ME? THIS IS A TRUE HAUNTED HOUSE, NIC. YOU CAN'T ASK FOR BETTER THAN THAT.
WHATEVER. DID ANYONE BRING ALCOHOL?
WHAT THE--
WHAT'S WRONG, T?
THE PAINTING...
IT CHANGED.

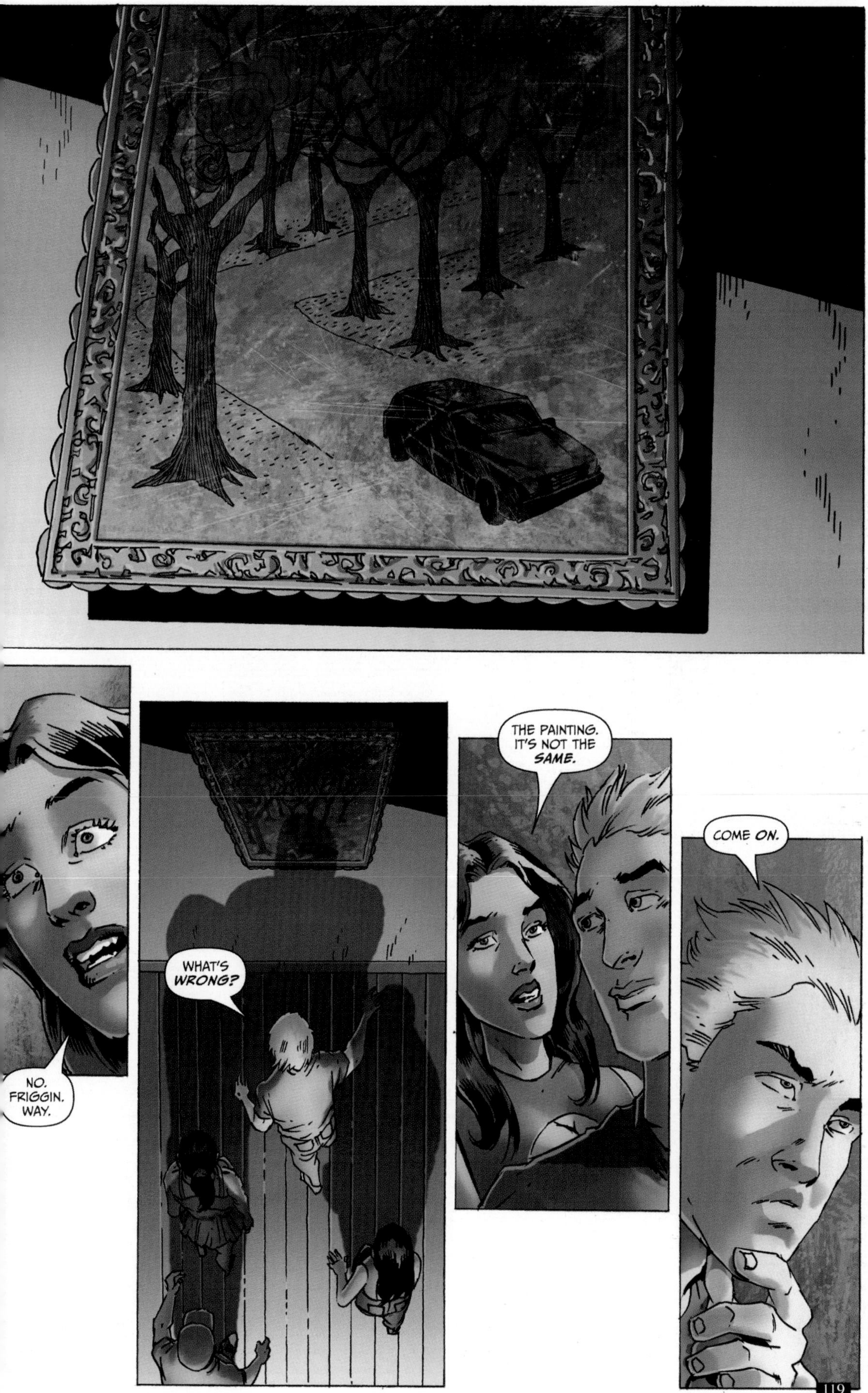
NO. FRIGGIN. WAY.
WHAT'S WRONG?
THE PAINTING. IT'S NOT THE SAME.
COME ON.

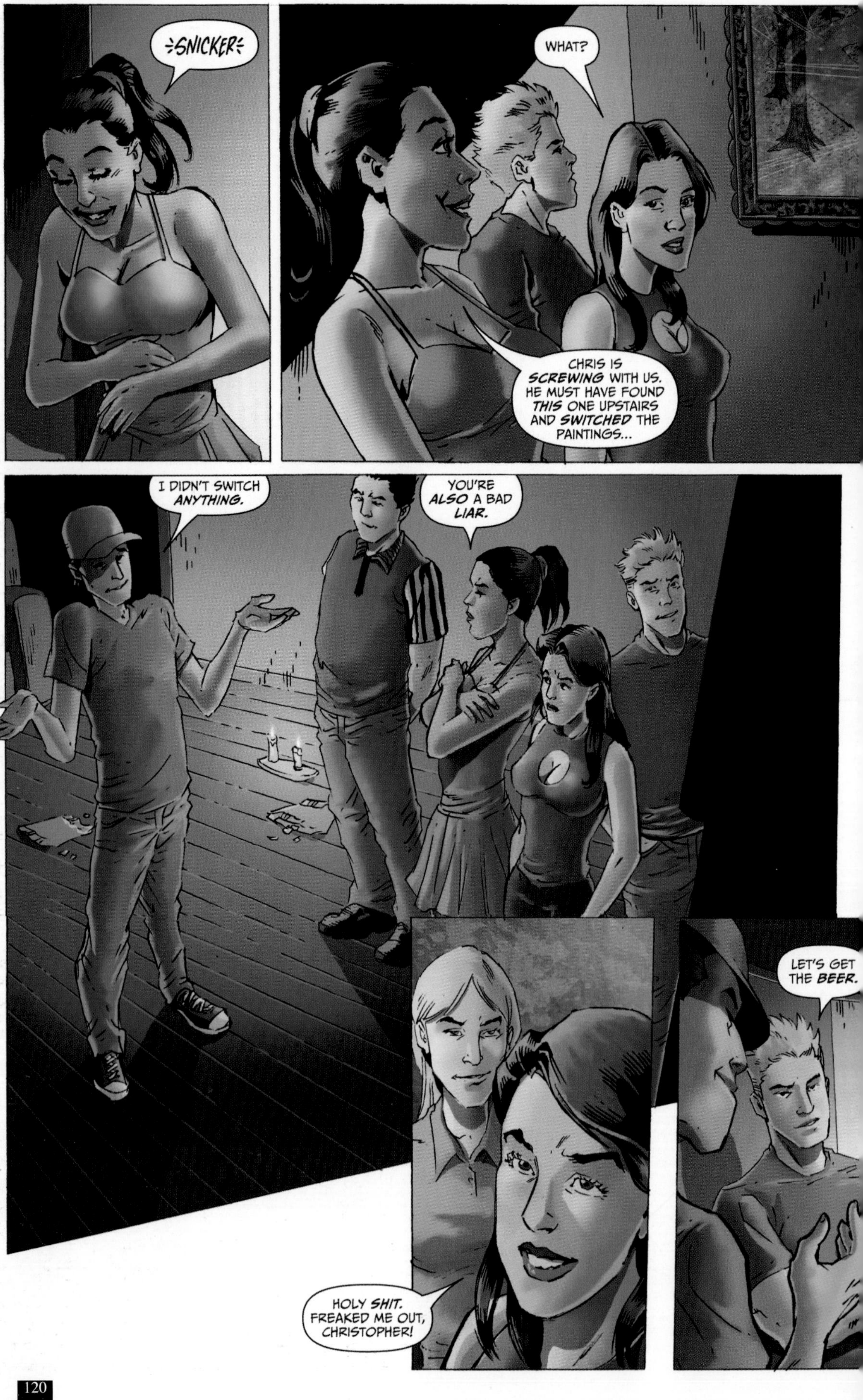
SNICKER
WHAT?
CHRIS IS SCREWING WITH US. HE MUST HAVE FOUND THIS ONE UPSTAIRS AND SWITCHED THE PAINTINGS...
I DIDN'T SWITCH ANYTHING.
YOU'RE ALSO A BAD LIAR.
HOLY SHIT. FREAKED ME OUT, CHRISTOPHER!
LET'S GET THE BEER.

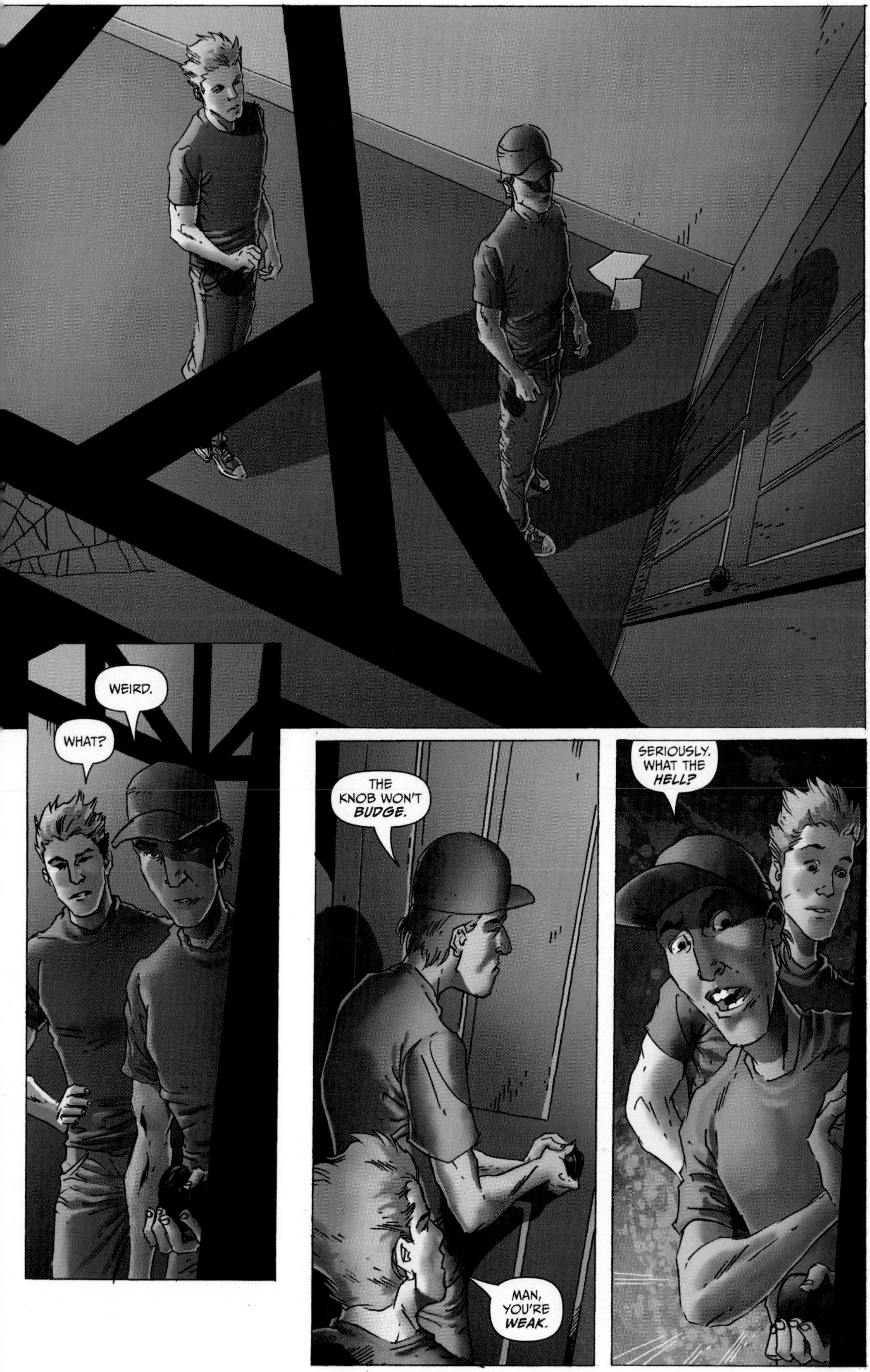
WEIRD.
WHAT?
THE KNOB WON'T BUDGE.
MAN, YOU'RE WEAK.
SERIOUSLY. WHAT THE HELL?

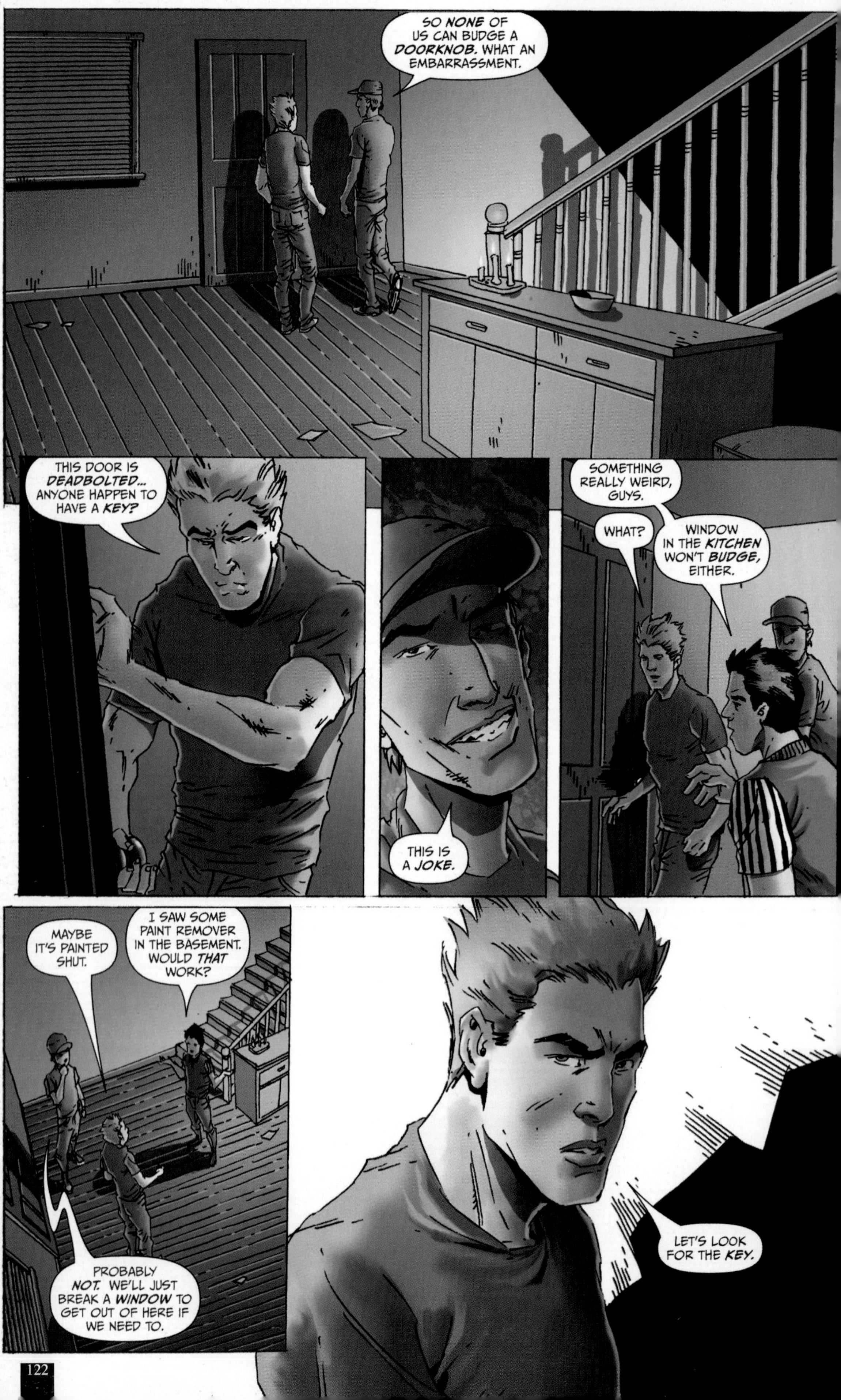
SO NONE OF US CAN BUDGE A DOORKNOB. WHAT AN EMBARRASSMENT.
THIS DOOR IS DEADBOLTED... ANYONE HAPPEN TO HAVE A KEY?
THIS IS A JOKE.
SOMETHING REALLY WEIRD, GUYS.
WHAT?
WINDOW IN THE KITCHEN WON'T BUDGE, EITHER.
MAYBE IT'S PAINTED SHUT.
I SAW SOME PAINT REMOVER IN THE BASEMENT. WOULD THAT WORK?
PROBABLY NOT. WE'LL JUST BREAK A WINDOW TO GET OUT OF HERE IF WE NEED TO.
LET'S LOOK FOR THE KEY.

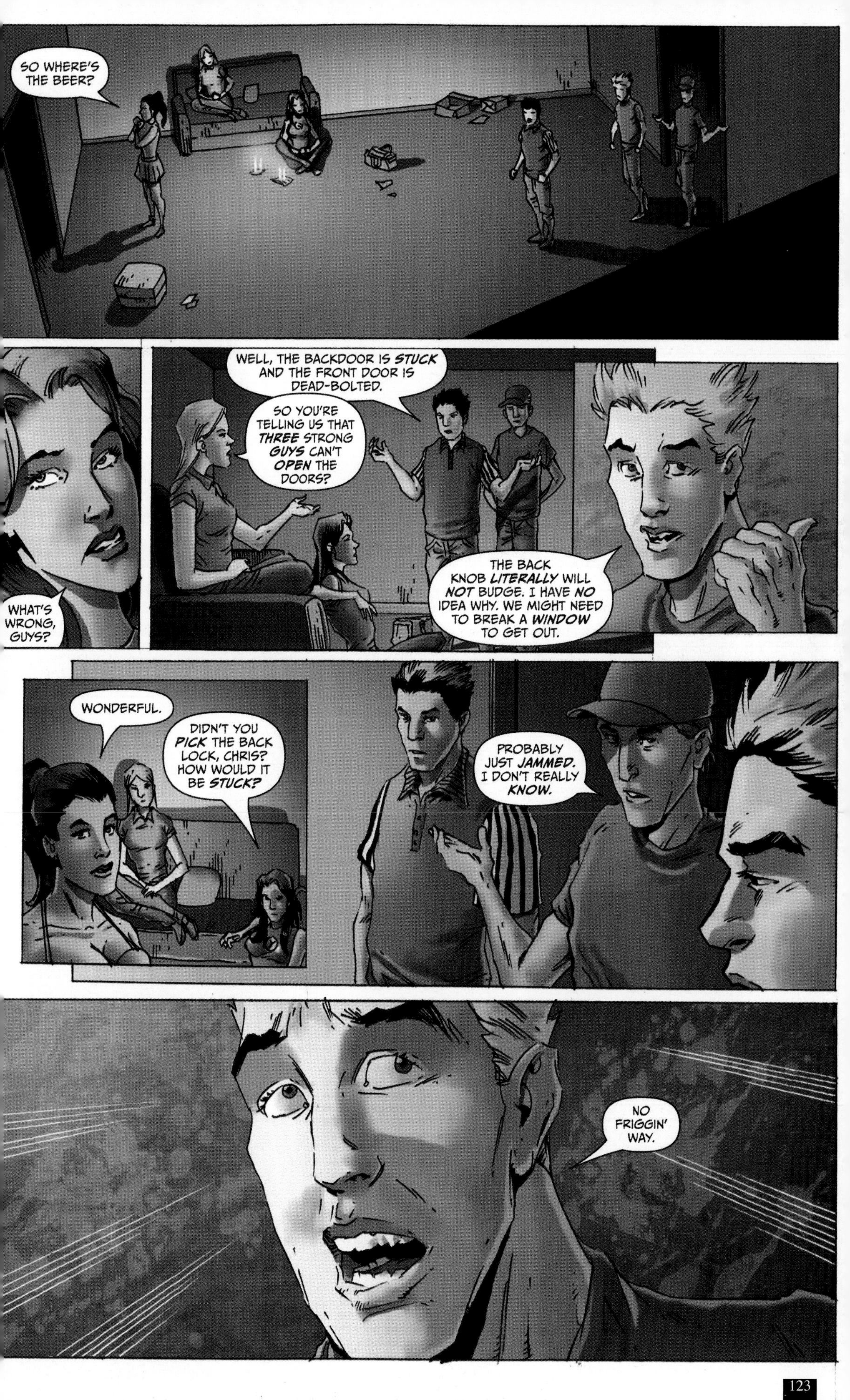
SO WHERE'S THE BEER?
WHAT'S WRONG, GUYS?
WELL, THE BACKDOOR IS STUCK AND THE FRONT DOOR IS DEAD-BOLTED.
SO YOU'RE TELLING US THAT THREE STRONG GUYS CAN'T OPEN THE DOORS?
THE BACK KNOB LITERALLY WILL NOT BUDGE. I HAVE NO IDEA WHY. WE MIGHT NEED TO BREAK A WINDOW TO GET OUT.
WONDERFUL.
DIDN'T YOU PICK THE BACK LOCK, CHRIS? HOW WOULD IT BE STUCK?
PROBABLY JUST JAMMED. I DON'T REALLY KNOW.
NO FRIGGIN' WAY.

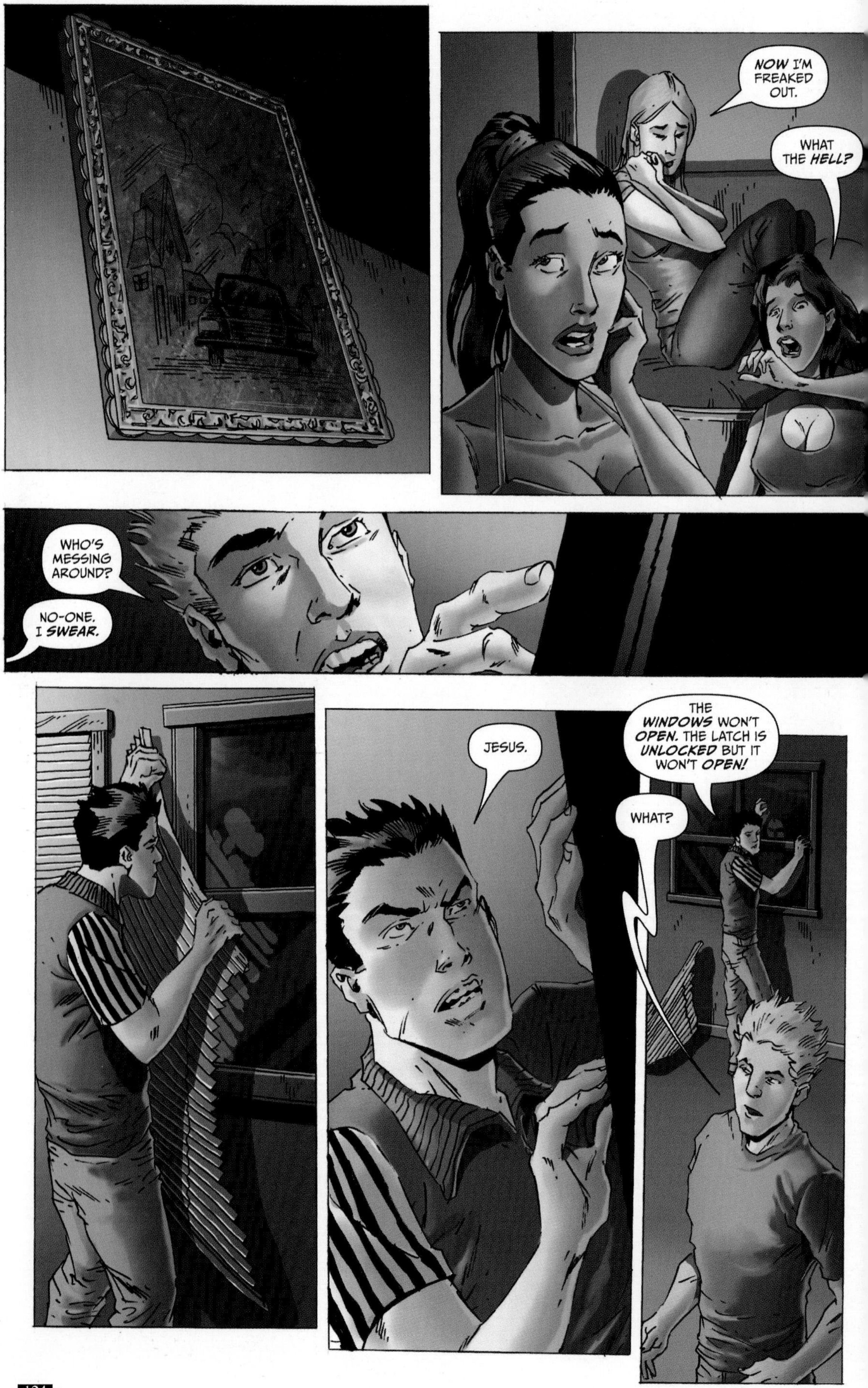

NOW I'M FREAKED OUT.
WHAT THE HELL?
WHO'S MESSING AROUND?
NO-ONE. I SWEAR.
JESUS.
THE WINDOWS WON'T OPEN. THE LATCH IS UNLOCKED BUT IT WON'T OPEN!
WHAT?

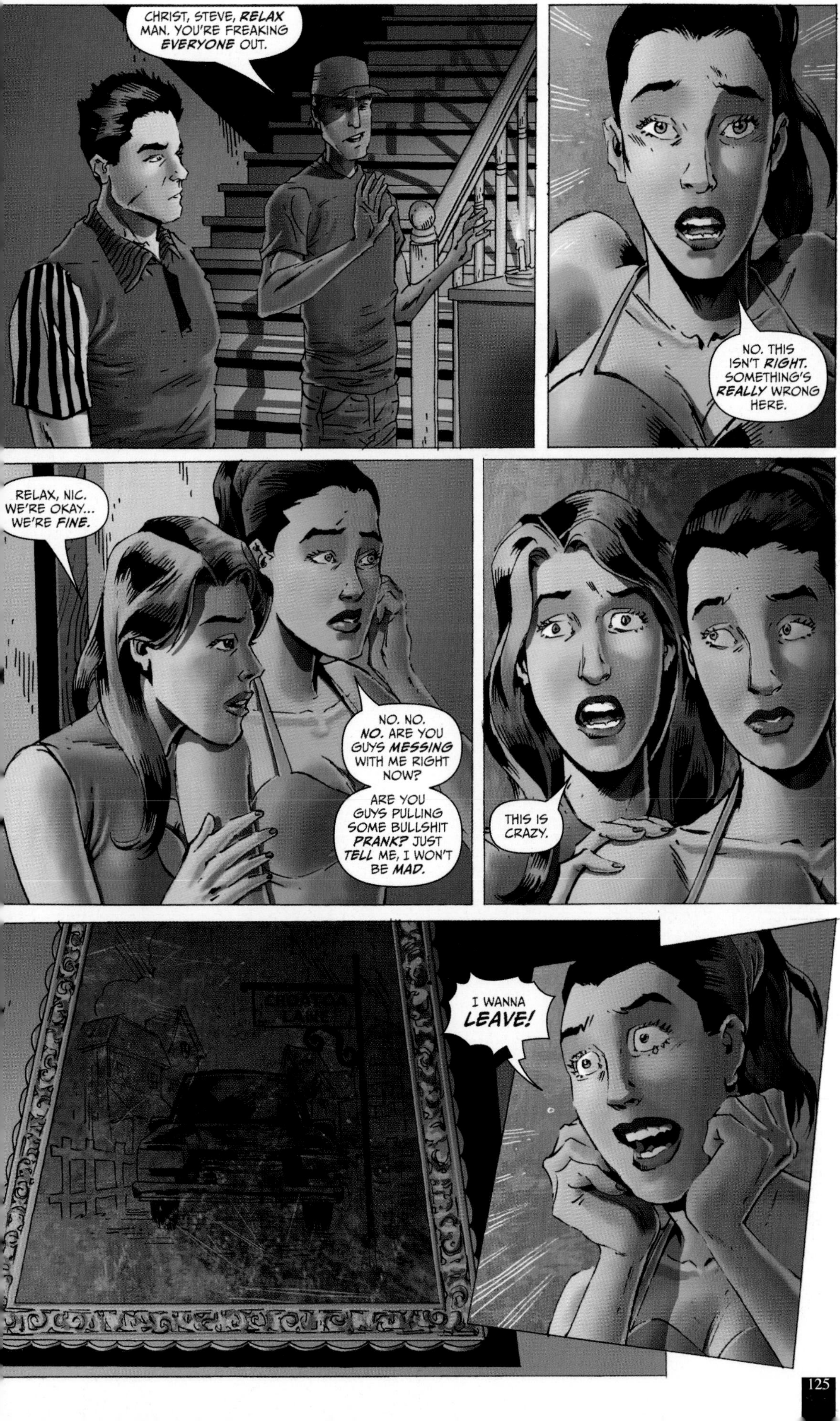
CHRIST, STEVE, RELAX MAN. YOU'RE FREAKING EVERYONE OUT.
NO. THIS ISN'T RIGHT. SOMETHING'S REALLY WRONG HERE.
RELAX, NIC. WE'RE OKAY... WE'RE FINE.
NO. NO. NO. ARE YOU GUYS MESSING WITH ME RIGHT NOW?
ARE YOU GUYS PULLING SOME BULLSHIT PRANK? JUST TELL ME, I WON'T BE MAD.
THIS IS CRAZY.
I WANNA LEAVE!

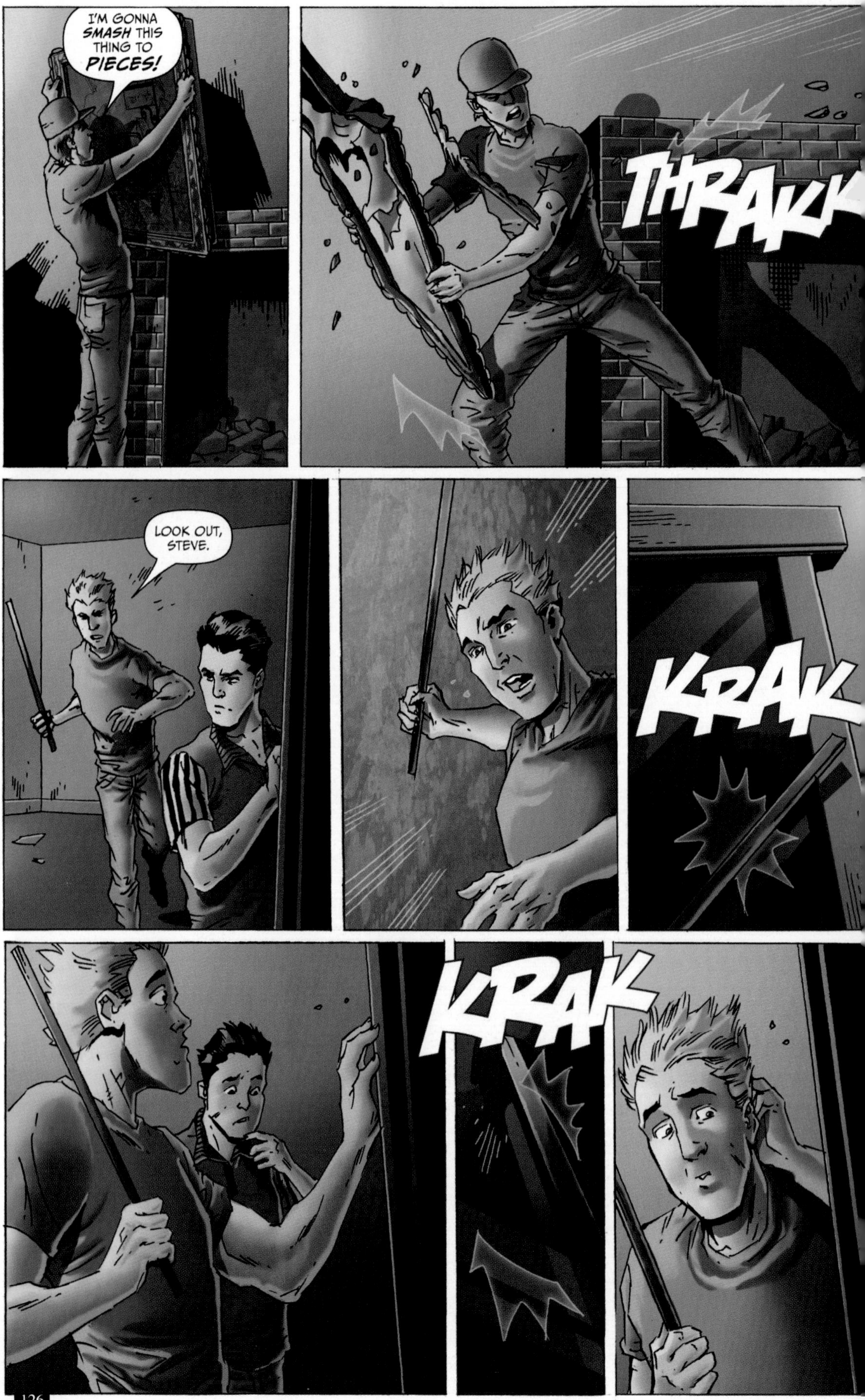

I'M GONNA SMASH THIS THING TO PIECES!
THRAKK
LOOK OUT, STEVE.
KRAK
KRAK

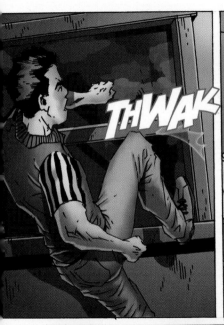

THWAK

THERE'S NO WAY, MAN. IS THIS BULLETPROOF GLASS?

THERE'S A CAR PULLING UP!

HEY!

HEY!

GET AWAY FROM THE WINDOW!

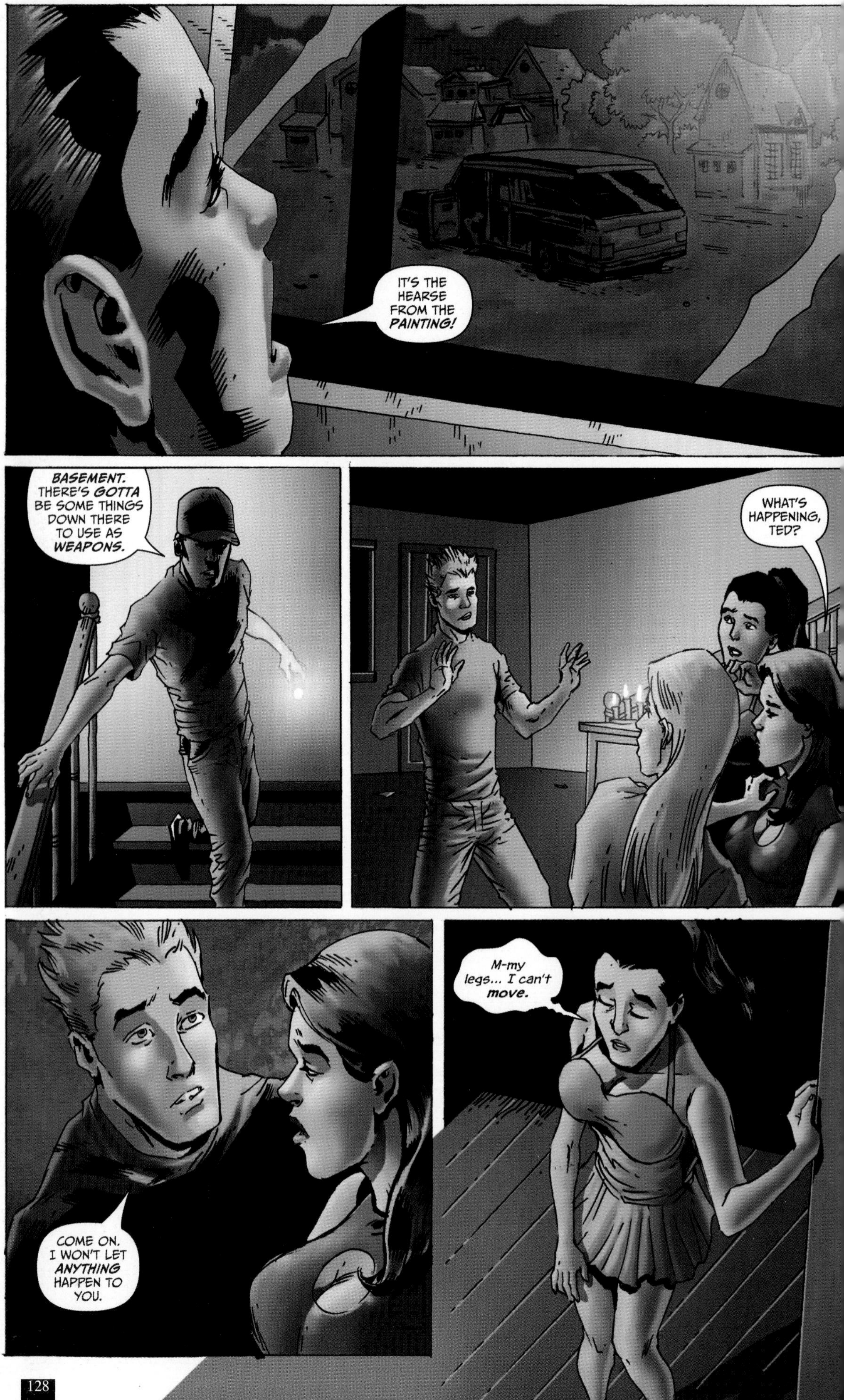
IT'S THE HEARSE FROM THE *PAINTING!*
BASEMENT. THERE'S *GOTTA* BE SOME THINGS DOWN THERE TO USE AS *WEAPONS.*
WHAT'S HAPPENING, TED?
COME ON. I WON'T LET *ANYTHING* HAPPEN TO YOU.
M-my legs... I can't ***move.***

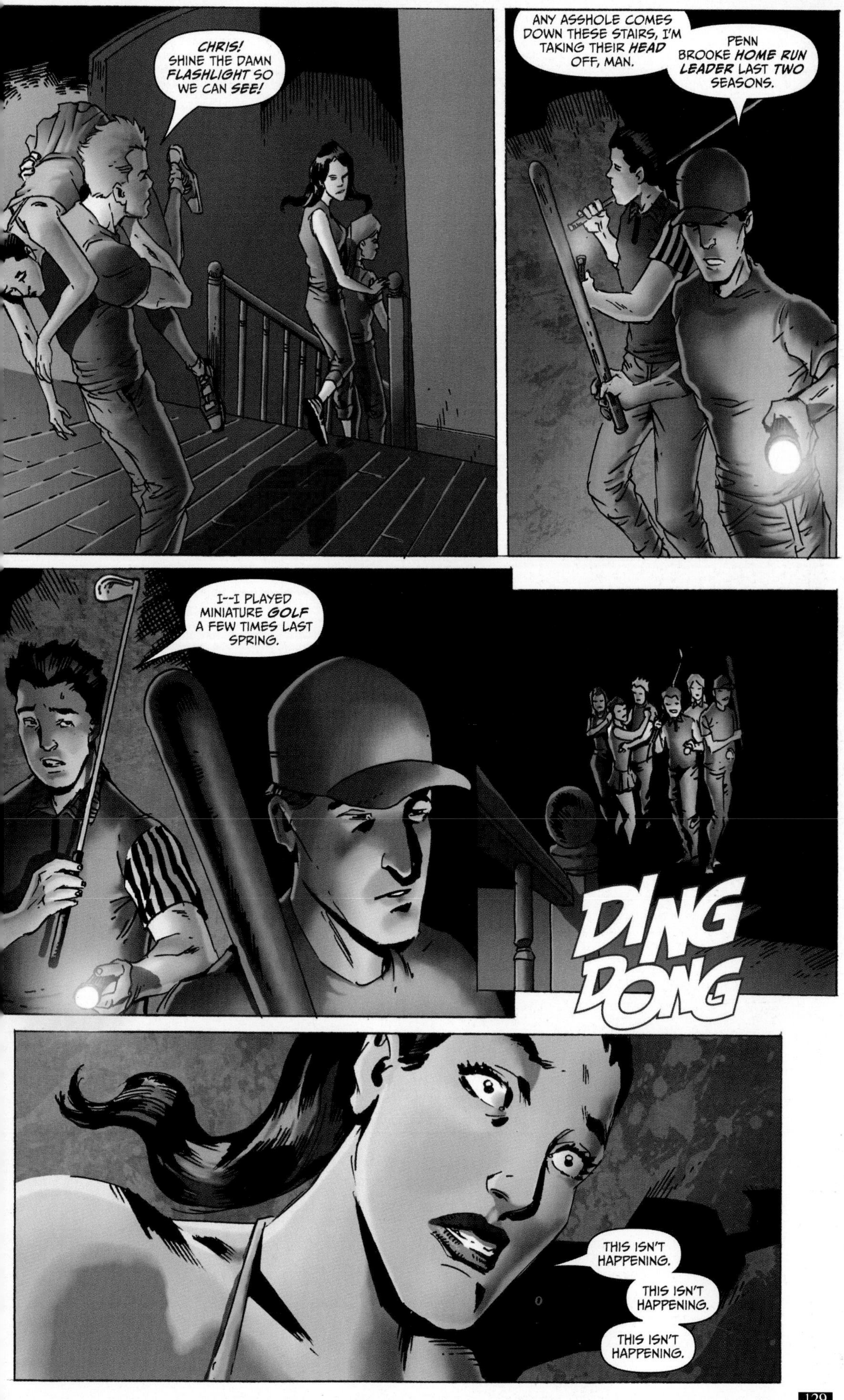
CHRIS! SHINE THE DAMN FLASHLIGHT SO WE CAN SEE!
ANY ASSHOLE COMES DOWN THESE STAIRS, I'M TAKING THEIR HEAD OFF, MAN.
PENN BROOKE HOME RUN LEADER LAST TWO SEASONS.
I--I PLAYED MINIATURE GOLF A FEW TIMES LAST SPRING.
DING DONG
THIS ISN'T HAPPENING.
THIS ISN'T HAPPENING.
THIS ISN'T HAPPENING.

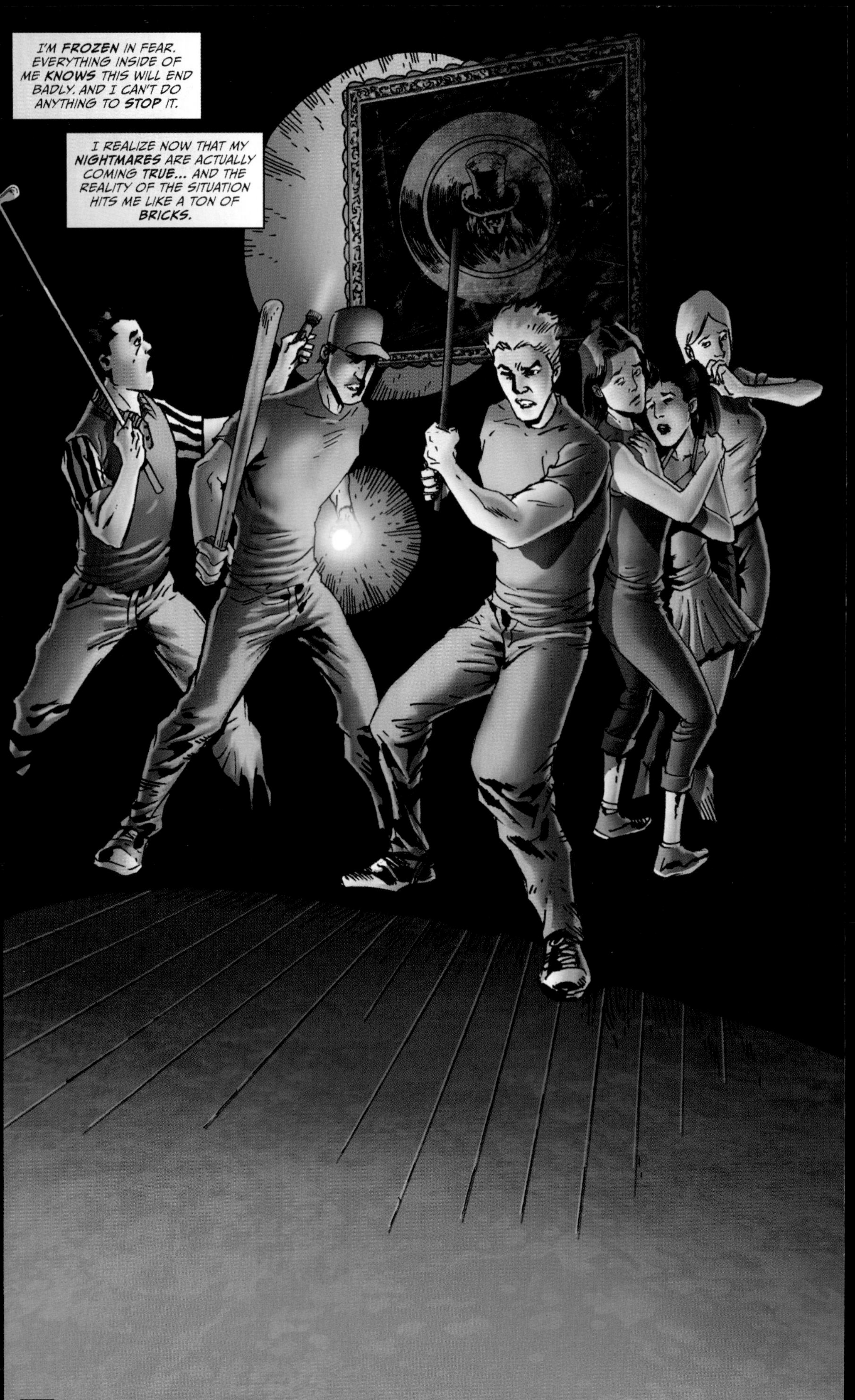
I'M FROZEN IN FEAR. EVERYTHING INSIDE OF ME KNOWS THIS WILL END BADLY. AND I CAN'T DO ANYTHING TO STOP IT.
I REALIZE NOW THAT MY NIGHTMARES ARE ACTUALLY COMING TRUE... AND THE REALITY OF THE SITUATION HITS ME LIKE A TON OF BRICKS.

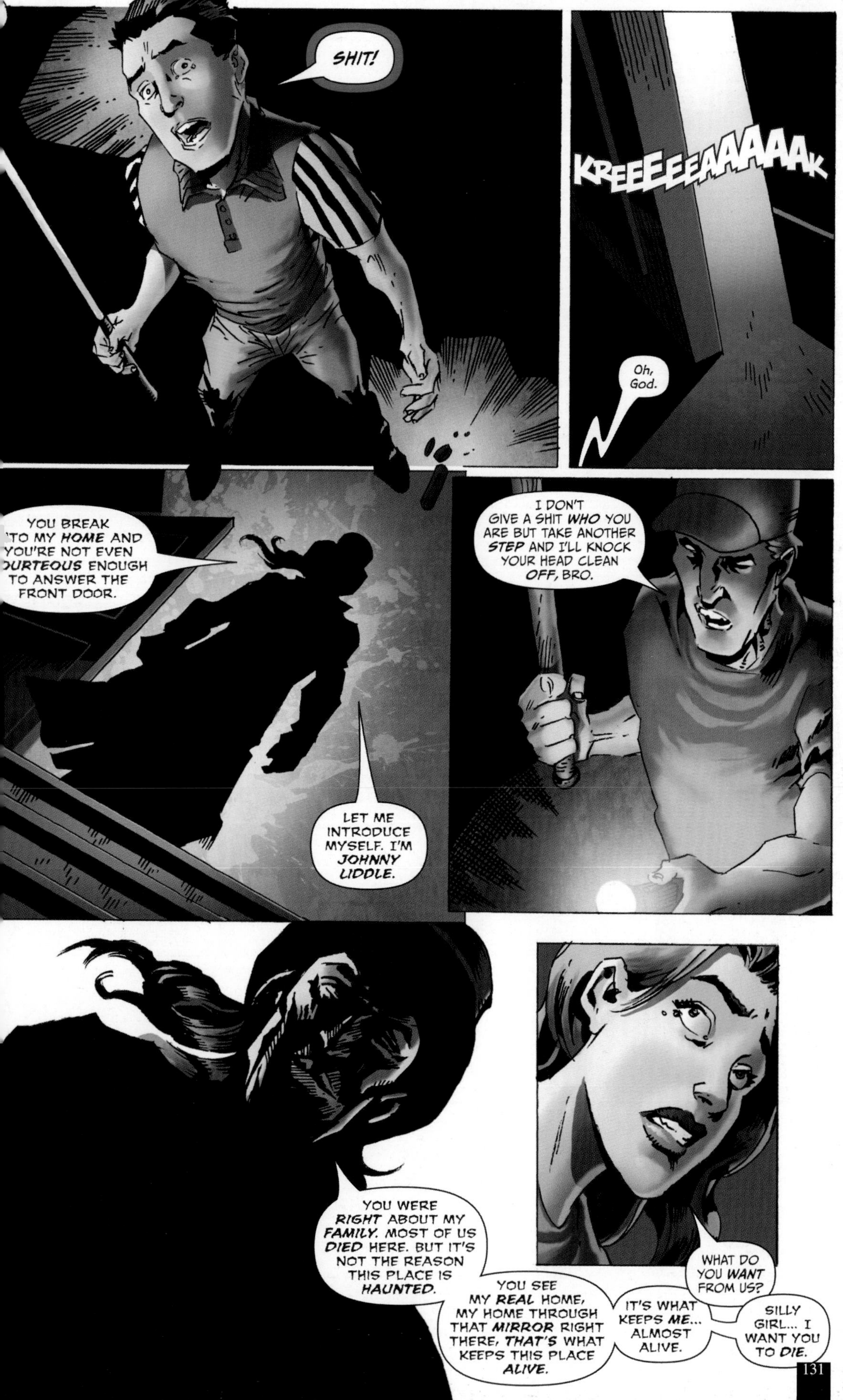

SHIT!
KREEEEEAAAAAK
Oh, God.
YOU BREAK 'TO MY HOME AND YOU'RE NOT EVEN OURTEOUS ENOUGH TO ANSWER THE FRONT DOOR.
I DON'T GIVE A SHIT WHO YOU ARE BUT TAKE ANOTHER STEP AND I'LL KNOCK YOUR HEAD CLEAN OFF, BRO.
LET ME INTRODUCE MYSELF. I'M JOHNNY LIDDLE.
YOU WERE RIGHT ABOUT MY FAMILY. MOST OF US DIED HERE. BUT IT'S NOT THE REASON THIS PLACE IS HAUNTED.
YOU SEE MY REAL HOME, MY HOME THROUGH THAT MIRROR RIGHT THERE, THAT'S WHAT KEEPS THIS PLACE ALIVE.
IT'S WHAT KEEPS ME... ALMOST ALIVE.
WHAT DO YOU WANT FROM US?
SILLY GIRL... I WANT YOU TO DIE.

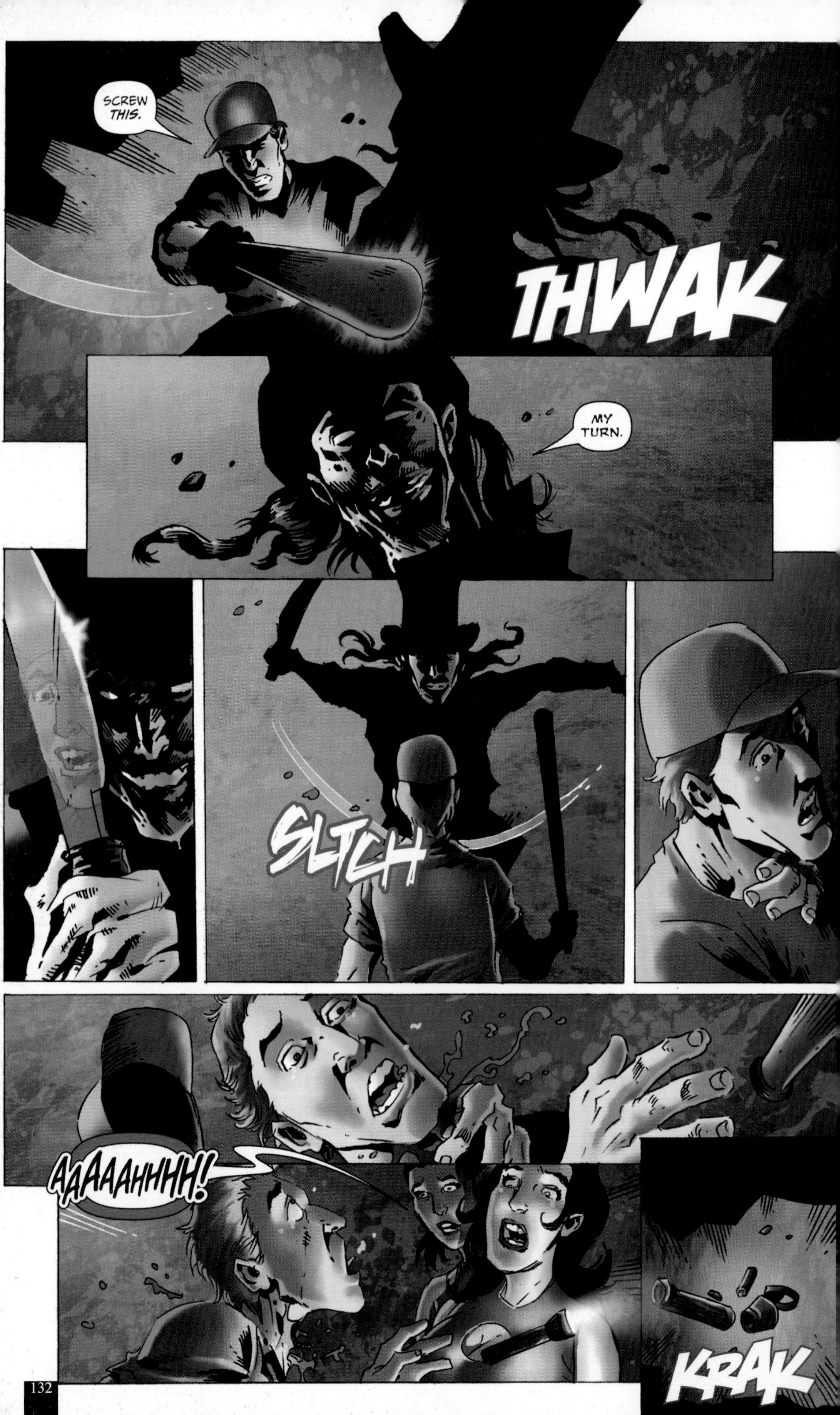
SCREW THIS.
THWAK
MY TURN.
SLTCH
AAAAAHHHH!
KRAK

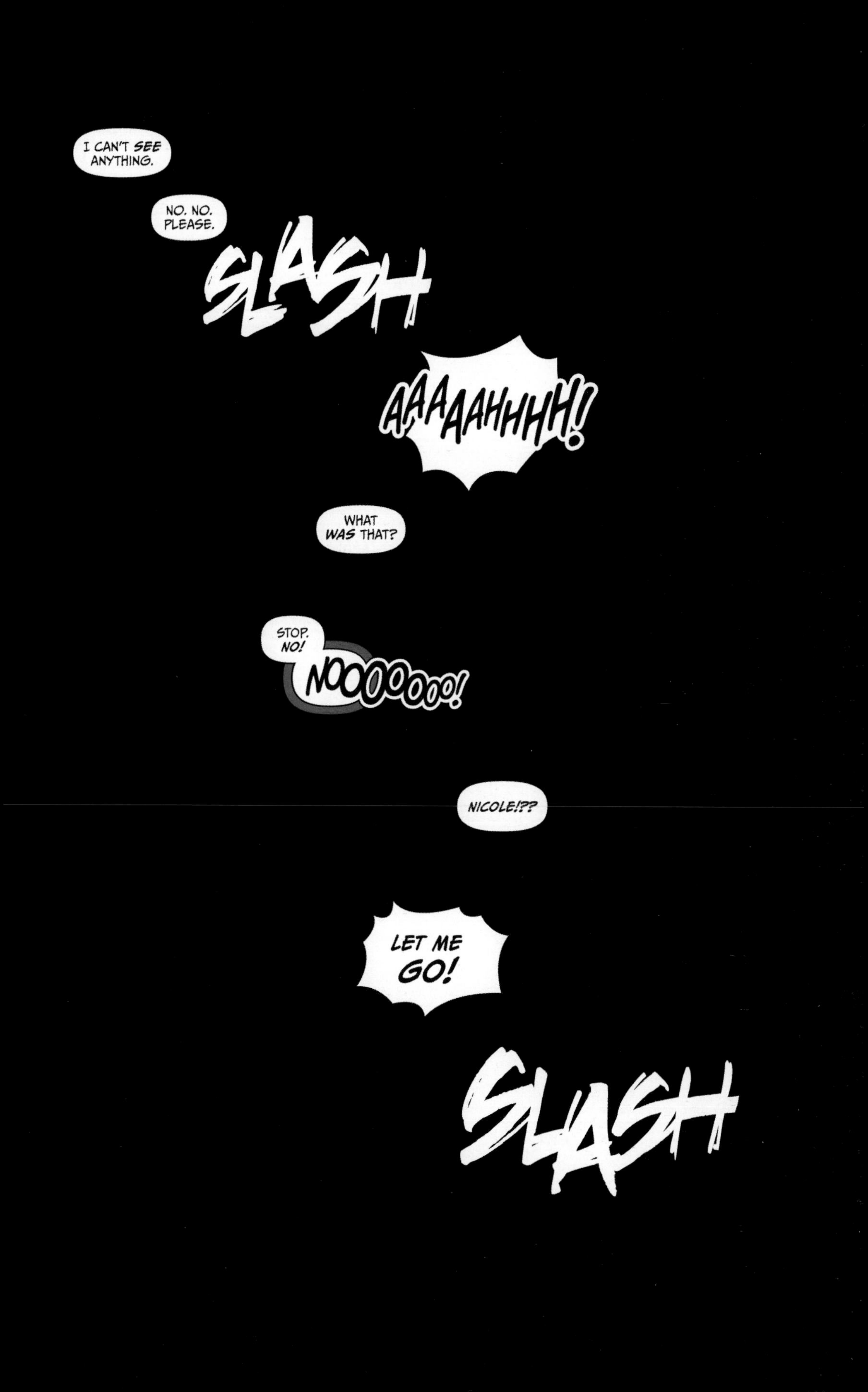
I CAN'T SEE ANYTHING.
NO. NO. PLEASE.
SLASH
AAAAAHHHH!
WHAT WAS THAT?
STOP. NO!
NOOOOOOO!
NICOLE!??
LET ME GO!
SLASH

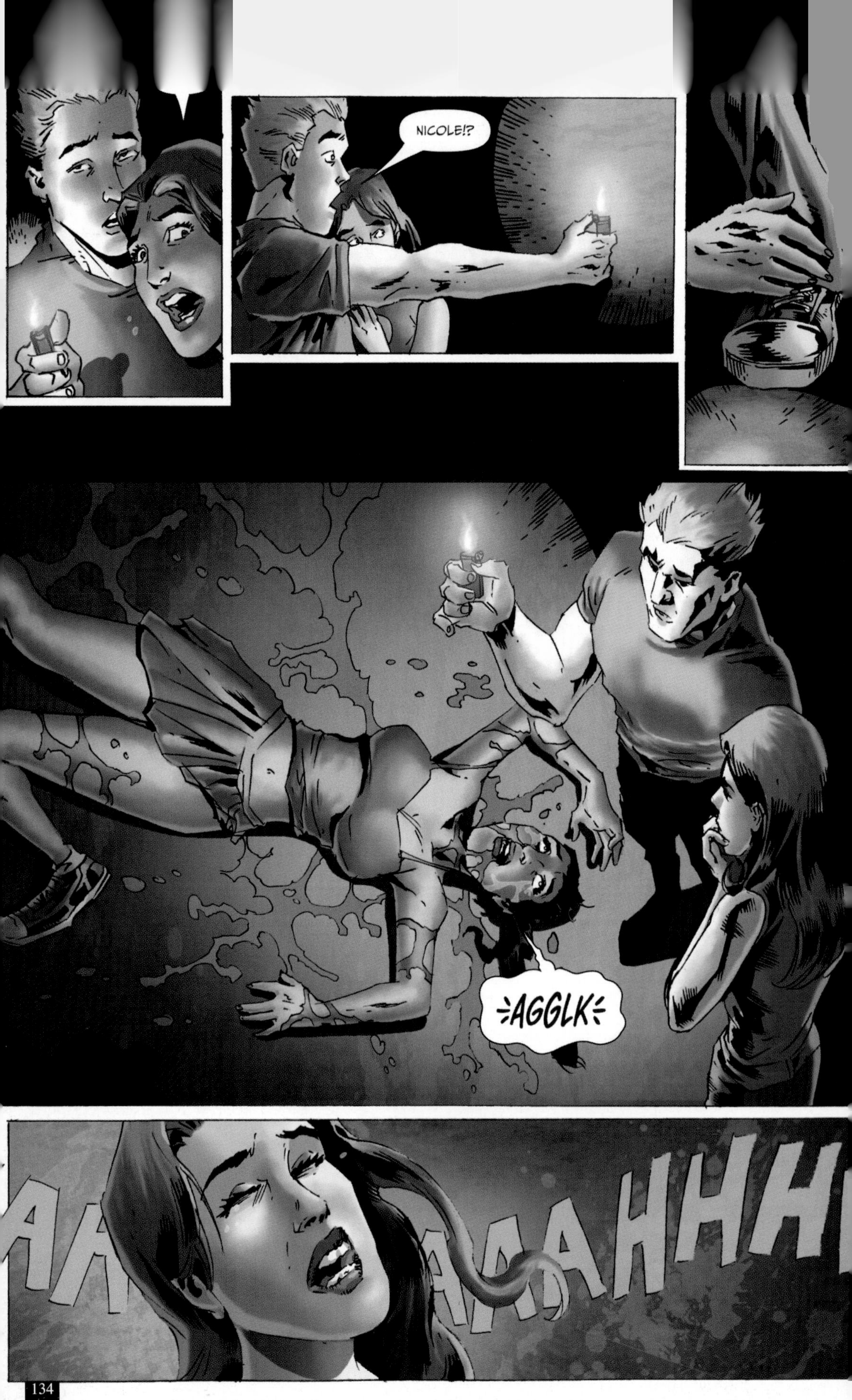
NICOLE!?
AGGLK
AAAAAAAHHHH

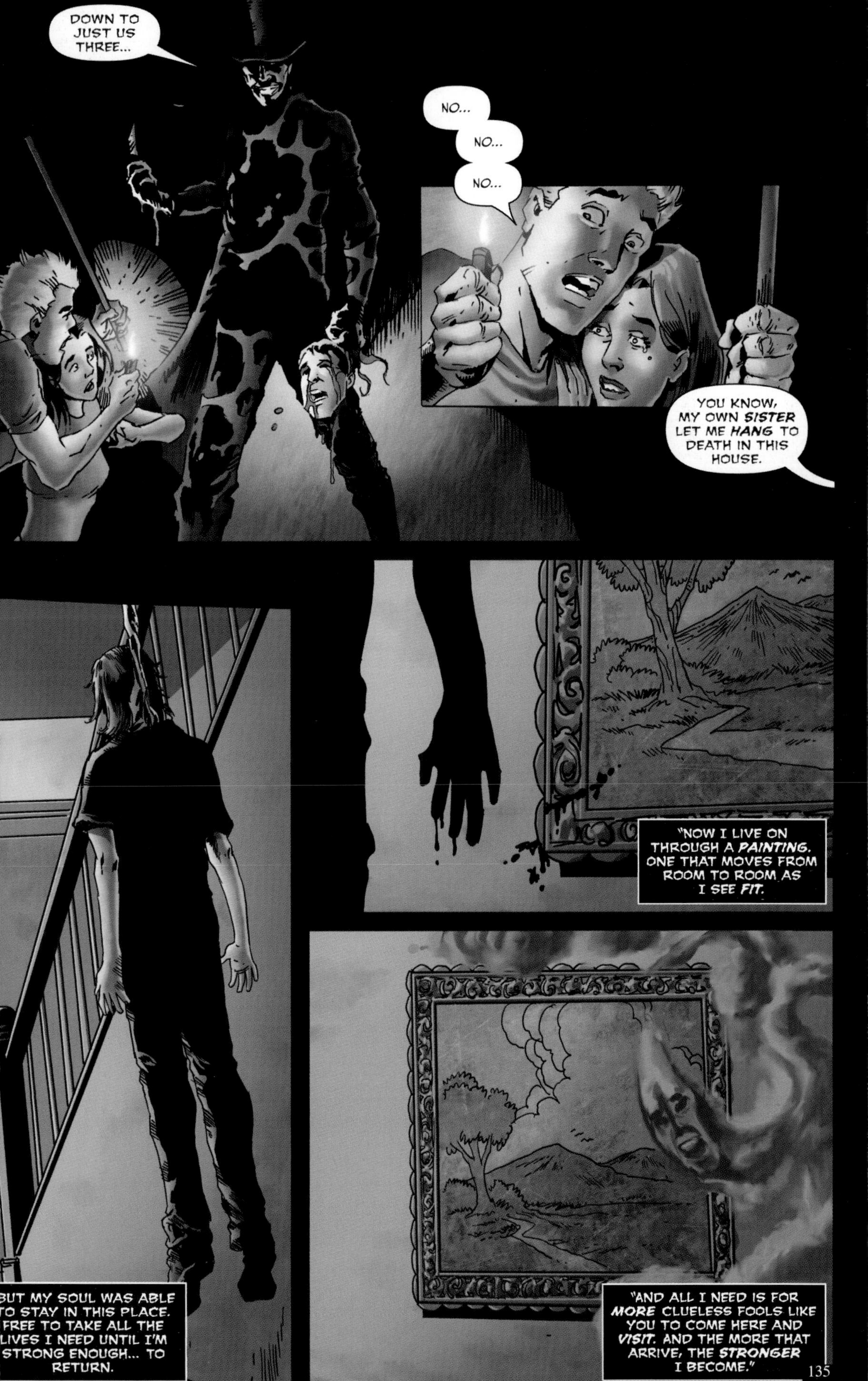
DOWN TO JUST US THREE...
NO...
NO...
NO...
YOU KNOW, MY OWN SISTER LET ME HANG TO DEATH IN THIS HOUSE.
BUT MY SOUL WAS ABLE TO STAY IN THIS PLACE. FREE TO TAKE ALL THE LIVES I NEED UNTIL I'M STRONG ENOUGH... TO RETURN.
"NOW I LIVE ON THROUGH A PAINTING. ONE THAT MOVES FROM ROOM TO ROOM AS I SEE FIT.
"AND ALL I NEED IS FOR MORE CLUELESS FOOLS LIKE YOU TO COME HERE AND VISIT. AND THE MORE THAT ARRIVE, THE STRONGER I BECOME."

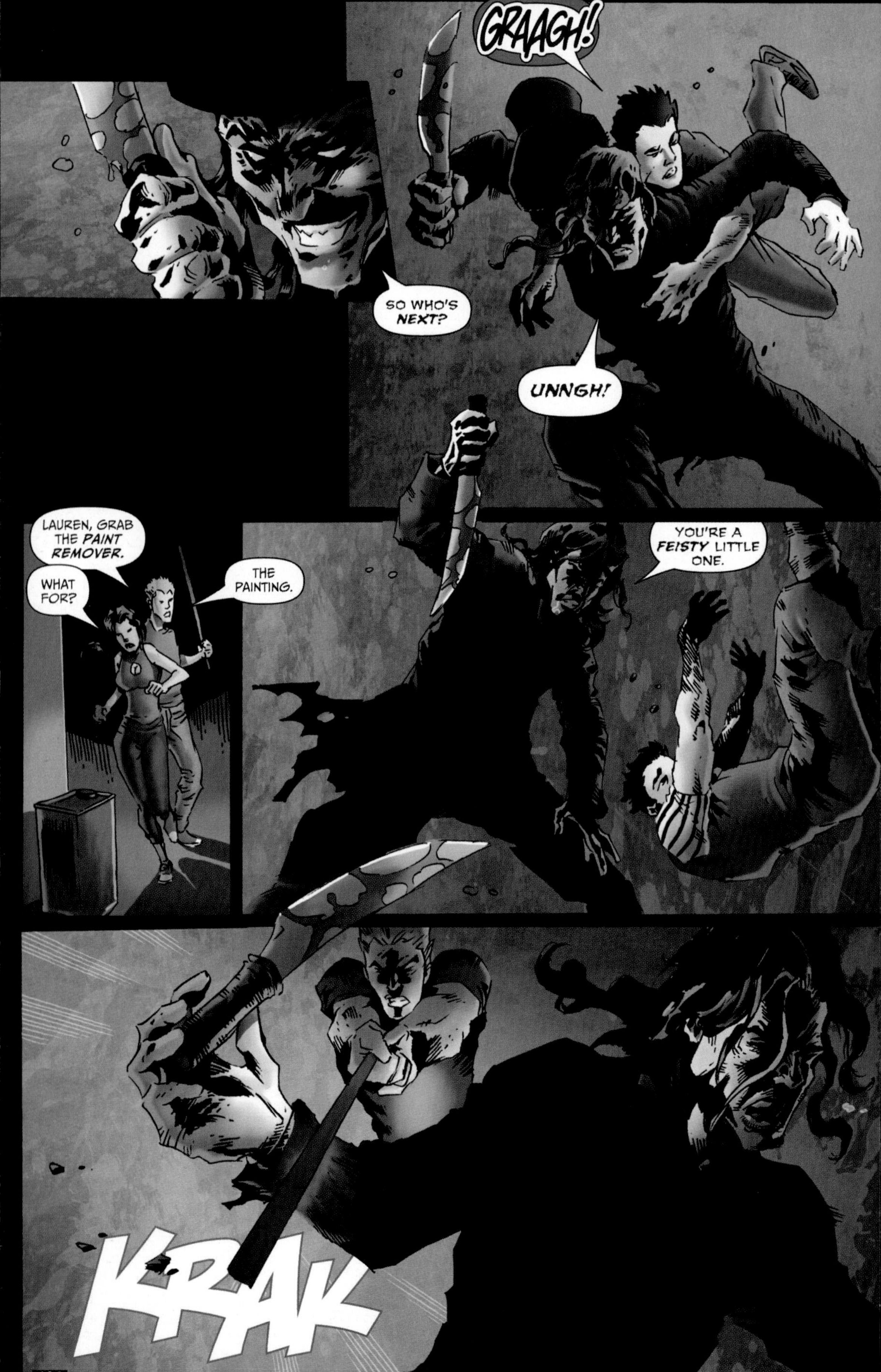
GRAAGH!
SO WHO'S NEXT?
UNNGH!
LAUREN, GRAB THE PAINT REMOVER.
WHAT FOR?
THE PAINTING.
YOU'RE A FEISTY LITTLE ONE.
KRAK

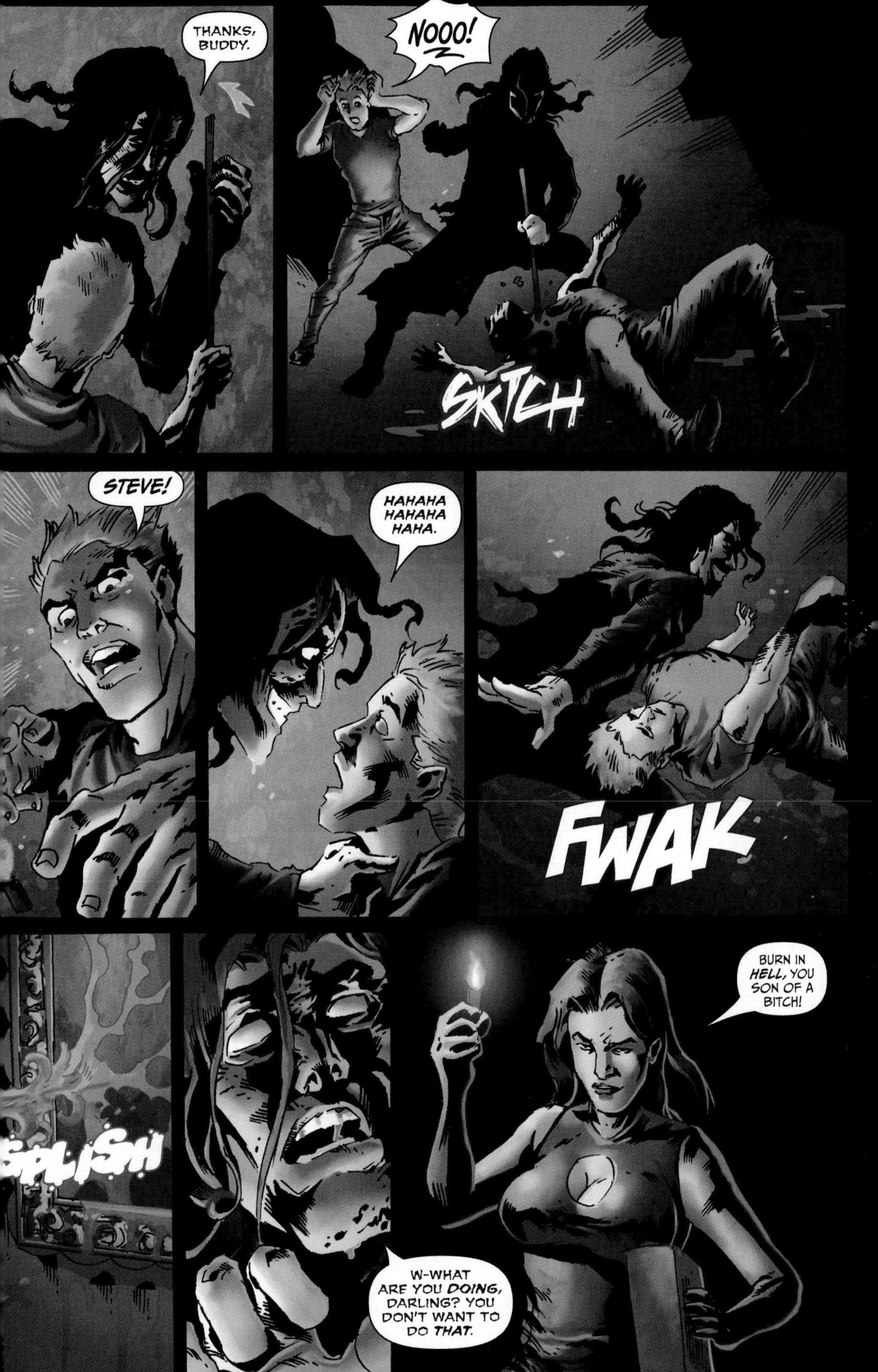

THANKS, BUDDY.
NOOO!
SKTCH
STEVE!
HAHAHA HAHAHA HAHA.
FWAK
SPLISH
W-WHAT ARE YOU DOING, DARLING? YOU DON'T WANT TO DO THAT.
BURN IN HELL, YOU SON OF A BITCH!

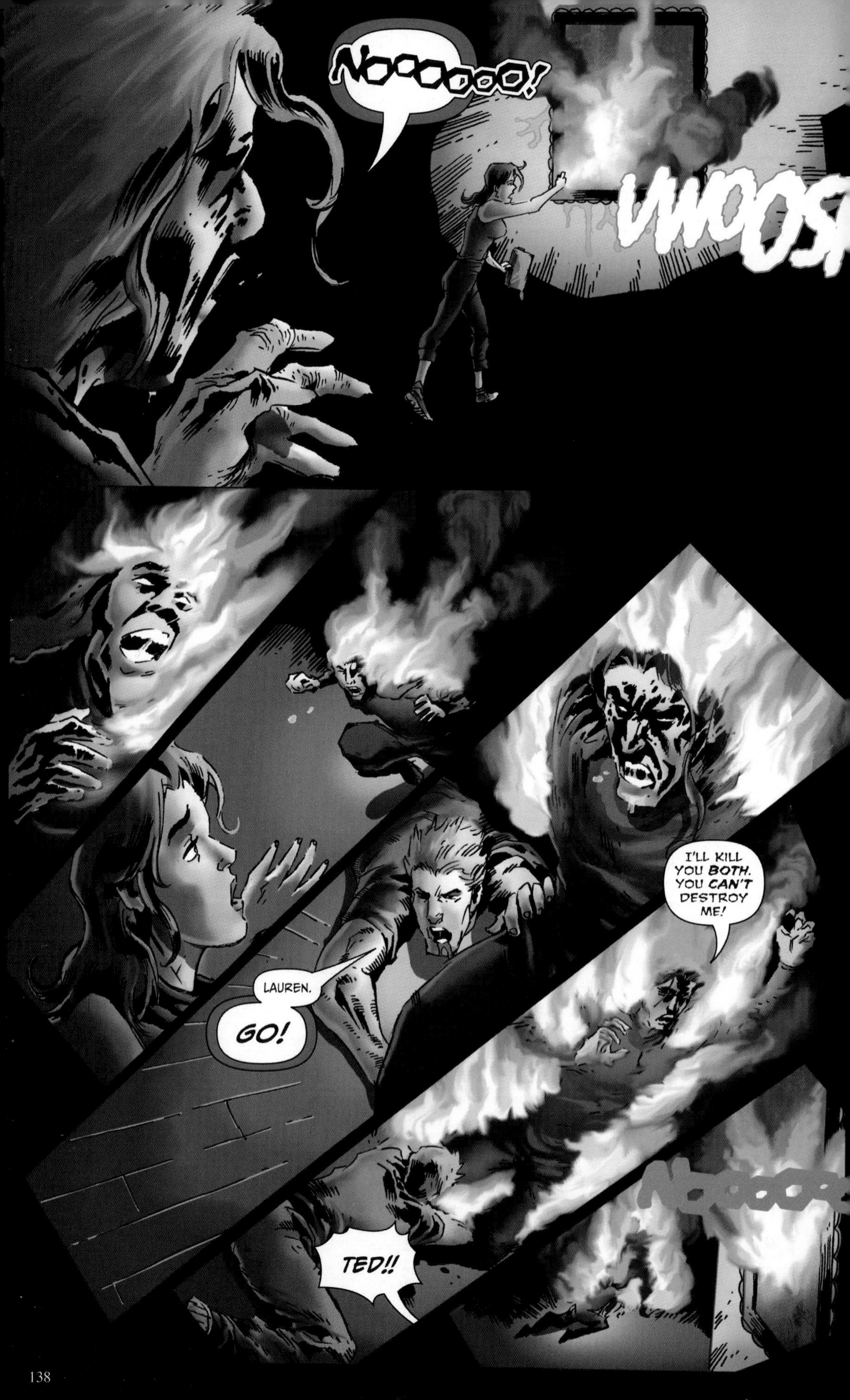
NOOOOOOO!
WOOSH
LAUREN.
GO!
I'LL KILL YOU BOTH. YOU CAN'T DESTROY ME!
TED!!

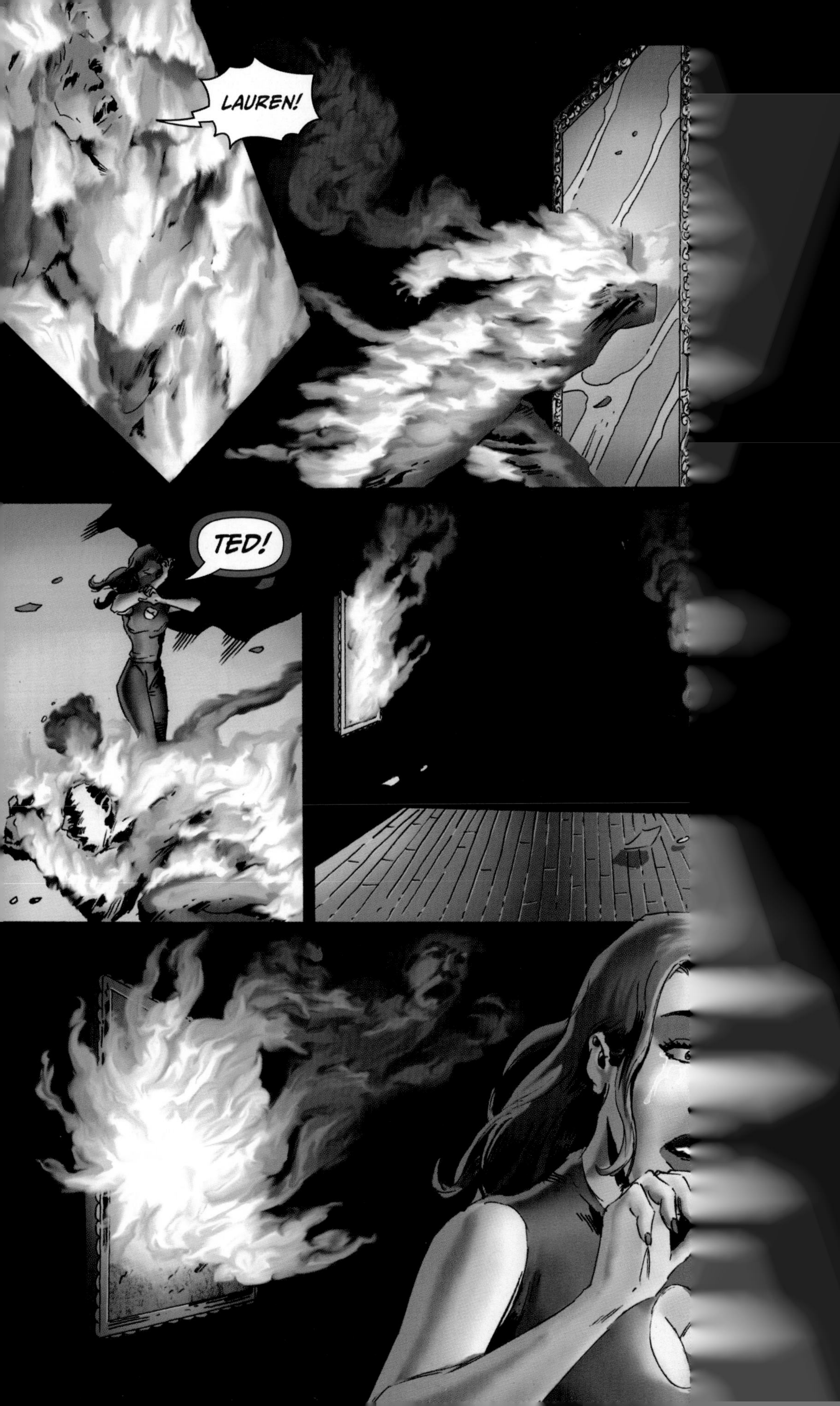
LAUREN!
TED!

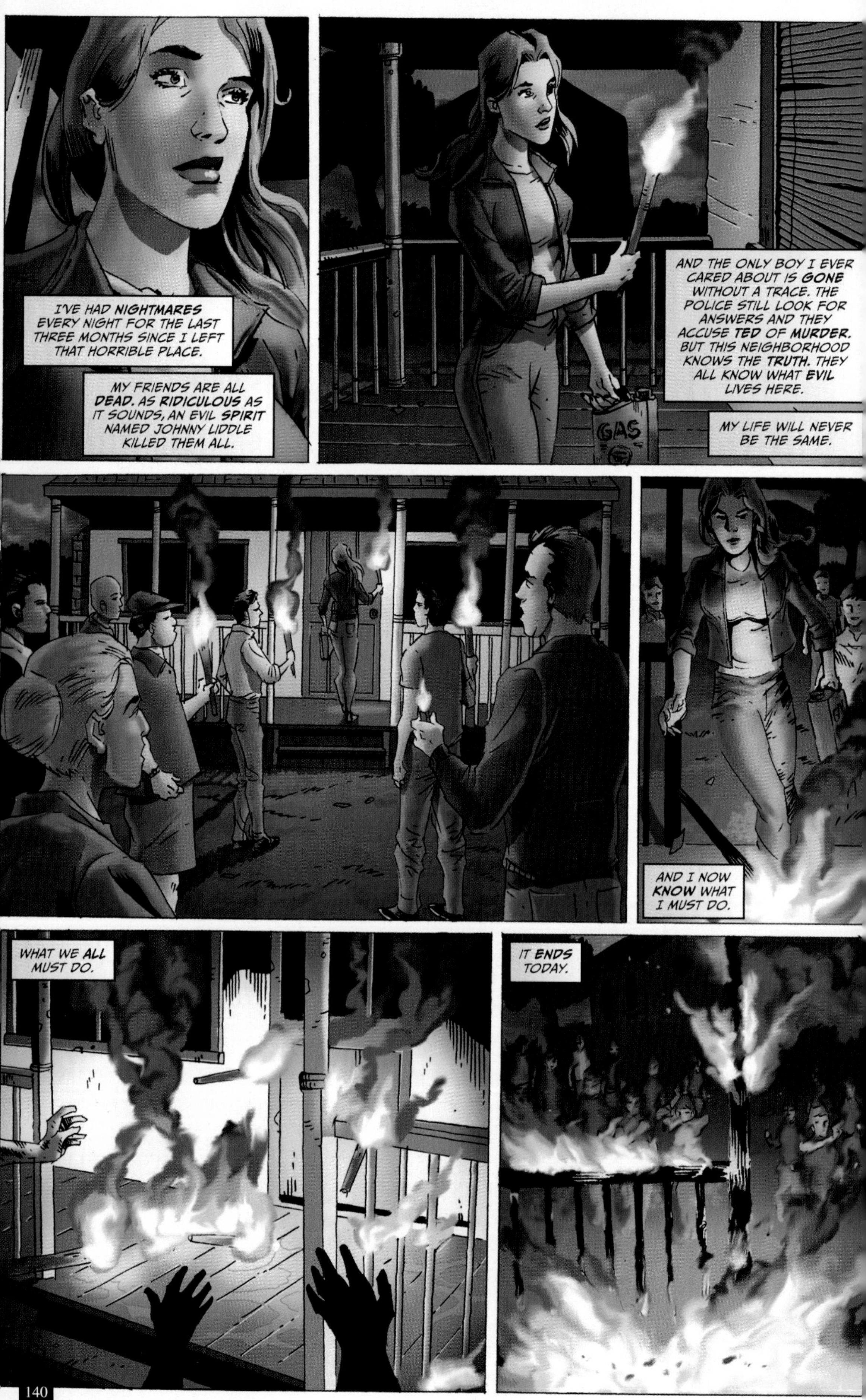
I'VE HAD **NIGHTMARES** EVERY NIGHT FOR THE LAST THREE MONTHS SINCE I LEFT THAT HORRIBLE PLACE.
MY FRIENDS ARE ALL **DEAD**. AS **RIDICULOUS** AS IT SOUNDS, AN EVIL **SPIRIT** NAMED JOHNNY LIDDLE KILLED THEM ALL.
AND THE ONLY BOY I EVER CARED ABOUT IS **GONE** WITHOUT A TRACE. THE POLICE STILL LOOK FOR ANSWERS AND THEY ACCUSE **TED** OF **MURDER**. BUT THIS NEIGHBORHOOD KNOWS THE **TRUTH**. THEY ALL KNOW WHAT **EVIL** LIVES HERE.
GAS
MY LIFE WILL NEVER BE THE SAME.
AND I NOW **KNOW** WHAT I MUST DO.
WHAT WE **ALL** MUST DO.
IT **ENDS** TODAY.

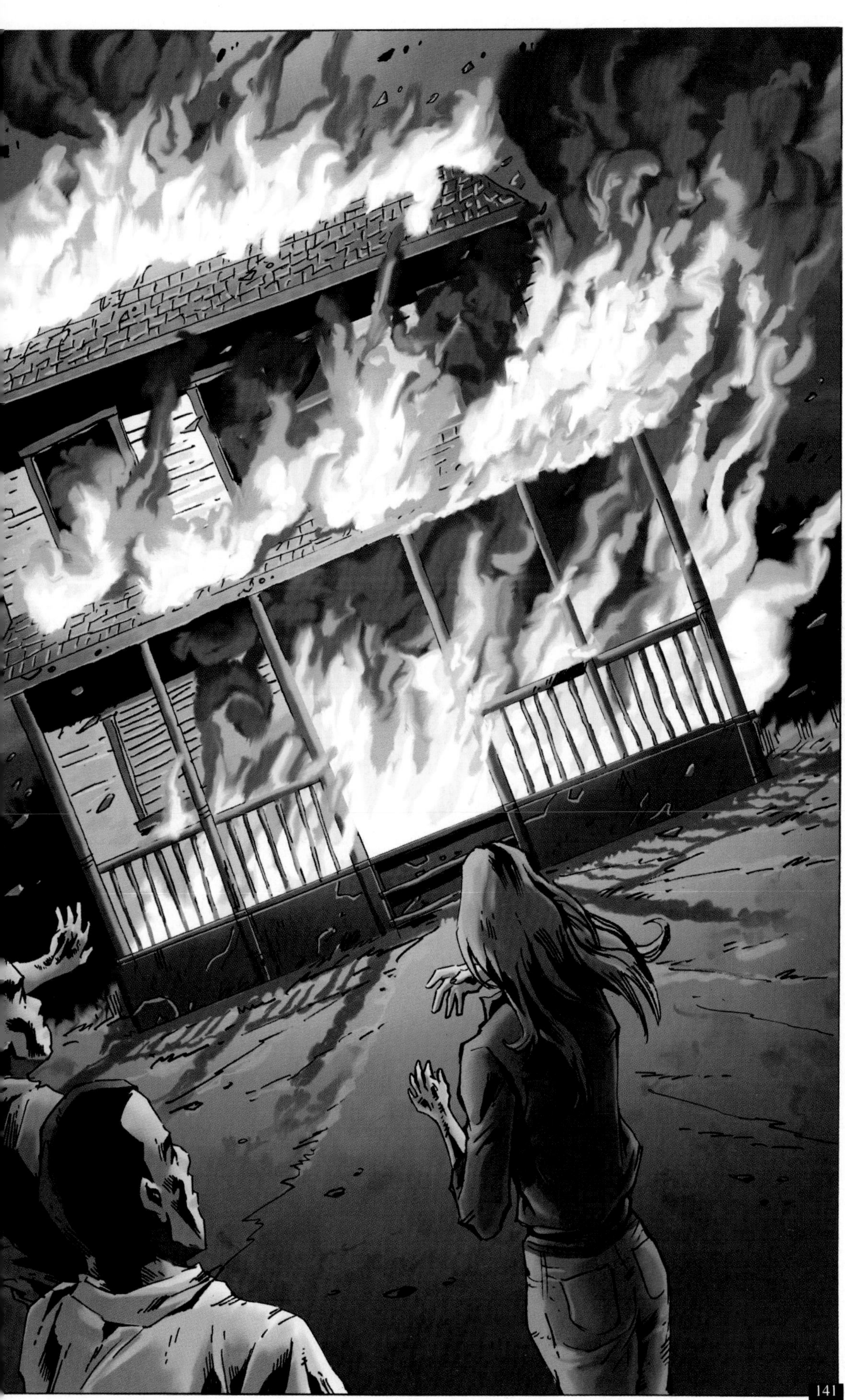

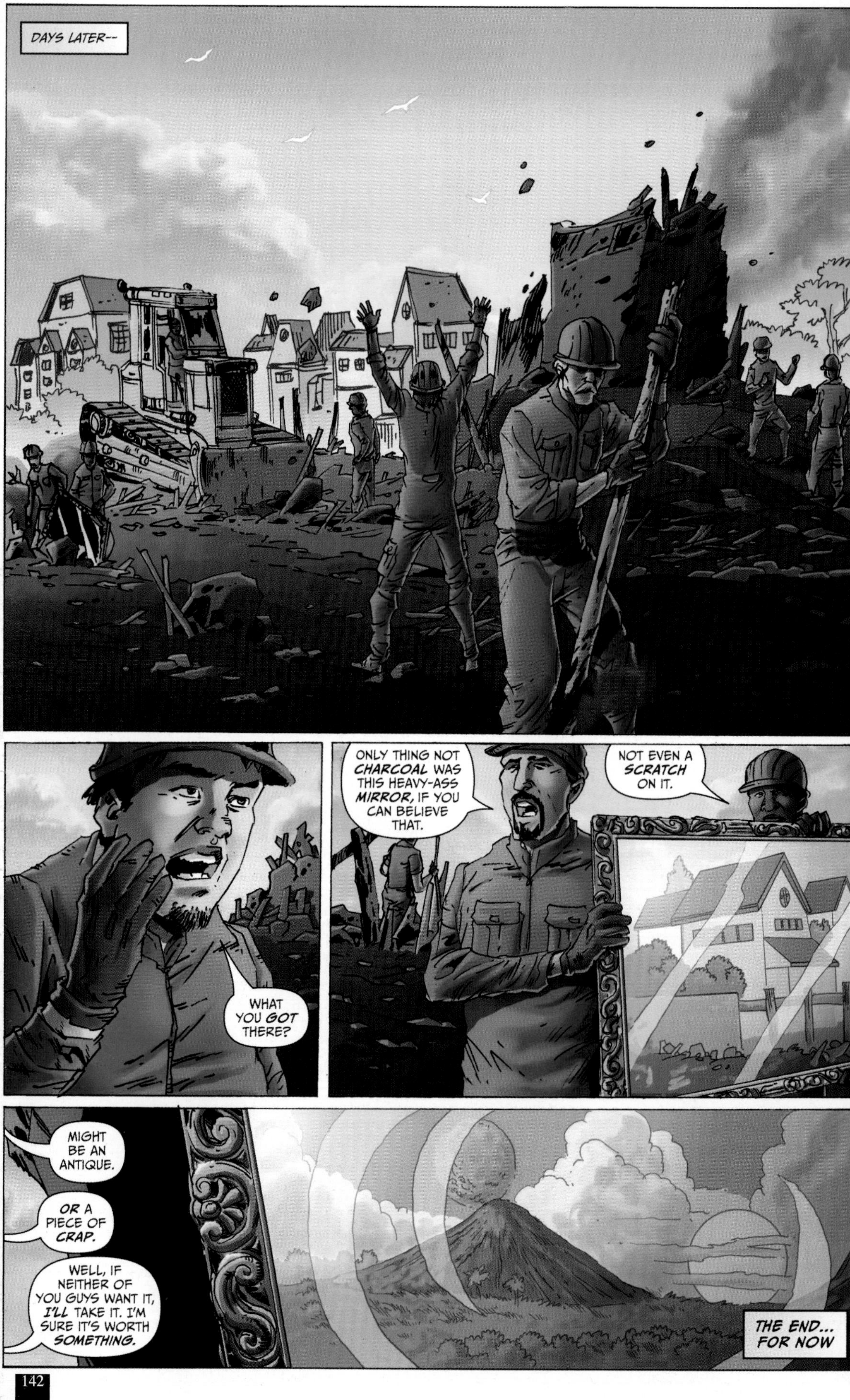
DAYS LATER--
WHAT YOU GOT THERE?
ONLY THING NOT CHARCOAL WAS THIS HEAVY-ASS MIRROR, IF YOU CAN BELIEVE THAT.
NOT EVEN A SCRATCH ON IT.
MIGHT BE AN ANTIQUE.
OR A PIECE OF CRAP.
WELL, IF NEITHER OF YOU GUYS WANT IT, I'LL TAKE IT. I'M SURE IT'S WORTH SOMETHING.
THE END... FOR NOW

Lauren Nelman "Nelly"

Activities: Science Club, Varsity Basketball (Captain), Field Hockey, Volleyball, French Club
Favorite Class: Chemistry
Favorite School Memory: Junior Prom
Future Plans: Attend college and law school then join the FBI.

Ted Franklin

Activities: Varsity Football (co-captain; all-star), Varsity Baseball (regional all-star), Track & Field, Varsity Basketball
Favorite Class: English with Ms. Gary
Favorite school memory: Football!!Regional Champs 2010!!
Future Plans: College at UCLA, graduate with a business degree and we'll see what happens...

Nicole Antonio "Nic"

Activities: Cheerleading, Softball, Soccer, Field Hockey
Favorite Class: English
Favorite school memory: Hangin with my girls Nelly and Tina! Junior Prom with Mike
Future Plans: graduate from USC with a marketing degree, get married and have a huge family!

Steve Marra "Shmoo"

Activities: Student Council, Soccer, Spanish Club
Favorite Class: Spanish with Mr. Garcia
Favorite school memory: Parties in my basement with my crew!
Future Plans: To attend college in New York City and become an architect

Tina D'Amico "T"

Activities: Cooking Club, Student Council, French Club, Varsity Soccer
Favorite Class: French
Favorite school memory: Making bratwursts with Nina in 5th period!!
Future Plans: To own my own Italian restaurant in Los Angeles

Chris Malloy "Malloy"

Activities: Basketball, Baseball (regional All-Star)
Favorite Class: Lunch
Favorite school memory: Cutting Sophmore year with Griggs
Future Plans: Pro Baseball player... 'Nuff said!

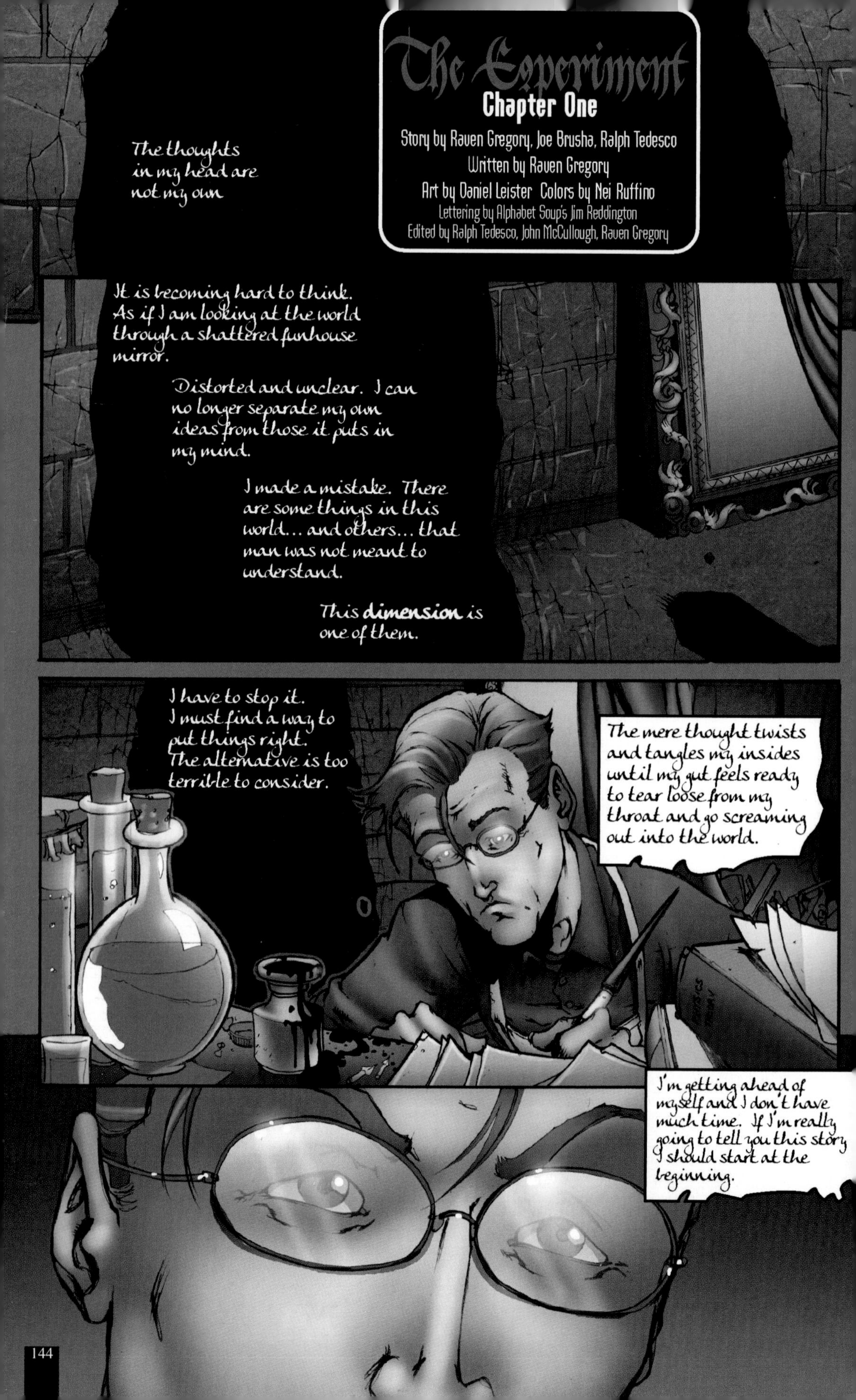
The Experiment
Chapter One
Story by Raven Gregory, Joe Brusha, Ralph Tedesco
Written by Raven Gregory
Art by Daniel Leister Colors by Nei Ruffino
Lettering by Alphabet Soup's Jim Reddington
Edited by Ralph Tedesco, John McCullough, Raven Gregory
The thoughts in my head are not my own
It is becoming hard to think. As if I am looking at the world through a shattered funhouse mirror.
Distorted and unclear. I can no longer separate my own ideas from those it puts in my mind.
I made a mistake. There are some things in this world... and others... that man was not meant to understand.
This **dimension** is one of them.
I have to stop it. I must find a way to put things right. The alternative is too terrible to consider.
The mere thought twists and tangles my insides until my gut feels ready to tear loose from my throat and go screaming out into the world.
I'm getting ahead of myself and I don't have much time. If I'm really going to tell you this story I should start at the beginning.

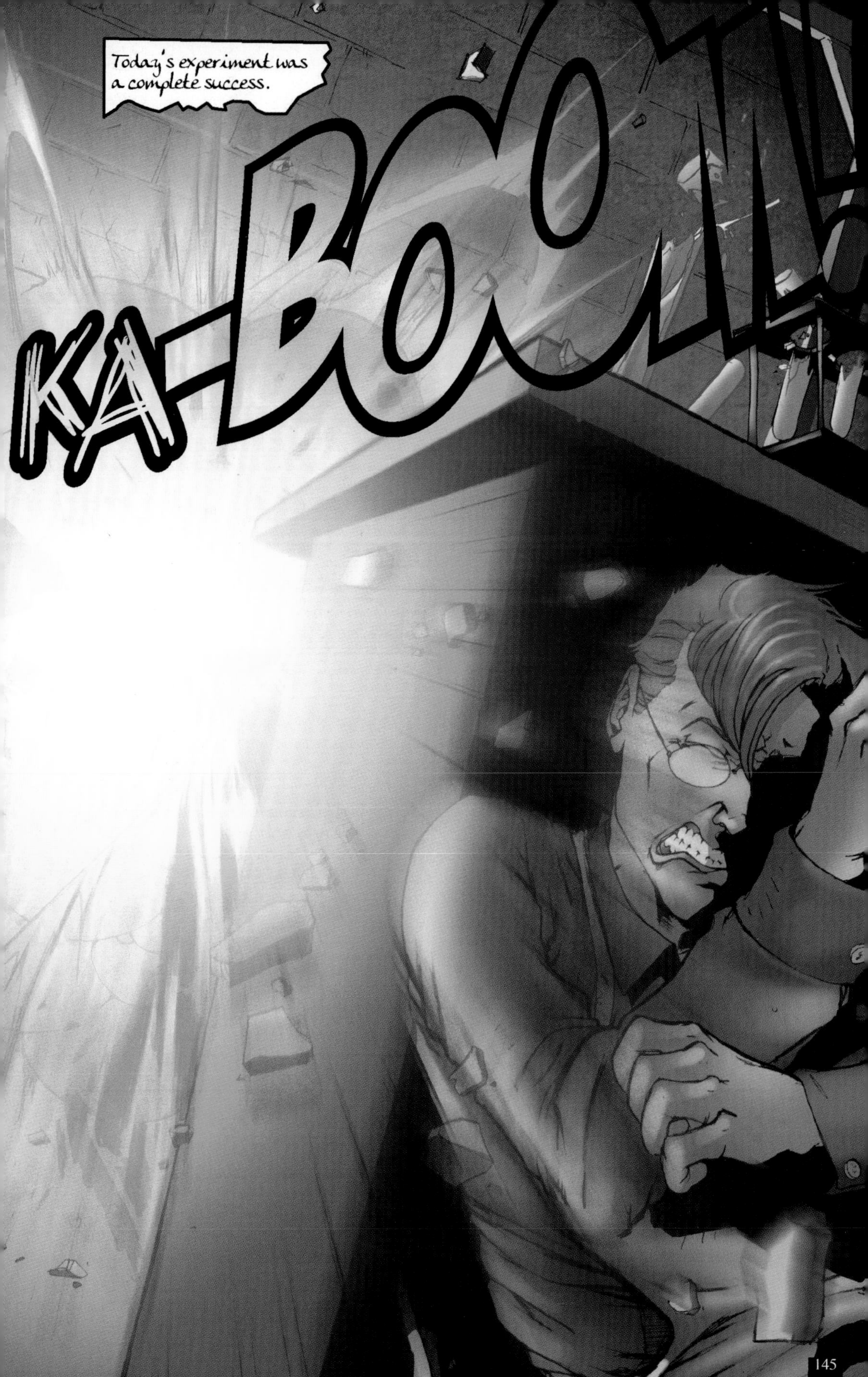
Today's experiment was a complete success.
KA-BOOM!

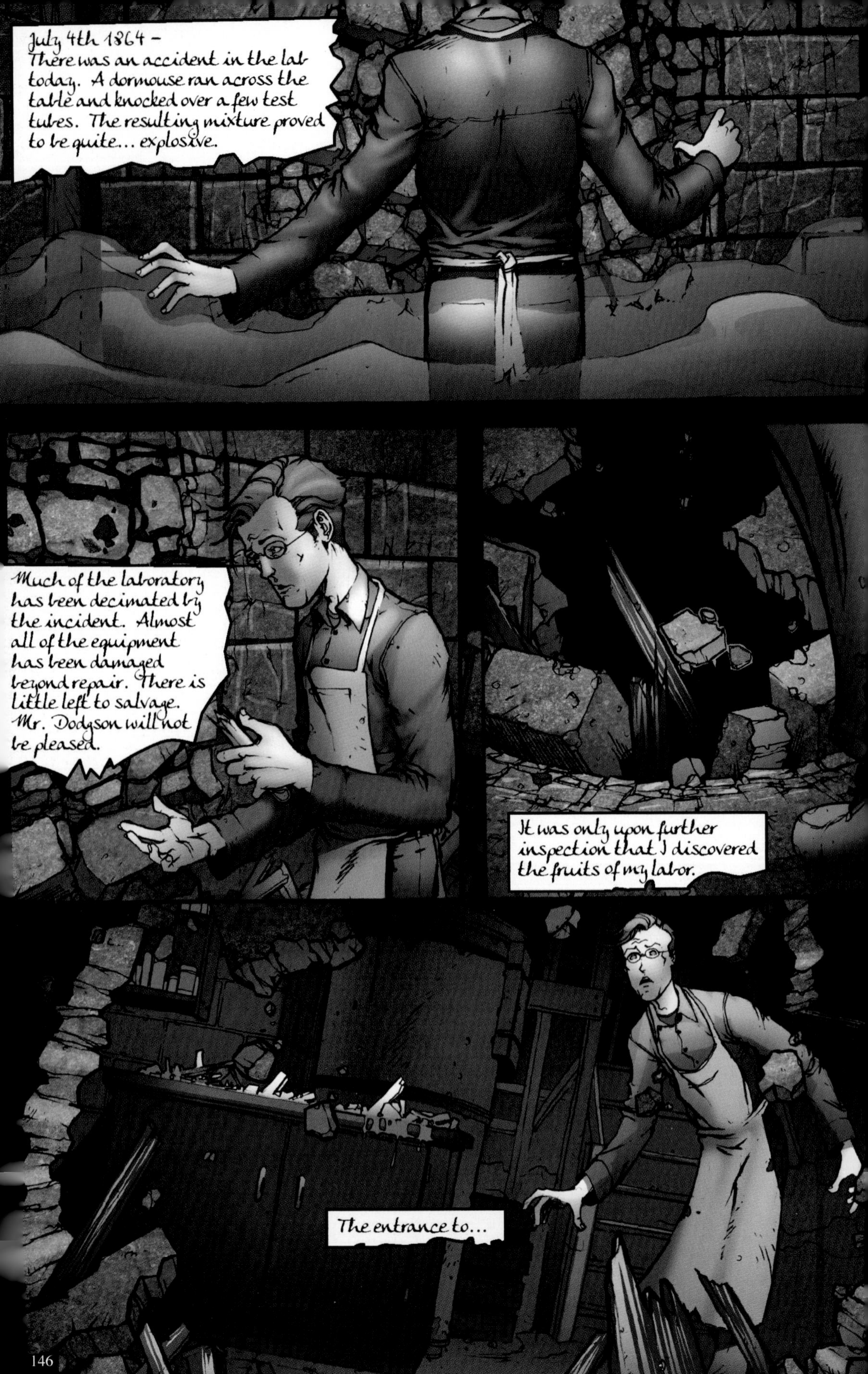
July 4th 1864 –
There was an accident in the lab today. A dormouse ran across the table and knocked over a few test tubes. The resulting mixture proved to be quite... explosive.
Much of the laboratory has been decimated by the incident. Almost all of the equipment has been damaged beyond repair. There is little left to salvage. Mr. Dodgson will not be pleased.
It was only upon further inspection that I discovered the fruits of my labor.
The entrance to...

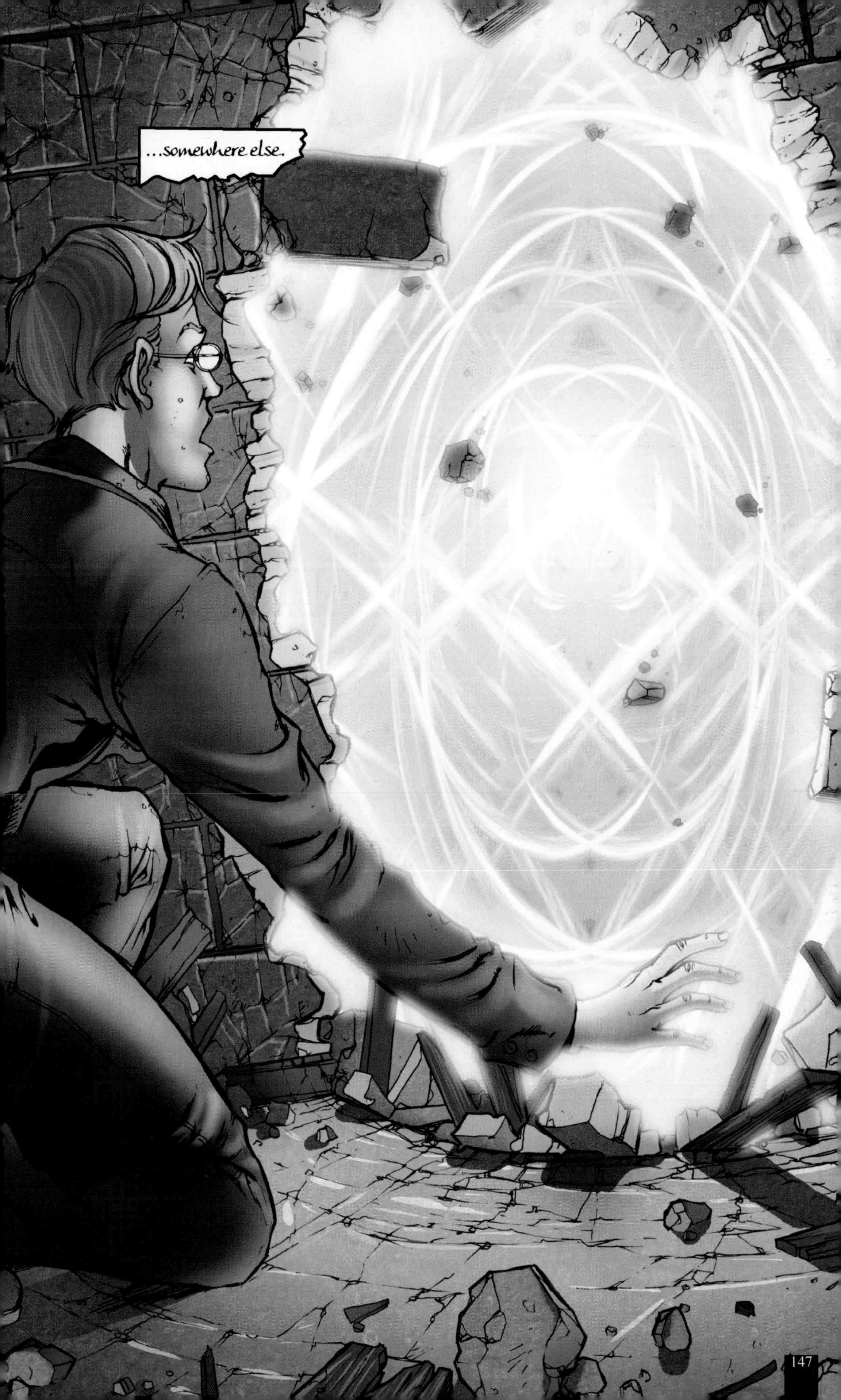
...somewhere else.

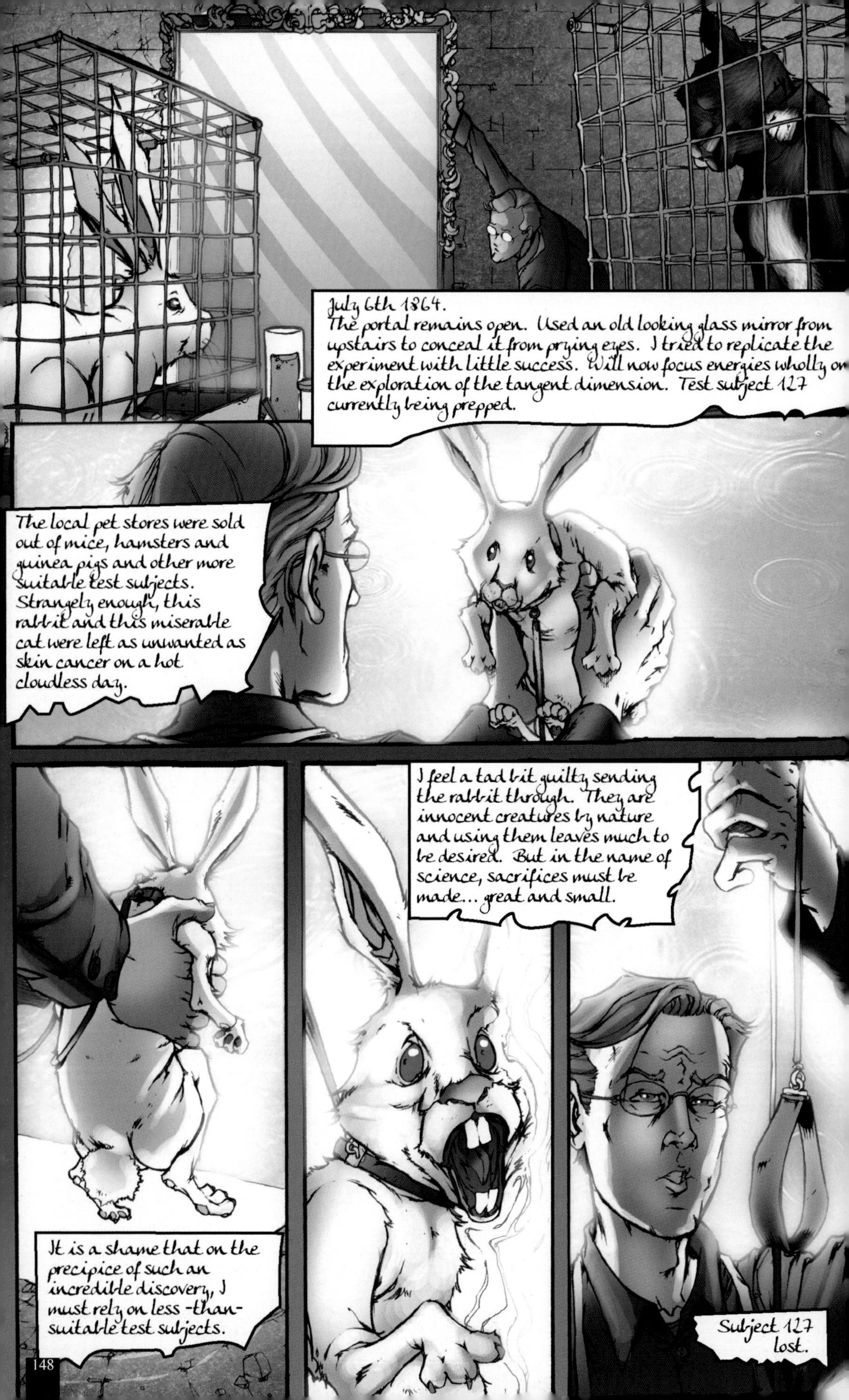
July 6th 1864.
The portal remains open. Used an old looking glass mirror from upstairs to conceal it from prying eyes. I tried to replicate the experiment with little success. Will now focus energies wholly on the exploration of the tangent dimension. Test subject 127 currently being prepped.
The local pet stores were sold out of mice, hamsters and guinea pigs and other more suitable test subjects. Strangely enough, this rabbit and this miserable cat were left as unwanted as skin cancer on a hot cloudless day.
It is a shame that on the precipice of such an incredible discovery, I must rely on less -than-suitable test subjects.
I feel a tad bit guilty sending the rabbit through. They are innocent creatures by nature and using them leaves much to be desired. But in the name of science, sacrifices must be made... great and small.
Subject 127 lost.

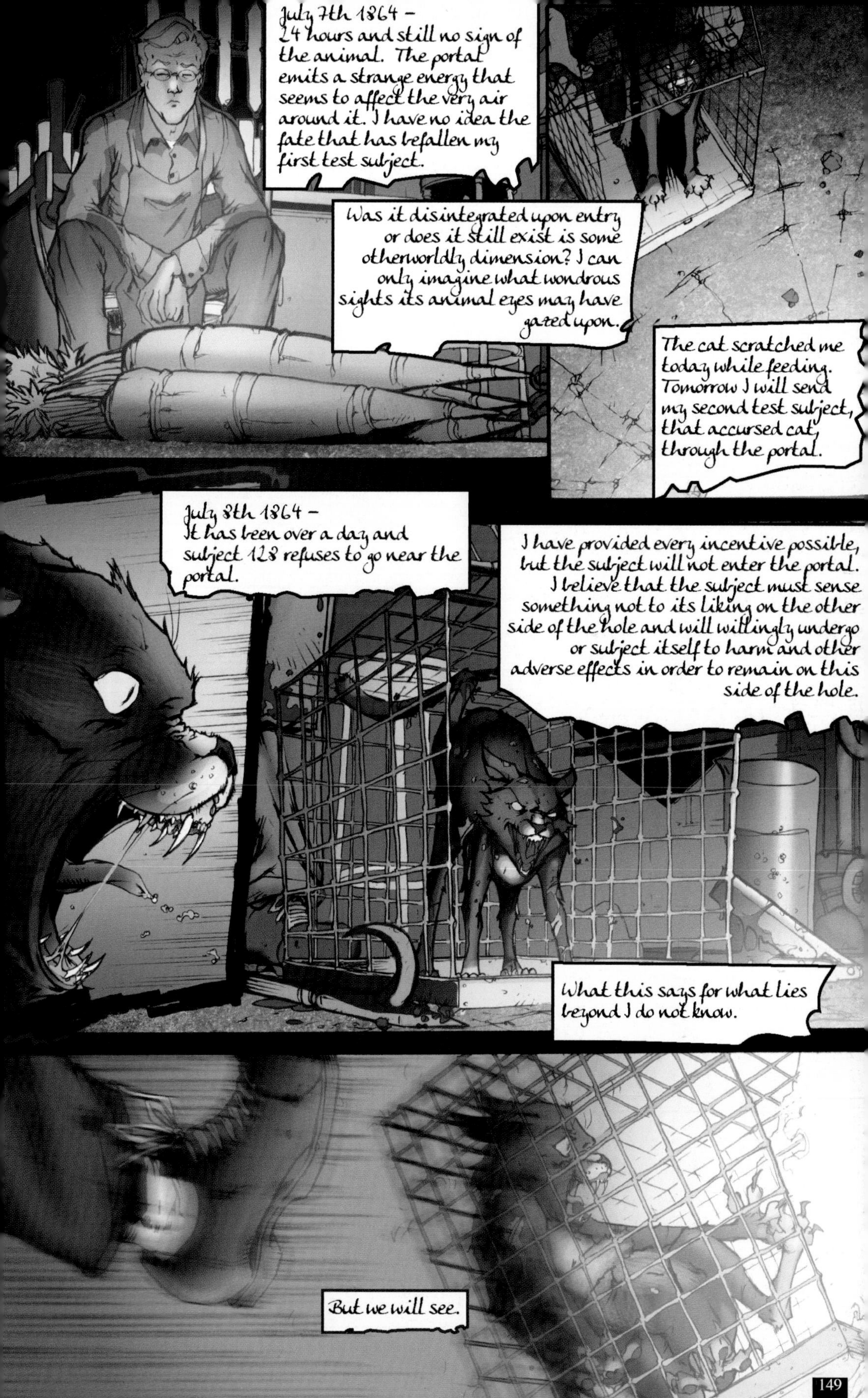
July 7th 1864 – 24 hours and still no sign of the animal. The portal emits a strange energy that seems to affect the very air around it. I have no idea the fate that has befallen my first test subject.
Was it disintegrated upon entry or does it still exist is some otherworldly dimension? I can only imagine what wondrous sights its animal eyes may have gazed upon.
The cat scratched me today while feeding. Tomorrow I will send my second test subject, that accursed cat, through the portal.
July 8th 1864 – It has been over a day and subject 128 refuses to go near the portal.
I have provided every incentive possible, but the subject will not enter the portal. I believe that the subject must sense something not to its liking on the other side of the hole and will willingly undergo or subject itself to harm and other adverse effects in order to remain on this side of the hole.
What this says for what lies beyond I do not know.
But we will see.

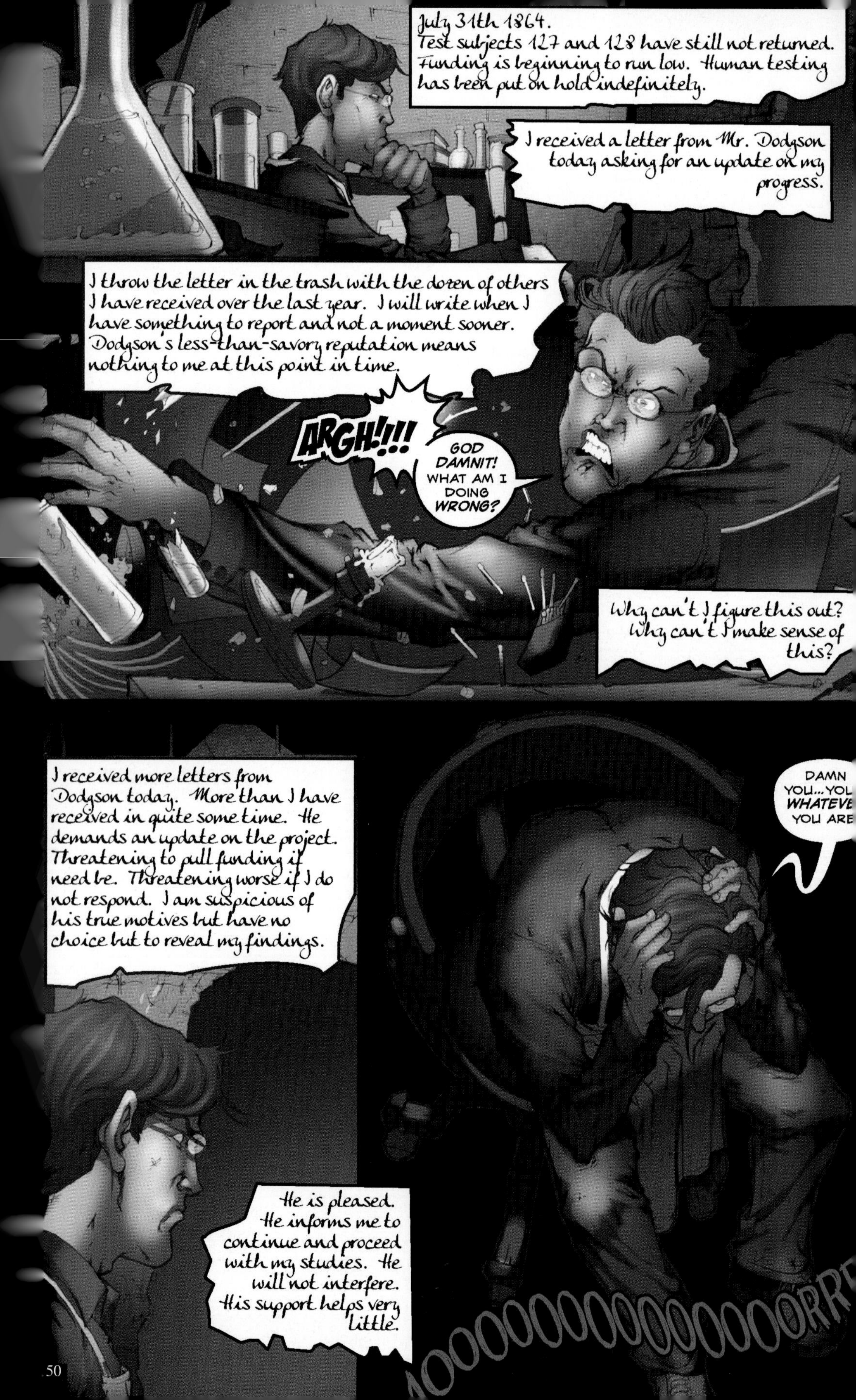
July 31th 1864.
Test subjects 127 and 128 have still not returned. Funding is beginning to run low. Human testing has been put on hold indefinitely.
I received a letter from Mr. Dodgson today asking for an update on my progress.
I throw the letter in the trash with the dozen of others I have received over the last year. I will write when I have something to report and not a moment sooner. Dodgson's less-than-savory reputation means nothing to me at this point in time.
ARGH!!!!
GOD DAMNIT! WHAT AM I DOING WRONG?
Why can't I figure this out? Why can't I make sense of this?
I received more letters from Dodgson today. More than I have received in quite some time. He demands an update on the project. Threatening to pull funding if need be. Threatening worse if I do not respond. I am suspicious of his true motives but have no choice but to reveal my findings.
DAMN YOU...YOU WHATEVE YOU ARE
He is pleased. He informs me to continue and proceed with my studies. He will not interfere. His support helps very little.
OOOOOOOOOOOOOOOOOOORRR

...rhaps the answer ...es in a dream.

Nine, eight, seven...

DAD! DAD!

WAKE UP!

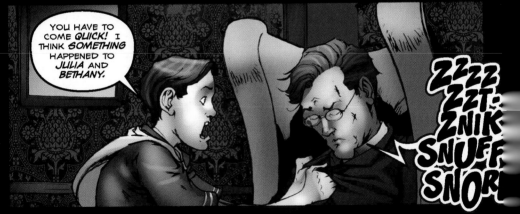

YOU HAVE TO COME *QUICK!* I THINK *SOMETHING* HAPPENED TO *JULIA* AND *BETHANY.*

ZZZZ ZZT. ZNIK SNUFF SNOR

DAD...

ARGH.

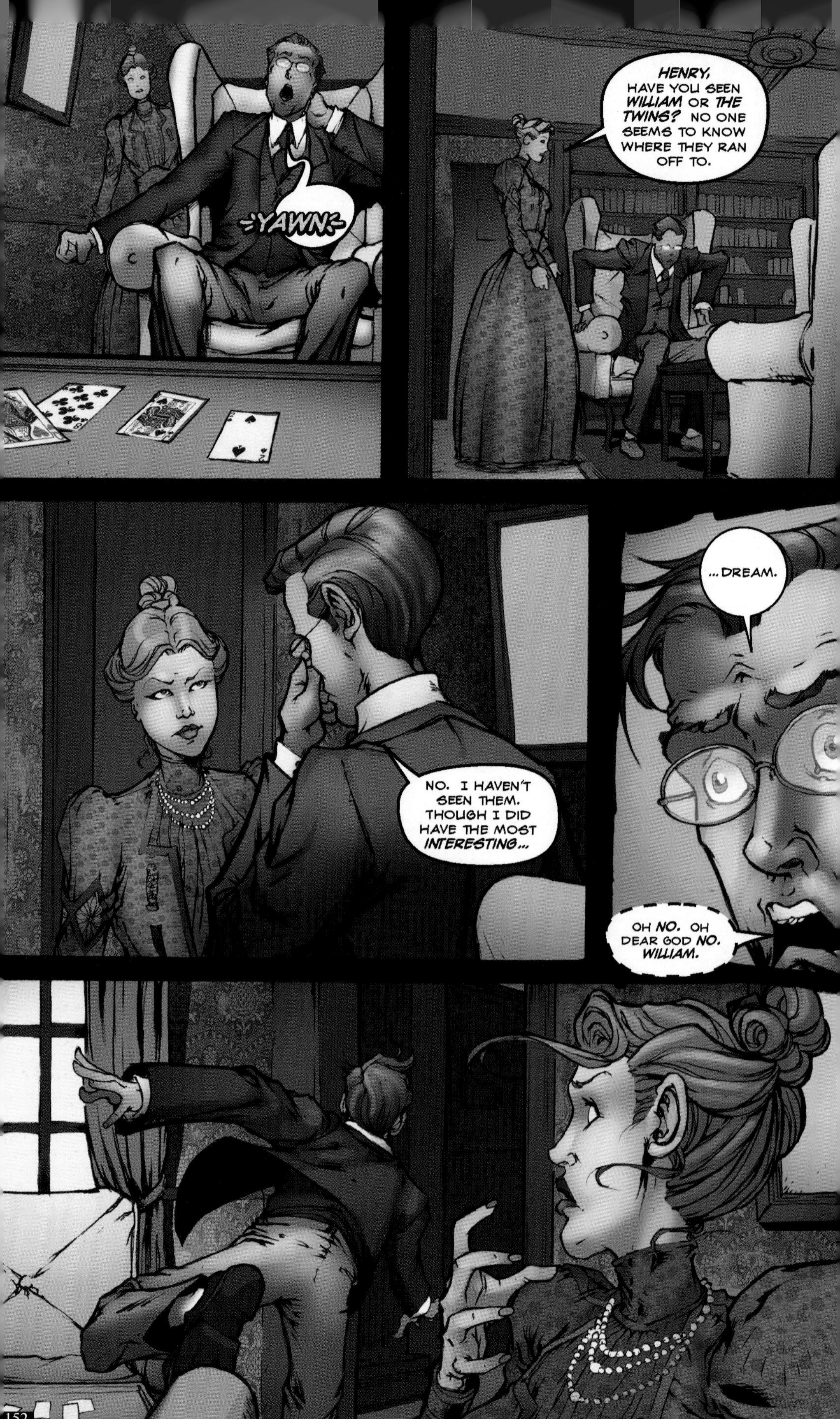

YAWN
HENRY, HAVE YOU SEEN WILLIAM OR THE TWINS? NO ONE SEEMS TO KNOW WHERE THEY RAN OFF TO.
NO. I HAVEN'T SEEN THEM. THOUGH I DID HAVE THE MOST INTERESTING...
...DREAM.
OH NO. OH DEAR GOD NO. WILLIAM.

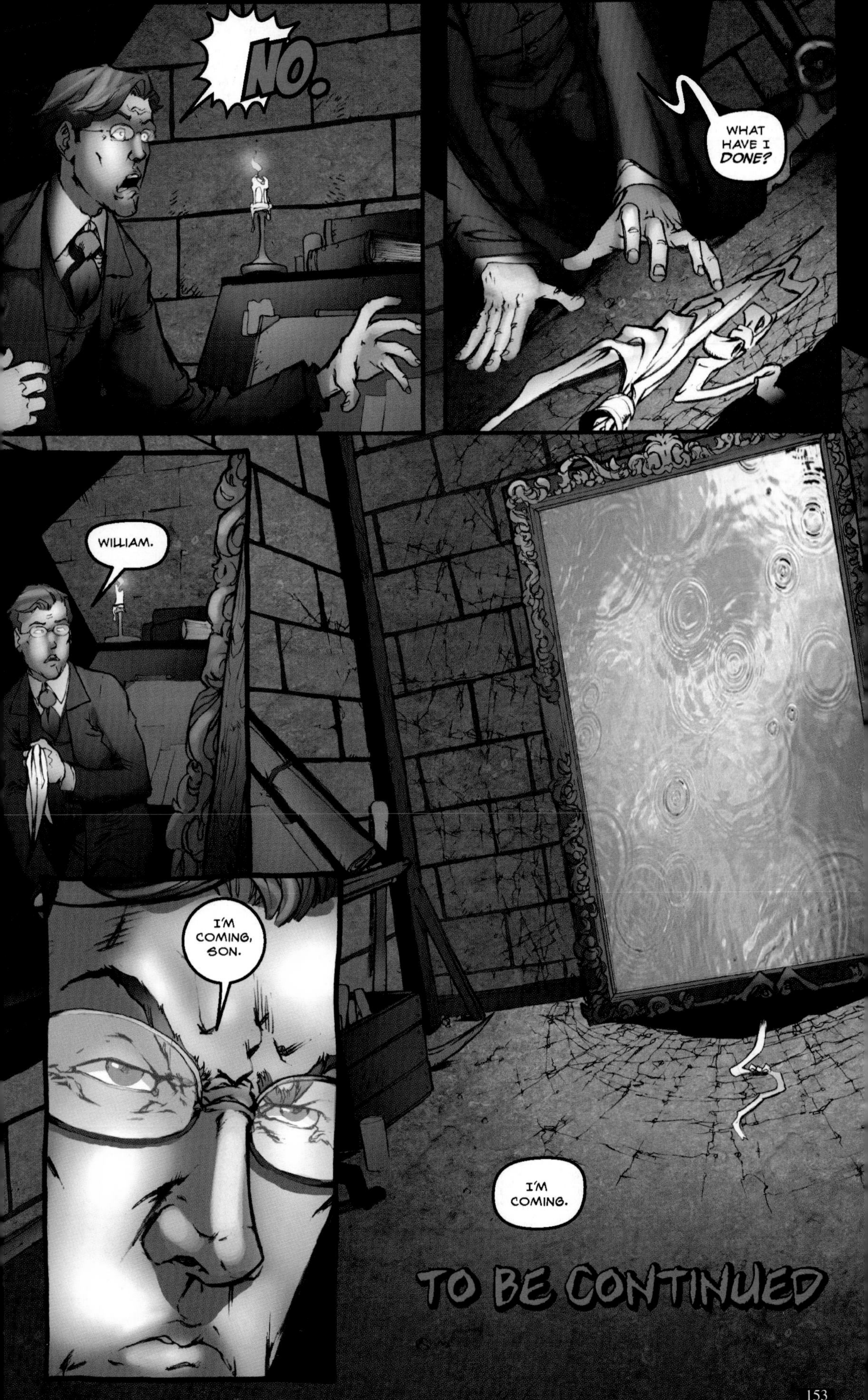
NO.
WHAT HAVE I DONE?
WILLIAM.
I'M COMING, SON.
I'M COMING.
TO BE CONTINUED

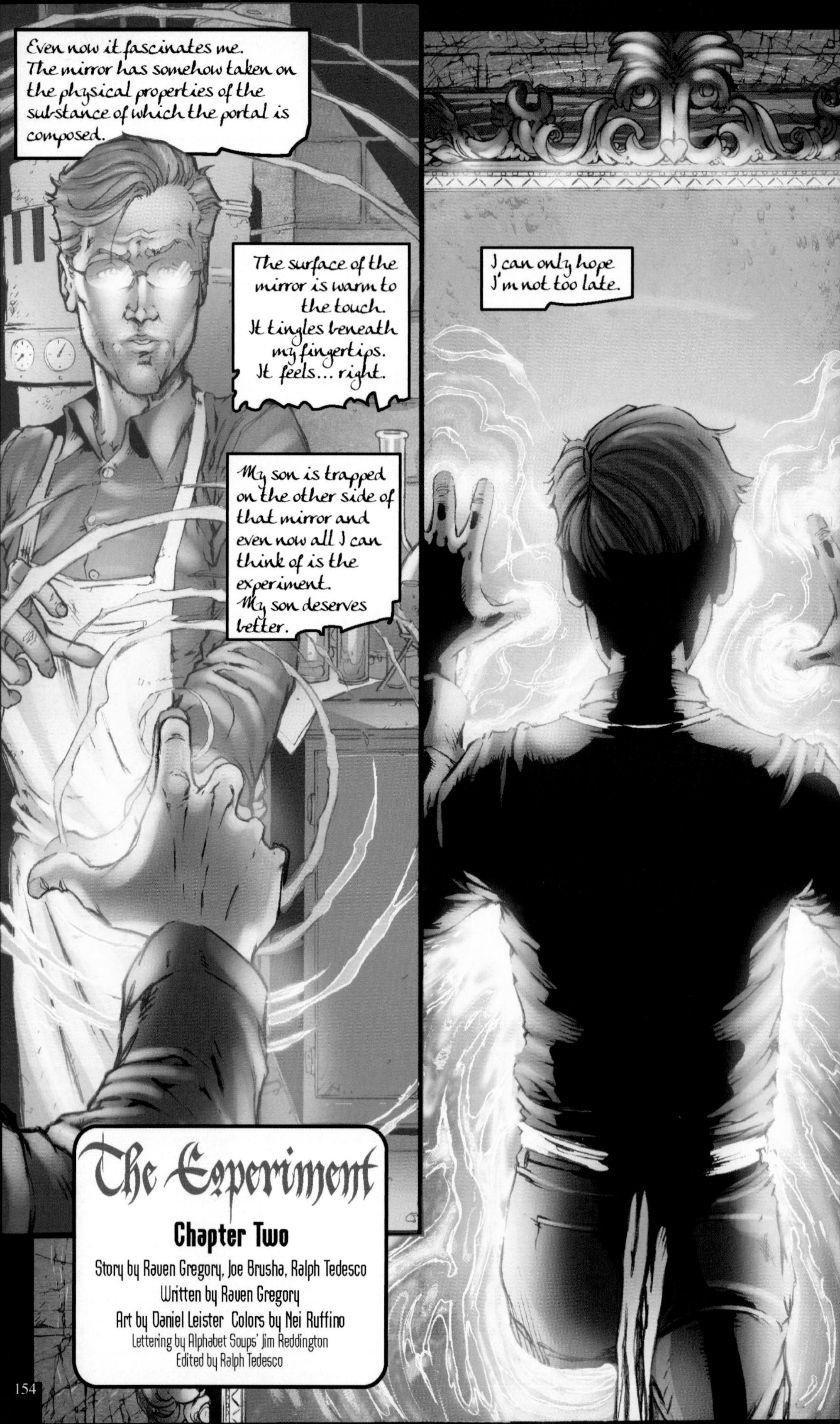
Even now it fascinates me. The mirror has somehow taken on the physical properties of the substance of which the portal is composed.
The surface of the mirror is warm to the touch. It tingles beneath my fingertips. It feels... right.
My son is trapped on the other side of that mirror and even now all I can think of is the experiment. My son deserves better.
I can only hope I'm not too late.
The Experiment
Chapter Two
Story by Raven Gregory, Joe Brusha, Ralph Tedesco
Written by Raven Gregory
Art by Daniel Leister Colors by Nei Ruffino
Lettering by Alphabet Soups' Jim Reddington
Edited by Ralph Tedesco

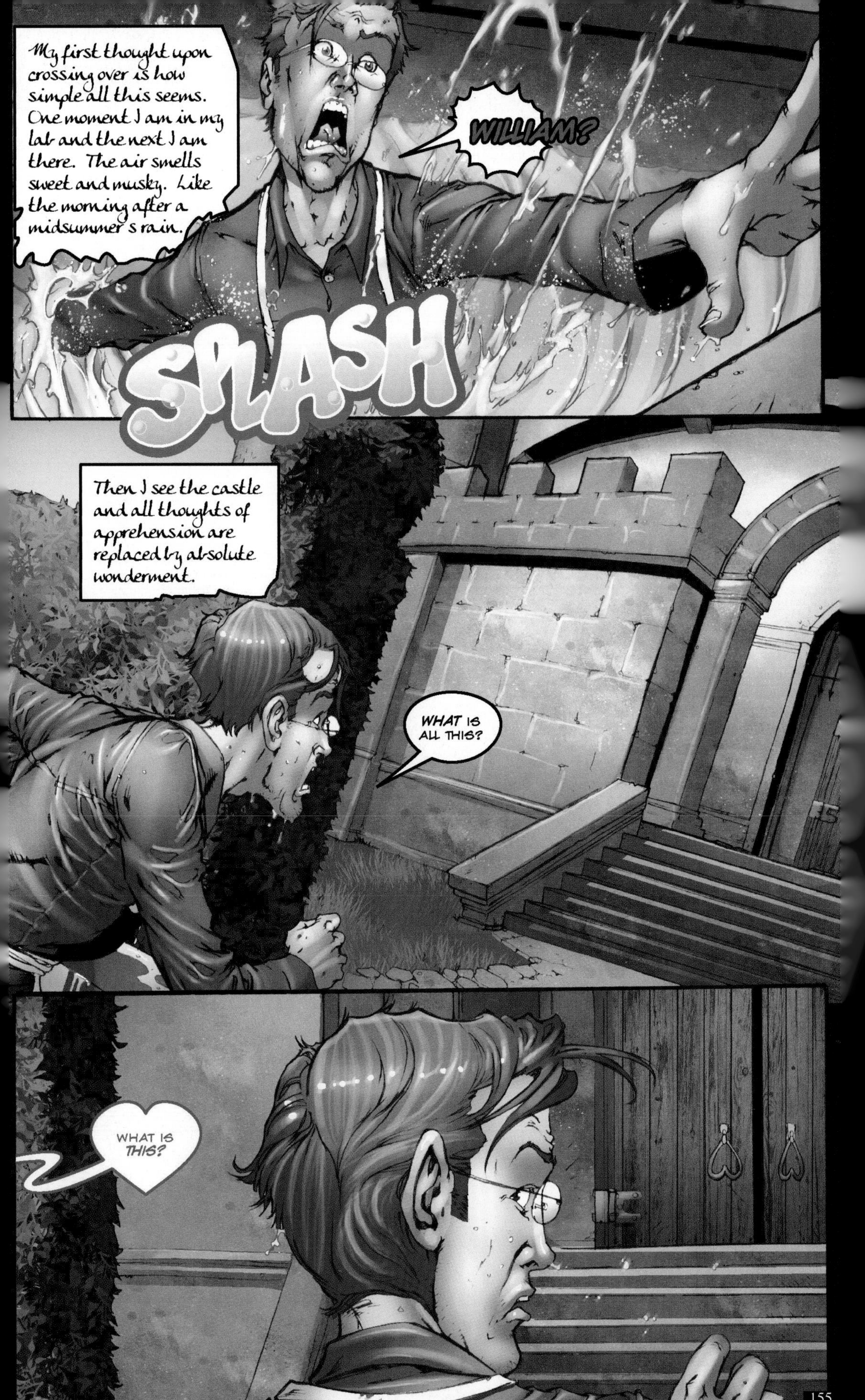
My first thought upon crossing over is how simple all this seems. One moment I am in my lab and the next I am there. The air smells sweet and musky. Like the morning after a midsummer's rain.
WILLIAM?
SPLASH
Then I see the castle and all thoughts of apprehension are replaced by absolute wonderment.
WHAT IS ALL THIS?
WHAT IS THIS?

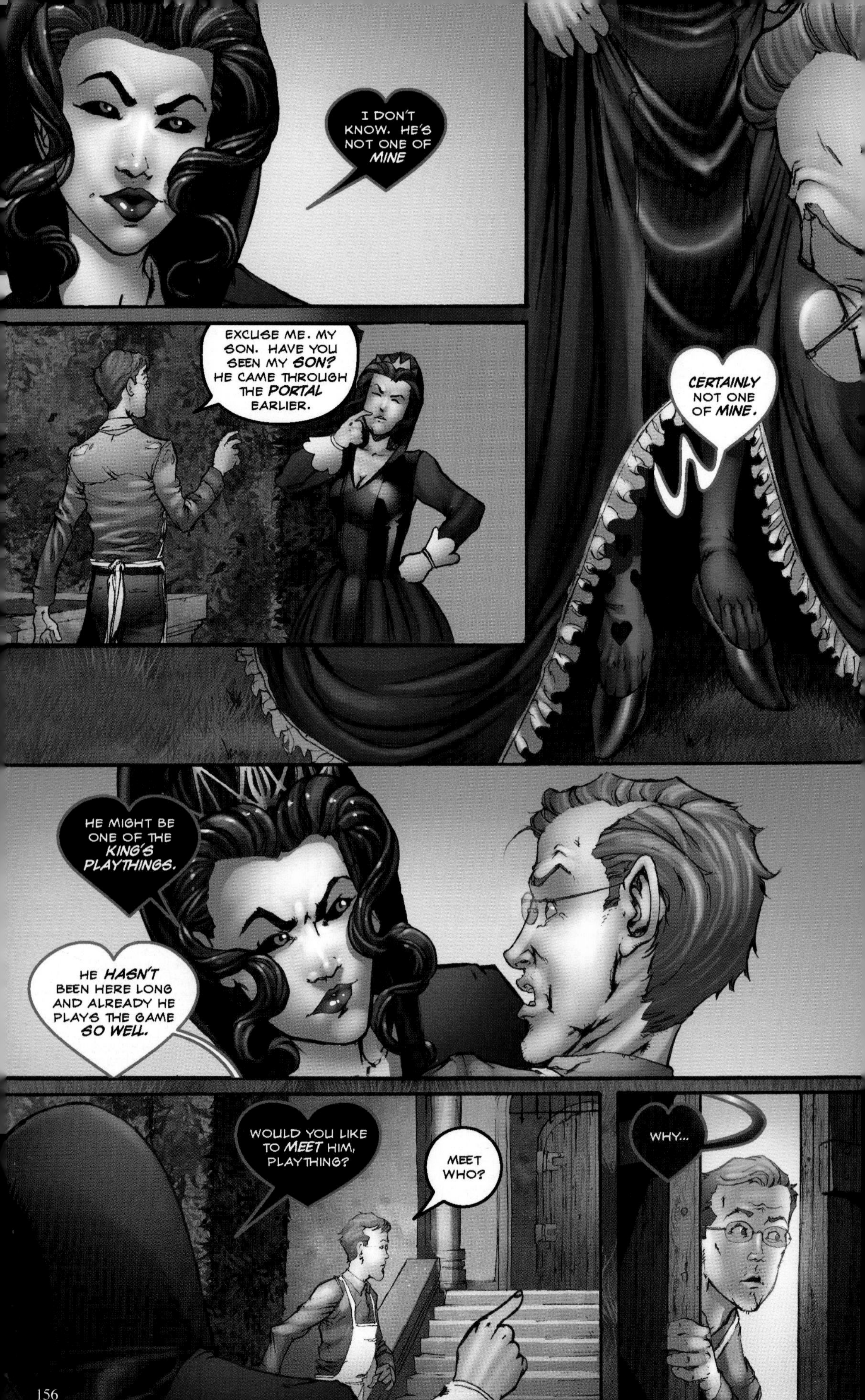
I DON'T KNOW. HE'S NOT ONE OF *MINE*
EXCUSE ME. MY SON. HAVE YOU SEEN MY *SON?* HE CAME THROUGH THE *PORTAL* EARLIER.
CERTAINLY NOT ONE OF *MINE*.
HE MIGHT BE ONE OF THE *KING'S PLAYTHINGS*.
HE *HASN'T* BEEN HERE LONG AND ALREADY HE PLAYS THE GAME *SO WELL*.
WOULD YOU LIKE TO *MEET* HIM, PLAYTHING?
MEET WHO?
WHY...

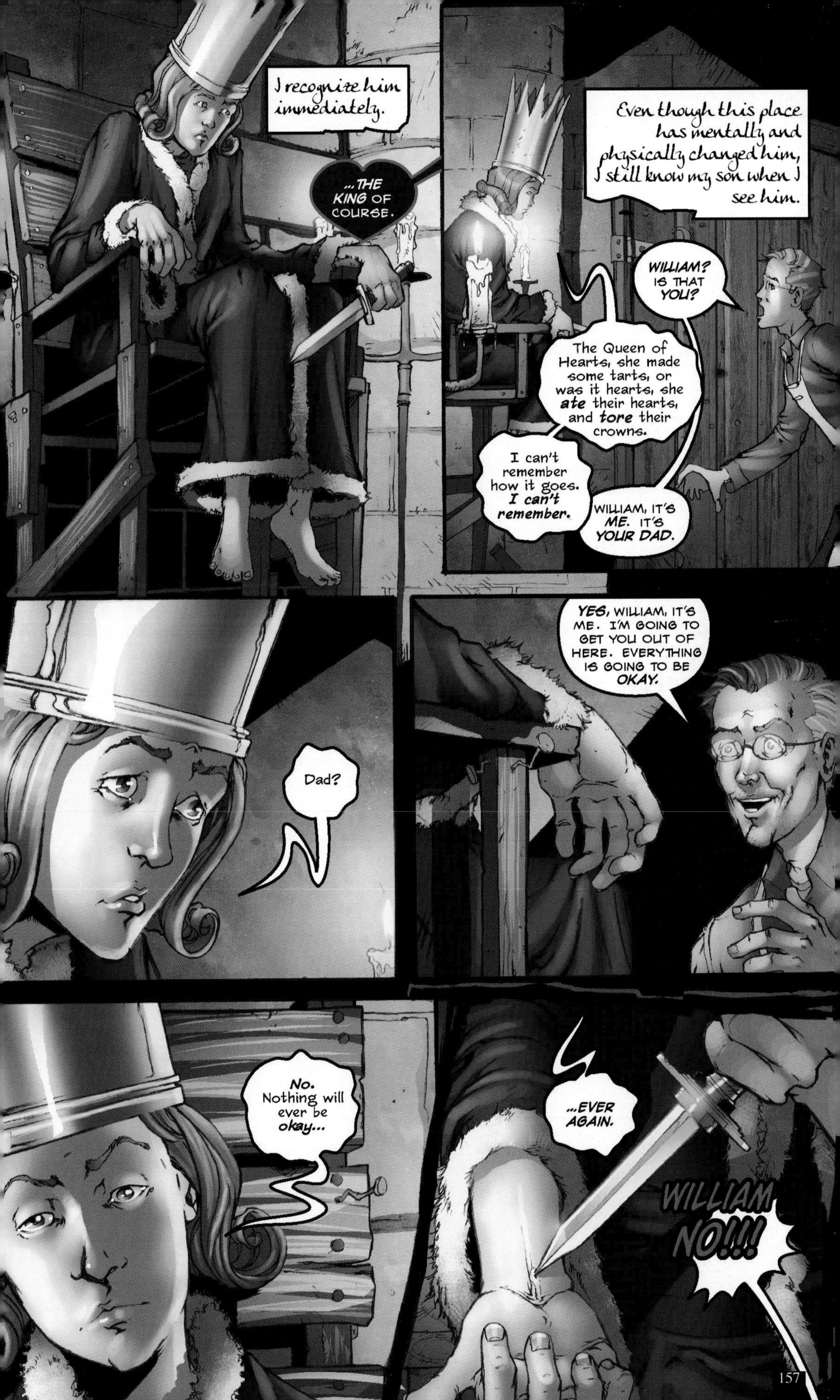

I recognize him immediately.
...THE KING OF COURSE.
Even though this place has mentally and physically changed him, I still know my son when I see him.
WILLIAM? IS THAT YOU?
The Queen of Hearts, she made some tarts, or was it hearts, she ate their hearts, and tore their crowns.
I can't remember how it goes. I can't remember.
WILLIAM, IT'S ME. IT'S YOUR DAD.
Dad?
YES, WILLIAM, IT'S ME. I'M GOING TO GET YOU OUT OF HERE. EVERYTHING IS GOING TO BE OKAY.
No. Nothing will ever be okay...
...EVER AGAIN.
WILLIAM NO!!!

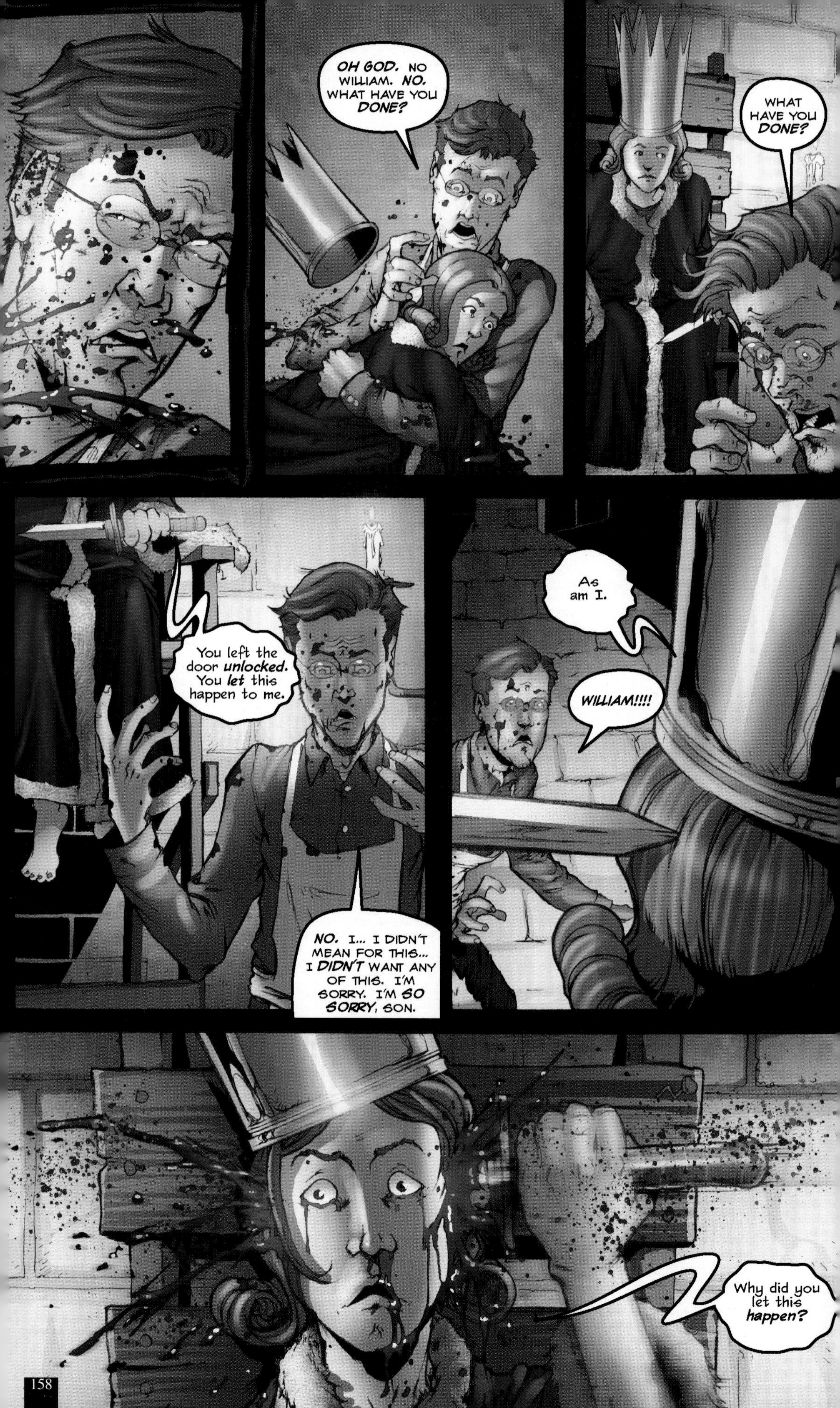
OH GOD. NO WILLIAM. NO. WHAT HAVE YOU DONE?
WHAT HAVE YOU DONE?
You left the door unlocked. You let this happen to me.
NO. I... I DIDN'T MEAN FOR THIS... I DIDN'T WANT ANY OF THIS. I'M SORRY. I'M SO SORRY, SON.
As am I.
WILLIAM!!!!
Why did you let this happen?

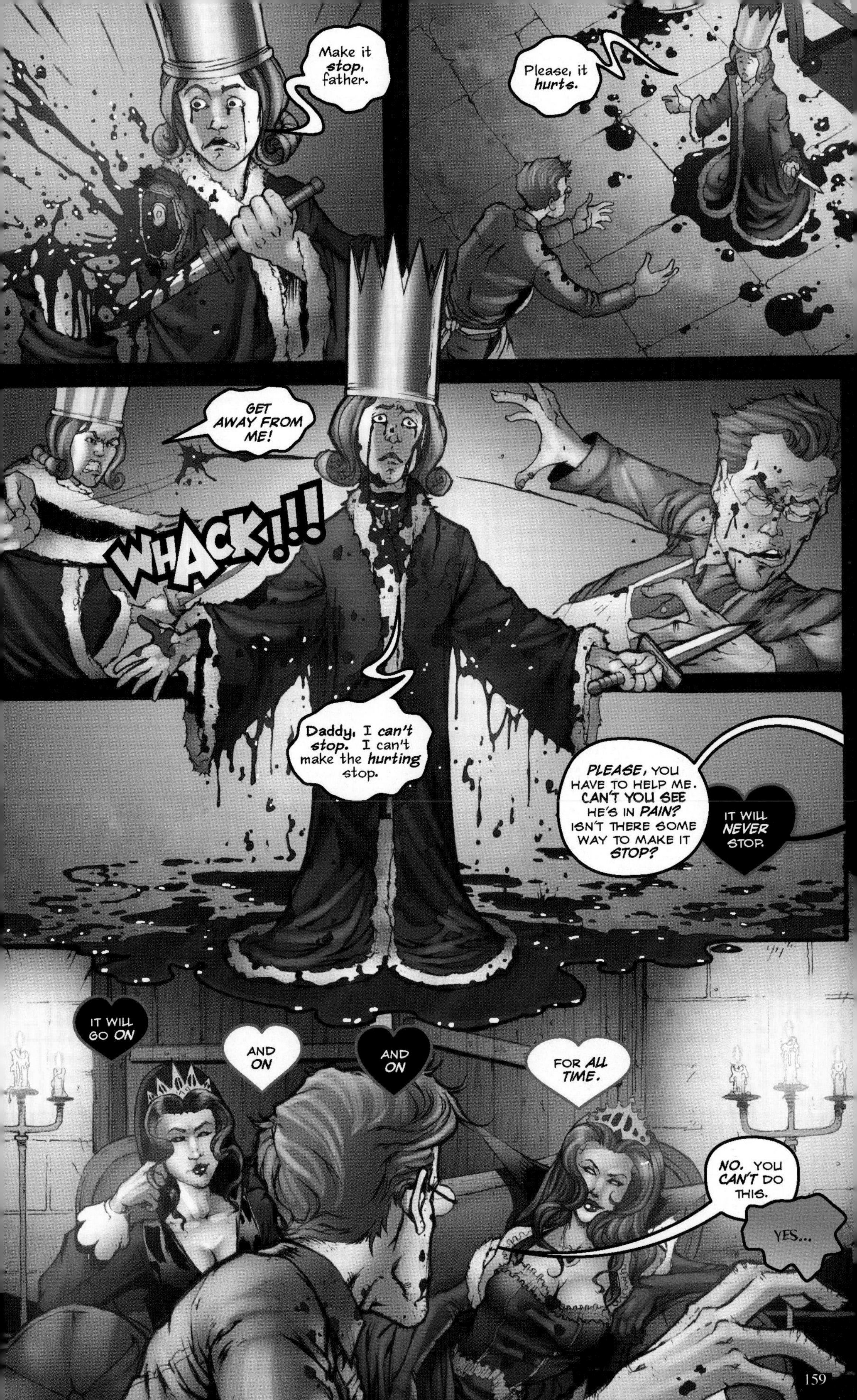

Make it stop, father.
Please, it hurts.
GET AWAY FROM ME!
WHACK!!!
Daddy, I can't stop. I can't make the hurting stop.
PLEASE, YOU HAVE TO HELP ME. CAN'T YOU SEE HE'S IN PAIN? ISN'T THERE SOME WAY TO MAKE IT STOP?
IT WILL NEVER STOP.
IT WILL GO ON
AND ON
AND ON
FOR ALL TIME.
NO. YOU CAN'T DO THIS.
YES...

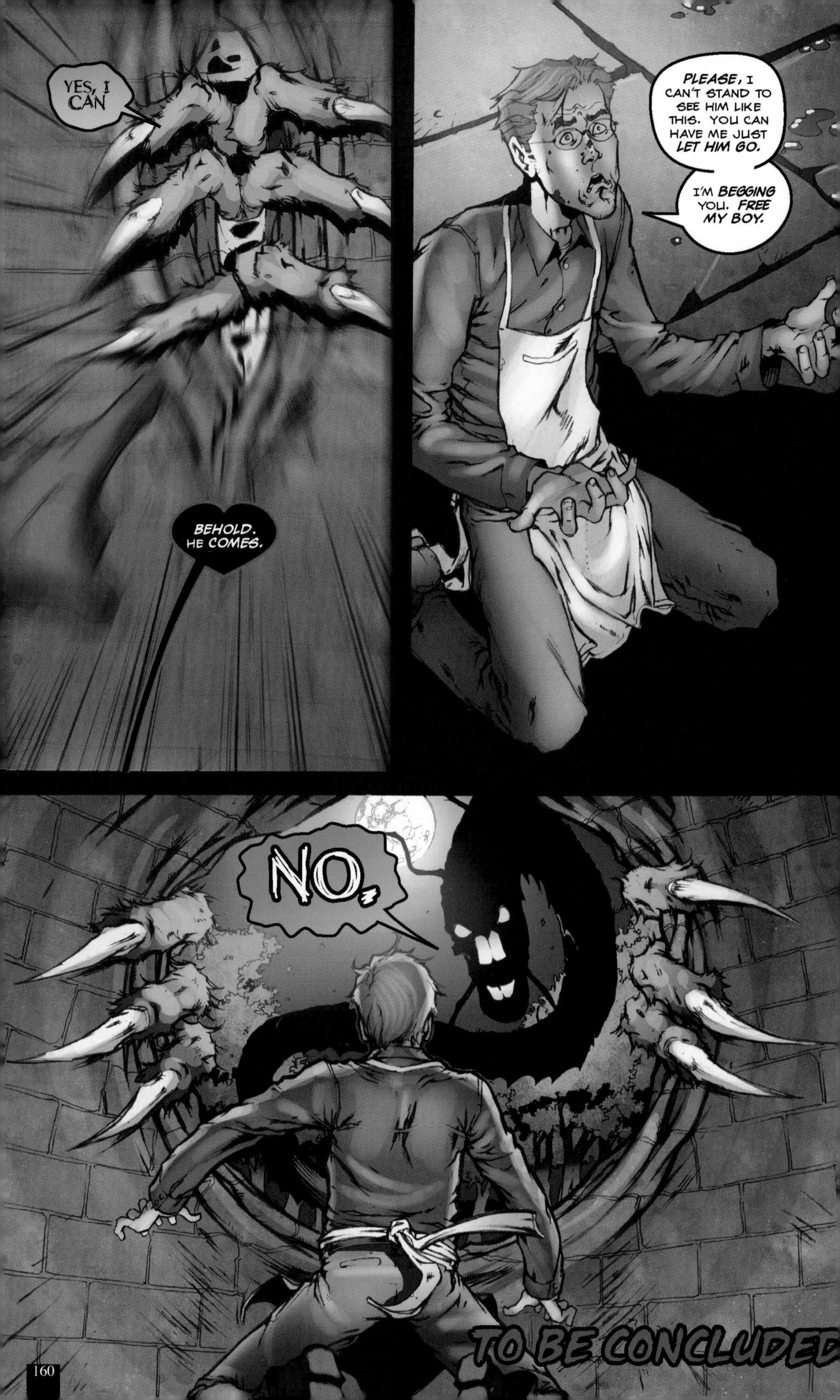
YES, I CAN
BEHOLD. HE COMES.
PLEASE, I CAN'T STAND TO SEE HIM LIKE THIS. YOU CAN HAVE ME JUST LET HIM GO.
I'M BEGGING YOU. FREE MY BOY.
NO,
TO BE CONCLUDED

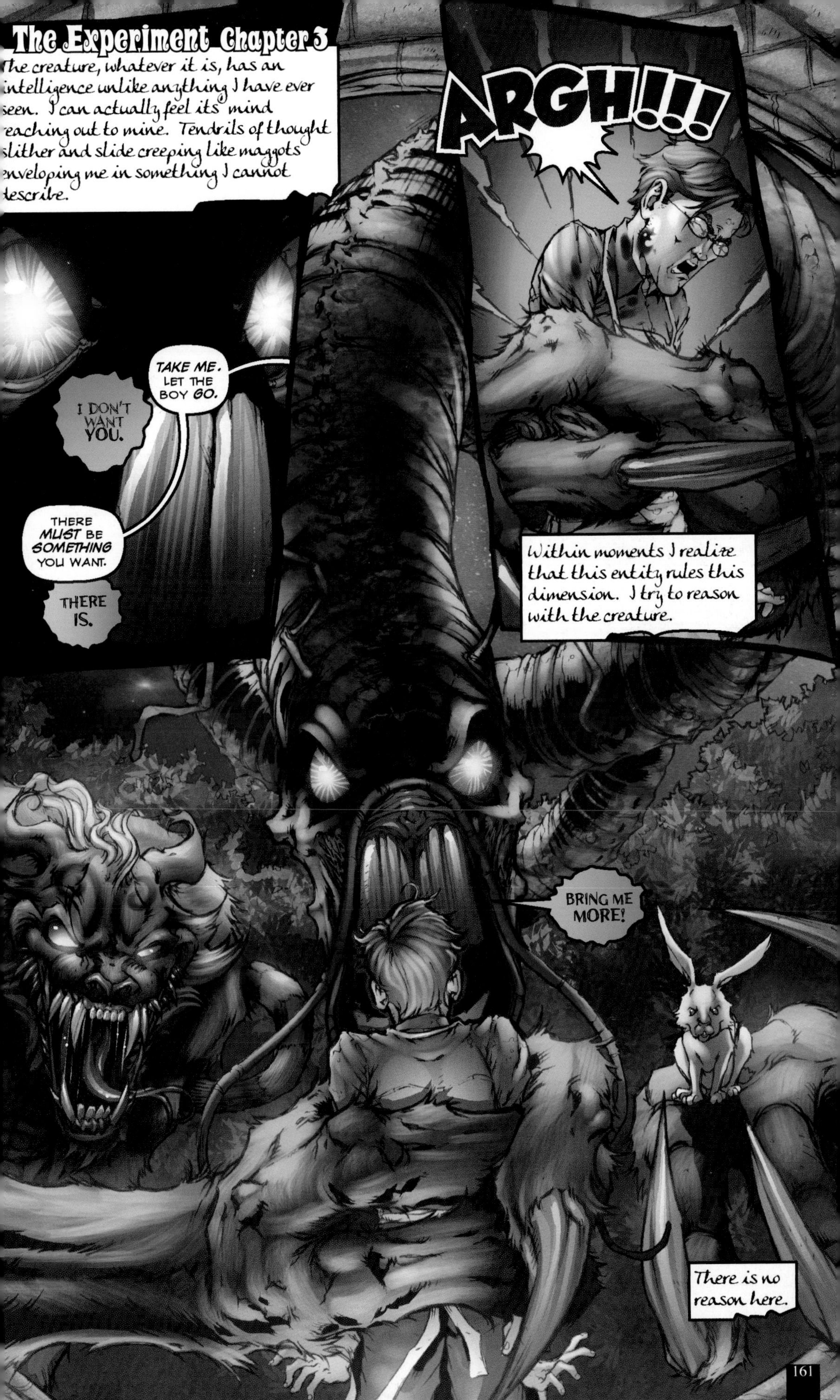
The Experiment Chapter 3
The creature, whatever it is, has an intelligence unlike anything I have ever seen. I can actually feel its mind reaching out to mine. Tendrils of thought slither and slide creeping like maggots enveloping me in something I cannot describe.
ARGH!!!
Within moments I realize that this entity rules this dimension. I try to reason with the creature.
TAKE ME. LET THE BOY GO.
I DON'T WANT YOU.
THERE MUST BE SOMETHING YOU WANT.
THERE IS.
BRING ME MORE!
There is no reason here.

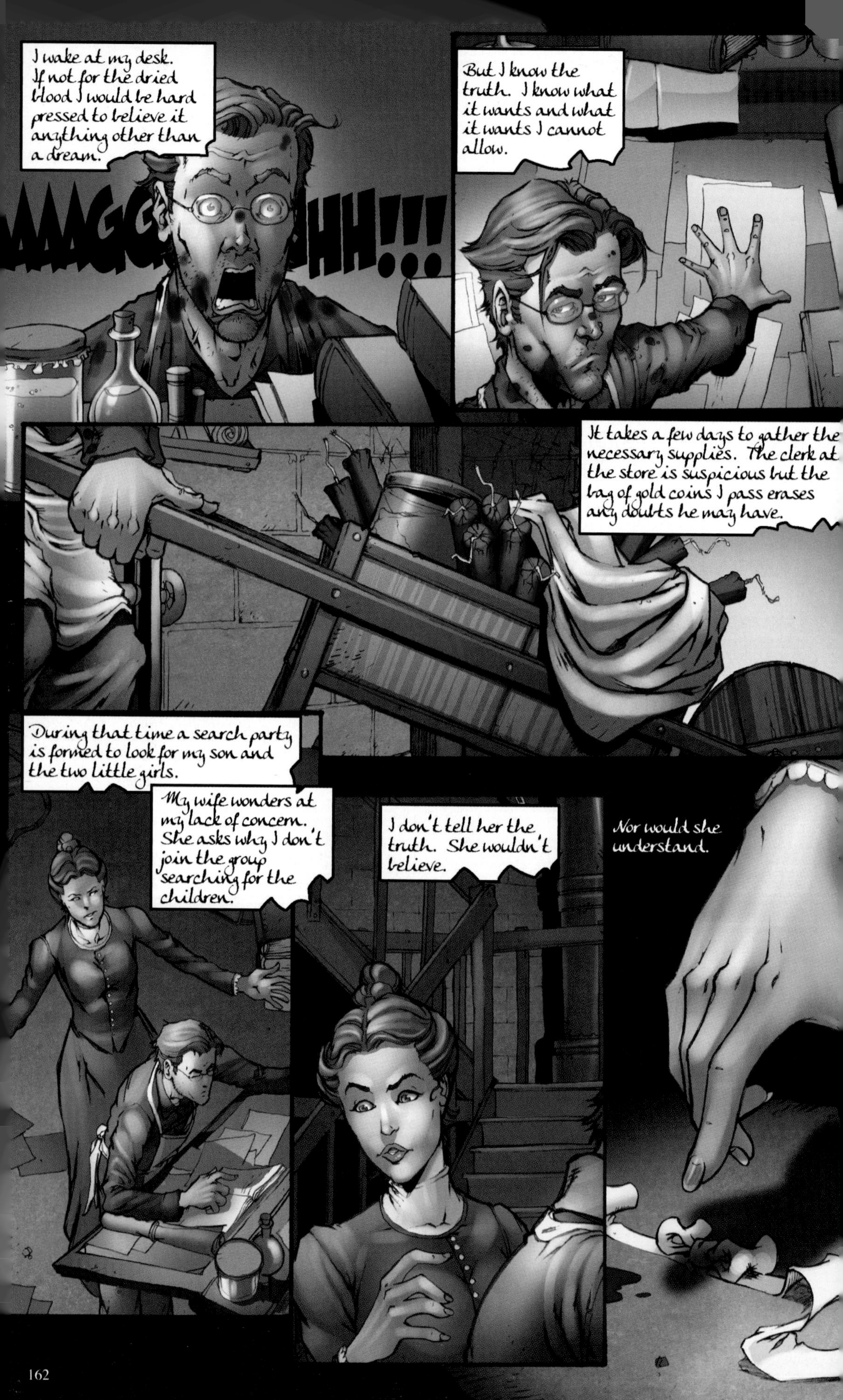
I wake at my desk. If not for the dried blood I would be hard pressed to believe it anything other than a dream.
AAAAGG...HH!!!
But I know the truth. I know what it wants and what it wants I cannot allow.
It takes a few days to gather the necessary supplies. The clerk at the store is suspicious but the bag of gold coins I pass erases any doubts he may have.
During that time a search party is formed to look for my son and the two little girls.
My wife wonders at my lack of concern. She asks why I don't join the group searching for the children.
I don't tell her the truth. She wouldn't believe.
Nor would she understand.

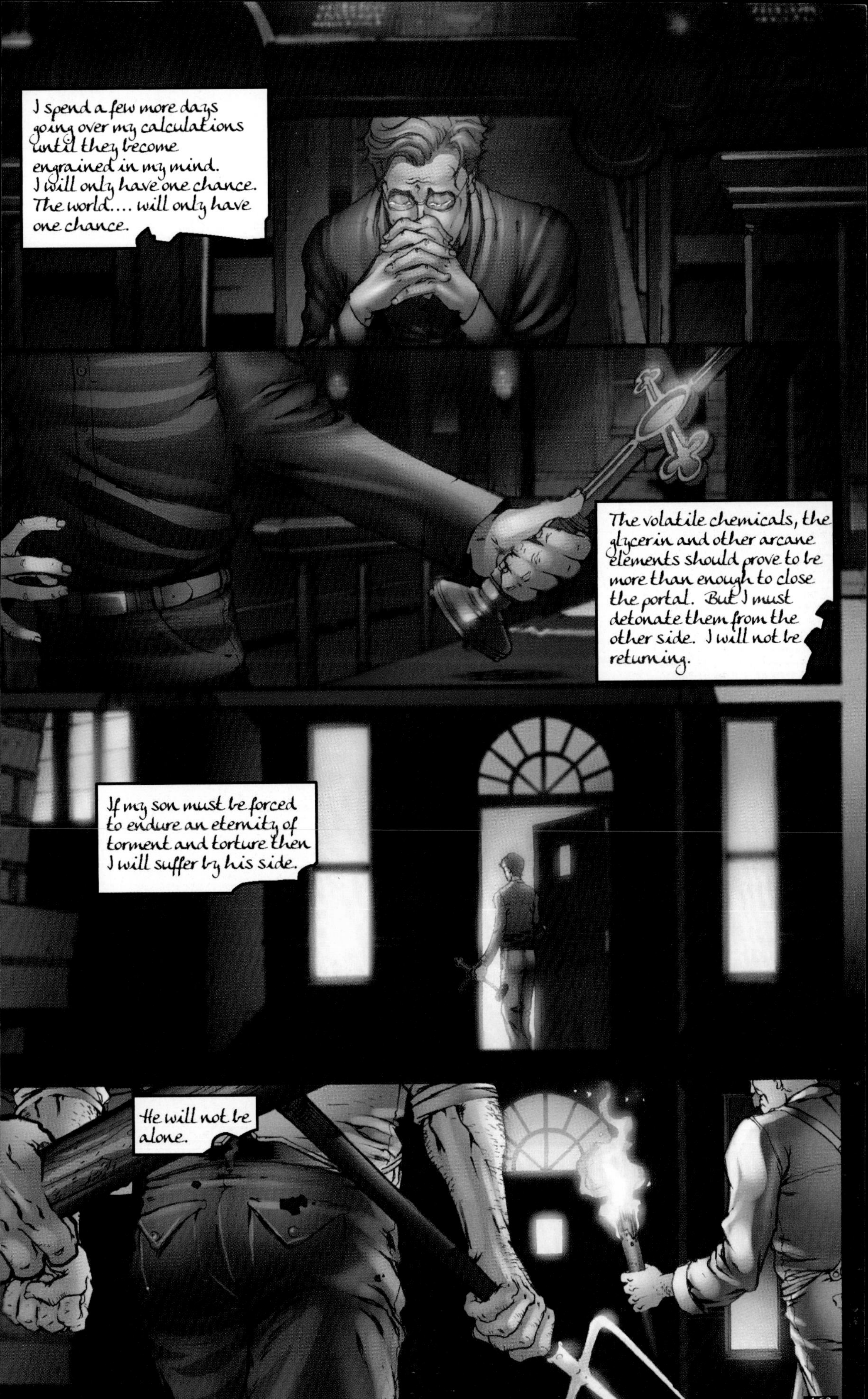
I spend a few more days going over my calculations until they become engrained in my mind. I will only have one chance. The world.... will only have one chance.
The volatile chemicals, the glycerin and other arcane elements should prove to be more than enough to close the portal. But I must detonate them from the other side. I will not be returning.
If my son must be forced to endure an eternity of torment and torture then I will suffer by his side.
He will not be alone.

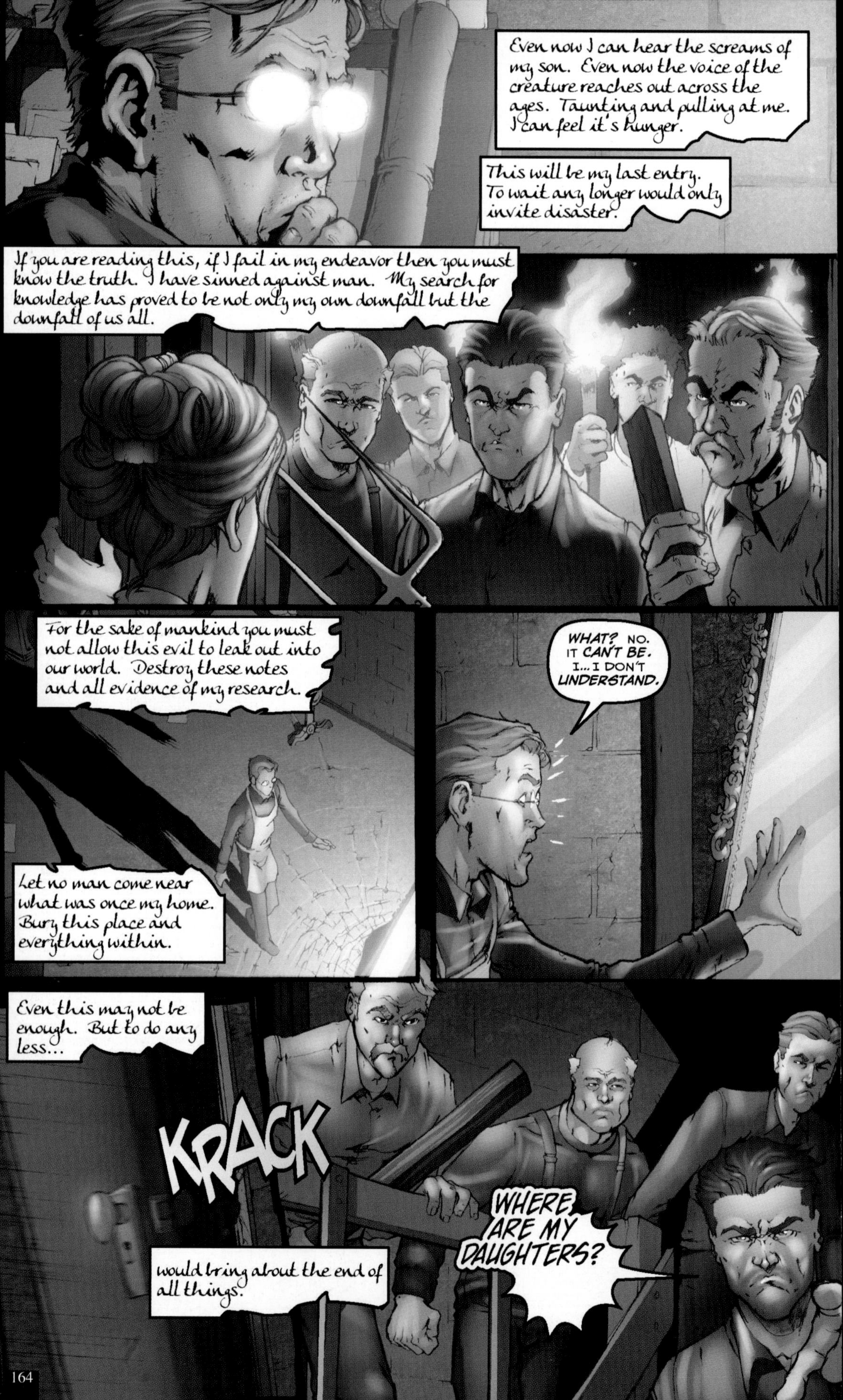
Even now I can hear the screams of my son. Even now the voice of the creature reaches out across the ages. Taunting and pulling at me. I can feel it's hunger.
This will be my last entry. To wait any longer would only invite disaster.
If you are reading this, if I fail in my endeavor then you must know the truth. I have sinned against man. My search for knowledge has proved to be not only my own downfall but the downfall of us all.
For the sake of mankind you must not allow this evil to leak out into our world. Destroy these notes and all evidence of my research.
Let no man come near what was once my home. Bury this place and everything within.
WHAT? NO. IT CAN'T BE. I... I DON'T UNDERSTAND.
Even this may not be enough. But to do any less...
KRACK
WHERE ARE MY DAUGHTERS?
would bring about the end of all things.

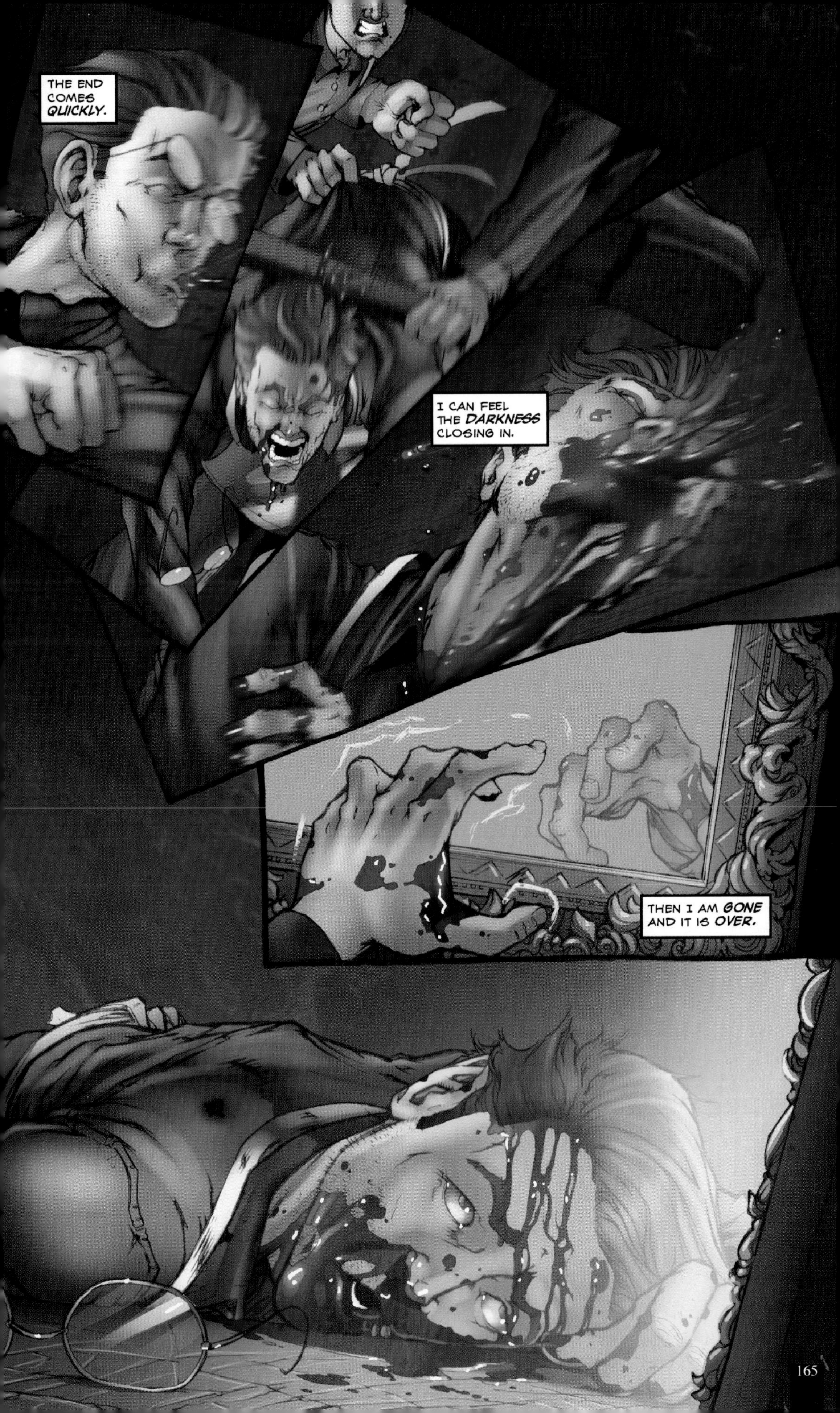
THE END COMES *QUICKLY*.
I CAN FEEL THE *DARKNESS* CLOSING IN.
THEN I AM *GONE* AND IT IS *OVER*.

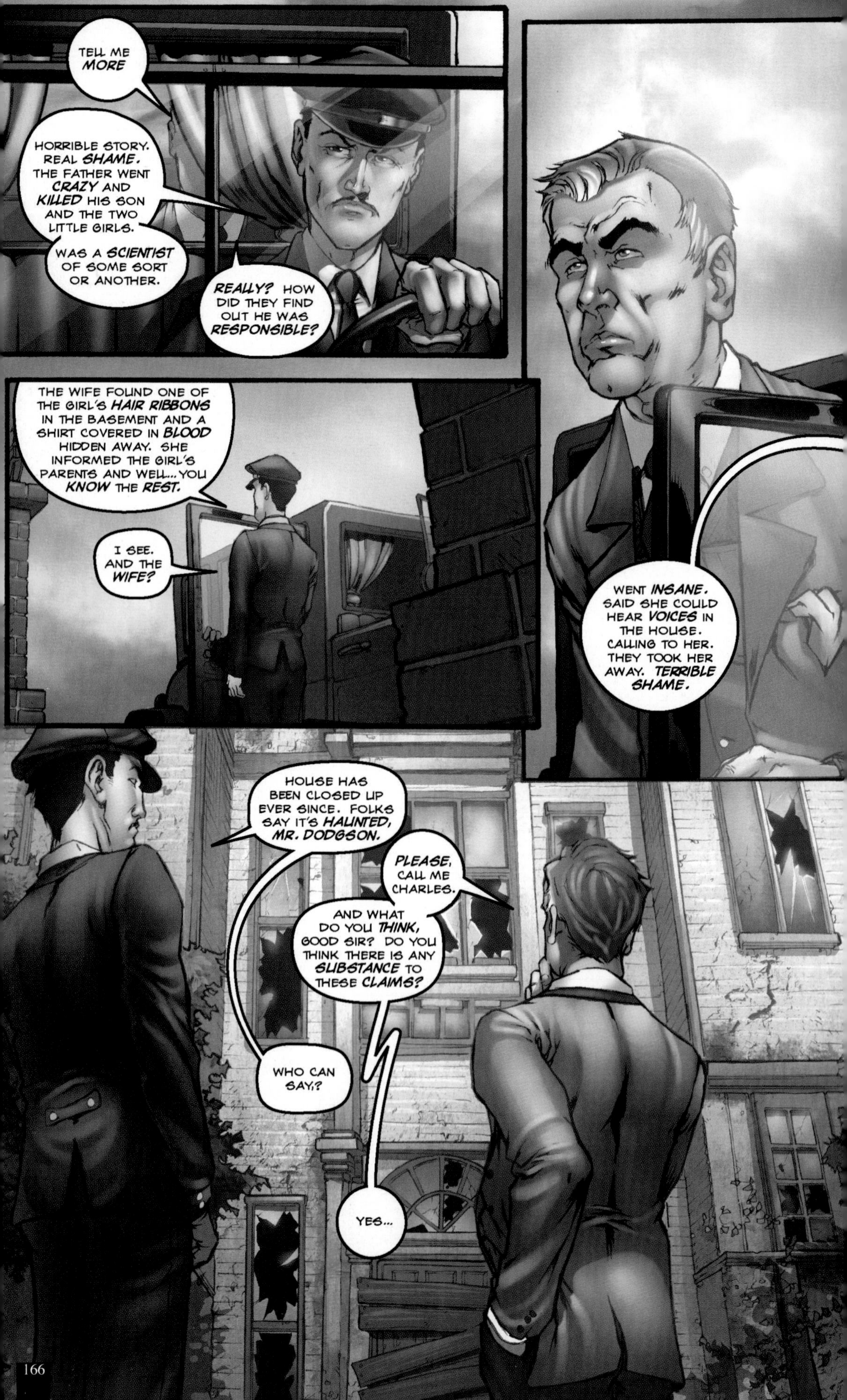
TELL ME MORE
HORRIBLE STORY. REAL SHAME. THE FATHER WENT CRAZY AND KILLED HIS SON AND THE TWO LITTLE GIRLS.
WAS A SCIENTIST OF SOME SORT OR ANOTHER.
REALLY? HOW DID THEY FIND OUT HE WAS RESPONSIBLE?
THE WIFE FOUND ONE OF THE GIRL'S HAIR RIBBONS IN THE BASEMENT AND A SHIRT COVERED IN BLOOD HIDDEN AWAY. SHE INFORMED THE GIRL'S PARENTS AND WELL... YOU KNOW THE REST.
I SEE. AND THE WIFE?
WENT INSANE. SAID SHE COULD HEAR VOICES IN THE HOUSE. CALLING TO HER. THEY TOOK HER AWAY. TERRIBLE SHAME.
HOUSE HAS BEEN CLOSED UP EVER SINCE. FOLKS SAY IT'S HAUNTED, MR. DODGSON.
PLEASE, CALL ME CHARLES.
AND WHAT DO YOU THINK, GOOD SIR? DO YOU THINK THERE IS ANY SUBSTANCE TO THESE CLAIMS?
WHO CAN SAY,?
YES...

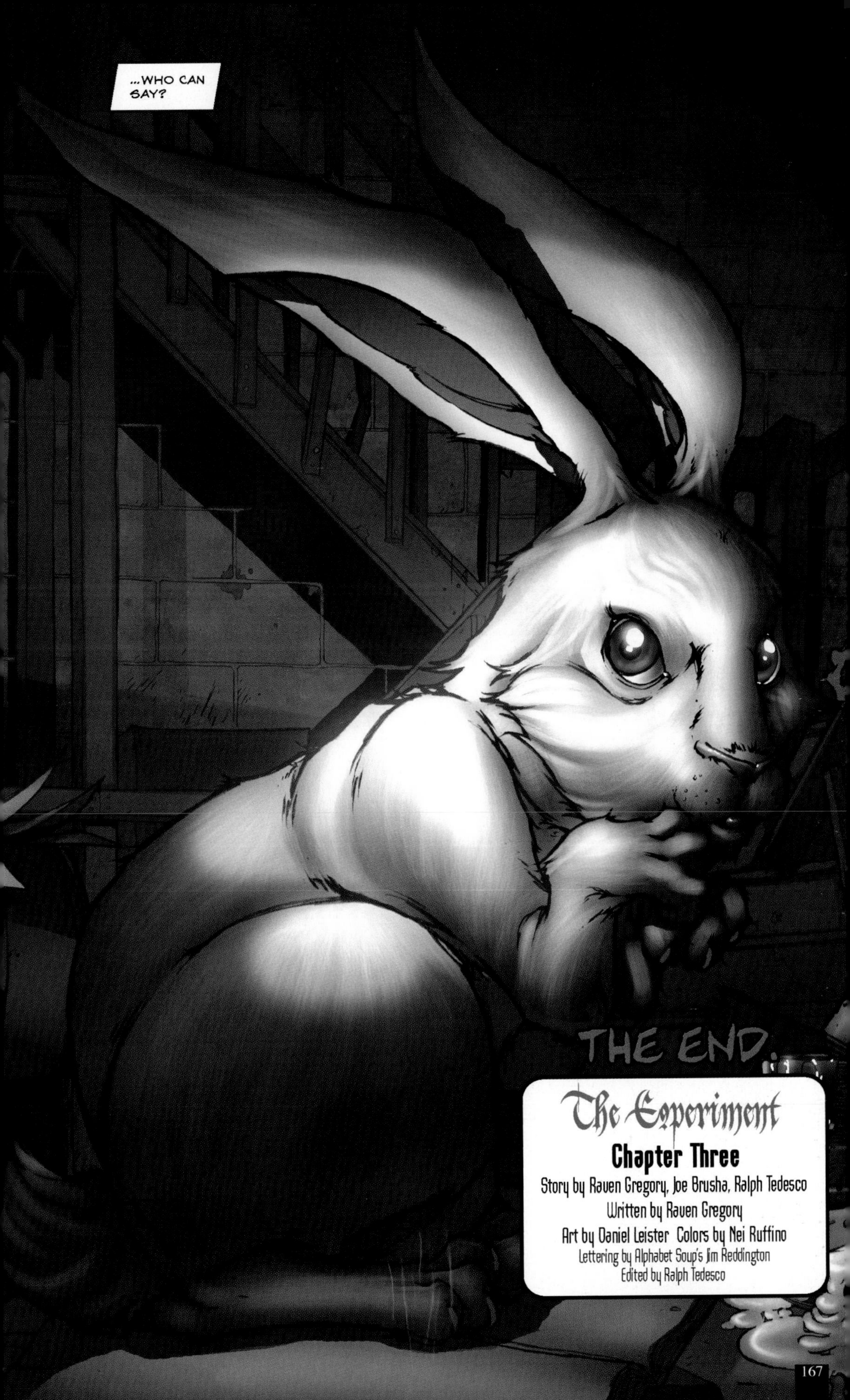
...WHO CAN SAY?
THE END.
The Experiment
Chapter Three
Story by Raven Gregory, Joe Brusha, Ralph Tedesco
Written by Raven Gregory
Art by Daniel Leister Colors by Nei Ruffino
Lettering by Alphabet Soup's Jim Reddington
Edited by Ralph Tedesco

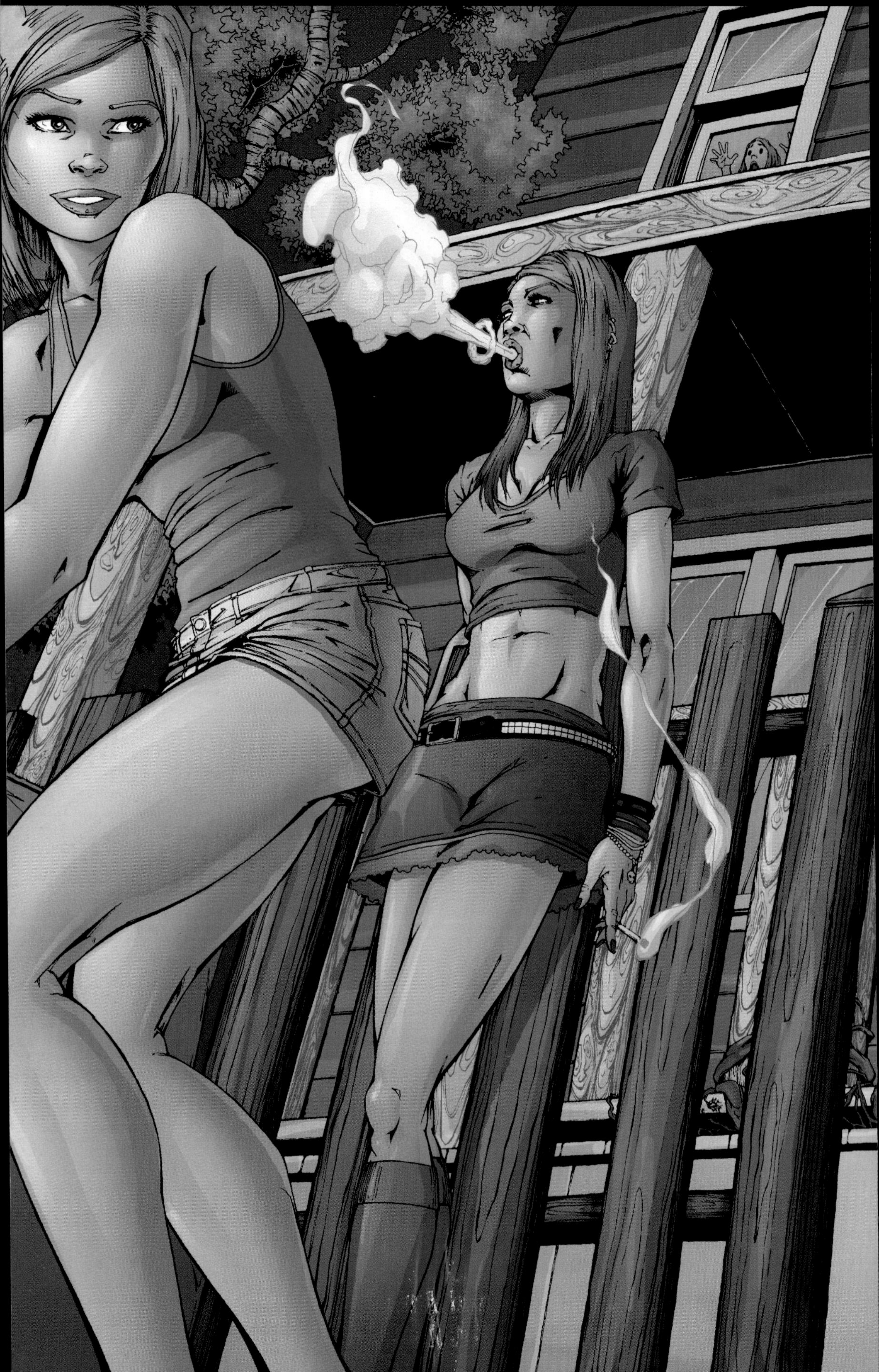

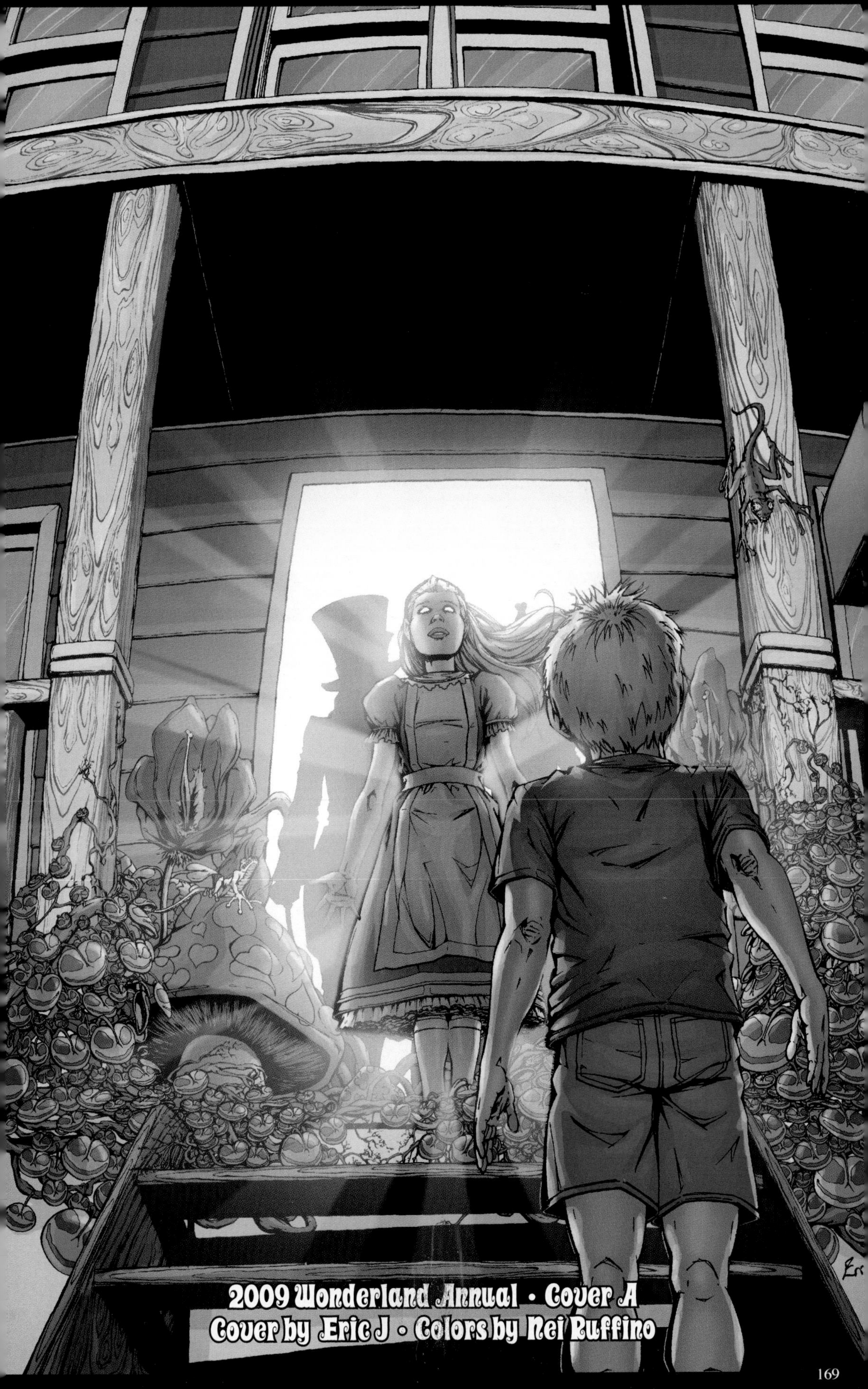

2009 Wonderland Annual • Cover A
Cover by Eric J • Colors by Nei Ruffino

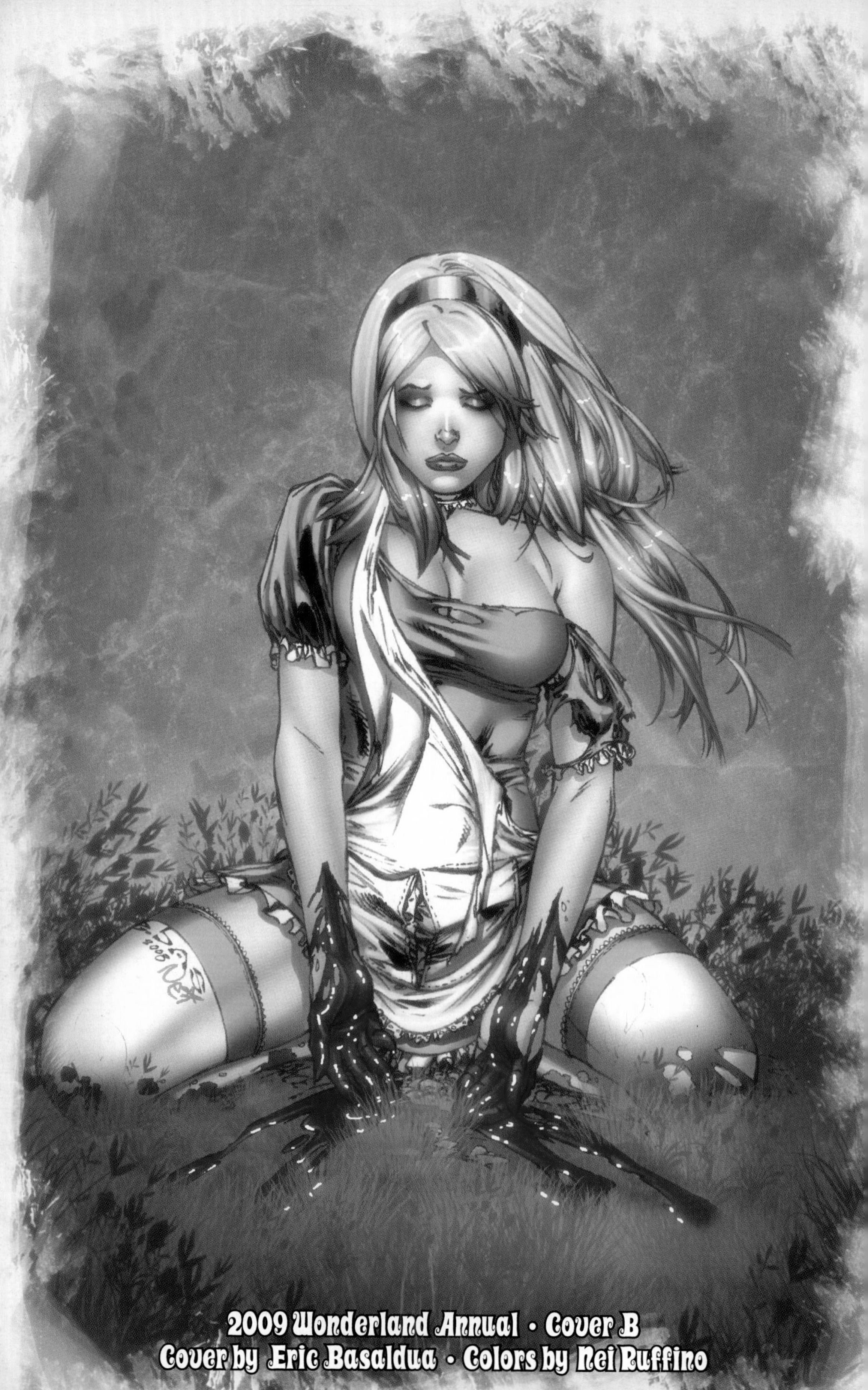

2009 Wonderland Annual • Cover B
Cover by Eric Basaldua • Colors by Nei Ruffino

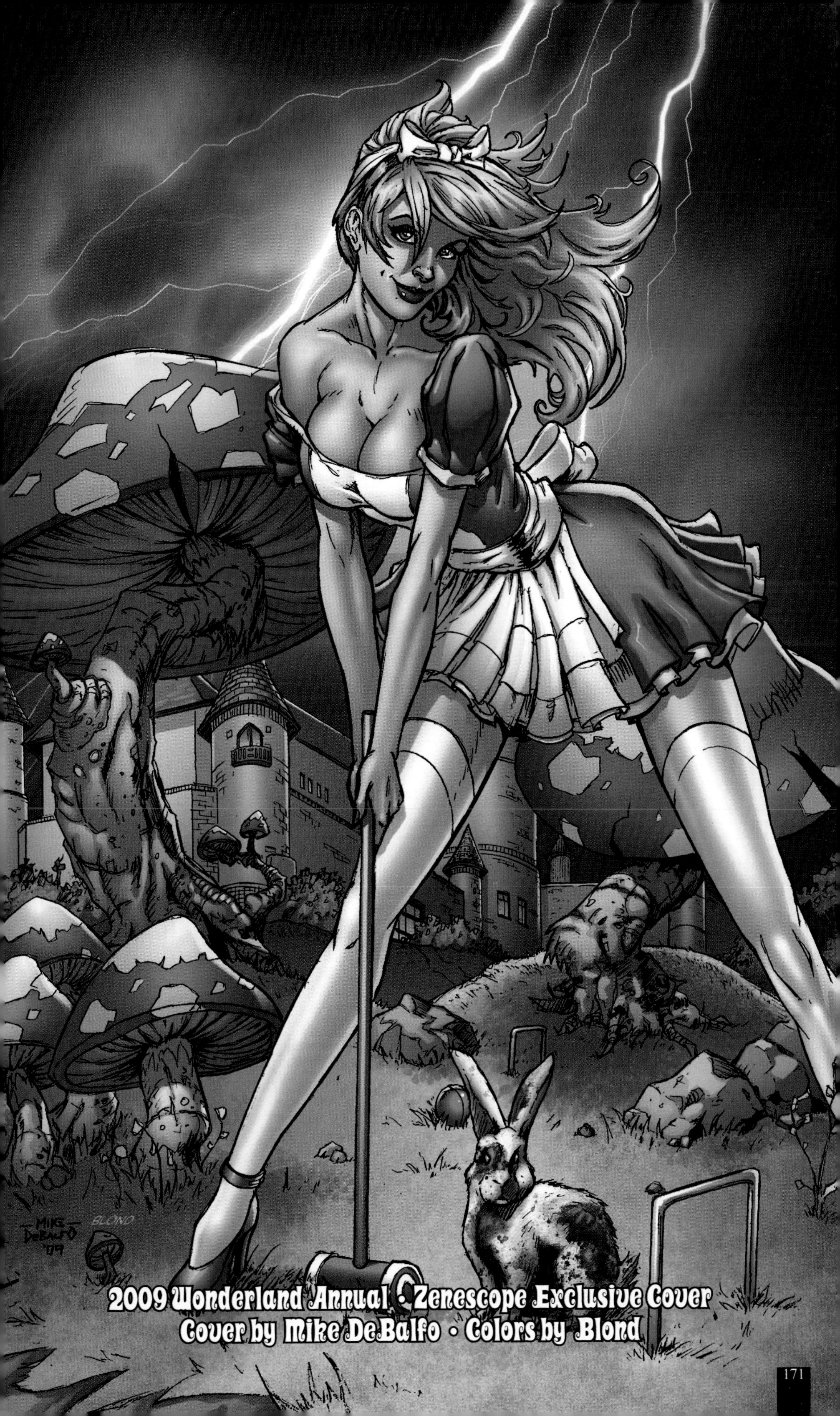
MIKE DeBALFO '09
BLOND

2009 Wonderland Annual • Zenescope Exclusive Cover
Cover by Mike DeBalfo • Colors by Blond

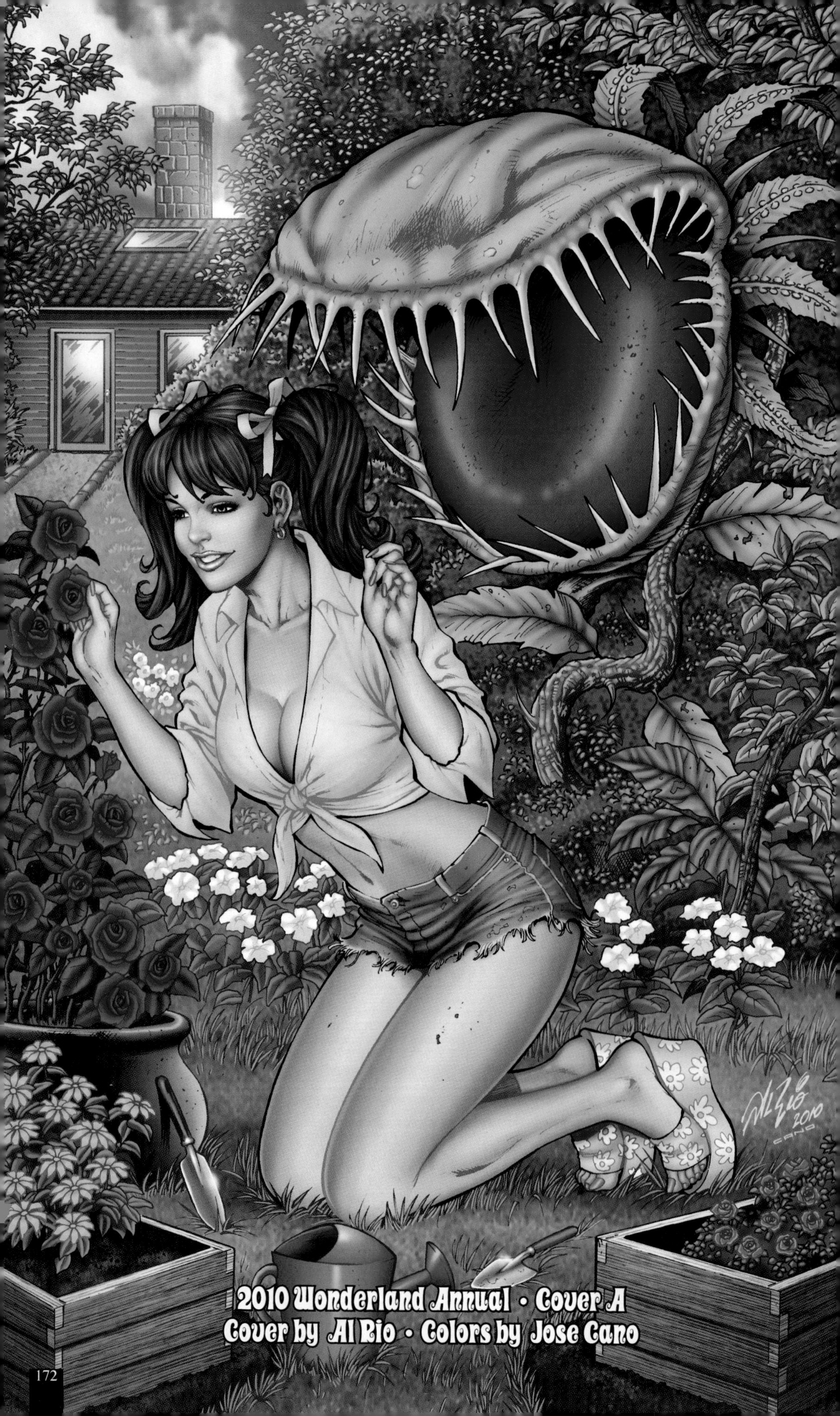

2010 Wonderland Annual • Cover A
Cover by Al Rio • Colors by Jose Cano

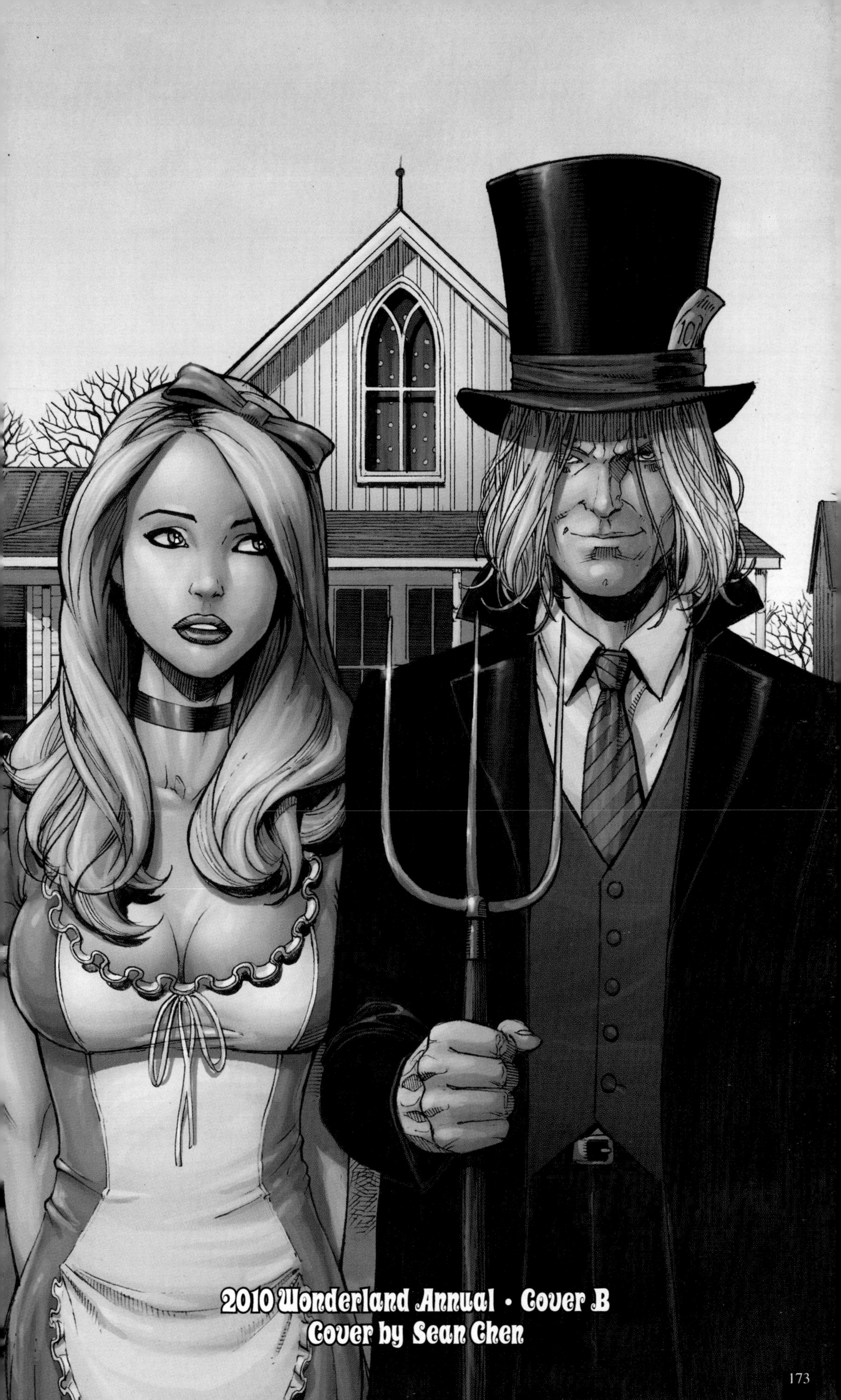

2010 Wonderland Annual • Cover B
Cover by Sean Chen

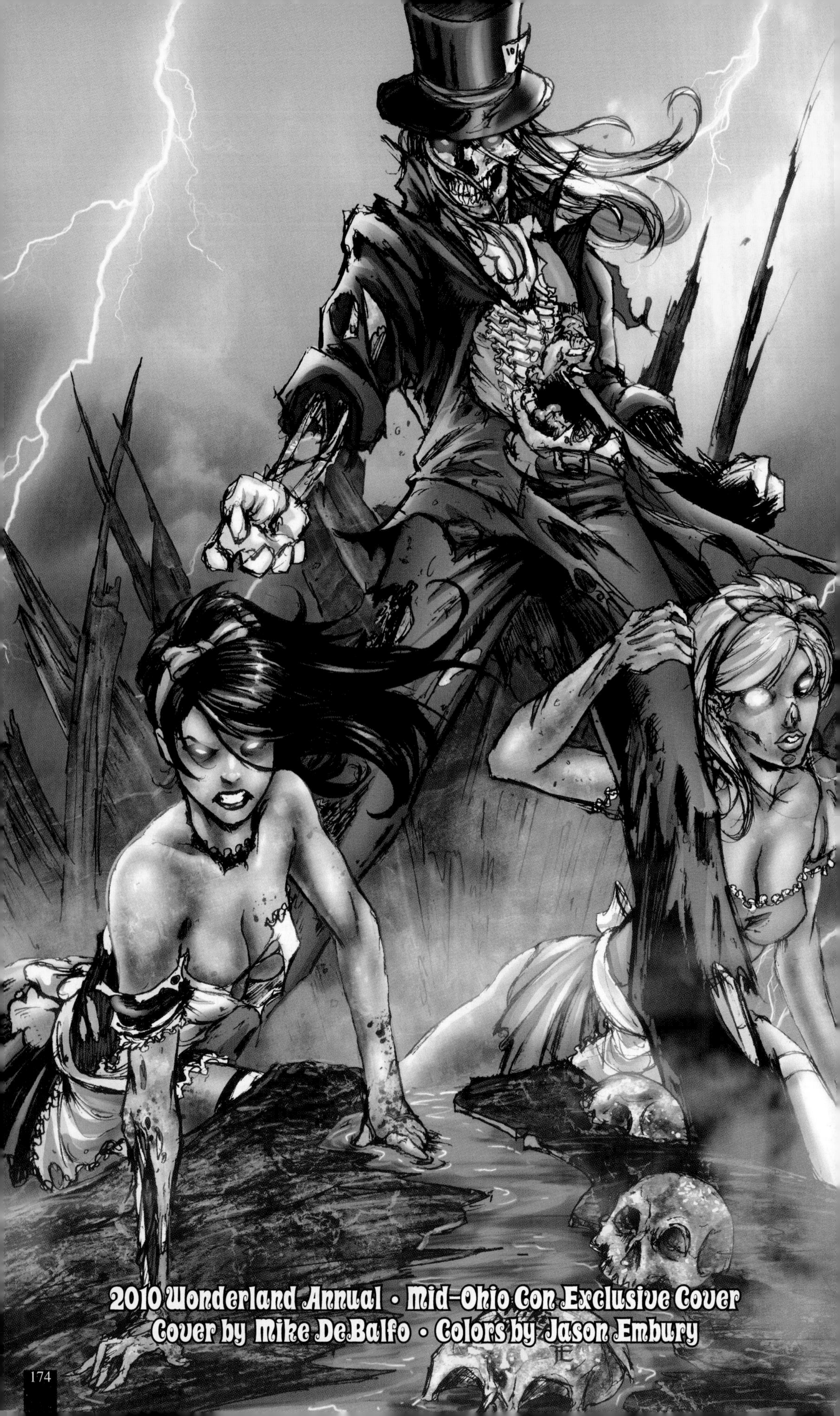

2010 Wonderland Annual • Mid-Ohio Con Exclusive Cover
Cover by Mike DeBalfo • Colors by Jason Embury

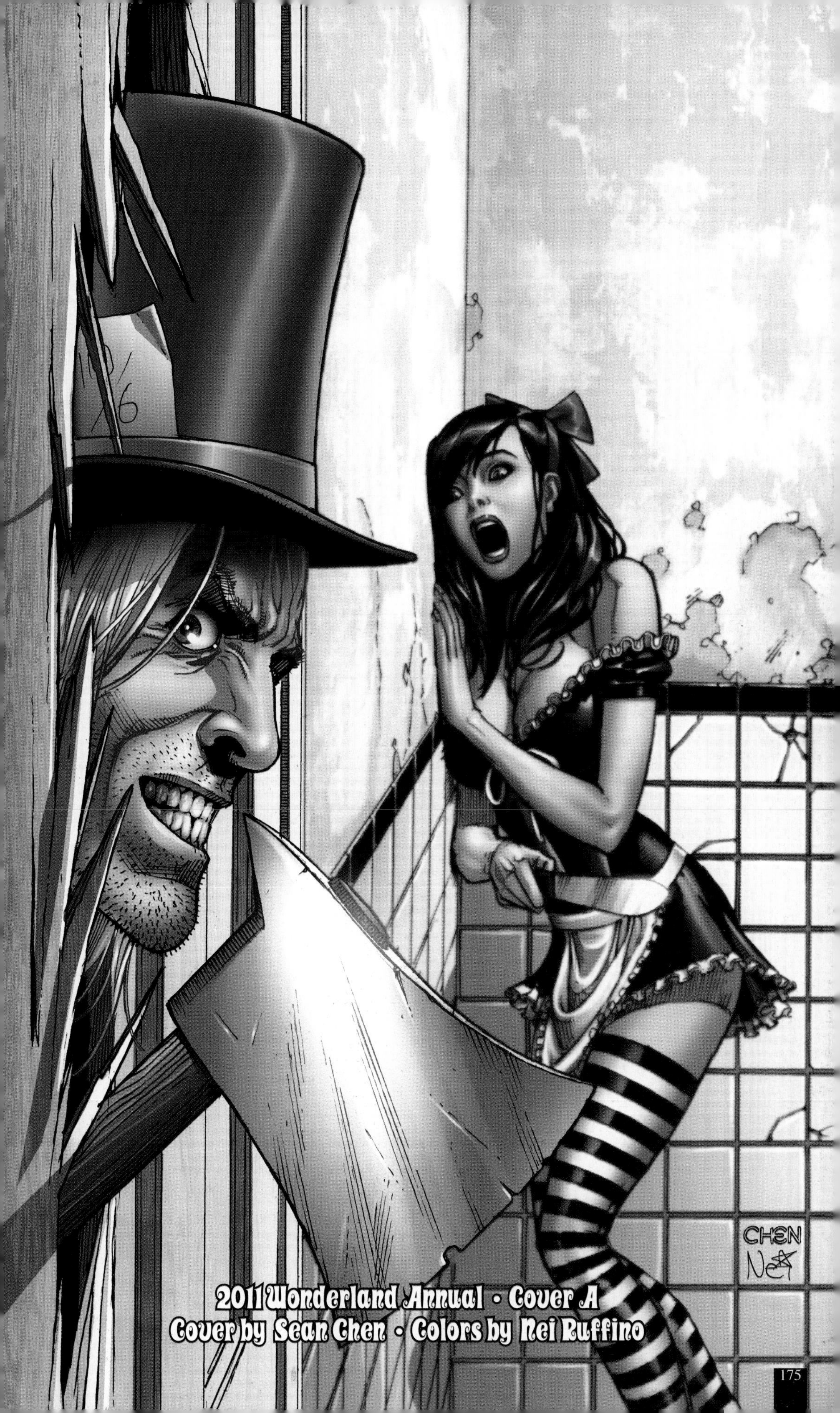
CHEN
Nei

2011 Wonderland Annual • Cover A
Cover by Sean Chen • Colors by Nei Ruffino

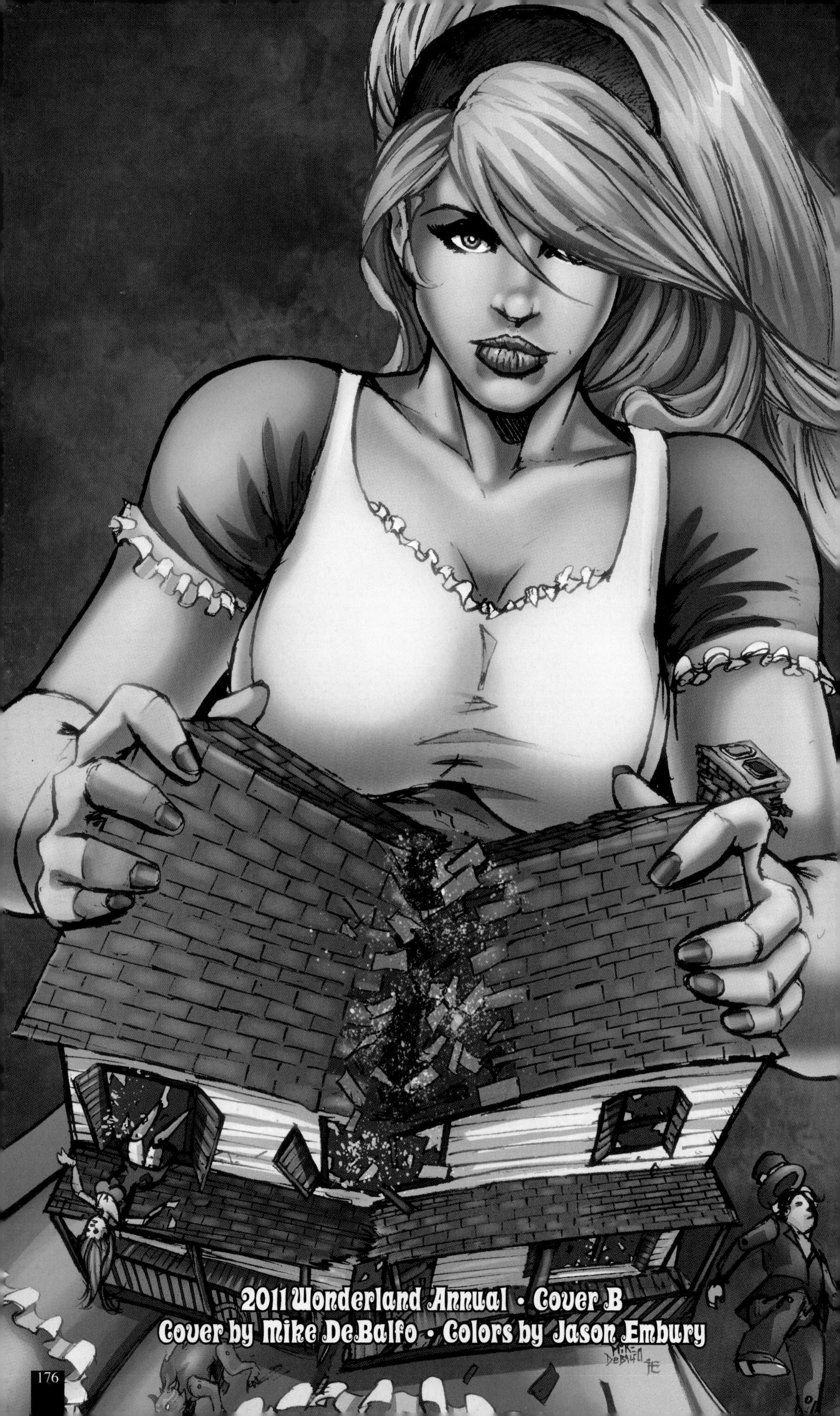

2011 Wonderland Annual • Cover B
Cover by Mike DeBalfo • Colors by Jason Embury

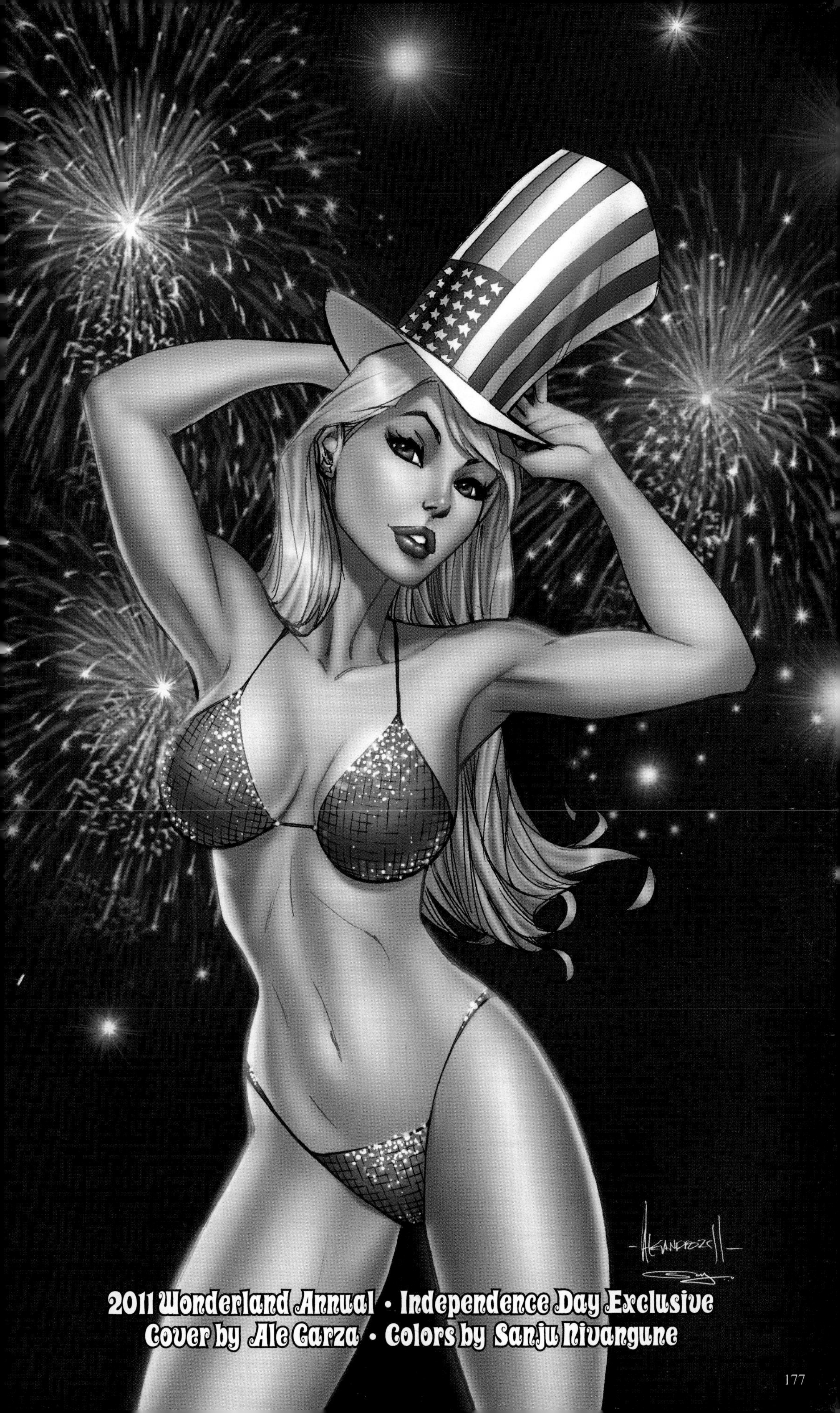

2011 Wonderland Annual • Independence Day Exclusive
Cover by Ale Garza • Colors by Sanju Nivangune

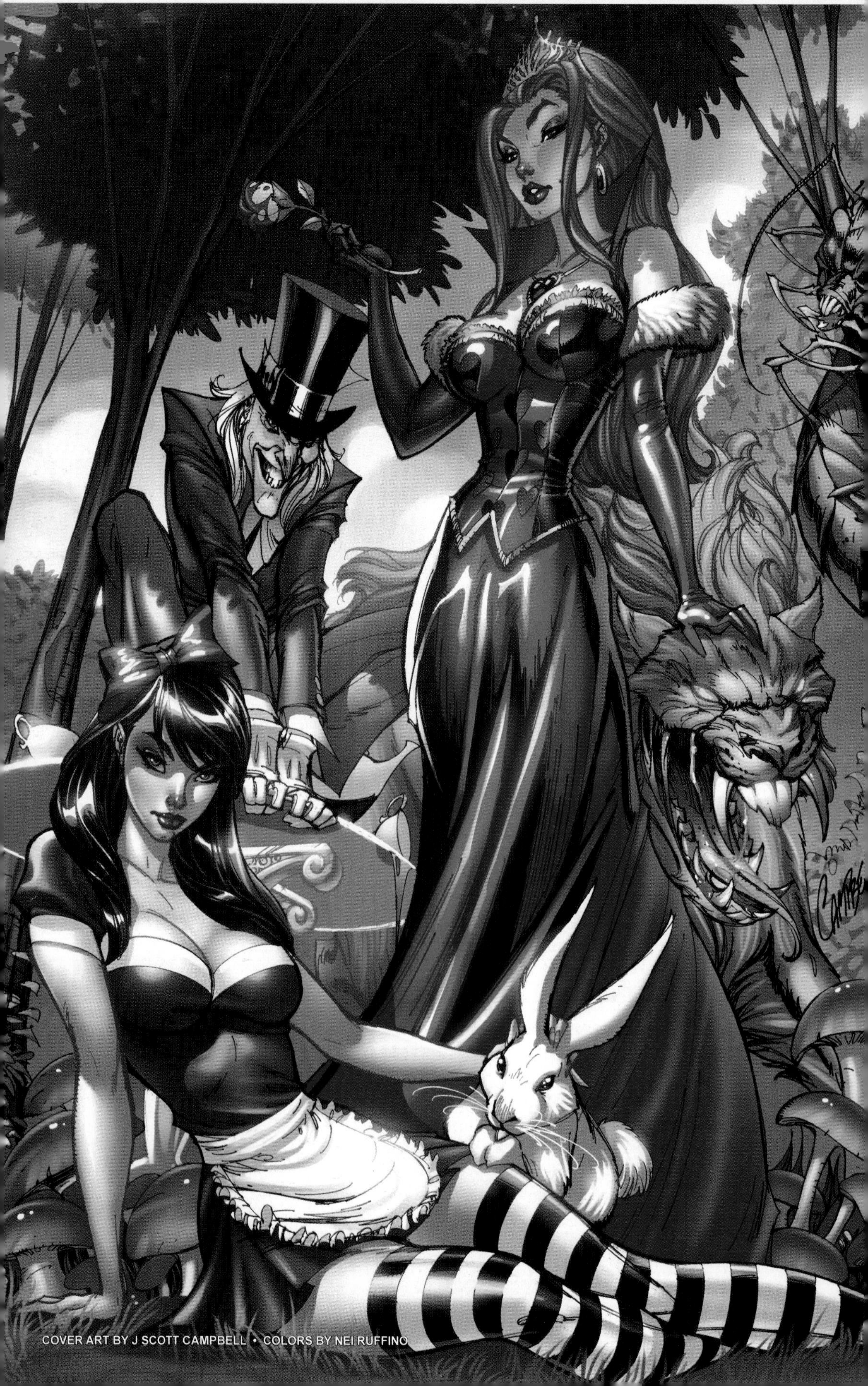

COVER ART BY J SCOTT CAMPBELL • COLORS BY NEI RUFFINO

Wonderland

Wonderland is a present day, horror-filled reinvention of the classic Alice's Adventures in Wonderland; a classic story retold for a new generation of reader. Alice is no longer the little girl you once knew. Years have passed since she took her trip down the mysterious rabbit hole. A grown woman now, with a husband and kids of her own, Alice has everything a person could want...aside from her sanity. Now Alice's daughter, Calie, will be forced to take the same journey as her mother did years before. It's a journey into a place full of horror where the adventures of Alice were only the beginning.

Return to Wonderland
Trade Paperback
Diamond ID #MAY091119

Beyond Wonderland
Trade Paperback
Diamond ID # JUN101206

Tales From Wonderland
Vol. 1 Trade Paperback
Diamond ID #NOV084364

Tales From Wonderland
Vol. 2 Trade Paperback
Diamond ID #AUG091146

Tales From Wonderland
Vol. 3 Trade Paperback
Diamond ID #JUL101202

Escape From Wonderland
Trade Paperback
Diamond ID # FEB111236

FACEBOOK.COM/ZENESCOPE

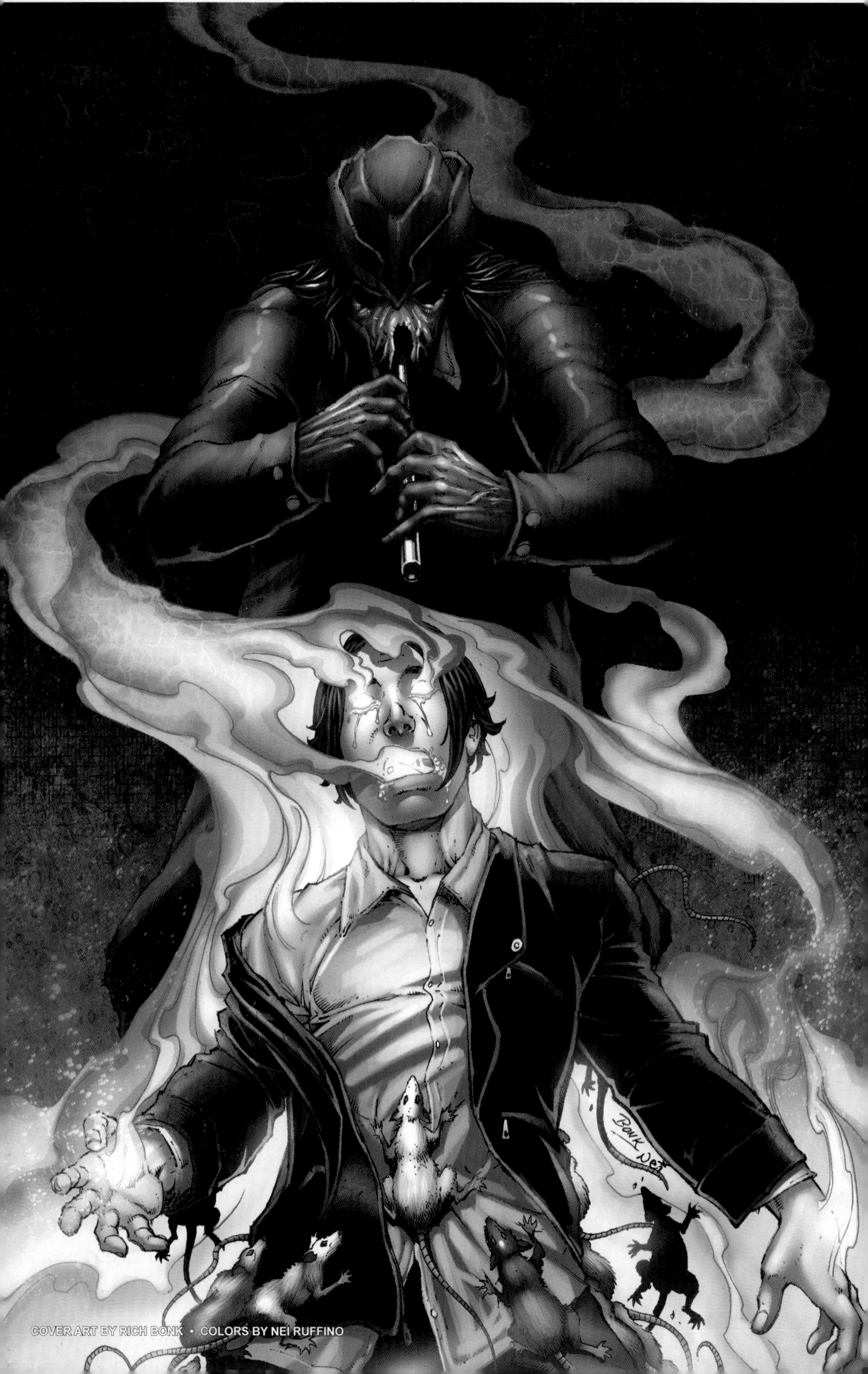
BONK NEI

COVER ART BY RICH BONK • COLORS BY NEI RUFFINO

FACEBOOK.COM/ZENESCOPE

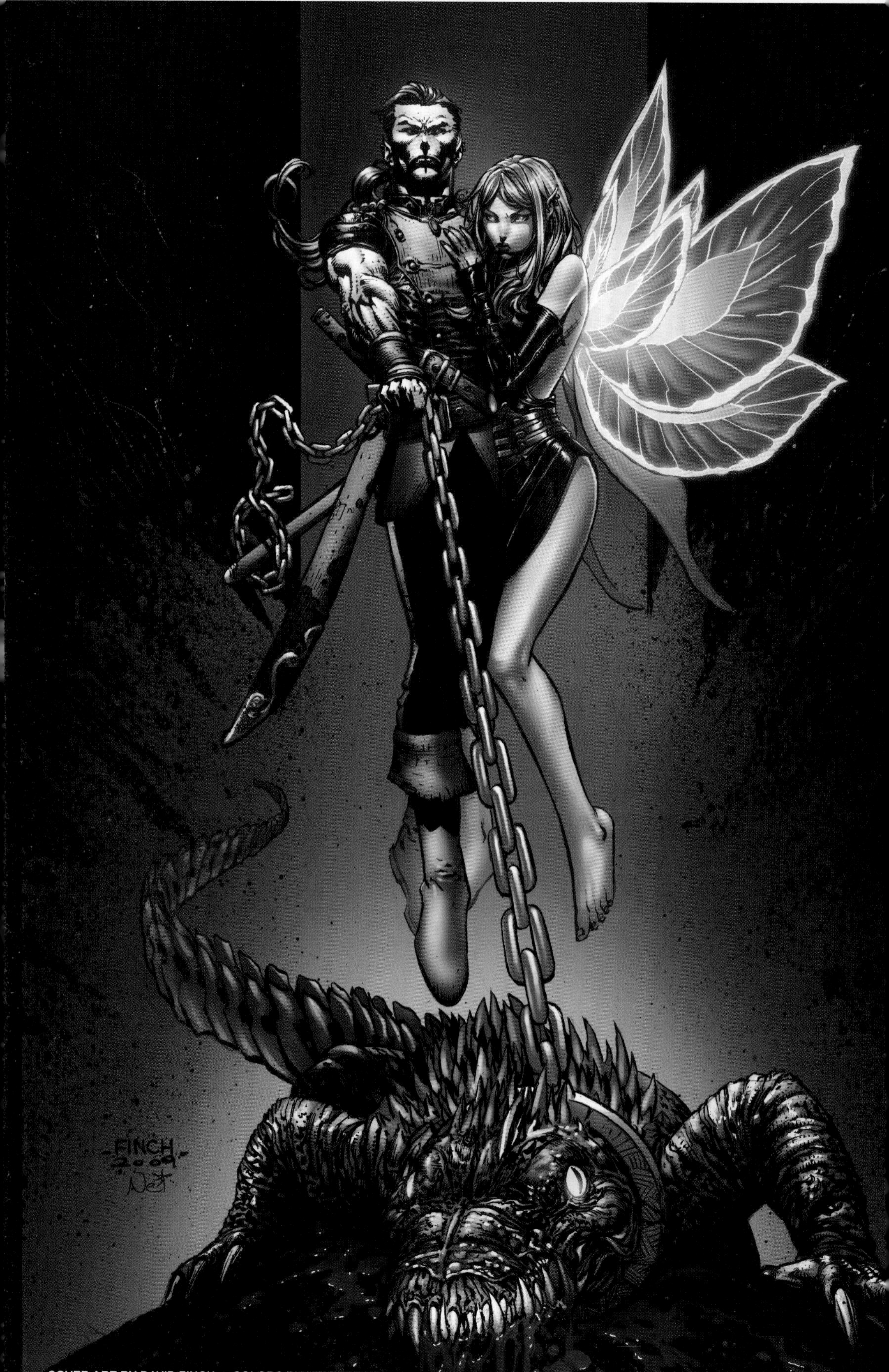

FINCH
2009

COVER ART BY DAVID FINCH • COLORS BY NEI RUFFINO

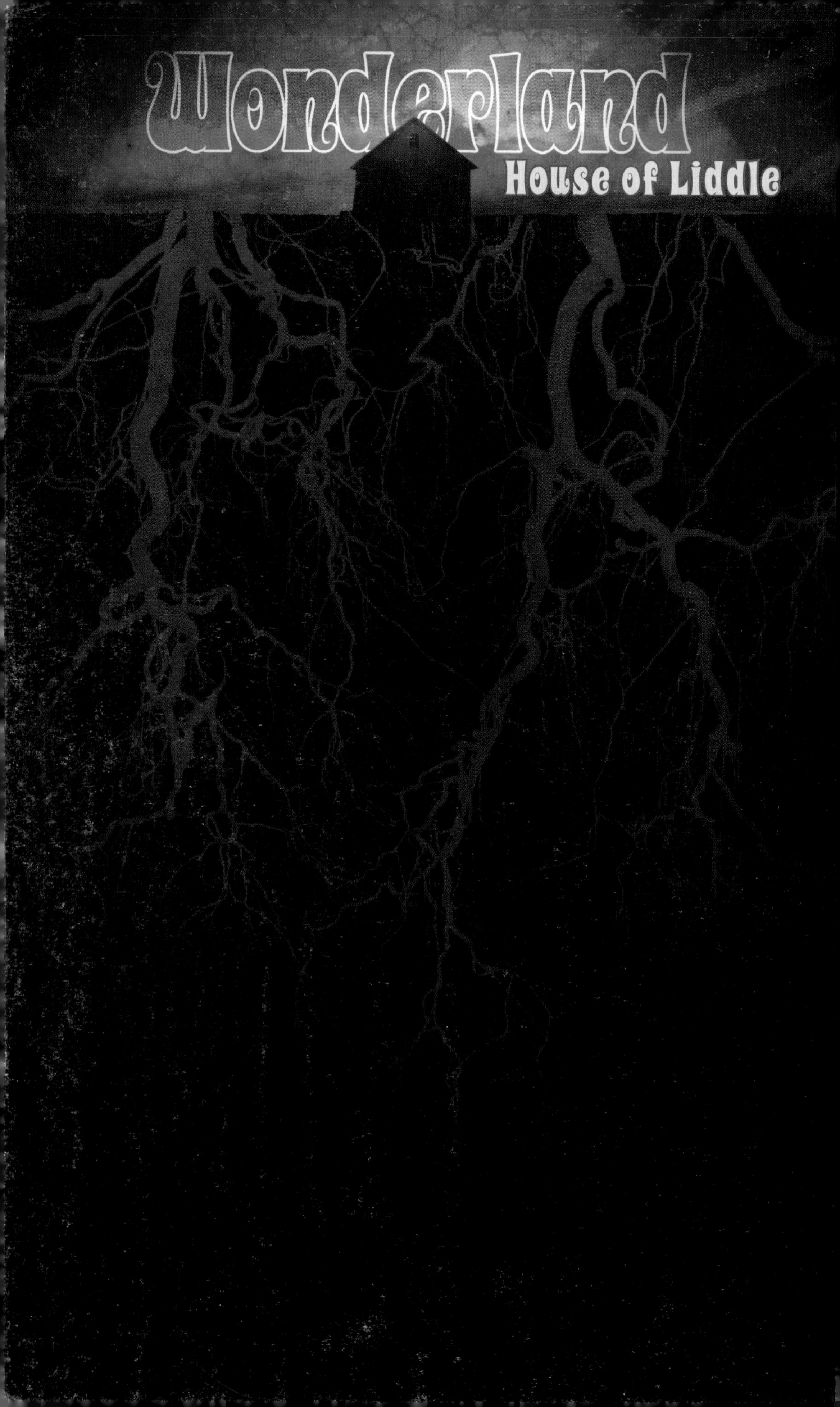
Wonderland
House of Liddle